The Rating Guide to

FRANCHISES

The Rating Guide to

FRANCHISES

by
Dennis L. Foster

Facts On File Publications
New York, New York • Oxford, England

The Rating Guide to Franchises

This publication is designed to provide accurate and authoritative information in regard to the subject matter. It is sold with the understanding that the publisher is not engaged in rendering legal advice. If legal advice is required, the services of a competent attorney should be sought.

Library of Congress Cataloging-in-Publication Data

Foster, Dennis L.
The rating guide to franchises.

Includes index.
1. Franchises (Retail trade) I. Title.
HF5429.23.F676 1989 381'.13'0973 88-3740
ISBN 0-8160-1891-X

British CIP data also available on request.

Printed in the United States of America

10 9 8 7 6 5 4 3 2

Many of the designations used by franchises, manufacturers, and sellers to distinguish their businesses, products, or services are claimed as trademarks. Where those designations appear in this book, and the author was aware of a trademark claim, the designations have been printed in initial caps, i.e., Kentucky Fried Chicken.

Contents

Introduction

By the end of the century, franchising will be the primary method of conducting business in North America. Franchise establishments already account for more than a third of all retail sales — nearly $700 billion annually. Seven million members of the work force are employed by franchise businesses, and the number of people who are actively interested in franchise opportunities is at an unsurpassed high. According to the U.S. Department of Commerce, buying a franchise is the average person's most viable avenue to owning a business.

Yet, until now, there has been no single reference that offers unbiased, in-depth profiles of America's leading franchisors and best franchise opportunities.

The Rating Guide to Franchises is an indispensible reference for anyone thinking about or currently involved in franchising. It is the first and only book that offers expert ratings and objective evaluations of major franchising companies.

Unlike the many franchise directories and magazine listings that are currently in print, this book goes far beyond mere names, addresses, fees, and royalties. In these pages, we analyze such vital information as the franchisor's range of services, advertising effectiveness, training program, past franchise disputes, litigation record, highlights of the franchise agreement, and the satisfaction level of current franchisees. We did not simply reproduce information from brochures or press releases, or sell advertising space to companies reviewed in this book. Instead, we conducted an exhaustive, independent research effort, to compile an objective comparison of the major franchisors in North America. Our research uncovered facts about each company's business history, financial and legal status, and relative position in the marketplace.

The Rating Guide to Franchises will steer you through the jungle of franchise statistics and legal terminology, sorting out the facts that are most important to anyone contemplating a franchise investment.

Franchise Background and Terminology

As you investigate franchise opportunities, you will find that certain terms are used repeatedly.

The word 'franchise' means a right or privilege. Thus, acquiring a franchise simply means obtaining the right to use a particular trademark or trade name, usually in conjunction with a ready-to-go business system or a unique product or service. The company that sells franchises to others is a 'franchisor,' and an individual, group, or company that purchases a franchise is a 'franchisee.'

The 'franchise agreement' is a written contract detailing the mutual responsibilities of the parties. The agreement usually has a definite 'term' — a time period in which the contract remains in effect. When the term is up, the contract expires and must be renewed. Some state laws require all franchise agreements to be renewable at the franchisee's option. Commonly, a franchise is granted to a specific individual; it may not be sold, transferred, or otherwise assigned to anyone else, without the franchisor's permission.

In the United States, franchisors are regulated by the Federal Trade Commission and 15 individual states: California, Connecticut, Illinois, Indiana, Maryland, Michigan, Minnesota,

Nebraska, New York, North Dakota, Rhode Island, South Dakota, Virginia, Washington, and Wisconsin. The regulations vary, but in most of these states, franchisors must register with a government authority, such as the attorney general or securities division, before offering franchises for sale.

All franchisors operating in the U.S. must comply with Federal Trade Commission Rule 436.1. This important regulation requires the franchisor to give a written prospectus to prospective franchisees at the earlier of the first personal meeting, or at least ten days 'before the signing of any franchise or related agreement or the making of any payment.' The prospectus prescribed by the FTC is called the Uniform Franchise Offering Circular, or UFOC. This document contains explicit information about the franchisor's background, important provisions of the franchise agreement, and existing franchisees.

Federal regulations also require that if a franchisor claims that a franchisee can achieve a certain level of sales or profits, the claim must be backed up by hard facts and figures. The figures must be contained in a special Earnings Claim Document. In the past, the rules were so complex, that most franchisors simply kept mum about the franchisee's projected sales or profits. In October, 1987, the regulations were relaxed, to encourage franchisors to supply prospective franchisees with an Earnings Claim Document. As a result, the number of franchisors who make earnings claims is increasing.

Franchising in Canada

By and large, business practices in Canada are identical to those in the United States. But Canadian businesspeople are generally more conservative and less prone to risk-taking ventures. Eighty percent of the franchisors operating in Canada are owned and managed by Canadian corporations. The failure rate of U.S.-based franchises entering the Canadian marketplace is high.

In Canada, franchisors are regulated by the Department of Industry, Trade, and Commerce, which also provides financial assistance to indigent Canadian businesspeople. The government frequently reviews foreign investment in Canadian-based businesses. A franchise must be 'effectively controlled' by an indigent Canadian businessperson or investment group. A U.S. corporation operating in Canada generally must disclose its shareholders and officers to the government. Businesses in Canada are also governed by the Department of Consumer and Corporate Affairs, which issues federal charters for incorporation, presides over bankrupcty proceedings, and oversees the 'orderly conduct of business.'

Franchise practices come under the scrutiny of the Competition Policy Branch, which has the authority to regulate agreements, mergers, price discrimination, promotional allowances, misrepresentations, false or misleading advertising, and retail price fixing. Under the Bilingual Act, all official documents, including franchise agreements, must be rendered in both English and French — the two official languages of Canada. The Province of Alberta has enacted local legislation requiring prior registration and filing of franchise offerings.

How To Use This Book

This book is divided into broad industrial categories. Each franchise profile contains the following sections:

Comparative Rating

Each franchisor has been rated according to the following criteria: industry experience, franchising experience, financial strength, training and services, fees and royalties, and satisfied franchisees. Each criterion receives a rating between one and four stars — with one denoting the lowest rating, four the highest.

Franchise Overview

Each profile is preceded by an introduction, containing a brief overview of the franchising company. The overview touches on the main historical events and characteristics of the franchise company.

Franchise Description

This section of each profile explains the business conducted by franchisees, describing a typical outlet, its products, services, and operating methods. The description provides a basic understanding of the franchise and how it may differ from others.

Franchisee Profile

This section describes the type of person that the franchisor is actively seeking as prospective franchisees, including any special training or background that may be required. The franchisee profile provides readers with a quick indication of their suitability for the franchise.

Projected Earnings

In this section, the profile presents the franchisor's statement of a franchisee's projected earnings. Many franchisors do not furnish prospective franchisees with any earnings claim at all. In some cases, we looked to independent sources for financial information about the franchising company and calculated the average volume of a franchisee's outlet. In other cases, we asked current franchisees to tell us how much they make.

Franchisor's Services

In this section of each profile, we examine the type of services provided to franchisees, including training, pre-opening assistance, and ongoing management support. Here are some key questions we answer about each franchisor: How long is the training program? Who pays for the franchisee's travel expenses? What kind of ongoing support will the franchisor provide after the franchisee's business is open?

Advertising

Advertising and name recognition are high on the list of things a prospective franchisee looks for in a franchise opportunity. This section synopsizes the advertising support that the franchisor supplies to franchisees and the cost to franchisees. The objective is to make the reader aware of any competitive advantages, or disadvantages, associated with the franchise program.

Disputes and Litigation

In this section, the profile delves into the franchisor's track record, focusing on franchisee disputes and litigation. We focus on major court decisions and disputes that have a strong bearing on the franchisor's relationship with its franchisees, recognizing that we live in an era when frivolous lawsuits are commonplace.

Investment Breakdown

This section contains a breakdown of the initial investment required to develop and open a franchise outlet. Where the information was available, the breakdown includes both high and low estimates. Bear in mind that considerable variation exists in the expense items included in different franchisors' estimates of the franchisee's initial investment. Some include only the minimum costs of acquiring the franchise and purchasing equipment or inventory. Others include working capital required to sustain the business until it becomes profitable. In some cases, we consulted current franchisees and other independent sources to estimate the cost of getting into the business.

Fees and Royalties

This section of each profile analyzes the fees and royalties charged by the franchisor, stressing any 'hidden' fees above and beyond the initial fee. Check this section carefully for any monetary obligations which might not be mentioned in the franchisor's advertisments or directory listings.

Contract Highlights

This section summarizes the important provisions of the franchise agreement. You will find matters relating to the term of the franchise, territorial protection, and conditions for selling or assigning the business to someone else.

Summary

The final section of each profile summarizes the franchisor's primary characteristics, benefits, strengths, and, in some cases, weaknesses.

Franchise Highlights

Each profile is followed by a table that summarizes the highlights of the franchise opportunity. The table shows the year in which the company began operating, the year it began selling franchises, the number of outlets currently open, the minimum and maximum franchise fee charged by the franchisor, the amount of the monthly royalty or other ongoing charge, the advertising fee, the length of time spent in training at the franchisor's headquarters, and the term of the franchise. The highlights provide the reader with basic facts and figures at a glance. In the interest of including as many franchising companies as possible, in some profiles the information has been consolidated, to save space.

The profiles are classified into 12 categories, each prefaced by an introduction. The categories include: apparel and soft goods franchises; automotive services; business services; construction, decoration, and maintenance; educational services; electronics, video, and appliance franchises; food service; lodging franchises; personal services; real estate; recreation and amusement; and retail and convenience stores. Each section contains a brief overview of the industry, including its overall economic status and current trends within the field.

The back matter includes two indexes. The first is a cross-reference index permitting readers to locate franchise profiles according to field of specialization. For example, Retail Franchises are broken down into listings such as Art Goods, Book Stores, and Convenience Markets; Food Service Franchises are segmented into Pizza Restaurants, Mexican Food Restaurants, Hamburger Restaurants, and so forth. The second index is an alphabetical listing of all the franchisors profiled in this book.

Evaluating Franchise Opportunities

There are literally thousands of franchise opportunities, but only a handful that are well suited to any particular individual. The decision to purchase a franchise should be based on several factors, including certain aspects of both the franchisor and the prospective franchisee. The following guidelines may help you narrow the selection and identify the opportunities best suited for your own personal aptitudes, ambitions, and financial qualifications.

1. Evaluate your credentials.

Begin by identifying the industry or field in which you are most interested. Some franchisors require previous training or experience in a particular business or trade, but many franchise advertisements claim 'anyone can learn the business.' In truth, simply being able to learn the business is hardly enough: starting a business involves emotional and financial decisions, as well as rational ones. Acquiring a franchise usually means committing the majority of one's waking hours — possibly, those of one's family, as well — to managing and operating the business. Starting any business is a mistake unless the owner/operator can derive emotional and psychological benefits.

2. Study the field.

Examine each franchise profile in your preferred field(s), and decide which ones have the most appeal. Then select the investments you believe you can handle, with or without financial assistance. The initial investment does not necessarily have to be paid entirely in cash. Financing for franchises is available from numerous sources, including banks that participate in SBA-guaranteed loan programs, Small Business Investment Companies (SBICs), venture capital groups, and conventional lending institutions.

3. Study your market.

Before pursuing a particular franchise opportunity, check the territory where you are most interested in opening the business. Find out the answers to the following questions: Does the franchisor already have existing outlets in your chosen market? If so, are you willing to consider another territory? Where? Are there enough customers in the market to support a business of this type?

4. Study the competition.

What other, competing businesses are already operating in the market? Is the franchise capable of dominating the competition? Is the market already saturated with comparable businesses? Are there already too many outlets of this kind in the territory?

5. Contact the franchisors.

When franchisors recruit prospective franchisees, they typically solicit applications from a large number of candidates, often weighing each individual's credentials against the others'. Turnabout is not only fair play, but — in this case — common sense. Even if you are keen on a particular franchisor, contact several different franchising companies in the same, or a related, field, as a basis for comparison.

Franchisors usually have two different vehicles for providing information to prospective franchisees. One is the Uniform Franchise Offering Circular (UFOC), prescribed by the Federal Trade Commission and/or state agencies that regulated franchisors. The UFOC is prepared by legal experts and, consequently, lacks promotional impact. The second vehicle is a franchise information kit, usually containing colorful brochures, reprints of publicity about the franchisor, and franchisee application forms. The franchisor will not normally furnish a UFOC until the time required by state or federal regulations — ten business days prior to the signing of the franchise agreement.

To establish contact with a prospective franchisor, call the phone number or write to the address shown in the franchisor's profile, and request a franchise information kit.

6. Rate each franchisor.

Compare each franchisor's information kit to the others you have solicited. Consider the important factors that will determine your success — among them, your personal suitability for the franchise, the franchisor's experience and name recognition, the type of assistance provided to franchisees, and the initial investment.

7. Complete the application form, and request a UFOC.

If you are interested in pursuing a particular opportunity, complete the franchise application and submit it to the franchisor. In most cases, the franchisor will supply a UFOC only to candidates that have completed the application forms. This process permits the company to perform preliminary background and credit checks before sending out the UFOC. In some instances, the UFOC is handed to the prospective franchee in person at the beginning of a personal interview.

8. Study the UFOC

By law, the UFOC must be in your hands a minimum of ten business days prior before you sign the franchise agreement or make any payment related to the franchise. Under no circumstances should you sign any contract related to the franchise, including a purchase or deposit agreement, until you have studied the UFOC. If a franchise salesman pressures you to pay a deposit to 'hold the territory' before the required waiting period has lapsed, it may very well be a violation of federal franchise regulations.

Study the contents of the UFOC carefully. Pay particular attention to the franchisor's background, disputes with other franchisees, and any obligations to purchase equipment or supplies from the franchisor of a designated supplier.

9. Share the UFOC with an attorney and an accountant.

Regardless of your personal impressions about a franchise opportunity, be sure to obtain competent financial and legal advice before making a final decision to purchase the franchise.

10. Visit other franchise outlets.

If possible, visit other franchise outlets besides the one the franchisor shows you. Very often, the franchise salesman will showcase an outlet that has been specially groomed to show off the program's best features, or one that has unusually high customer traffic. Are other outlets also teeming with customers? Are the employees reasonably content with their jobs and with management? Project yourself into the outlet: Is the business a place where you will be happy spending the majority of your time over the next five or ten or twenty years? Is the image of the business conducive with your own?

11. Contact other franchisees.

Whether or not you are able to visit other franchise outlets, call or write to other franchisees. The UFOC contains a list of the franchisor's established outlets, including the names, addresses, and telephone numbers of the owners. Find out how satisfied they are with the franchise and with the franchising company. What do they perceive to be the franchisor's main strengths and weaknesses in dealing first-hand with franchisees? Was any aspect of the business exaggerated or misrepresented by the franchise salesman? Given the chance to do it all over again, would they still still buy their franchises?

The Importance of Diligence

Perhaps the most highly publicized aspect about franchises is the Department of Commerce statistic that two thirds of all independent businesses fail — most of them during the first year of operation — whereas 95 percent of the franchises that were open three years ago are still in business today. Nevertheless, it is worth remembering that no statistics are kept regarding the number of franchises that continue to stay in business, while operating at a loss or by barely breaking even. To be sure, some franchisees do not ever make the kind of profits they envisioned at the outset.

The number of reported franchise failures is at an unsurpassed high. Moreover, although state and federal governments regulate franchisors, the regulatory agencies do not have nearly enough manpower to police all the business practices of the nation's thousands of franchising companies.

The Rating Guide to Franchises was written to provide an unbiased source of information about franchisors, not to promote, advertise, or recommend any particular franchise opportunity. The appearance of a franchise profile in this book should not be construed as a form of recommendation or endorsement.

No book, including this one, can substitute for the exercise of diligence, research, common sense, and reason in the quest for personal and financial independence through franchising. All other factors being equal, the ideal franchisor is the one whose own management personality and chemistry are ideally suited to those of the individual franchisee.

The authors have exercised great care to assure the accuracy of the information in this book. But you should be aware that it is the nature of franchise programs to change, often very rapidly, especially with respect to such data as the number of outlets, franchise fees or royalties, or the location of the company's headquarters. The authors and publisher cannot be held responsible for any errors or discrepancies that may appear, nor for any liability or loss incurred as a direct or indirect result arising out of the use of any information contained in this book.

Apparel and Soft Goods Franchises

Two interrelated factors ignited the explosive growth of apparel franchises in the 1980s: the Baby Boom of the 70s and the two-decade-long health and fitness craze. Throughout the 1970s, the U.S. population increased by 3.15 million babies every year. Most of those future consumers are teens or preteens today, accounting for 40 percent of all retail clothing sales in America. In the 1980s, the annual birth rate has actually increased — promising a snug fit for today's apparel chains in search of expansion.

The new Baby Boomers and their 1940s counterparts share at least one fashion trend in common — the exercise fad. It began with jogging in the mid 1970s and spread to aerobic dancing, weight lifting, and tennis in the 80s. With the fashion scene shifting from night clubs to health clubs, even people who don't exercise regularly want to look like they do.

America spends over $2 billion on sneakers every year, from traditional tennis shoes to costly designer models. Enough fashion sportswear is sold every two years to completely clothe every man, woman, and child in the United States.

The burgeoning youth market has also favored retailers in more traditional fields, such as formal wear. Gingiss International, the nation's oldest and largest tuxedo specialist, rents and sells annually to 600,000 men and boys dressing up for high school proms, weddings, conventions, and banquets.

The social hots spots for the apparel-buying youth crowd are America's sprawling shopping malls, where small, independently owned specialty boutiques compete on equal footing with giant department store chains.

Most apparel franchises are purchased by self-motivated entrepreneurs with a fashion bent. It doesn't take a Paris- trained designer to be successful in a clothing boutique, but it certainly helps if the owner truly loves the business.

ACA Joe

Industry experience:	★★★	*Franchising experience:*	★★
Financial strength:	★★★	*Training & services:*	★★★
Fees & royalties:	★★★	*Satisfied franchisees:*	★★★

ACA Joe
915 Front Street
San Francisco, California 91411
U.S. (800) 422-2563
Calif. (415) 986-5850

In an era of colorful polyester, ACA Joe has built a small retail empire by disdaining synthetic fabrics. Founded in 1983, the apparel chain blossomed in four short years to 170 outlets, of which nearly 60 percent are operated by independent franchisees. The heart of the ACA Joe store concept is an inventory of all natural-fibre casual apparel.

The Franchise: The franchisee operates a retail apparel store, specializing in adult casual wear, under the trade name ACA Joe. A typical outlet is situated in a strip center, retail building, shopping mall, or other suitable site. Franchisees sell a broad range of casual clothing for both men and women, focusing on apparel manufactured completely from all-natural fibres.

Franchisee Profile: A background in apparel merchandising is preferred, but not mandatory.

Projected Earnings: The franchisor does not provide a statement of projected earnings.

Franchisor's Services: Franchisees receive training at the company's headquarters in San Francisco. Attendees are responsible for their own travel and lodging expenses. The curriculum includes merchandising techniques, marketing, sales, and business operations. Additional on-site orientation is provided at the franchisee's outlet. All franchisees receive copies of the confidential ACA Joe store operations manual, which details the management and conduct of the business.

Initial Investment: New ACA Joe franchisees should be prepared to handle an investment up to $200,000 to establish the business. The amount includes the initial franchise fee, site acquisition and development, fixtures and improvements, initial inventory requirements, and working capital. ACA Joe does not offer any direct financial assistance to franchisees.

Contract Highlights: The term of the franchise is ten years. The contract may be renewed for an additional five-year term, at the franchisee's option. The franchise may not be sold or assigned without franchisor's consent.

Fees and Royalties: The $30,000 initial franchise fee is on the high side for the retail apparel industry. The total royalty burden is only three percent. ACA Joe derives profits from the sale of merchandise to franchisees.

Summary: The ACA Joe franchise offers a unique format catering to an established, steadily increasing niche in the retail apparel market. Franchisees benefit from consolidated purchasing and personal support from a young, growth-oriented organization.

Franchise Highlights

Began operating: 1983	**Monthly royalty: None**
Began franchising: 1983	**Advertising fee: 3%**
Outlets currently open: 170	**Training program: Varies**
Initial franchise fee: $30,000	**Term: 10 years**

Allison's Place

Industry experience: ★ ★ *Franchising experience:* ★ ★
Financial strength: ★ ★ ★ ★ *Training & services:* ★ ★
Fees & royalties: ★ ★ ★ *Satisfied franchisees:* ★ ★ ★

Allison's Place
3161 E. Washington Street
Los Angeles, California 90023
(213) 267-0663

Founded in 1980, Allison's Place bulged from 40 company-owned outlets in 1984 to 250 retail sites today. About a third of the chain's women's clothing stores are franchise operations.

The Franchise: The franchisee operates a retail apparel store, specializing in women's clothing and accessories and doing business under the trade name Allison's Place. Franchisees purchase merchandise from the franchisor.

Franchisee Profile: A background in retail merchandising is beneficial, but not mandatory.

Projected Earnings: Based on the company's reported annual sales, the average volume of an Allison's Place outlet is about $105,700 per year, before expenses. This figure does not distinguish between company-owned stores and franchise outlets, and does not take into account individual variables such as outlet size or location. The estimate is not based on any projected earnings statement furnished by the franchisor.

Franchisor's Services: Allison's franchisees attend a three-day training seminar in Los Angeles before opening their doors for business. An additional seven days of training and grand opening assistance are provided at the franchisee's own site.

Each franchisee receives a set of comprehensive operations manuals detailing store operations, management, purchasing, merchandising, sales, and inventory control. An Allison's field specialist provides ongoing assistance in periodic visits to the store. The franchisor operates a centralized purchasing system to supply franchisees with merchandise at volume discounts.

Initial Investment: The total start-up investment for a new store is estimated at around $95,000. Allison's does not offer any direct financial assistance to franchisees.

Fees and Royalties: The initial franchise fee of $89,500 covers the franchisee's turnkey start-up costs. The total royalty obligation, including a 3.5 percent monthly franchise royalty and a two percent advertising fee, is less than six percent of gross sales.

Summary: A public corporation in reasonably good financial condition, Allison's has enjoyed one of the highest growth rates of any retail chain - 580 percent over the last three years. The franchise program offers growing name recognition, consolidated purchasing power, and merchandising support from a savy organization.

Franchise Highlights

Began operating: 1980
Began franchising: 1985
Outlets currently open: 250
Initial franchise fee: $89,500
Monthly royalty: 3.5%
Advertising fee: 2%
Training program: 3 days
Term: 10 years

Athletic Attic

Industry experience: ★★★ *Franchising experience:* ★★
Financial strength: ★★★ *Training & services:* ★★★
Fees & royalties: ★★★★ *Satisfied franchisees:* ★★★★

Athletic Attic Marketing
P. O. Box 14503
Gainesville, Florida 32604
(904) 377-5289

In 1973, collegiate track coach Jimmy Carnes and famed runner Marty Liquori joined forces to create Athletic Attic, a retail store devoted entirely to sports apparel and shoes. Carnes went on to coach the 1980 U.S. Olympic track team. Liquori was once one of the world's fastest milers and later, a popular TV sports announcer. Today, Carnes's and Liquori's public image is as integral a part of the Athletic Attic franchise as the company's colorfully stocked mall outlets.

Since launching their franchise effort in 1974, the illustrious team has pursued a cautious track, opening close to 100 stores in 12 years. The company is currently seeking new franchisees in all major U.S. markets.

The Franchise: The franchisee operates a retail sports apparel store under the trade name Athletic Attic. A typical outlet is situated in a shopping mall or strip center, with three or more full-time employees. Additional part-time help may be required during the holiday season. Athletic Attic outlets cater to sports and fitness fashion trends, as well as to legitimate athletic apparel needs. A typical outlet sells sneakers, cleats, jogging suits, and athletic shirts and jackets.

Franchisee Profile: A background in retail merchandising is beneficial, but not mandatory. Absentee ownership is discouraged. Preference is given to prospective franchisees who are willing to manage the business personally.

Projected Earnings: Based on the company's reported annual sales, the average gross revenues of an Athletic Attic outlet are about $300,000 per year, before expenses. Net profits average around 12 percent.

Franchisor's Services: Athletic Attic provides an intensive two-week training course at the company's headquarters in Gainesville, Florida. Attendees are responsible for their own travel and lodging expenses. The curriculum includes first-hand exposure to an operating Athletic Attic retail outlet. An additional five days of on-the-job training take place at the franchisee's place of business.

A franchise representative will assist with selecting the optimal site for the outlet and negotiating a lease for the premises. Franchisees also receive assistance with store layout and inventory planning. When the site is open for business, an Athletic Attic field consultant will make periodic visits to the store to check on inventory and offer on-site assistance. Athletic Attic operates a centralized purchasing system to enable franchisees to take advantage of wholesale discounts on approved sportswear. The support package also includes a franchisee newsletter, ongoing training, and special promotions. The franchisor sponsors world-class athletes in competition, through the National Track Club.

Initial Investment: Athletic Attic franchisees must invest from $150,000 to as much as $220,000. The investment amount includes lease deposits, site improvements, fixtures, inventory, miscellaneous startup costs, and working capital requirements. The franchisor does not offer any direct financial assistance to franchisees.

Advertising: Athletic Attic franchisees contribute one half of one percent of their of gross sales to the franchisor's advertising fund. The ad pool is used to develop materials for national, regional, and local campaigns.

Contract Highlights: The Athletic Attic franchise has a 30-year term — three times the average term of a retail franchise. The contract may be renwed for another 30 years at the franchisee's option. The franchisee receives a protected territory, with the right to open additional outlets. Area franchises are available under a separate agreement.

Fees and Royalties: The initial franchise fee of $10,000 is commensurate with other franchises in the field. The three percent monthly royalty and the one half percent advertising fee closely parallel the competition.

Summary: The Athletic Attic franchise may rank second among athletic footwear and apparel chains, but it outclasses the field in the use of company profits to sponsor amateur track and field competition.

Franchise Highlights

Began operating: 1973	**Monthly royalty: 3%**
Began franchising: 1974	**Advertising fee: .5%**
Outlets currently open: 240	**Training program: 2 weeks**
Initial franchise fee: $7,500	**Term: 30 years**

The Athlete's Foot

Industry experience:	★★★	*Franchising experience:*	★★★
Financial strength:	★★★	*Training & services:*	★★★
Fees & royalties:	★★★	*Satisfied franchisees:*	★★★★

The Athlete's Foot
3735 Atlanta Industrial Parkway
Atlanta, Georgia 30331
(404) 696-3400

Riding the crest of the personal fitness wave, The Athlete's Foot surged from humble origins to the stature of an American retail giant. Founded in 1972, The Athlete's Foot has established nearly 500 athletic footwear and clothing stores across America and in more than 80 foreign countries. Fewer than a fourth are company owned. Specializing in sneakers and exercise apparel, the prolific chain is still seeking new franchisees in all areas of the U.S., Western Europe, and the Netherlands. A separate franchise organization in Ontario (no relation to the American retailer) administers a small system of The Athlete's Foot stores in Canada.

The Franchise: The franchisee operates a retail apparel store devoted to sports footwear and operated under the trade name The Athlete's Foot. A typical outlet is situated in a shopping mall, strip center, or other suitable retail site, with a staff of two full-time and two part-time employees. Franchisees sell all types and styles of athletic shoes and sneakers, presumably selected on the basis of stringent research and testing. Customers of the outlet include the fashion-conscious as well as the fitness- oriented.

Franchisee Profile: A background in retail merchandising or the footwear business is not required. The company is seeking prospective franchisees who can handle the investment and are willing to do whatever it takes to succeed in the business. The company is not currently seeking absentee owners.

Projected Earnings: The franchisor does not provide a statement of projected earnings.

Franchisor's Services: The franchisor provides a one-week training program at the company's headquarters in Atlanta. Attendees are responsible for their own travel and lodging expenses. The curriculum includes merchandising, inventory control, advertising, budgeting and retail operations. An additional week of on-the-job training is provided at the franchisee's place of business.

The franchisor will assist with selecting a site, negotiating a lease, and acquiring fixtures for the store. The Athlete's Foot also helps plan and order the opening inventory and participates in Grand Opening activities.

An area manager will visit the store periodically to offer on-site assistance. The franchisor works closely with its designated sportswear vendors to assure quality control and availability. Franchisees realize significant discounts on equipment and supplies purchased from the franchisor, but the franchise agreement does not prohibit the store owner from using other suppliers. The Athlete's Foot publishes a monthly franchisee newsletter and produces a series of videotapes for continuing education.

Initial Investment: New franchisees should be prepared to invest from $90,000 to $180,000, depending on the location and size of the outlet. The amount includes lease deposits, improvements, fixtures, and an opening inventory of sportswear. The Athlete's Foot does not offer any form of direct financial assistance to franchisees.

Advertising: Franchisees contribute just one half of one percent of gross monthly revenues for advertising. The franchisor provides ad slicks, radio and television commercials, point-of- sale materials, and public relations aids.

Contract Highlights: The term of the franchise is eight years. The contract may be renewed for an additional five-year term, at the franchisee's option. The franchisee receives a protected territory, guaranteeing that The Athlete's Foot will not open another store within the designated boundaries. The franchisee in turn is prohibited from engaging in any business which is in direct competition with the franchise outlet while the franchise agreement is in effect.

Fees and Royalties: The initial fee of $10,000 is average for a retail sportwear franchise. The three percent monthly royalty is low. Including the one half percent advertising contribution, the total royalty bite is a mere three and one half percent of gross sales.

Summary: The Athlete's Foot ran up impressive statistics during the personal fitness craze of the early 1970s, but more importantly, sustained its track record into the fashion- conscious 80s. Swelling at the rate of 30 new stores per year, the franchise system offers a proven retail format supported by the resources of an industry leader. Low royalties help offset the steep fees charged by shopping malls for high-traffic retail sites.

Franchise Highlights

Began operating: 1972
Began franchising: 1973
Outlets currently open: 480
Initial franchise fee: $10,000

Monthly royalty: 3%
Advertising fee: .5%
Training program: 1 week
Term: 8 years

The Athlete's Foot (Canada)

Industry experience:	★ ★ ★	*Franchising experience:*	★ ★
Financial strength:	★ ★ ★	*Training & services:*	★ ★ ★
Fees & royalties:	★ ★ ★	*Satisfied franchisees:*	★ ★ ★ ★

The Athelete's Foot
57 King Street
Kitchener, Ontario Canada N2G 1A1
(519) 576-9300

Founded in 1974, The Athlete's Foot of Kitchener, Ontario is the Candian counterpart to the phenomenally successful American retail footwear chain of the same name. The franchisor operates 22 franchises and eight company-owned stores.

The Franchise: The franchisee conducts a retail apparel store, specializing in athletic footwear and accessories, under the trade name The Athlete's Foot.

Franchisee Profile: Franchisees do not need any special qualifications.
Projected Earnings: A projected earnings claim is not available.

Franchisor's Services: Prior to opening, the franchisee receives two weeks of on-site training. The program covers retail merchandising, purchasing, inventory, advertising, and daily operating procedures. The franchisor provides each franchisee with a copy of its confidential operations manual. After the store has opened, a field representative calls on the outlet periodically, to offer guidance and troubleshooting. The Athlete's Foot operates a centralized purchasing program for supplies and inventory. The company also publishes a monthly franchisee newsletter and conducts ongoing seminars and workshops to keep franchisees abreast of new products and consumer trends. A toll-free hotline puts franchise owners and their staffs in touch with company operations experts.

Initial Investment: The initial investment for a Canadian franchise is estimated at $60,000, including the initial franchise fee, lease deposits, improvements, fixtures, and inventory. The franchisor does not offer financial assistance to franchisees.

Advertising: The monthly advertising royalty in Canada is one percent of the gross monthly revenues of the outlet. Contract Highlights: The term of the franchise is ten years. The contract may be renewed for ten more years, if the franchisee is in compliance with all material provisions. The franchisee receives an exclusive territory in conjunction with the franchise.

Fees and Royalties: The initial franchise fee of $10,000 is average for the industry. The three percent monthly royalty, added to the one percent advertising royalty, exacts just four percent of gross sales.

Summary: In Canada, The Athlete's Foot franchise offers fair name recognition, a moderate investment, and a low royalty structure, encouraging the rapid development of new outlets.

Franchise Highlights:

Began operating: 1974	**Monthly royalty: 3%**
Began franchising: 1975	**Advertising fee: 1%**
Outlets currently open: 30	**Training program: As needed**
Initial franchise fee: $10,000	**Term: 10 years**

Fashion Crossroads

Industry experience:	★★★★	*Franchising experience:*	★★★★
Financial strength:	★★★	*Training & services:*	★★★
Fees & royalties:	★★★★	*Satisfied franchisees:*	★★★

Fashion Crossroads
2130 North Hollywood Way
Burbank, California 91505
U.S. (800) 423-2607 Calif. (818) 843-4340

Fashion Crossroads also operates the Mode O Day women's apparel chain, with a combined total of 450 outlets nationwide. More than 90 percent of the firm's outlets are owned by independent franchisees. The company is currently converting Mode O Day stores to the Fashion Crossroads name and motif.

The Franchise: The franchisee operates a retail apparel store, specializing in women's fashions, and doing business under the trade name Fashion Crossroads. A typical outlet is situated in a high-traffic shopping mall or retail strip center, using the franchisor's standardized layout, inventory, and merchandising concepts.

Franchisee Profile: A background in apparel merchandising is beneficial, but not mandatory.

Projected Earnings: A written statement of projected earnings was not available at press time.

Franchisor's Services: Franchisees receive two weeks of training at the Fashion Crossroads flagship in Burbank, California. An additional two weeks of training and pre-opening assistance are provided at the franchisee's site. A set of confidential operating manuals provides background in apparel merchandising and details the management and operation of the retail outlet. A Fashion Crossroads representative provides ongoing management inventory, and merchandising support in periodic visits to the outlet. The franchisor provides merchandise to franchise outlets on a consignment basis, with franchisees paying for their inventories item by item upon sale to the public. This technique keeps the franchisee's initial investment low, while standardizing the merchandise mix throughout the chain.

Initial Investment: The start-up investment is estimated at around $21,000, including lease deposits, fixtures, signs, and an opening inventory. The franchisor does not offer any direct financial assistance to franchisees, but does not require store merchandise to be paid for until sold.

Fees and Royalties: The $3,000 initial fee is exceptionally low for a retail franchise. Fashion Crossroads franchisees do not pay any ongoing royalties or fees, other than the franchisor's margin on merchandise sold by the outlet.

Summary: The Fashion Crossroads franchise is characterized by high visibility and professional merchandising suppport from one of the oldest women's apparel retailers in North America.

Franchise Highlights

Began operating: 1933	**Monthly royalty: None**
Began franchising: 1940	**Advertising fee: None**
Outlets currently open: 450	**Training program: 2 weeks**
Initial franchise fee: $3,000	**Term: 5 years**

Gingiss Formalwear

Industry experience:	★★★★	*Franchising experience:*	★★★★
Financial strength:	★★★	*Training & services:*	★★★
Fees & royalties:	★★★	*Satisfied franchisees:*	★★★

Gingess Formalwear
180 N. LaSalle Street
Chicago, Illinois 60601
(800) 621-7125

If the name Gingiss calls to mind adolescent memories of high school proms and graduation dances, it is because America's best known tuxedo retailer has been dressing up boys and men for more than 50 years. Founded in 1936, Gingess International has established a respectable chain of 240 stores in 40 states — most of them franchises. Gingess stores both sell and rent tuxedoes, enjoying the past patronage of such luminaries as Conrad Hilton, Liberace, and Bob Hope.

The Franchise: The franchisee operates a retail store specializing in men's formal aparel and doing business under the trade name Gingess Formalwear. A typical outlet operates with two full-time and four part-time employees, offering tuxedo sales and rentals to the general public.

Franchisee Profile: A background in sales, marketing, or public relations is desirable. The company is seeking prospective franchisees who can work effectively with the public and present a strong personal image. Absentee ownership is prohibited.

Projected Earnings: Gingiss will provide a written statement of projected earnings prior to the personal interview.

Franchisor's Services: The franchisor provides an intensive two-week training program at the company's headquarters in Chicago. One week is spent at an operating Gingiss Formalwear outlet, for observing store operations first-hand. Attendees are responsible for their own travel and lodging expenses. While the tuition for the training program is included in the initial franchise fee, the costs of travel, lodging, and meals are the franchisee's responsibility. The curriculum covers retail procedures, merchandising techniques, financial administration, staff hiring and training, and marketing.

Gingiss selects the site for the outlet, based on the company's predefined location criteria. A field consultant helps prepare the outlet for opening and is present during the kickoff marketing campaign. An area manager calls on each store periodically, to inspect the operation and offer on-site guidance. The franchisor publishes a newsletter for franchisees and occasionally conducts continuing education seminars. A franchise hotline provides access to company retail operations experts.

Initial Investment: New Gingiss franchisees should be prepared to invest from $125,000 to $160,000. The amount includes lease deposits, fixtures, inventory, and miscellaneous start-up costs. The franchisor offers financial assistance to qualified franchisees.

Advertising: Franchisees contribute three percent of gross monthly revenues for advertising. The franchisor conducts aggressive ad campaigns on behalf of all Gingiss outlets, using magazines such as Cosmopolitan and Modern Bride. The company also makes extensive use of newspapers and radio to promote the Gingiss name. Franchisees receive ad materials for conducting local campaign, as well.

Contract Highlights: The term of the Gingiss franchise is ten years. The contract may be renewed for an additional ten-year term, without the payment of a renewal fee. The franchisee receives a protected territory for the duration of the agreement.

Fees and Royalties: The initial franchise fee of $15,000 is average for the retail trade. The six to ten percent monthly royalty is on the high side. Including the three percent advertising fee, the total royalty burden is from nine to 13 percent of the gross revenues of the outlet.

Summary: The Gingiss franchise is characterized by sound management, a stable history, and a product with consistent consumer demand resistant to fluctuating economic conditions.

Franchise Highlights

Began operating: 1936
Began franchising: 1968
Outlets currently open: 240
Initial franchise fee: $15,000
Monthly royalty: Min. 6%
Max 10%

Advertising fee: 3%
Training program: 2 weeks
Term: 10 years

Just Pants

Industry experience:	★ ★ ★	*Franchising experience:*	★ ★ ★
Financial strength:	★ ★ ★	*Training & services:*	★ ★ ★
Fees & royalties:	★ ★ ★ ★	*Satisfied franchisees:*	★ ★ ★ ★

Just Pants
201 N. Wells Street, Ste. 1530
Chicago, Illinois 60606
(312) 346-5020

Riding high on the casual fashion trend of the late 1960s, Just Pants successfully adapted to the fashion-conscious 70s and 80s, with a mix of jeans, slacks, sweaters, shirts, and blouses. The company has established 120 outlets since the company began franchising in 1969.

The Franchise: The Just Pants franchisee conducts a retail apparel store, focusing primarily on casual trousers for men and women. A typical outlet is situated in approximately 1,750 sq. ft. of space in a shopping mall or strip center, with a staff of two full-time and eight part-time employees. Besides jeans and slacks, franchisees sell a variable selection of shirts, blouses, and accessories.

Franchisee Profile: A background in retail merchandising is preferred, but not mandatory. Absentee ownership is not prohibited.

Projected Earnings: Based on reported sales figures, the average revenues of a Just Pants outlet are about $350,000 before expenses.

Franchisor's Services: The franchisor conducts a two-day training seminar at the company's headquarters in Chicago, supplemented by a week of first-hand observation at an operating Just Pants outlet. Attendees are responsible for their own travel and lodging expenses.

Franchisees have the option of subleasing a turnkey store from Just Pants or developing a new site. The franchisor will assist with selecting a site for the outlet and negotiating a lease for the premises. A field representative will oversee the design and construction of improvements and help set up inventory, bookkeeping, and purchasing systems. When the store is open, an area advisor will provide periodic on-site assistance and training. Just Pants operates a centralized purchasing system for franchisees, working closely with manufacturers to obtain favorable pricing. Franchisee conferences are held twice yearly.

Initial Investment: The franchisor estimates the franchisee's initial investment as follows:

	Low	High
Preliminary deposits	10,500	11,500
Promotion fee	500	1,500
Equipment & fixtures	7,500	10,000
Construction & improvements	50,000	95,000
Opening inventory	40,000	70,000
Miscellaneous	10,000	15,000
Total	118,500	203,000

A portion of the amount for preliminary deposits may be refunded to the franchisee after the lease is secured. The franchisor does not offer any form of direct financial assistance to franchisees.

Advertising: Just Pants franchisees contribute three percent of gross monthly revenues for advertising. The franchisor's advertising programs rely heavily on radio and newspaper promotions. The company occasionally co-sponsors rock concerts to promote the Just Pants name to its target audience of young consumers. The franchisor also participates in manufacturers' co-op advertising programs.

Contract Highlights: The term of the franchise lasts for the lifetime of the store lease. The franchisee does not receive a protected territory for the store. Franchisees are not obligated to purchase inventories from Just Pants.

Fees and Royalties: Just Pants franchisees do not pay any initial franchise fee, other than the first month's lease payment. The five percent monthly royalty is moderate. Including the three percent advertising royalty, the total royalty bite is eight percent of gross sales.

Summary: With a youth-oriented image and marketing strategy, the Just Pants franchise offers a standardized vehicle for entering the retail apparel trade. Franchisees benefit from a manageable initial investment, an proven mall concept, and keen personal attention, especially during the critital start-up period.

Franchise Highlights

Began operating: 1969
Began franchising: 1969
Outlets currently open: 120
Initial franchise fee: None

Monthly royalty: 5%
Advertising fee: 3%
Training program: 10 days
Term: Same as lease

Linda's Love Lace

Industry experience:	★★★	*Franchising experience:*	★
Financial strength:	★★	*Training & services:*	★★★
Fees & royalties:	★★★	*Satisfied franchisees:*	★★★

Linda's Love Lace
P. O. Box 53292
New Orleans, Louisiana 70153
(504) 595-5020

Linda's Love Lace may not be one of the most prolific franchisors in North America, but it certainly has one of the most intriguing names. The trade name capitalizes on the mid 1970s fame of a former adult film actress who recently testified before Congress to protest the pornographic exploitation of women. But the Linda's Love Lace franchise is neither pornographic nor exploitative. The tiny chain of retail lingerie outlets caters to an established consumer market which has been cultivated for years with unqualified success by such illustrious merchandisers as Frederick's of Hollywood and Cosmopolitan magazine.

The Franchise: The franchisee conducts a retail lingerie sales business, operated under the trade name Linda's Love Lace. Franchisees conduct private 'lingerie parties' to demonstrate their wares and recruit customers.

Franchisee Profile: The franchisor stresses the importance of the willingness to invest hard work and effort to make the business succeed.

Projected Earnings: The franchisor does not provide a statement of projected earnings.

Franchisor's Services: The franchisor provides a three-day training program at the company's headquarters in New Orleans. Attendees are responsible for their own travel and lodging expenses. The curriculum presumably covers all aspects of operating a retail lingerie business. An additional week of on-the-job training is provided at the franchisee's place of business.

A Linda's Love Lace representative will visit the outlet periodically, to offer on-site guidance and ongoing training, as needed. The franchisor helps plan the franchisee's inventory requirements and provides purchasing assistance. The company publishes a monthly franchisee newsletter and conducts occasional sales seminars.

Initial Investment: The total investment, including site acquisition, fixtures, inventory, and working capital, is estimated at between $125,000 and $150,000. Linda's Love Lace does not offer any form of financial assistance.

Advertising: Linda's Love Lace franchisees contribute two percent of gross monthly revenues for advertising.

Contract Highlights: The term of the franchise is ten years. The contract may be renewed for an additional term, if the franchisee is in compliance with all material provisions.

Fees and Royalties: The initial franchise fee of $15,000 is average for the retail industry. The five percent monthly royalty, added to the two percent advertising fee, exacts just seven percent of gross sales.

Summary: The Linda's Love Lace franchise offers a unique retail format with a product of demonstratable demand. The company is a small franchisor with limited resources, but franchisees are assured of a high level of personal attention.

Franchise Highlights

Began operating: 1976
Began franchising: 1980
Outlets currently open: 5
Initial franchise fee: $15,000
Monthly royalty: 5%
Advertising fee: 2%
Training program: 3 days
Term: 10 years

T-Shirts Et Cetera

Industry experience:	★★	*Franchising experience:*	★★
Financial strength:	★★★	*Training & services:*	★★★
Fees & royalties:	★★★	*Satisfied franchisees:*	★★★

T-Shirts Et Cetera
5475 Crestview
Memphis, Tennessee
(901) 682-7712

T-Shirts Et Cetera has established 85 outlets since the company began franchising in 1978, opening an average of almost ten new stores each year.

The Franchise: The franchisee operates a retail apparel store, specializing in T-shirts, with or without imprints, and doing business under the trade name T-Shirts Et Cetera. A typical outlet is situated in a retail shopping mall, with a staff of two full-time employees and one part-time. Franchisees offer T-shirts and related merchandise. Customers of the franchise business include mall patrons and consumers.

Franchisee Profile: A background in retail merchandising is beneficial, but not mandatory. Absentee ownership is permitted.

Projected Earnings: The franchisor does not provide a statement of projected earnings.

Franchisor's Services: T-Shirts Et Cetera conducts a three-day training seminar at the company's headquarters in Memphis, Tennessee. Attendees are responsible for their own travel and lodging expenses. The curriculum includes retail operations, merchandising, T-shirt imprinting, and sales promotion. An additional three days of on-the-job training are provided at the franchisee's place of business.

The franchisor will assist with selecting a site for the outlet and negotiating a lease for the premises. When the business is open, a field representative will visit the outlet periodically, to offer guidance and troubleshooting. The franchisor operates a centralized purchasing system to supply franchisees' inventories. T-Shirts Et Cetera publishes a monthly newsletter and offers continuing education for established franchisees. A franchisee hotline puts franchise owners and their staffs in touch with company operations experts.

Initial Investment: The initial investment is estimated at $30,000, including lease deposits, fixtures, equipment, and opening inventory. The franchisor does not offer any form of direct financial assistance to franchisees.

Advertising: T-Shirts Et Cetera franchisees do not pay any monthly advertising royalty, but are responsible for promoting their own outlets. The franchisor supplies sign specifications and point-of-sale materials.

Contract Highlights: The term of the franchise is 20 years. The contract may be renewed for ten more years, at the franchisee's option. The franchisee does not receive a protected territory for the outlet.

Fees and Royalties: The initial franchise fee of $10,000 is low for the industry. The seven percent monthly royalty is average, although there is no separate advertising royalty. Summary: T-Shirts Et Cetera offers an easy-to-operate business format with high visibility, a moderate investment, and a trendy product with demonstrated public appeal.

Franchise Highlights

Began operating: 1978
Began franchising: 1978
Outlets currently open: 85
Initial franchise fee: $10,000
Monthly royalty: 7%
Advertising fee: None
Training program: 3 days
Term: 10 years

T-Shirts Plus

Industry experience:	★★★	*Franchising experience:*	★★★
Financial strength:	★★★	*Training & services:*	★★★
Fees & royalties:	★★★	*Satisfied franchisees:*	★★★

T-Shirts Plus
P. O. Box 20608
Waco, Texas 76702
(800) 433-3307

Capitalizing on the imprinted T-shirt craze of the mid 1970s, T-Shirts Plus has established slighty more than 300 outlets since the company began franchising in 1975 — an average of almost 30 new stores per year.

The Franchise: The franchisee conducts a retail apparel store specializing in T-shirts and other sports wear and doing business under the trade name T-Shirts Plus. A typical outlet is situated in a shopping mall or retail strip center, with a staff of two full-time and four part-time employees. Customers of the outlet include mall patrons and other retail consumers.

Franchisee Profile: A background in apparel retailing is beneficial, but not mandatory. Absentee ownership is a possibility.

Projected Earnings: The franchisor will furnish prospective franchisees with a written projected earnings claim on request.

Franchisor's Services: New franchisees receive training at the company's headquarters in Waco, Texas. Attendees are responsible for their own travel and lodging expenses. The seminar covers general merchandising, purchasing, imprinting techniques, and sales promotion. Additional on-the-job training is provided at the franchisee's place of business.

The franchisor will assist with selecting a site for the outlet and negotiating a lease for the T-shirt store. A field adviser participates in opening activities. When the business is operational, a T-Shirts Plus representative will visit the outlet periodically, to offer troubleshoote operations. The franchisor operates a centralized purchasing program for inventory items, publishes a franchisee newsletter, and organizes continuing education seminars. Company advisers are available by phone as required.

Initial Investment: Prospective franchisees should be able to handle an investment of from $50,000 to $100,000. The amount includes lease deposits, improvements, fixtures, inventory purchases, and working capital requirements. T-Shirts Plus does not offer any direct financial assistance to franchisees.

Advertising: T-Shirts Plus franchisees contribute two percent of gross monthly revenues for advertising. In return, the franchisor supplies point-of-sale materials, commercials, sign designs, and public relations aids.

Contract Highlights: The term of the franchise is 20 years, twice the national average. The contract may be renewed for an additional term, at the franchisee's option. The franchisee does not receive a protected territory for the store. The owner is prohibited from engaging in any business activity that competes directly with the T-Shirts Plus outlet while the contract is in effect.

Fees and Royalties: The initial franchise fee of $17,500 is slightly high for the apparel industry, reflecting, in part, the franchisor's stature as the largest chain of its kind in America. The five percent monthly royalty plus the two percent advertising royalty create a moderate royalty burden of just seven percent of gross sales.

Summary: The T-Shirts Plus franchise offers a ready-made retail system for entering the specialty apparel trade, backed by a professional training program and the competitive benefits of an expansion-oriented chain.

Franchise Highlights

Began operating: 1975
Began franchising: 1975
Outlets currently open: 320
Initial franchise fee: $17,500

Monthly royalty: 5%
Advertising fee: 2%
Training program: 3 days
Term: 10 years

Automotive Franchises

Since the first Ford automobile was assembled in a shed in 1896, the franchise method has been used to sell, fuel, service, repair, paint, rustproof, equip, customize, restore, and tow America's cars. The first horseless carriage was too big to fit through the shed door, and before long, the automobile industry grew too big to define. When the FTC introduced sweeping franchise reforms in 1980, most auto sales and petroleum franchises were excluded from regulation. But car rental agencies, auto service businesses, and paint-and-body shops continue to flourish under the franchise flag.

Franchising has long been a favorite marketing strategy in the car rental industry. The Big Four in the field are Hertz, Avis, National, and Budget, in order of total fleet size and system-wide revenues. But a new, second tier arose in the last decade to fuel competition. The relative newcomers include American International, Thrifty, Dollar, and Alamo. Clearly, the industry as whole is in a state of transition. In 1986, United Airlines (UAL) purchased the Hertz system from its former parent, RCA. A year later, United decided to sell off its non-airline holdings. Avis was recently taken over by Wesray Capital, an investment group headed by former Presidential adviser William Simon. More ownership transfers are in the works as this book goes to press.

The car rental market topped $5 billion in annual revenues for the first time in 1985. Major chains are expanding their fleets by an average of 14 percent per year. But fierce competition among the Big Four and from the second tier have eroded industry-wide profits. The costs of fleet insurance and reservations soared dramatically in the last two years, increasing overhead in a period of dwindling rates.

The automobile aftermarket — including auto parts, repair, rustproofing, and painting businesses — enjoyed a boom period in the recessionary 70s and high-interest 80s, as consumers put off new car purchases and opted to keep their old cars running. Lower interest rates in recent years have revitalized sales and prompted service companies to alter their tactics. The most dramatic growth in this industry over the last three years was exhibited by specialty service boutiques offering such services as speedy oil changes and tune-ups.

AAMCO Transmissions

Industry experience:	★ ★ ★ ★	*Franchising experience:*	★ ★ ★ ★
Financial strength:	★ ★ ★ ★	*Training & services:*	★ ★ ★ ★
Fees & royalties:	★ ★ ★	*Satisfied franchisees:*	★ ★ ★

AAMCO Transmissions, Inc.
1 Presidential Boulevard
Bala Cynwyd, Pennsylvania 19004
(215) 668-2900

AAMCO enjoys the largest share of the world's auto transmission service market. Established as a franchise operation in 1963, the company boasts nearly 1,000 outlets today, none of which are company-owned.

The Franchise: The franchisee operates a retail automobile service business specializing in transmission repair and maintenance, using the franchisor's trade name and trademarks. AAMCO transmission shops must meet company standards for service and sell only authorized products. A typical outlet employs four full-time mechanics and one part-time mechanic.

Franchisee Profile: AAMCO trains franchisees in both transmission service and business management. Technical experience is unnecessary. The company is currently seeking applicants with general management backgrounds.

Projected Earnings: AAMCO does not furnish prospective franchisees with a written statement of projected earnings.

Franchisor's Services: The franchisor provides a four-week training program at Bala Cynwyd, Pennsylvania. Franchisees are responsible for travel and lodging expenses. Besides auto transmission repair and service, the curriculum covers all phases of business administration. An additional week of on-the-job training is provided at the franchisee's place of business. A field representative assists with personnel recruitment and Grand Opening promotions.

Initial Investment: The total investment is estimated at from $100,000 to $110,000.

Advertising: The franchisor conducts aggressive national advertising campaigns on behalf of all AAMCO outlets. The advertising royalty varies depending on location.

Contract Highlights: The franchise term is 15 years, with the option to renew the contract for an additional 15 years. The franchisee does not receive an exclusive territory.

Fees and Royalties: The initial franchise fee of $25,000 covers opening training and support, but not franchisee travel expenses. The nine percent franchise royalty is slightly higher than the industry average, reflecting, in part, a premium on the AAMCO name and reputation.

Summary: AAMCO is an established franchisor with a highly developed training and support system, bolstered by continuing public demand for auto transmission service.

Franchise Highlights

Began operating: 1963	**Monthly royalty: 9%**
Began franchising: 1963	**Advertising fee: Varies**
Outlets currently open: 920	**Training program: 5 weeks**
Initial franchise fee: $25,000	**Term: 15 years**

Ajax Rent A Car

Industry experience:	★ ★ ★	*Franchising experience:*	★ ★ ★
Financial strength:	★ ★ ★	*Training & services:*	★ ★ ★
Fees & royalties:	★ ★ ★	*Satisfied franchisees:*	★ ★ ★

Ajax Rent A Car
1801 Century Park East
Los Angeles, California 90067
(213) 552-9300

Headquartered near Los Angeles International airport, Ajax Rent A Car boasts locations in principal travel destinations, with ample representation at airports. The company participates in major airline and travel agency reservation programs, assuring a consistent stream of new and repeat business. Ajax is currently seeking prospective franchisees in all U.S. and Canadian markets, as well as in selected overseas territories.

The Franchise: The franchisee conducts an automobile rental business, supported by a national toll-free reservation system and operated under the trade name Ajax Rent A Car. A typical outlet offers a broad range of passenger automobiles for daily, weekly, and monthly rental, from economy size cars to luxury sedans.

Franchisee profile: Some prior experience in the automobile rental business is preferred, but not mandatory. Absentee ownership is not encouraged. Preference is given to applicants who will operate and manage the franchise business themselves.

Projected Earnings: Ajax does not provide a written statement of projected earnings.

Franchisor's Services: The franchisor's training program consists of one week of first-hand experience at the Ajax outlet at Los Angeles International airport, plus an additional week of on-the- job assistance at the franchisee' place of business.

Ajax will assist new franchisees with selecting a site for the outlet and negotiating a lease for the premises. The support package also includes periodic visitations by a field representative and annual conferences. A purchasing co-op permits vehicles and supplies to be acquired at a discount.

Initial Investment: Depending on the size of the rental fleet, franchisees should be prepared to spend between $50,000 and $300,000 to establish and develop the outlet. The total includes the initial franchise fee, lease deposits, vehicles, fixtures, and supplies.

Advertising: The franchisor offers promotional materials, such as fliers and approved advertising designs, and conducts periodic advertising campaigns on behalf of franchisees. Ajax franchisees are not required to pay a monthlty advertising fee. Franchisees derive leads from the franchisor's 24-hour toll free reservation system, as well as from airline and travel agency computers.

Contract Highlights: The term of the franchise is ten years, the industry average. At the end of the term, the franchise may be renewed if the franchisee is substantially in compliance with the terms and provisions of the franchise agreement. Ajax designates an exclusive territory for the outlet, promising not to sell or open other outlets within the protected area. Area franchises are available, subject to negotiation.

Fees and Royalties: The seven percent franchise royalty is moderate by industry standards, but the initial franchise fee tends to the high side. Because there is no mandatory advertising royalty, the overall royalty picture is favorable to franchisees.

Summary: Ajax is an established car rental franchisor with a solid base of outlets and a capable reservation system. Desirable territories in major markets are still available.

Franchise Highlights

Began operating: 1969
Began franchising: 1971
Outlets currently open: 190
Initial franchise fee: Min $15,000
Max. $99,000

Monthly royalty: 7%
Advertising fee: None
Training program: 2 weeks
Term: 10 years

American International Rent A Car

Industry experience:	★★★★	*Franchising experience:*	★★★★
Financial strength:	★★★	*Training & services:*	★★★★
Fees & royalties:	★★★	*Satisfied franchisees:*	★★★★

American International Rent A Car Corporation
4801 Spring Valley Road
Suite 120-B
Dallas, Texas 75244
(214) 233-6530

To compete with the established giants of the car rental industry, American International Rent A Car emphasizes discount prices, achieved in part by the use of off-airport locations. Since 1969, American has steadily gained ground in the market, with approximately 1,500 franchises operating in 38 states and 25 foreign countries.

American International is a uniquely democratic franchise system. None of its outlets are company-owned, and corporate officers and directors are elected by franchise owners.

The Franchise: The typical American International outlet is located at an airport, or in an urban area with dense traffic characteristics, with a staff of from five to 12 full-time employees. The objective of each franchisee is to offer comfortable, reliable rental transportation at competitive prices. The franchisor stresses customer service above all other considerations in the business. The franchisee's fleet may vary from 75 to 200 vehicles.

Franchisee Profile: Experience in car rental service and/or business management is helpful but not a prerequisite. American International is not currently seeking absentee owners, preferring instead that franchisees manage their outlets personally.

Projected Earnings: The franchisor does not provide a written statement of projected earnings. Based on the company's reported annual sales, the average gross of an American International franchise is about $154,000 per year. That average factors in outlets in North America, South America, and Europe.

Franchisor's Services: As soon as the franchise contract is signed, company representatives assist the new franchisee in selecting a suitable site for the outlet, obtaining financing for the rental fleet, and procuring insurance.

Franchisees have the option of receiving complete or partial training. Field representatives will spend up to nine days at the franchisee's place of business reviewing agency operations. In addition, an intensive two-day workshop is conducted at company headquarters in Dallas, Texas. The curriculum includes fleet planning, sales and marketing, customer service, and accounting.

The support package also includes ongoing training and on-site consultation. Franchisees have unlimited access to a company operations expert by phone.

Initial Investment: Depending on the initial fee and the size of the rental fleet, new franchisees should be prepared to invest from $30,000 to $400,000 to get the business off the ground. Some direct financial assistance is available.

Advertising: All franchises benefit from a centrally administered co-op ad program, but there is no mandatory advertising royalty. The company operates a national toll-free reservation system and is represented in major airline and travel agency computer systems. American International advertises extensively in airline in-flight magazines and publications that cater to travel agents.

Contract Highlights: The term of the franchise is five years. The contract is renewable if the franchisee is in compliance with all material provisions. The franchisee receives exclusive rights to a specified territory. An option to expand or subfranchise within a large geographic region may be negotiated. Whereas many franchisors discourage absentee ownership, American Internation offers the option of hiring a qualified manager to run the business. The outlet must be open within six months after the franchise agreement has been signed.

Fees and Royalties: The initial fee varies, depending on the territory and fleet size. Existing franchisees paid between $5,000 to as much as $175,000 to establish their outlets. Franchise royalty fees run seven percent of gross monthly revenues — average for the industry — but the company does not exact advertising royalties.

Summary: American International Car Rental has steadily increased its share of the rental car market during its 15 years of franchise expansion. The democratic organization of this franchisee-shared corporation gives it a special appeal. In a recent survey of overall customer satisfaction, *Consumer Reports* gave high marks to American International, which tied for second place with Budget, Hertz, and Avis.

Franchise Highlights

Began operating: 1969
Began franchising: 1969
Outlets currently open: 1,500
Initial franchise fee: Min. $5,000
Max. $400,000

Monthly royalty: 2% to 7%
Advertising fee: None
Training program: 11 days
Term: 5 years

Avis Rent A Car

Industry experience:	★ ★ ★ ★	*Franchising experience:*	★ ★ ★ ★
Financial strength:	★ ★ ★ ★	*Training & services:*	★ ★ ★ ★
Fees & royalties:	★ ★ ★	*Satisfied franchisees:*	★ ★ ★ ★

Avis Rent A Car System
900 Old Country Road
Garden City, New York 11530

To Warren Avis, the nation's second largest car rental chain has seemed like 'a lost girlfriend,' since he sold the business to a Hertz franchisee in 1954. In April of 1986, the Avis system was purchased for $250 million by Wesray Capital, marking the fifth time that the company's ownership had changed hands since 1975. About half of the Avis car rental agencies operating in North America are franchised outlets. New franchises are presently unavailable, but occasionally an established Avis franchisee may place his or her outlet(s) up for sale. Even in those cases, the franchisor may exercise the right of first refusal to buy back the franchise, making the purchase of an independent Avis outlet a rare opportunity.

The Franchise: The franchisee conducts an automobile and truck rental business, operated under the Avis trademarks. A typical outlet maintains a fleet of economy, compact, full size, and luxury automobiles, plus selected trucks, vans, and specialty vehicles. Franchisees may also derive profits from the sale of insurance, arrangements with tour operators, long-term auto leasing, and used cars sales. Corporate customers account for more than 60 percent of the outlet's business.

Franchisee Profile: Business and management skill are considered more important than a background in the rent-a-car industry.

Projected Earnings: Based on system-wide sales, the average volume of an Avis outlet is about $800,000 per year, before expenses. This figure does not distinguish between company-owned outlets and franchises, nor take into consideration such variables as on-premises airport locations or fleet size.

Franchisor's Services: Although Avis is not currently recruiting new franchisees, established outlets benefit from one of the most aggressive corporate accounts programs in the car rental industry. By guaranteeing discount rates to management and employees of major corporations, the company cultivates repeat business on behalf of all Avis locations.

Initial Investment: At present, the only viable avenue to owning an Avis franchise is to purchase an existing agency. A survey of Avis franchisees reveals some outlets valuated as high as a million dollars, with most falling in the $500,000 to $900,000 range.

Advertising: Avis is a leading national advertisor, making extensive use of television, radio, magazines, and newspapers. The franchisor operates a national toll-free reservation system in which all Avis agencies participate. The chain is also represented by major airline and travel agency computers.

Summary: To purchase an established Avis franchise, the buyer must meet the franchisor's standard qualifications for Avis franchisees and agree to assume all obligations of the existing franchise agreement. Although Avis is one the second largest chain in its field, locations in major markets are rarely available. In a recent *Consumer Reports* survey, Avis ranked second — tied with Budget, American International, and Hertz — in overall customer satisfaction.

Franchise Highlights

Outlets currently open: 1200
Initial franchise fee: Varies
Monthly royalty: Varies

Big O Tires

Industry experience:	★ ★ ★ ★	*Franchising experience:*	★ ★ ★
Financial strength:	★ ★ ★ ★	*Training & services:*	★ ★ ★
Fees & royalties:	★ ★ ★ ★	*Satisfied franchisees:*	★ ★ ★ ★

Big O Tire Dealers, Inc.
P. O. Box 3206
Englewood, Colorado 80155
(303) 779-9991

Although lacking the name recognition of Goodyear or Goodrich, Big O Tires has built a successful franchise system on the premise of a premium tire dealership. Like most of their competitors, Big O franchisees offer an exclusive line of tires for passenger cars, trucks, and industrial equipment.

The Franchise: The Big O franchisee operates a retail tire store, typically with six full-time employees, selling the franchisor's private brand of tires and performing related services, such as wheel alignments, tire rotation, and balancing. The outlet purchases its inventories from the franchisor.

Franchisee Profile: Previous experience in the tire industry or automotive services field is preferred, but not mandatory. The company is not currently considering absentee owners or area franchisees.

Projected Earnings: The franchisor does not make any statement regarding projected earnings of the outlet.

Franchisor's Services: Big O conducts a two-week training program at the company's headquarters near Denver, Colorado. The franchisor assists with selecting a site for the outlet and negotiating the lease. The company also helps plans the franchisee's inventory requirements, based on local market conditions and budget considerations. A centralized purchasing system expedites re-ordering. A Big O field consultant visits each outlet periodically to provide on-site assistance in the day-to-day operation of the tire store.

Initial Investment: Although there is no initial franchise fee, Big O franchisees must invest from $100,000 to $160,000 to open a new outlet. The total includes the lease deposits, site improvements, tools and equipment, an opening inventory, and working capital. Big O does not currently offer any form of direct financial assistance to franchisees.

Advertising: Franchisees contribute four percent of their gross revenues to a co-op advertising fund, which the franchisor uses to conduct national and regional campaigns. Representative media include major newspapers, television, and radio. Franchisees also receive ad mattes, logo art, and promotional aids for use in local advertising efforts.

Contract Highlights: The term of the franchise is ten years — the same as the industry average. The contract may be renewed for an additional ten-year term, providing that the franchisee is in compliance with all material provisions. The franchisee does not receive a protected territory. No area or subfranchising rights are granted by the franchise agreement.

Fees and Royalties: Besides the two percent monthly franchise royalty, the franchisor derives profits from the sale of tires to Big O dealers. Coupled with the four percent advertising contribution, the franchisee's royalty burden is still relatively light.

Summary: Big O franchisees benefit from increasing name recognition, a growing base of franchised dealerships, and a manageable royalty burden.

Franchise Highlights

Began operating: 1962
Began franchising: 1964
Outlets currently open: 250
Initial franchise fee: None
Monthly royalty: 2%
Advertising fee: 4%
Training program: 2 weeks
Term: 10 years

Budget Rent A Car

Industry experience:	★★★★	*Franchising experience:*	★★★★
Financial strength:	★★★★	*Training & services:*	★★★★
Fees & royalties:	★★★★	*Satisfied franchisees:*	★★★★

Budget Rent A Car
200 N. Michigan Avenue
Chicago, Illinois 60601
(312) 580-5000

The fourth largest automobile rental chain, Budget Rent A Car boasts over 3,000 outlets in more than 100 countries. The company's orange and black logo can be seen in such remote places as the jungles of Bora Bora and the silent volcanoes of Huahine. Founded in 1958 and sold to the Transamerica conglomerate ten years later, Budget is now owned by a large investment bank. The company has an aggressive corporate account program and a cooperative business arrangement with Sears Roebuck, the nation's largest retailer. With locations still available in desirable markets and solid name recognition in the business travel market, the Budget franchise must be considered one of premier franchise opportunities in the rental car trade.

The Franchise: The franchisee operates an automobile rental business, offering economy, compact, and standard size cars, in addition to selected luxury sedans, sports cars, and specialty vehicles. The typical Budget Rent A Car outlet maintains a fleet of between 20 and 50 passenger cars and from five to ten trucks and vans. Customers of the outlet include business travelers, vacationing family units, and corporate accounts. Budget Rent A Car outlets service the nationwide Sears Car and Truck Rental network.

Franchisee Profile: Prior experience in car or truck rentals is preferred, but not mandatory. Absentee ownership is permitted.

Projected Earnings: Budget does not provide a written claim of estimated or anticipated profits of the franchise outlet. However, based on reported annual sales, the average gross revenues of a Budget outlet are about $300,000 before expenses. This figure includes both company-operated and franchised agencies, regardless of location.

Franchisor's Services: The franchisor provides a one-week training program at the corporate headquarters in Chicago. Additional on-the-job training may be provided at the franchisee's place of business, as required. If the franchisee will operate the business as an absentee owner, both the owner and the designated manager must attend the mandatory training program. The curriculum includes fleet operations, vehicle purchasing and maintenance, safety procedures, marketing techniques and record keeping.

The franchisor operates an efficient, toll free reservation system, which is tied into major airline and travel agency networks. Budget will assist the new franchisee with selecting a site for the outlet and negotiating a lease for the premises. Periodic visitations from a field representative and ongoing advice and consultation are part of the support package. Budget also operates a cooperative vehicle purchasing program to assist franchisees with obtaining credit and acquiring vehicles for their fleets.

Initial Investment: The Budget Rent A Car franchisee must invest from $250,000 to $750,000 in the business, including the initial fee, lease of the premises, equipment, fixtures, signs, vehicles, and insurance. Although the franchisor does not formally finance any part of the investment, the company may be willing to defer partial payment of the initial franchise fee.

Advertising: Franchisees contribute two percent of gross monthly revenues to a national co-op ad fund, which the franchisor uses to conduct promotional campaigns on behalf of all Budget Rent A Car outlets. The franchisor is a 'partner' in United Airline's Mileage Plus program for frequent fliers and aggressively markets the Budget name to travel agencies and airline customers. The franchisor may also assist with Yellow Pages advertising and other local promotions.

Contract Highlights: The term of the franchise is five years, half the ten-year industry average. The contract is renewable on expiration, assuming the franchisee is not in default of any material provisions.

Fees and Royalties: The five percent monthly franchise royalty is low by industry standards. Coupled with the two percent co-op advertising contribution, the franchisee's royalty burden is relatively moderate. Although the minimum franchise fee is $15,000, most of the locations that are still available are more costly.

Summary: One of the oldest and most easily recognized car rental chains, Budget enjoys good franchisee satisfaction, excellent advertising reach, and extensive cooperative benefits commensurate with the company's stature as one of the 'Big Four' of the rental car industry. *Consumer Reports* rated Budget second in the industry with regard to overall customer satisfaction — in a tie with American International, Hertz, and Avis.

Franchise Highlights

Began operating: 1958
Began franchising: 1960
Outlets currently open: 3,100
Initial franchise fee: Min $15,000

Monthly royalty: Min. 7.5%
Advertising fee: 2%
Training program: 1 week
Term: 5 years

Champion Auto

Industry experience:	★★★★	*Franchising experience:*	★★★★
Financial strength:	★★★	*Training & services:*	★★★★
Fees & royalties:	★★★★	*Satisfied franchisees:*	★★★

Champion Auto Stores, Inc.
5520 N. County Road 18
New Hope, Minnesota 55428
(612) 535-5984

The Champion Auto franchise sprang up in 1961 as an outgrowth of the trend in do-it-yourself retailing of all types. Rather than catering to repair garages and service stations, Champion set out to establish a chain of stores that would sell auto parts and supplies directly to the consumer. Over the last 25 years, the franchise system has enjoyed a steady growth rate to more than 110 outlets in major U.S. markets. More than 90 percent of the Champion Auto stores operating today are franchised stores.

The Franchise: The franchisee is engaged in the retail automobile parts business for the fix-it-yourself auto repair market, operating under the trade name Champion Auto Store. Automated accounting, purchasing, and inventory systems free the franchisee to focus on customer service and volume selling. According to a company spokesman, the Champion outlet is a 'parts supermarket,' stocking and merchandising a comprehensive array of automotive parts, accessories, and supplies.

Franchisee Profile: Prior experience in the auto parts business is not required. Preference is given to prospective franchisees who demonstrate the qualities of good retail salesmanship.

Franchisor's Services: The franchisor conducts a training program at the company's headquarters in Minneapolis. Franchisees are responsible for their own travel and lodging expenses. The curriculum includes first-hand observation of an operating Champion Auto Store. The length of the program depends on the amount of training required by each franchisee — normally, from eight to ten days. The program may be expanded as needed.

The franchisor selects the site for the outlet, negotiates the lease, and plans the store's layout and improvements. Franchisees also receive help with inventory planning and opening promotions. The ongoing support package includes periodic inspections and advice from a Champion field representative, computerized accounting and inventory systems, in-store promotional aids, and advertising assistance.

Initial Investment: The total investment is estimated at $130,000, including deposits, site buildout, fixtures, displays, and an opening inventory.

Advertising: Although the franchisor does not charge an advertising royalty, Champion aggressively conducts national, regional, and local advertising campaigns on behalf of all outlets. Target media include television, radio, and major metropolitan newspapers.

Contract Highlights: The franchise does not have a definite term. In effect, the contract remains in force as long as both parties are in compliance and agreement. The franchise is not accompanied by an exclusive territory.

Fees and royalties: Champion Auto franchisees do not pay either an initial franchise fee or any monthly royalties. The franchisor derives its primary profits by supplying merchandise to franchisees for resale.

Summary: Champion Auto franchisees benefit from good name recognition in markets where outlets are already operating, a moderate initial investment, an aggressive and effective advertising program, and consistent demand sustained by a repeat customer base of fix-it-yourself car owners.

Franchise Highlights

Began operating: 1956
Began franchising: 1961
Outlets currently open: 115
Initial franchise fee: None
Monthly royalty: None
Advertising fee: None
Training program: 10 days
Term: None

Classic Car Wash

Industry experience: ★ ★ ★
Financial strength: ★ ★ ★
Fees & royalties: ★ ★ ★
Franchising experience: ★ ★ ★
Training & services: ★ ★ ★ ★
Satisfied franchisees: ★ ★ ★ ★

Classic Car Wash
871 E. Hamilton Avenue
Campbell, California 95008
(408) 538-7836

In the past decade, Classic Car Wash has successfully expanded in California, Illinois, and Texas, where name recognition is strongest. The franchise concept is based on a totally automated car wash system housed in a standardized facility with a high-tech image.

The Franchise: The franchisee operates a retail car wash business, offering complete interior cleaning and exterior washing, polishing, and waxing in an automated facility. The outlet conforms to the franchisor's specifications for architecture, design, furnishing, and signage.

Franchisee Profile: Some experience in managing a car wash or supervising employees is preferable, but not mandatory. The company will consider granting area franchises to develop a large territory or region.

Earnings Projection: Classic will provide a written statement of projected earnings to prospective franchisees on request.

Franchisor's Services: Classic conducts a two-week training program at the company's headquarters in Campbell, California, just east of Los Angeles. The curriculum includes car wash techniques, equipment maintenance, marketing, and business administration. An additional week of on-the-job training is provided at the franchisee's place of business.

The franchisor assists in selecting a site for the outlet, negotiating a lease for the premises, and preparing the business for opening. A field representative provides ongoing guidance and assistance in periodic visits to the outlet. In addition, the Classic conducts seminars and workshops and offers centralized purchasing of car wash supplies at special prices.

Initial Investment: Franchisees must be prepared to invest between $500,000 and $1 million to establish and develop the outlet. The total includes the initial franchise fee, build-up of the site, and the Classic automated car wash system. The franchisor does directly finance any part of the investment, but Classic will assist franchisees with obtaining financial assistance from a third party.

Advertising: All Classic franchisees contribute one percent of their gross monthly revenues to fund advertising campaigns.

Contract Highlights: The term of the franchise is 20 years, twice the industry average. The contract is renewable at the end of the term, if the franchisee is in compliance with all material provisions. The franchisee receives a protected territory along with the franchise.

Fees and Royalties: The initial fee is moderate to high for the industry. The six and a half percent monthly royalty is low, particularly since the advertising bite is only one percent.

Summary: An automated car wash business represents a ponderable investment, but customer demand is consistently strong, particularly in the Sun Belt where the Classic name is best known. Classic franchises are typified by a well conceived operating format, uniform standards, and a strong base of repeat customers.

Franchise Highlights

Began operating: 1978
Began franchising: 1979
Outlets currently open: 90
Initial franchise fee: Min $15,000
Monthly royalty: 6.5%
Advertising fee: 1%
Training program: 2 weeks
Term: 20 years

Dollar Rent A Car

Industry experience:	★★★★	*Franchising experience:*	★★★★
Financial strength:	★★★★	*Training & services:*	★★★★
Fees & royalties:	★★★	*Satisfied franchisees:*	★★★★

Dollar Systems
6141 W. Century Boulevard
Los Angeles, California 90045
(213) 776-8100

The service objective of the Dollar Rent A Car system is to provide full-service automobile and truck rentals at competitive rates. The company's reputation as a discount source for quality car rentals has spurred the Dollar system's growth from a single lot in 1966 to about 550 outlets today. Although individual outlets are available from master franchisees and subfranchisors, the parent company, Dollar Systems, primarily markets area franchises with subfranchising rights within set geographical boundaries.

The Franchise: The company is currently emphasizing area franchises, in which a 'master' franchisee agrees to sell or open outlets within a large regional territory. Each outlet operates a car and truck rental business offering a full range of vehicles, from economy cars to utility vans, backed by the franchise's reputation as a discount agency. A typical Dollar Rent A Car outlet is located at a major airport or downtown location, catering to business travelers.

Franchisee Profile: No previous experience in the car or truck rental trade is required. The franchisor is currently interested in applicants with general business experience, with a preference for prospective area franchisees.

Franchisor's Services: Dollar Systems does not operate a formal franchise training school at its corporate headquarters, preferring instead to orient and train new franchisees at their places of business. The franchisor assists with selecting a site for the outlet, negotiating a lease for the premises, and acquiring a fleet of vehicles no older than two years. The on-site training program includes sales personnel training, rental car coordination, and assistance in planning local advertising campaigns.

Dollar also conducts national advertising programs on behalf of franchisees, targeting publications read by business travelers. A field representative makes periodic visits to each franchise outlet and counsels franchisees on business operations. The franchisor conducts frequent seminars and refresher courses to keep franchisees abreast of new developments and techniques. An international reservation system provides a continuous source of leads to franchisees.

Initial Investment: Dollar franchisees should be prepared to invest at least $50,000 per outlet. A credit line of $500,000 to $1 million is also required.

Advertising: Although Dollar Systems does not levy an ongoing advertising fee, the franchisor conducts co-op ad programs on behalf of its franchisees. Target media include in-flight magazines and metropolitan newspapers. The franchisor will also reimburse franchisees for approved ads placed in local media.

Contract Highlights: The franchise agreement does not have a definite term. The franchisee receives a protected territory in which Dollar Systems will not grant other franchises or compete with the franchisee.

Fees and Royalties: The nine percent franchise royalty on gross revenues of the outlet includes co-op advertising. The initial franchise fee is calculated on the basis of $150 for each 1,000 residents in the designated territory. Thus, a territory with a population of 500,000 would be worth $75,000. The minimum franchise fee is $7,500.

Summary: Dollar receives high marks for first-hand franchisee assistance, a respectable base of outlets, and attention to detail. One of the company's strengths is its focus on simplifying the day-to-day aspects of conducting the business. Its worldwide reservation ties offers a competitive edge in reaching the foreign traveler.

Franchise Highlights

Began operating: 1966
Began franchising: 1969
Outlets currently open: 550
Initial franchise fee: Min $7,500
Max Varies

Monthly royalty: 9%
Advertising fee: None
Training program: On-the-job, as needed
Term: None

Endrust

Industry experience:	★ ★ ★ ★	*Franchising experience:*	★ ★ ★
Financial strength:	★ ★ ★	*Training & services:*	★ ★ ★ ★
Fees & royalties:	★ ★ ★ ★	*Satisfied franchisees:*	★ ★ ★ ★

Endrust Industries
1725 Washington Road
Pittsburgh, PA 15241
(412) 831-1255

Pennsylvania-based Endrust Industries has franchised extensively in the Ohio Valley since 1978, specializing in automobile rustproofing and reconditioning. Today, Endrust boasts system-wide revenues in excess of $3 billion per year. Franchisees may operate either as standalone car detailing operations, or as adjuncts to related automotive services. The one-time licensing fee covers the greater part of the franchisee's initial investment. The franchisor does not charge an ongoing royalty of any kind, instead relying on profits from the sale of merchandise and supplies to franchisees.

The Franchise: The franchisee operates a retail automobile detailing and reconditioning service under the name Endrust Car Care Center. Absentee ownership is discouraged, although the franchisor may allow the franchise business to be conducted in association with an existing, related business, such as an auto glass or upholstering service.

Endrust franchisees channel Endrust products to the retail market, using the trade and service marks Endrust (rustproofing products and services), End-A-Stain (fabric protection service), and End-A-Flat (sealant products). Franchisees may also offer theft protection products.

Franchisee Profile: Prior experience in auto detailing or a related service is considered a plus, but not mandatory.

Projected Earnings: The franchisor provides a projected earnings claim to prospective franchisees prior to signing the franchise agreement. A franchisee who charges a retail price of $210 and services three vehicles per day would realize approximately $150,000 in gross sales. Established franchisees report annual profits of $80,000 or more, with some realizing twice that amount.

Franchisor's Services: The franchisor provides a one-week training program at the franchisee's place of business. In addition, Endrust offers assistance in selecting a site for the franchise operation. After the outlet has opened for business, an area manager periodically visits each outlet to provide on-site troubleshooting and guidance. The company operates a franchisee hotline to provide access to key support personnel, and publishes a newsletter to inform franchisees of industry trends and developments.

Initial Investment: The franchisee's total initial investment is estimated at between $30,000 and $50,000. The amount includes a startup equipment package and opening inventory of Endrust products, warranty slips, and promotional items.

Fees and Royalties: Aside from the initial investment, there are no other fees or royalties.

Advertising: The franchisor does not presently administer a co-op advertising program on behalf of Endrust franchisees. Advertising assistance consists of preprinted promotional aids, such as bumperstickers and warranty fliers, which the franchisee may purchase for dissemination to prospective customers.

Contract Highlights: The Endrust franchise agreement specifies an exclusive territory in which the franchising corporation agrees it will not compete with the franchisee. The contract does not have a specific term.

Summary: Endrust has a high level of franchisee satisfaction, based on the company's perceived reputation and ongoing support. In effect, the franchisee receives a lifetime grant of franchise, entitling him or her to almost unlimited distribution rights to Endrust products and access to advice and counsel from the franchisor's field staff. The low initial investment and absence of ongoing royalties make the Endrust franchise an easy business to establish and develop.

Franchise Highlights

Began operating: 1969
Began franchising: 1978
Outlets currently open: 80
Initial franchise fee: Min $30,000
Monthly royalty: None
Advertising fee: None
Training program: 1 week
Term: None

Firestone Tire Centers

Industry experience: ★ ★ ★ ★
Financial strength: ★ ★ ★ ★
Fees & royalties: ★ ★ ★ ★
Franchising experience: ★ ★ ★ ★
Training & services: ★ ★ ★ ★
Satisfied franchisees: ★ ★ ★ ★

Firestone Tire and Rubber Company
P. O. Box 81073
Brook Park, Ohio 44142

One of the oldest tire companies in America, Firestone has opened more than 24,000 dealerships since 1900. Franchisees and authorized dealers market Firestone tires, auto parts and supplies, and related services.

The Franchise: The franchisee operates an automotive tire and automotive service business under the name Firestone Tire Center. In addition to the Firestone line of tires, the outlet may also offer automotive services, such as tune-ups, front end alignment, and brake service.

Franchisee Profile: Prior experience in the tire industry is considered beneficial, but not mandatory.

Projected Earnings: The franchisor does not provide a written earnings claim for prospective franchisees.

Franchisor's Services: The franchisor assists franchisees with inventory and sales planning, and provides point-of-sale merchandising aids. Periodic visits by a field representative and franchisee seminars are also part of the support program.

Initial Investment: The total investment is estimated at $65,000.

Advertising: Firestone conducts aggressive national advertising campaigns, using television, radio, and major metropolitan newspapers. In addition, the franchisor provides franchisees with in-store promotional aids and brochures.

Franchise Highlights

Began operating: 1900
Outlets currently open: 24,000

B F Goodrich

Industry experience:	★ ★ ★ ★	*Franchising experience:*	★ ★ ★ ★
Financial strength:	★ ★ ★ ★	*Training & services:*	★ ★ ★ ★
Fees & royalties:	★ ★ ★ ★	*Satisfied franchisees:*	★ ★ ★

Uniroyal Goodrich
600 S. Main Street
Akron, Ohio 44318
(800) 321-1800

Though it does not appear on any blimp, the Goodrich name was once displayed on the suits worn into space by astronauts. The B F Goodrich franchise, a.k.a Uniroyal Goodrich, is devoted to the merchandising and installation of Goodrich tires. All of the company's 2,200 outlets are franchised dealers. Goodrich and Uniroyal outlets are all part of the same system, products of a 1984 merger between the nation's second and fourth largest tire companies.

The Franchise: The Goodrich franchisee operates a retail tire store, typically with three full-time and two part-time employees, selling Goodrich merchandise for passenger cars, trucks, farm equipment, and industrial vehicles. The outlet purchases inventories from the franchisor at wholesale prices based on volume commitments.

Franchisee Profile: Previous experience in the tire industry or automotive services field is considered valuable, but not mandatory. The company is not currently considering absentee owners. The person who is awarded the franchise is responsible for managing the outlet.

Projected Earnings: The franchisor does not make any statement regarding projected earnings of the outlet.

Franchisor's Services: Goodrich provides from four to eight weeks of training at the franchisee's place of business. The franchisee is responsible for selecting a site for the premises, although the franchisor will offer guidance and assist in negotiating the lease. The Goodrich National Order Processing Center dispatches inventory purchases and monitors the status of each shipment. The company also provides inventory planning assistance, promotional aids, periodic seminars and workshops.

Initial Investment: Although there is no initial franchise fee to open a Goodrich tire center, franchised dealers should be prepared to invest about $100,000 to open a new outlet. The franchisor does not currently offer any direct form of financial assistance, but will help prospective franchisees apply for loans from a third party.

Advertising: Although the company does not exact an advertising royalty, the franchisor aggressively promotes the Goodrich name and products in national ad campaigns, including television, radio, newspapers, and magazines.

Contract Highlights: The franchise must be renewed every year, giving each party ample opportunity to review the performance of the other. Renewal may not be unreasonably denied, if both parties are substantially in compliance with all the provisions. Area franchises are not currently available.

Fees and Royalties: There are no formal franchise fees or royalties connected with the Goodrich franchise, but the company derives profits from equipment, supplies, and inventory sold to franchisees. All new franchisees must purchase an opening inventory of Goodrich merchandise.

Summary: Solid name recognition, a healthy base of franchise outlets, and the absence of a royalty burden give the Goodrich franchisee stable footing in an intensely competitive market.

Franchise Highlights

Began operating: 1900
Began franchising: 1925
Outlets currently open: 2,200
Initial franchise fee: None
Monthly royalty: None
Advertising fee: None
Training program: 4 weeks
Term: 1 year

Goodyear Tire Centers

Industry experience:	★ ★ ★ ★	*Franchising experience:*	★ ★ ★
Financial strength:	★ ★ ★ ★	*Training & services:*	★ ★ ★ ★
Fees & royalties:	★ ★ ★ ★	*Satisfied franchisees:*	★ ★ ★ ★

Goodyear Tire and Rubber Company
144 E. Market Street
Akron, Ohio 44316
(216) 796-3467

Founded in 1898, 'the company with the blimp' has one of the most recognizable names in American commerce. The Goodyear system boasts more than 5,000 authorized tire dealers and 620 franchisees through which the parent company channels its products. Launched in 1968, the franchise program is characterized today by one of the most comprehensive training programs in the industry, computer-based bookkeeping, and an exclusive focus on Goodyear merchandise.

The Franchise: The franchisee operates an automotive tire and service business under the name Goodyear Tire Center. The outlet sells only Goodyear products and other merchandise specified by the franchisor. Besides tires, the product/service mix may include light auto maintenance, such as tune-up service and brake repair. The typical franchisee leases both the business premises and all related service equipment from the franchisor.

Franchisee Profile: The ideal franchisee should possess relevant business experience and essential sales skills. Previous management or supervisory experience is also stressed.

Projected Earnings: The franchisor does not provide prospective franchisees with a projected earnings claim.

Franchisor's Services: Goodyear provides a comprehensive 12-week training program in Akron, Ohio. The franchisee is required to pay for travel expenses, although the franchisor will handle lodging and meals. The curriculum is divided into two months of franchise school and one month of on-the-job training at an actual Goodyear store.

The franchisor selects the site for the outlet and leases the premises, along with fixtures and equipment, to the franchisee. When the outlet is operational, a field consultant calls on the franchisee's store periodically to offer on-site assistance. A computerized bookkeeping and inventory system is available to franchisees at additional cost. Goodyear conducts frequent refresher courses to maintain the proficiency of franchisees and their staffs.

Initial Investment: Although Goodyear does not charge an initial franchise fee, the total investment is estimated at $65,000. The franchise offers several financial assistance programs, ranging from conventional business loans to credit on inventory purchases.

Advertising: The Goodyear name is one of the most heavily promoted in the automobile industry. The company conducts aggressive, mass-market advertising campaigns on behalf of all Goodyear outlets, and provides slickly produced merchandising aids for use in the showroom.

Contract Highlights: The term of the franchise is ten years, the industry average. The franchise agreement includes a lease of the premises, and further obligates the franchisee to lease equipment, supplies, and merchandise from Goodyear.

Fees and Royalties: There is no initial franchise fee to open a Goodyear Tire Center. However, the company is very selective about the franchisees it chooses to enroll. The three percent monthly royalty is the lowest in the automotive service and accessories trade.

Summary: With a sizeable network of franchisees and dealerships, excellent name recognition, a moderate investment, and the availability of financial assistance, the Goodyear Tire Center has all the trappings of a successful franchise.

Franchise Highlights

Began operating: 1898	**Monthly royalty: 3%**
Began franchising: 1968	**Advertising fee: None**
Outlets currently open: 620	**Training program: 12 weeks**
Initial franchise fee: None	**Term: 10 years**

Grease Monkey

Industry experience:	★ ★ ★	*Franchising experience:*	★ ★ ★
Financial strength:	★ ★ ★	*Training & services:*	★ ★ ★
Fees & royalties:	★ ★ ★ ★	*Satisfied franchisees:*	★ ★ ★ ★

Grease Monkey International
1660 Wynkoop, # 960
Denver, Colorado 80202
(303) 543-1660

Perhaps the most striking aspect of the Grease Monkey franchise is its award-winning advertising themes, the most memorable of which is the service slogan 'We lube you truly.' A company that recently teetered on the brink of failure, Grease Monkey International successfully emerged from dire financial straits to maintain its share of the trendy 'instant' auto oil change market.

The Franchise: The franchisee operates a quick automobile oil change and lubrication business, based on a standardized site design and equipment package, and using the trade name Grease Monkey. The outlet may offer related services such as air filter replacement, brake fluid replenishment, and interior cleaning. The typical outlet has from one to three service bays in a 1400 sq. ft. shop facility and employs five full-time service specialists. Multiple unit ownership is common.

Franchisee Profile: No prior auto mechanics experience is required. The company is currently emphasizing business, managerial, and supervisory qualifications and prefers active participation in the management of the outlet, rather than absentee ownership. However, the company offers special incentives for franchisees interested in opening more than one outlet.

Projected Earnings: The franchisor does not provide a written statement of projected earnings or anticipated profits. Based on the company's reported annual sales, the average gross volume of a Grease Monkey franchise is about $250,000 per year, before expenses.

Franchisor's Services: Grease Monkey provides a one-week training program at the company's headquarters in Denver. The curriculum includes both technical and business aspects of the franchise operation. A field representative is present during the Grand Opening of the outlet.

The franchisor assists in selecting a site, negotiating a lease, and building out the premises. A Grease Monkey consultant regularly visits each franchise shop to offer on-site troubleshooting and guidance. The franchisor conducts a series of annual seminars and workshops to keep franchisees abreast of new techniques and trends. The company also operates a centralized purchasing system to enable franchisees to take advantage of volume price discounts. The Grease Monkey support staff is available for telephone consultation as required.

Initial Investment: The franchisor estimates the franchisee's initial investment as follows:

	Low	High
Initial franchise fee	$7,500	$25,000
Lease deposits	5,000	9,000
Improvements	14,500	19,750
Furnishings	1,000	2,000
Inventory	6,000	9,000
Miscellaneous	1,750	3,500
Working capital	14,000	17,500
Total	49,750	81,550

The figure for working capital includes initial advertising expenses, as well as funds required to sustain the business during the startup period.

Advertising: Grease Monkey franchisees contribute four percent of gross monthly revenues to a co-op ad fund. Target media include radio, television, and newspapers.

Contract Highlights: The term of the franchise is ten years, renewable for an additional ten-year term if the franchisee is in compliance with all material provisions of the contract. Franchisees do not receive a protected territory.

Fees and Royalties: The $25,000 initial fee and five percent franchise royalty are moderate for the industry. A franchisee who purchases more than three outlets at the standard initial fee can obtain rights to additional outlets at a reduced fee of $7,500 each.

Summary: Backed by award-winning ad campaigns and a change of top level management, the Grease Monkey franchise appears to have emerged unscathed from the verge of bankruptcy. With a stable base of outlets and a modest fee and royalty structure, the system is currently seeking new franchisees in all U.S. and Canadian markets.

Franchise Highlights

Began operating: 1978
Began franchising: 1978
Outlets currently open: 82
Initial franchise fee: Min. $7,500
Max. $25,000

Monthly royalty: 5%
Advertising fee: 4%
Training program: 1 week
Term: 10 years

Hertz Rent A Car

Industry experience:	★★★★	*Franchising experience:*	★★★★
Financial strength:	★★★★	*Training & services:*	★★★★
Fees & royalties:	★★★	*Satisfied franchisees:*	★★★★

Hertz Corporation
7 Entin Road
Parsippany, New Jersey 07054

Widely recognized as the dominant force in the automobile rental industry, Hertz was put up for sale by Allegis Corporation (a.k.a. United Airlines) in early 1987. The company continues to operate 605 franchises and approximately 1,050 company-owned agencies in the United States and Canada. Although the most desirable locations have already been franchised — or occupied by company-owned outlets — from time to time established Hertz agencies are available for purchase from their previous owners.

The Franchise: The franchisee operates a full-service car and truck rental business using the Hertz trademark. The rental fleet typically includes economy, compact, standard size, and luxury automobiles, in addition to a small selection of trucks and utility vans. Specialty vehicles may be offered on request.

Franchisee Profile: No previous experience in car or truck rental is necessary, but the franchisor stresses the need for sound business know-how and a financial aptitude.

Projected Earnings: The franchisor does not make any statement regarding projected earnings of the outlet. Based on the company's reported annual sales, the average gross revenues of a Hertz outlet are close to a million dollars before expenses. However, this figure includes both company-operated and franchised outlets, with no consideration for location. According to a former Hertz franchisee, the actual gross varies significantly from one outlet to another, with airport locations reaping the highest share.

Initial Investment: Hertz franchisees invest from $100,000 to $700,000, depending on the location of the outlet and the size of the rental fleet. The franchisor does not offer any direct or indirect form of financial assistance to franchisees.

Advertising: The franchisor conducts aggressive advertising campaigns on behalf of all Hertz outlets, including both franchisees and company-owned rental lots. The system is prominently represented on major airline and travel agency computers, and participates in the United Airlines Mileage Plus program for frequent fliers.

Summary: The purchaser of an existing Hertz franchise must be prepared to meet the company's standard qualifications for Hertz franchisees and to assume all the obligations of the franchise agreement. The purchaser must normally execute a new contract. Although Hertz is commonly regarded as the world leader in its field, desirable locations are sparsely available. Still, the company's unparalleled name recognition, massive advertising reach, and customer appeal offer a strong assurance of new and repeat business. In a *Consumer Reports* survey of overall customer satisfaction, was ranked second in a tie with Budget, American International, and Avis.

Franchise Highlights

Began operating: 1918
Began franchising: 1921
Outlets currently open: 1,655
Initial franchise fee: Varies
Monthly royalty: Varies
Advertising fee: Varies
Training program: Not available
Term: Not available

Holiday-Payless Rent-A-Car

Industry experience:	★★★	*Franchising experience:*	★★★
Financial strength:	★★★	*Training & services:*	★★★
Fees & royalties:	★★★★	*Satisfied franchisees:*	★★★★

Holiday-Payless Rent-A-Car System
5510 Gulfport Boulevard
St. Petersburg, Florida 33707
(813) 381-2758

The Holiday-Payless system consists of Holiday Rent-A-Car and Payless Rent-A-Car outlets, which, combined, constitute the sixth largest U.S. car rental chain. Taking advantage of low property rents at off-airport locations, the company has successfully penetrated the market for economy priced automobile rentals, with 200 outlets in 38 states today. All Holiday-Payless car rental agencies are franchises, and more than twenty percent operate in Canada, Florida, and the Caribbean, where recognition of the Holiday name is strongest.

The Franchise: The franchisee operates a car rental outlet catering to business travelers and vacationing families, under the trade name Holiday-Payless Rent-A-Car. A typical outlet is located near (but not at) a major airport or in a high-traffic commercial or resort area, with three full-time and two part-time employees. Besides car rentals, franchisees may also derive income from automobile and liability insurance, sales of used fleet cars, long-term auto leases, and point-to-point drive-away services.

Franchisee Profile: Prior experience in the automobile or rental trade is preferred, but not mandatory. The company is not currently seeking absentee owners or area franchisees.

Projected Earnings: The franchisor does not provide a statement of projected earnings or anticipated profits.

Franchisor's Services: Holiday-Payless conducts a one-week training program in St. Petersburg, Florida. The curriculum includes customer relations and sales, fleet management, personnel administration, and business operations. Attendees are responsible for travel and lodging expenses. An additional week of on-the-job training is provided at the franchisee's place of business.

The franchisor will assist with selecting a site for the outlet, negotiating a lease for the premises, planning the rental fleet, and acquiring vehicles. Franchisees also benefit from consolidated purchasing and a computerized accounting system which is available at extra cost. A field representative helps recruit customer prospects to get the business off the ground, and provides on-site troubleshooting and advice in periodic visits to the franchisee's outlet.

Holiday-Payless operates a national toll-free reservation system, which produces a continual stream of new business. Business customers are cultivated through the company's Passport Club program, which caters to corporate accounts. The support program also includes biannual franchisee conferences, monthly reports on competition, and telephone access to corporate experts. A computer-based bookkeeping system is available at additional cost to franchisees.

Initial Investment: New franchisees should be prepared to spend from $40,000 to $125,000, depending on the location and fleet size. The initial costs include lease deposits, improvements, insurance, and rental vehicles. The franchisor does not offer direct financial assistance to franchisees.

Advertising: Holiday-Payless franchisees contribute three percent of gross monthly revenues to a co-op advertising fund. The franchisor conducts national and regional advertising programs, and is represented in all major airline and travel agency reservation computers. Franchisees receive an ad kit containing prepared promotional materials and guidelines for conducting local campaigns.

Contract Highlights: The term of the franchise five years, with a five-year renewal option. The franchise is accompanied by a protected territory. The franchisee does not have any subfranchising rights whatsoever.

Fees and Royalties: The initial franchise fee varies, depending on the location and size of the outlet, from $10,000 to as much as $50,000. The monthly franchise royalty is a moderate five percent of gross sales.

Summary: The merger of Holiday and Payless, two young but aggressive car-rental chains, bolstered franchisee benefits and created a new industry contender overnight. Yet the system still retains its original values of a moderate investment, a manageable royalty structure, and personalized support from the franchise staff.

Franchise Highlights

Began operating: 1971	**Monthly royalty: 5%**
Began franchising: 1971	**Advertising fee: 3%**
Outlets currently open: 200	**Training program: 1 week**
Initial franchise fee: Min $12,000	**Term: 5 years**
Max. $75,000	

Jiffy Lube

Industry experience:	★ ★ ★	*Franchising experience:*	★ ★ ★
Financial strength:	★ ★ ★	*Training & services:*	★ ★ ★
Fees & royalties:	★ ★ ★	*Satisfied franchisees:*	★ ★ ★ ★

Jiffy Lube International
7008 Security Boulevard
Baltimore, Maryland 21207
(301) 298-8200

Jiffy Lube was one of the first franchise chains to capitalize on the gushing 'instant oil change' market of the 1970s. Demand for quick oil change and lubrication service remains strong today, as evidenced by Jiffy Lube's track record. Since 1973, the system has grown by an average of 17 outlets per year.

The Franchise: The franchisee operates a quick-change oil and lubrication business. The typical outlet employs three full-time and two part-time specialists, offering related services such as replenishing brake, transmission, and battery fluid and replacing air filters and windshield wiper blades.

Franchisee Profile: Prior experience in auto maintenance or repair is not required. Preference is given to applicants who will manage the business themselves. The company will consider granting area franchises to develop large territories.

Projected Earnings: The franchisor does not furnish prospective franchisees with a written statement of projected earnings.

Franchisor's Services: Jiffy Lube provides a two-week training program at the company's headquarters in Baltimore. The curriculum focuses on both technical and business aspects of running a profitable franchise shop. The franchisee is responsible for selecting a site for the outlet, but a Jiffy Lube consultant will offer advice and guidance. The franchisor also assists with building out the outlet and planning Grand Opening promotions.

After the shop has opened for business, a field manager periodically inspects the operation and provides on-site troubleshooting. The outlet's inventory level receives special attention. Jiffy Lube operates a centralized purchasing system through which franchisees may order accessories, parts and supplies at competitive wholesale prices.

Initial Investment: The total investment is estimated at $90,000, including lease deposits, site buildout, equipment, supplies, and working capital.

Advertising: Jiffy Lube franchisees contribute six percent of gross monthly revenues to fund advertising. In lieu of co-op advertising, the franchisee has the option of spending an equivalent amount on local promotions.

Contract Highlights: The term of the franchise is 20 years, twice the national average. The contract may be renewed upon expiration, providing the franchisee is in compliance with all material provisions. The franchisee receives a protected territory in which no other Jiffy Lube outlets will be sold or opened while the contract is in force. Area franchising rights are available under a separate agreement.

Fees and Royalties: The $35,000 initial fee reflects the franchisor's investment in pre-opening training and assistance, and the added value of a growing chain. The five percent monthly royalty is low for the industry, although the six percent advertising royalty is on the high side.

Summary: In number of units, Jiffy Lube is the largest chain of auto service centers specializing in ten-minute oil change and lubcrication service. The company is keen on first-hand support and guidance, with the intention of making the business as easy to run as possible. The franchisor offers the flexibility of a small or expanded shop, with the possibility of conducting related service businesses on the same premises.

Franchise Highlights

Began operating: 1972
Began franchising: 1973
Outlets currently open: 270
Initial franchise fee: $35,000

Monthly royalty: 5%
Advertising fee: 8%
Training program: 2 weeks
Term: 10 years

King Bear

Industry experience:	★★★	*Franchising experience:*	★★★
Financial strength:	★★★	*Training & services:*	★★★
Fees & royalties:	★★★	*Satisfied franchisees:*	★★★★

King Bear Auto Service Centers
1390 Jerusalem Avenue
North Merrick, New York 11566
(516) 483-3500

Established in 1973, King Bear has franchised extensively in New York and California, where the company's crowned-bear logo is a common sight perched atop franchisees' combination auto repair/parts centers. The franchisor is currently seeking new franchisees on the East Coast and in California.

The Franchise: The franchisee operates an automobile repair and maintenance shop, combined with an auto parts supply house. Customers of the franchise business include individual car owners, fleet operators, service stations, and independent garages and auto parts retailers.

Franchisee Profile: Prior experience in auto repair or parts retailing is preferred, but not mandatory. The company is primarily seeking full-time owner/operators, as opposed to absentee owners. However, King Bear will consider selling area franchises to develop large territories.

Franchisor's Services: The franchisor conducts a two-week training program at the corporate headquarters near New York City. Franchisees are responsible for travel and lodging expenses. King Bear will help select a site for the franchise outlet, negotiate a lease for the premises, and prepare the business for opening.

A King Bear field representative peridoically visits each franchise outlet to inspect the shop and advise the staff on operations and procedures. The company operates a computerized purchasing system to enable franchisees to take advantage of low prices on auto parts and accessories. Each outlet's inventory level is carefully monitored to assure availability of those parts which are most likely to be required in the day-to-day operation of the shop.

Initial Investment: The total investment is estimated at $70,000, including the initial franchise fee, lease deposits, fixtures, improvements, equipment, and opening inventory.

Advertising: King Bear conducts regional and local advertising campaigns, funded by a seven percent advertising royalty contributed by all franchisees.

Contract Highlights: The term of the franchise is 15 years, renewable for an additional ten-year term, providing that the franchisee remains in compliance with all the provisions of the contract. The franchisor grants a protected territory in which no other King Bear outlets will be sold or opened during the term of the franchise. A franchisee normally has no subfranchising rights within the territory. Area franchise rights may be acquired under a separate agreement.

Fees and royalties: The initial franchisee fee of $15,000 is moderate for an established franchisor. The five percent monthly royalty is on the low side, but, coupled with the seven percent advertising royalty, creates a hefty — but not unmanageable — 13-percent royalty burden.

Summary: King Bear enjoys the best market share and name recognition in New York and California, where the franchise opportunity is registered with state authorities. The system is characterized by steady growth, personal attention, and a manageable initial investment.

Franchise Highlights

Began operating: 1973
Began franchising: 1974
Outlets currently open: 60
Initial franchise fee: $15,000
Monthly royalty: 5%
Advertising fee: 7%
Training program: 2 weeks
Term: 15 years

Lee Myles Associates

Industry experience:	★★★★	*Franchising experience:*	★★★★
Financial strength:	★★★	*Training & services:*	★★★★
Fees & royalties:	★★★	*Satisfied franchisees:*	★★★★

Lee Myles Associates
25 E. Spring Valley Avenue
Maywood, New Jersey 07607
(201) 843-3200

Lee Myles Associates first began repairing auto transmissions shortly after the close of World War II. Since the company began franchising in 1964, more than 150 shops have opened in the Middle Atlantic and Southwestern states, where the Lee Myles name is the most familiar today.

The Franchise: The franchisee operates a retail auto transmission service shop, selling a broad range of related products and services. A typical outlet performs both major repair work and minor servicing on automatic transmissions for all makes and models of passenger cars. New franchisees receive a startup package consisting of tools, equipment, parts, and business forms.

Franchisee Profile: Prior experience or training in auto service or repair is not required. The company stresses personal, financial, and managerial qualifications.

Franchisor's Services: The franchisor provides a three-week training program in Maywood, New Jersey, and pays for the franchisee's travel and lodging expenses. Besides transmission repair, the curriculum covers business administration, marketing, and inventory management. An additional week of training is conducted at the franchisee's place of business.

The franchisee is responsible for selecting a site for the outlet and negotiating a lease, with the franchisor's guidance. A Grand Opening promotion includes a 13-week advertising campaign supplied by Lee Myles. The support program also includes periodic visitations from a field representative and an aggressive regional co-op advertising program.

Initial Investment: The total investment is estimated at $75,000, including the initial franchise fee, lease deposits, improvements, tools, equipment, and an opening inventory of parts and supplies.

Advertising: Lee Myles franchisees contribute a set amount for co-op advertising, ranging from $300 to $400 per week. The funds are pooled to finance intensive regional ad campaigns on television and radio.

Contract Highlights: The term of the franchise is 15 years. Although the franchisor supplies a mandatory initial inventory, the franchise agreement does not restrict the franchisee from purchasing on-going parts or equipment from other suppliers.

Fees and Royalties: The $20,000 initial fee is commensurate with other franchises of similar stature, as is the eight percent monthly royalty

Summary: The Lee Myles franchise is characterized by steady growth concentrated in a limited geographical market, a well-rounded training package, and effective use of co-op advertising funds.

Franchise Highlights

Began operating: 1947	
Began franchising: 1964	**Monthly royalty: 8%**
Outlets currently open: 150	**Advertising fee: Min. $300 per week**
Initial franchise fee: $20,000	**Training program: 3 weeks Term: 15 years**

MAACO

Industry experience:	★ ★ ★ ★	*Franchising experience:*	★ ★ ★ ★
Financial strength:	★ ★ ★ ★	*Training & services:*	★ ★ ★ ★
Fees & royalties:	★ ★ ★	*Satisfied franchisees:*	★ ★ ★ ★

MAACO Enterprises
381 Brooks Road
King of Prussia, Pennsylvania 19406
(800) 523-1180

MAACO Auto Painting and Bodyworks is one of the most illustrious success stories in franchising. MAACO founder Anthony A. Martino had previously started AAMCO Transmissions, one of the pioneering chains of the franchise boom of the late 1950s. Not by coincidence, the names of both companies are derived from their founder's initials. In the 25 years since MAACO painted its first used car, the company's trademark has become one of the best known in auto painting, body repair, and restoration — accounting for roughly $200 million in annual sales.

The Franchise: The franchisee operates a retail automobile painting and body repair shop, under the name MAACO Auto Painting and Bodyworks. The typical outlet is a 10,000 sq. ft. shop facility with ten full-time employees, in a commercial or industrial area. MAACO sells paint and shop equipment to franchisees at a profit, but does not attempt to restrict franchisees from purchasing these items elsewhere. The outlet offers body repair, restoration, and painting services to retail customers, with a significant proportion of revenues derived from insurance cases.

Franchisee profile: Previous experience in auto painting and/or body repair is considered beneficial, but not mandatory, depending on the applicant's other qualifications. The MAACO franchisee is required to participate full-time in the conduct of the business; absentee ownership is specifically prohibited by the franchise agreement.

Projected Earnings: The franchisor does not make a projected earnings claim. Based on the company's reported annual sales, the average gross volume of a MAACO outlet is about $540,000 per year, before expenses.

Franchisor's Services: MAACO provides an extensive four-week training program at the company's franchise school in King of Prussia, Pennsylvania, just outside Philadelphia. The franchisor pays for the attendee's travel and lodging expenses. In addition to painting technique and shop operations, the curriculum includes advertising methods, customer relations, inventory control, personnel and financial administration, and equipment maintenance and safety. The shop manager receives an additional week of management training. Retraining and refresher courses are offered periodically.

The franchisor offers site selection assistance, but does not specify the actual location. The site must be approved by the franchisor before the lease is executed. Company personnel will help plan the layout and construction of the outlet and purchase equipment and supplies.

MAACO provides Grand Opening assistance in a two week visitation by a field representative at the franchisee's place of business. In addition, the franchisor provides periodic field support, a franchisee newsletter, and unlimited telephone communications via a toll-free franchisee hotline.

Initial Investment: The franchisor estimates the initial investment at from $115,000 to about $135,000. Of this amount, $6,500 represents working capital, which must be deposited in an escrow-type account until the outlet is ready to open. The franchisor does not currently offer any direct assistance in financing either the initial fee or any part of the investment. However, the company may assist qualified candidates with obtaining financial assistance from a third party. A minimum cash investment of $45,000 is required.

Advertising: All new franchisees are obligated to spend $3,000 on a Grand Opening advertising campaign, administered by the franchising company. Thereafter, a set advertising fee of $500 per calendar week is levied, to support co-op advertising on behalf of all MAACO outlets.

Fees and Royalties: The initial franchise fee of $15,000 is moderate for franchises in this field, and low for a franchise with such a high level of name recognition and goodwill. The eight percent royalty on gross revenues of the outlet is average for the industry. New franchisees should also be prepared to pay $3,000 for the Grand Opening program and a $6,500 working capital deposit.

Contract provisions: The franchise agreement does not stipulate a protected territory for the franchise outlet. However, the franchisor does offer to assist in selecting a site, as well as negotiating a lease for the premises. No area or subfranchising rights are normally granted by the contract. The term of the franchise is 15 years, slightly higher than the industry average.

Summary: MAACO is a street-smart, experienced franchise operation headed by a bona fide industry pioneer. Unlike many well known chains, MAACO is firmly committed to franchising, with all but five of its 400-plus outlets operated by independent franchisees. The training program receives high marks for thoroughness, relevance, and duration.

Franchise Highlights

Began operating: 1972
Began franchising: 1973
Outlets currently open: 450
Initial franchise fee: Min $15,000
Monthly royalty: 8%
Advertising fee: $500 per week
Training program: 4 weeks
Term: 15 years

Meineke Discount Muffler

Industry experience:	★ ★ ★ ★	*Franchising experience:*	★ ★ ★
Financial strength:	★ ★ ★	*Training & services:*	★ ★ ★ ★
Fees & royalties:	★ ★	*Satisfied franchisees:*	★ ★ ★

Meineke Discount Muffler Shops, Inc.
128 S. Tyron Street, Suite 900
Charlotte, North Carolina 28202
(704) 377-8855

Meineke Discount Muffler, a subsidiary of Parts Industries, Inc., offers limited automotive maintenance and repair at discount rates. Established as a franchise operation in 1972, Meineke gradually built a positive reputation based on quality service at discount prices. In 1983, more than 300 shops carried the Meineke trademark. Today, more than 700 outlets service passenger automobiles in 35 states.

Meineke is registered in all states that require more than the standard FTC disclosure statement. The company is currently seeking new franchisees in the West, Midwest, and Canada.

The Franchise: The franchisee conducts a retail auto repair business specializing in exhaust systems, shock absorbers, and brake repairs, and operating under the trade name Meineke Discount Mufflers. The franchise system has enjoyed steady growth by establishing a reputation based on quality service at competitive prices. Franchise shops are geared for efficiency in both overhead and inventory, with limited service guarantees, to maximize profits while maintaining a discount price policy. The typical outlet has three service bays in a 2,500 sq. ft. repair facility employing at least two full-time mechanics. High-volume turnover is an essential ingredient in the Meineke franchise. Franchisees ostensibly realize significant savings from central purchasing and inventory control provided by the franchisor.

Franchisee Profile: Many of the company's existing franchisees had little prior experience in auto repair or maintenance. Some have professional or business backgrounds. The company is currently seeking franchisees who demonstrate personal pride, ambition, and a dedication to quality craftsmanship. Whereas Meineke does not require industry experience, the company does expect franchise owners to take an active part in the management of the business.

Projected Earnings: Based on the company's reported sales, the average gross volume of a Meineke outlet is about $165,000 per year. The average volume of outlets that have been open for two years or longer exceeds $280,000.

Franchisor's Services: New franchisees attend a three-week training program at the company's headquarters in Charlotte, North Carolina. Attendees must pay their own travel and lodging expenses. The curriculum covers financial accounting, inventory control, central purchasing, personnel relations, marketing, and mechanical service and repair techniques. An additional week of on-the-job training is provided at the franchisee's place of business.

Company representatives will assist with selecting a site for the outlet, negotiating a lease, and ordering equipment and supplies. The franchisor maintains a full-time staff of 60 industry professionals to provide ongoing support. In periodic visits to the outlet, a field representative keeps franchisees informed of new service techniques and helps plan for future inventory needs. Meineke encourages franchisee communication and interaction, through a Dealer Advisory Council. Weekly reports from company headquarters compare sales figures of other franchise outlets.

Initial Investment: Prospective franchisees should be prepared to invest a minimum of $45,000, plus an additional capital investment of $45,000. The company will assist the franchisee in obtaining financial assistance from a major lender and offers direct financing on the purchase of equipment.

Advertising: The company administers a national advertising campaign funded by advertising royalties. Target media include radio, television, newspapers, and magazines. Meineke also supplies franchisees with in-store promotional aids, catalogs, and brochures.

Contract Highlights: The contract period is 15 years with a 15-year first-renewal option. The franchisee is granted exclusive rights to territory and the option to expand, but not to subfranchise. The outlet must be open within seven months after the franchise agreement has been signed. Absentee ownership is prohibited; the franchisee must personally manage the business.

Fees and Royalties: The $22,500 initial fee is moderate to slightly high for the industry, reflecting the system's stature and maturity. The seven percent franchise royalty and 12 percent advertising royalty exact a hefty 19 percent of the gross revenues of the outlet. Franchisees who purchase more than two outlets may obtain rights to addititional shops at a reduced franchise fee of $16,875 per outlet.

Summary: Meineke Discount Muffler has a long and stable financial history with a recent period of intense growth. The royalty structure reflects the company's growth objectives. On the positive side, the initial investment and managerial controls optimize the franchisee's ability to turn a profit.

Franchise Highlights

Began operating: 1972	**Monthly royalty: 7%**
Began franchising: 1972	**Advertising fee: 12%**
Outlets currently open: 820	**Training program: 3 weeks**
Initial franchise fee: $22,500	**Term: 15 years**

Mister Transmission

Industry experience:	★★★	*Franchising experience:*	★★★
Financial strength:	★★★★	*Training & services:*	★★★
Fees & royalties:	★★★	*Satisfied franchisees:*	★★★★

Mister Transmission
50 Don Park Road
Markham, Ontario, Canada L3R 1J3
(416) 475-1511

With 120 outlets franchised since 1973, Mister Transmission (not to be confused with Nashville-based Mr. Transmission) is the largest chain of auto transmission service centers in Canada. Completely Canadian-owned and managed, the company is currently seeking new franchisees only in Canada.

The Franchise: The franchisee operates a retail auto transmission service shop, employing four full-time mechanics and performing major repairs in addition to routine servicing and adjustments.

Franchisee Profile: Prior experience or training in auto service or repair is beneficial, but not mandatory. The company is not actively seeking absentee owners or area franchisees.

Franchisor's Services: The franchisor provides a two-week training program in Markham, Ontario. The curriculum covers auto transmission service, repair procedures, pricing, invoicing, bookkeeping, and personnel administration. The franchisor helps select a site for the transmission shop and negotiate a lease for the premises. A Mister Transmission consultant is present on-site to help plan and implement Grand Opening activities.

A field representative periodically visits each shop to inspect the operation and provide ongoing advice and troubleshooting. Mister Transmission franchisees gather each year to exchange experiences and update their knowledge about the auto transmission trade.

Initial Investment: The total investment is estimated at $80,000, including the initial franchise fee, lease deposits, improvements, tools, equipment, and an inventory of transmission parts. The franchisor offers financial assistance to prospective franchisees who qualify.

Advertising: Mister Transmission franchisees pay a seven percent advertising royalty to fund national promotions. The company's reach extends across all Canadian provinces.

Contract Highlights: The term of the franchise is ten years. The contract is renewable for an additional ten-year term if the franchisee is not in violation of any material provision. The franchisee receives a protected territory in which Mister Transmission will not sell or open a competing auto transmission outlet.

Fees and Royalties: The $20,000 initial fee reflects the system's steady growth and maturity. The seven percent monthly royalty is average for the industry. Including the co-op ad contribution, the total royalty burden is 14 percent of gross revenues of the outlet.

Summary: Strong name recognition, effective advertising reach, and a solid base of outlets have contributed to Mister Transmission's successful exploitation of the Canadian auto transmission market.

Franchise Highlights

Began operating: 1963
Began franchising: 1973
Outlets currently open: 120
Initial franchise fee: $20,000
Monthly royalty: 7%
Advertising fee: 7%
Training program: 2 weeks
Term: 10 years

Midas International

Industry experience:	★★★★	*Franchising experience:*	★★★★
Financial strength:	★★★★	*Training & services:*	★★★★
Fees & royalties:	★★★	*Satisfied franchisees:*	★★★

Midas International Corporation
225 North Michigan Ave.
Chicago, Illinois 60601
(312) 565-7500

Was it the 'Midas touch' that changed a single Georgia muffler shop into an thriving international business empire, or was it entrepreneurial genuius? Undoubtedly, effective advertising played a major role in the longstanding success of Midas Muffler and Brake automotive service shops. Thirty years after its unimpressive beginning in 1956, Midas hosts more than 1,500 outlets throughout the United States and Canada, and in selected overseas markets. A subsidiary of IC Industries, Inc., Midas is a member of the International Franchise Association.

The Franchise: The franchisee conducts an automotive service and repair business under the trade name Midas Muffler and Brake. A typical outlet employs three full-time mechanics, servicing mufflers and other exhaust components, as well as suspension systems, brakes, and front-ends. Franchisees are obliged to purchase and sell a private line of auto parts marketed by the company.

Franchisee Profile: Midas looks for applicants with a successful business record. Previous mechanical experience is helpful but not required.

Franchisor Services: The company provides the new franchisee with a complete turnkey operation. The franchisor acquires the site and constructs improvements, then sublets the finished outlet to the franchisee for the duration of the franchise contract.

A two-week training program at the Midas Institute of Technology at Palatine, Illinois teaches franchisees how to plan, staff, and run the outlet. Trainees spend an additional two weeks gaining hands-on experience in a regional Midas service shop.

The franchisor assists in hiring and training employees, setting up the outlet's accounting system, and launching promotional campaigns. The franchisee receives ongoing advice on purchasing and inventory control, and continuing education at regional and national meetings.

Initial Investment: Besides the franchise license fee of $10,000, an initial charge of $75,000 covers site acquisition, training, and opening support. Midas requires evidence of $170,000 in working capital to start operations.

Advertising: Midas franchisees contribute a hefty ten percent of their gross sales for advertising. In return, the franchisor conducts aggressive ad campaigns at the national, regional, and local levels.

Contract Highlights: The term of the franchise is 20 years with a 20-year renewal option. The franchisee does not receive a protected territory for the franchise.

Fees and Royalties: The initial franchise fee ranges from $10,000 to $12,500. Including the franchise royalty and avertising fee, the total royalty burden is a ponderous 20 percent of gross monthly sales.

Summary: Despite high royalties, the Midas franchise offers excellent name recognition, a well-rounded training program, and the cooperative benefits of one of the largest franchise chains in North America.

Franchise Highlights

Began operating: 1956	**Monthly royalty: 10%**
Began franchising: 1956	**Advertising fee: 10%**
Outlets currently open: 1,508	**Training program: 2 weeks**
Initial franchise fee: Min. $10,000	**Term: 20 years**
Max. $12,500	

Mr. Transmission

Industry experience:	★ ★ ★ ★	*Franchising experience:*	★ ★ ★
Financial strength:	★ ★ ★	*Training & services:*	★ ★ ★ ★
Fees & royalties:	★ ★ ★	*Satisfied franchisees:*	★ ★ ★ ★

Mr. Transmission, Inc.
P. O. Box 111060
Nashville, Tennessee 37211
(615) 251-3504

Founded in 1962, Mr. Transmission has franchised more than 200 auto transmission centers since 1976 — most of them in Tennessee, Florida, and Texas, where the company's name is most widely reocgnized. The company is currently seeking new franchisees in all regions of the United States.

The Franchise: The franchisee operates a retail auto transmission service shop under the trade name Mr. Transmission. A typical outlet is a 10,000 sq. ft. repair facility with from three to eight bays and four full-time employees. Franchisees offer transmission repair, rebuilding, and reconditioning. Franchisees are not specifically obligated to purchase parts from the franchisor, but they are encouraged to do so by discount pricing made possible by consolidated purchasing.

Franchisee Profile: Prior experience or training in auto mechanics is not required, but successful applicants will possess sound management skills and dedication to personal accomplishment. Absentee ownership is a possibility.

Franchisor's Services: The franchisor provides three weeks of instruction at the company's training center in Nashville, plus an additional week of on-site instruction and assistance. Franchisees must pay for their own travel and lodging expenses while at the Mr. Transmission training center. The curriculum covers customer service, inventory management, administration, and financial planning, focusing on the business aspects of the franchise. Technical training is provided in a special course for the franchisee's designated transmission expert.

With the franchisor's guidance, the franchisee is responsible for selecting a site for the outlet and negotiating a lease for the facility. Mr. Transmission provides assistance with planning the shop's inventory, hiring personnel, and developing an advertising strategy. After the shop has opened for business, a field manager inspects the shop periodically and offers on-site guidance. Operations experts are also accessible by telephone.

Initial Investment: The total investment is estimated at $103,000 including the initial franchise fee, lease deposits, improvements, tools, equipment, opening inventory, and working capital.

Advertising: Mr. Transmission franchisees contribute ten percent of gross monthly revenues to a co-op ad fund. The royalty payments help finance national and regional ad campaigns.

Contract Highlights: The term of the franchise is 20 years, twice the national average. The franchise agreement does not restrict the franchisee from purchasing parts from other suppliers. The franchisee also receives a protected territory for his franchise.

Fees and Royalties: The $19,500 initial fee is average for a franchise in the auto transmission trade, as is the eight percent monthly royalty. The ten percent advertising fee is on the high side. Consider that the total royalty burden represents 18 percent of gross revenues of the outlet.

Summary: Mr. Transmission enjoys stable growth, a high level of franchisee satisfaction, and a training program highly rated by graduating franchisees.

Franchise Highlights

Began operating: 1962	**Monthly royalty: 8%**
Began franchising: 1976	**Advertising fee: 10%**
Outlets currently open: 210	**Training program: 4 weeks**
Initial franchise fee: $19,500	**Term: 20 years**

Precision Tune

Industry experience:	★ ★ ★	*Franchising experience:*	★ ★ ★ ★
Financial strength:	★ ★ ★	*Training & services:*	★ ★ ★ ★
Fees & royalties:	★ ★ ★	*Satisfied franchisees:*	★ ★ ★ ★

Precision Tune, Inc.
New Center Development
755 S. 11th Street, Suite 101
Beaumont, Texas 77701
(800) 231-0588

Predominately clustered in the Midwest and East Coast, Precision Tune has built a trustworthy name in auto tune-up service with an effective 'We Care' public relations policy. Founded in 1975, Precision has sold nearly 40 new franchises every year since 1977.

The Franchise: The franchisee operates a specialty auto tune-up business under the trade name Precision Tune. Many franchises are based in existing service station facilities. A typical standalone outlet has three to six mechanics working in a 2,500 sq. ft. facility. Service is backed by a six month/six thousand mile warranty on all parts and labor.

The Franchisee Profile: More than a third of existing Precision franchisees did not have previous auto service experience when they entered the business. Experience in auto mechanics or business is considered helpful but not necessary. Multiple unit ownership is common, but the company prefers franchisees who will actively participate in the management of the business, regardless of the number of outlets owned.

Projected Earnings: Based on the company's reported annual sales, the average volume of a Precision Tune outlet is around $300,000 per year, before expenses.

Franchisor's Services: The franchisor insists that franchise units adhere to standardized architectural and design schemes. The company must approve the site for the outlet, as well as any equipment and fixtures. PAC Manufacturing and Distributing Company, a subsidiary of the franchisor, offers to sell approved equipment and tools, although franchisees are free to purchase these items from independent suppliers.

The company training program is held either in Beaumont, Texas or at a qualified subfranchisor's facility. The cost of the training program is included in the license fee, but travel expenses must be borne by the franchisee. The curriculum covers automotive service and repair, business management, and marketing. An extensive film library is available for on-site staff training.

The company organizes annual franchisee conferences and publishes a bimonthly newsletter and a weekly technical bulletin to keep franchisees abreast of new developments. A company representative periodically inspects each outlet to offer advice and troubleshooting. Precision also operates a centralized purchasing and inventory system, and markets its own line of spark plugs and air filters.

Initial Investment: The total cash investment is estimated at from $100,000 to $120,000, including lease deposits, improvements, equipment, inventory, and working capital. The minimum cash investment with approved credit is $30,000. A third party lender may finance the balance.

Advertising: Precision Tune franchisees contribute nine percent of gross monthly revenues to a co-op ad fund, and receive radio and television commercials, approved Yellow Pages ads, and slicks for newspaper or magazine campaigns. The franchisor also supplies a videotape dealing with effective advertising techniques.

Contract Highlights: The Precision Tune franchise has a short term of five years with a five year renewal contract. The franchisee does not receive a protected territory, except in the case of an area franchise, which may be negotiated under a separate agreement. The franchisor has the right to approve the site and all signage and advertising related to the franchise. The outlet must be open within six months after the franchise agreement has been signed.

Fees and Royalties: The intitial franchise fee of $15,000 is moderate by industry standards. The 7.5 percent franchise royalty is slightly high. Including the nine percent advertising royalty, franchisees must be prepared to pay out 16.5 percent of their gross monthly revenues.

Summary: A solid base of outlets, a comprehensive training program, and aggressive advertising equip Precision Tune franchisees with a competitive edge in the lucrative market for routine auto care.

Franchise Highlights

Began operating: 1976	**Monthly royalty: 7.5%**
Began franchising: 1977	**Advertising fee: 9%**
Outlets currently open: 375	**Training program: 2 to 4 weeks**
Initial franchise fee: $15,000	**Term: 10 years**

Rent-A-Wreck

Industry experience: ★★★ *Franchising experience:* ★★★★
Financial strength: ★★★ *Training & services:* ★★★
Fees & royalties: ★★★★ *Satisfied franchisees:* ★★★★

Rent-A-Wreck
10889 Wilshire Boulevard, #12960
Los Angeles, California 90024
(800) 421-7253

The first successful used-car rental chain, Rent-A-Wreck profited as much from its colorful trade name as from its reputation for low rates. The name was the brainschild of David Schwartz, a Southern California used-car dealer who decided to rent out some of his merchandise at bargain rates to help offset lagging sales. In trend-conscious Los Angeles, Schwartz's new side business received an impetus from being patronized by famous Hollywood stars, catapulting Rent-A-Wreck into the national limelight.

Schwartz began selling franchises in 1980. Today, under the management of former media mogul Goeffrey Nathanson, Rent-A-Wreck boasts a respectable chain of more than 350 outlets.

The Franchise: The franchisee operates a used-car rental business with four full-time employees, either as a standalone operation or as an adjunct to a related automotive sales or service business. The system disdains many of the most rigid aspects of other car rental franchises, such as uniformed counter personnel, but requires rental vehicles to be clean and in good running condition.

Franchisee Profile: Prior experience in automobile rental, sales, or service is mandatory. Absentee ownership is a possibility.

Projected Earnings: Rent-A-Wreck does not make any statements regarding projected earnings of the outlet.

Franchisor's Services: The franchisor provides a five-day training program at company headquarters in Los Angeles. The curriculum includes vehicle acquisition and maintenance, marketing and sales techniques, financial controls, and security procedures.

The franchisor also offers ongoing support in the form of periodic visitations by a field consultant. Rent-A-Wreck conducts a series of technical and business seminars to provide continuing education to franchisees and their staffs. The franchisor also provides advertising materials and conducts co-op ad campaigns on behalf of franchisees.

Initial Investment: The total investment ranges from $75,000 to as much as $250,000, depending on the size of the rental fleet. The franchisor may finance the initial franchise fee.

Advertising: Franchisees pay an advertising royalty of two percent of gross sales. The royalty is pooled with payments from other franchisees to finance system-wide advertising campaigns.

Contract Highlights: The term of the franchise is ten years, the national average. The franchisee receives an exclusive territory in which Rent-A-Wreck will not sell or open another outlet while the contract is in force.

Fees and Royalties: The initial franchise fee is considered low to moderate, encouraging rapid growth. The combined royalty burden is a manageable eight percent, about average for the car rental trade.

Summary: Rent-A-Wreck franchisees rent cars that are 'pre-owned,' but in good running condition — not 'clunkers,' as implied by the trade name. With a respectable base of outlets and a track record of steady growth, Rent-A-Wreck enjoys a solid niche in a highly competitive market. In a Consumer Reports survey of rental car clients, Rent-A-Wreck was rated seventh in terms of overall customer satisfaction.

Franchise Highlights

Began operating: 1969
Began franchising: 1980
Outlets currently open: 355
Initial franchise fee: Min $5,000
Max. $50,000

Monthly royalty: 6%
Advertising fee: 2%
Training program: 5 days
Term: 10 years

Sparks Tune-Up

Industry experience:	★★★	*Franchising experience:*	★★★★
Financial strength:	★★★	*Training & services:*	★★★★
Fees & royalties:	★★★	*Satisfied franchisees:*	★★★

Sparks Tune-Up, Inc.
381 Brooks Road
King of Prussia, PA 19406
(800) 523-1180

Sparks Tune-Up is a young franchise business characterized by strong industry ties, aggressive management, and a solid track record. A subsidiary of MAACO Enterprises (the parent company to MAACO Auto Painting and Bodyworks), Sparks began franchising auto tune-up centers in 1983 with ten years of franchise experience already under its belt. Sparks remains strictly a franchise operation, with none of the company's 120 outlets company-owned. Sparks has been a member of the International Franchise Association since 1983.

The franchise: The franchisee operates an auto service outlet devoted primarily to tune-ups and light maintenance. Located in high density population areas, Sparks outlets cater to the demand for speedy ignition system maintenance. Franchisees promote fast service at a competitive price that includes both parts and labor, guaranteed for six months or 6,000 miles, whichever comes first. A typical outlet employs three full-time and five part-time employees.

Franchisee Profile: The franchisor suggests that experience in business and/or the automotive service industry is helpful, but not mandatory.

Franchisor's Services: A staff of 22 industry-trained professionals provide personal support and guidance in opening the new tune-up center. A Sparks representative participates in site acquisition and assists the franchisee with securing financial assistance from a major lender. The franchisor also provides construction guidelines and evaluates the site prior to opening.

New franchise owners attend a nine-day training program at King of Prussia, Pennsylvania, near Philadelphia, where they learn the business-management aspects of operating a Sparks tune-up center. Separate technical training is conducted at the franchisee's site shortly before opening.

Ongoing support includes centralized purchasing, data processing, and inventory control, company newsletters, telephone hotlines, and periodic visits from a field specialist.

Initial Investment: New franchisees should be prepared to invest at least $32,000. The total capital investment may run as high as $120,000.

Advertising: Sparks franchises contribute a set fee of $420 per month to a co-op advertising fund which the franchisor uses to conduct promotional campaigns on behalf of all Sparks tune-up centers.

Fee and Royalties: The initial franchise fee of $20,000 is somewhat high for a young franchise system, but not disproportionate to the number of outlets currently open. The seven percent monthly royalty is average for the industry.

Contract Highlights: The term of the franchise is 15 years with a renewal option for an additional 15-year term. Franchisees are granted rights to an exclusive territory, normally without expansion rights. The franchise may not be sold, assigned, or transferred without the consent of the franchisor. The franchisee is free to conduct a related business in conjunction with the franchise, but not one which would directly compete with the Sparks outlet.

Summary: Sparks outlets are currently concentrated in Ohio, Pennsylvania, and New York. Although the MAACO name enjoys strong name recognition among target customers, Sparks Tune-Up is less well known. The franchise is backed by a solid management team, a capable training program, and a rapidly expanding network of new outlets.

Franchise Highlights

Began operating: 1980	**Monthly royalty: 7%**
Began franchising: 1981	**Advertising fee: $420 per month**
Outlets currently open: 120	**Training program: 9 days**
Initial franchise fee: $20,000	**Term: 15 years**

Thrifty Rent-A-Car

Industry experience:	★★★★	*Franchising experience:*	★★★★
Financial strength:	★★★★	*Training & services:*	★★★
Fees & royalties:	★★★★	*Satisfied franchisees:*	★★★★

Thrifty Rent-A-Car System
P. O. Box 35250
Tulsa, Oklahoma 74135
(918) 665-3930

The success of Thrifty Rent-A-Car was forged on the idea of locating outlets close to, but not on the premises of, major airports. Space at airports is leased at premium rates, while properties in the immediate vicinity are usually sold or rented at bargain prices. Thrifty has traditionally passed along the savings to the public in the form of low rates on car and truck rentals. The company's signature is a chauffeur-driven limousine that picks up customers at the airport and deposits them at the rental office.

The Franchise: The Thrifty franchisee operates a full-service, off-airport car rental business, providing free customer transportation from airline terminals to the outlet. The rental fleet typically includes a broad range of passenger cars and utility vans.

Franchisee Profile: Prior experience in the rental car trade is preferred, but not mandatory.

Projected Earnings: The franchisor does not furnish a written claim of projected earnings of a franchise outlet.

Franchisor's Services: Thrifty provides a mandatory training program at Tulsa, Oklahoma. The cost of travel, lodging, and meals is borne by the franchisee. Additional training takes place at the franchisee's rental office. The franchisor assists in selecting a site for the outlet and offers advice in acquiring the rental fleet. The support program also includes frequent franchisee meetings and seminars, to keep franchisees abreast of industry trends and developments. A Thrifty field consultant periodically inspects each outlet to verify adherence to the franchisor's performance standards, and to provide on-site guidance and troubleshooting.

Thrifty operates a national reservation system and is represented by major airline and travel agency computers.

Initial Investment: The total investment ranges from $10,000 to $75,000, depending on the number of vehicles in the rental fleet.

Advertising: The franchisor conducts aggressive national advertising programs, funded by advertising royalties contributed by Thrifty franchisees. The toll free reservation system assures a steady stream of business clients.

Fees and Royalties: The $9,000 initial franchise fee and three percent monthly royalty are both low for the industry. Even with the five percent advertising royalty, the franchisee enjoys a light royalty burden.

Summary: A well entrenched franchisor with solid name recognition, Thrifty enjoys a unique niche in the rental market, combining the economy of off-airport premises with a national reputation. Low franchise fees and a flexible initial investment make a Thrifty Rent-A-Car outlet an affordable vehicle for quickly entering and penetrating a highly competitive market.

Franchise Highlights

Began operating: 1962
Began franchising: 1964
Outlets currently open: 500

Initial franchise fee: Min $9,000
Monthly royalty: 3%
Advertising fee: 5%

Tuff-Kote Dinol

Industry experience:	★ ★ ★ ★	*Franchising experience:*	★ ★ ★ ★
Financial strength:	★ ★ ★ ★	*Training & services:*	★ ★ ★
Fees & royalties:	★ ★ ★	*Satisfied franchisees:*	★ ★ ★

Tuff-Kote Dinol, Inc.
15045 Hamilton Avenue
Highland Park, Michigan 48203
(313) 867-4700

The Tuff-Kote Dinol franchise combines the brand recognition of Tuff-Kote sealing products with the chemical innovations of Astra-Dinol, a Swedish firm. In 1972, the two companies launched a joint franchising effort under the name Tuff-Kote Dinol. Since then, the company has licensed more than 3,600 dealers and sold more than 160 franchises based on its unique, two-step rustproofing system.

The Franchise: The franchisee operates a retail automobile rustproofing service, using the Tuff-Kote Dinol system and trade name. A typical outlet is a 2,500 sq. ft. facility in a standalone site in a commercial or light industrial area.

The heart of the business is a rust penetrant developed by Astra-Dinol and an aluminized sealant marketed by Tuff-Kote. The penetrant invades existing rust, while the sealant prevents future oxidation, providing a true remedy for rusting guaranteed for five years or 50,000 miles. In addition, franchisees may sell fabric protection services, sunroofs, and automobile trim accessories.

The business may be conducted as a self-sufficient operation or as a supplement to a related automotive service. The primary customers for the Tuff-Kote Dinol outlet include both individual car owners and fleet operators.

Franchisee Profile: Prior experience in auto rustproofing, reconditioning, or a related service is considered helpful, but not mandatory. Absentee ownership, while not prohibited, is discouraged by the franchisor.

Projected earnings: Based on the company's reported annual sales, the average volume of a Tuff-Kote Dinol outlet is about $156,000 per year, before expenses.

Franchisor's Services: Tuff-Kote Dinol provides five days of orientation at corporate headquarters in Michigan, plus three days of on-the-job training at the franchisee's place of business. The curriculum includes shop operations, rustproofing technique, business management, and marketing methods. Franchisees are required to pay their own travel and lodging expenses to attend the training program.

The franchisor provides site selection assistance, as well as help in negotiating a lease for the premises. The company will outfit the shop and prepare the business for opening at additional cost. Signage may be purchased or leased from the franchisor. All franchisees receive a Grand Opening promotional campaign. Field sales training, ongoing consultation from a field representative, annual meetings, and a franchise newsletter are also part of the franchisor's support package.

Initial Investment: Based on the maximum franchise fee of $11,000, the franchisee's initial investment is broken down as follows:

Initial franchise fee	$11,000
Lease deposits	3,000
Improvements and signs	5,000
Equipment and inventory	8,000
Working capital	16,000
Total	$43,000

The figure for working capital includes $1,000 for insurance and organizational expenses. The remainder represents employee wages and operating costs required to sustain the business during the startup period.

The franchisor offers to finance 50 percent of the initial franchise fee, although franchisees who pay only the minimum fee are not eligible for the financial assistance program.

Advertising: Franchisees contribute five percent of gross monthly revenues to a co-op ad fund used to conduct national and regional advertising campaigns on behalf of all Tuff-Kote outlets. The franchisor also supplies franchisees with radio and television commercials, Yellow Pages ads, and slicks for newspaper and magazine campaigns. In-store promotional materials may be purchased at nominal cost.

Contract Highlights: The term of the franchise is ten years, the industry average. The franchisee has an option to renew the contract on expiration for an additional ten-year term. In addition, the franchisee receives a protected territory in which Tuff-Kote Dinol will not sell or open a competing outlet. The franchise agreement does not grant any subfranchising rights whatsoever.

Fees and Royalties: The initial franchise fee is low to moderate, depending on the economic conditions of the local market. The eight percent franchise royalty is average, but the five percent co-op ad fee is on the high side, exacting a hefty 13 percent of the outlet's revenues before expenses.

Summary: Franchisee satisfaction, brand recognition, and the cooperative benefits of thousands of outlets (only about 170 are franchises) merit high marks. Tuff-Kote Dinol is arguably the best known trade mark in automobile rustproofing. In sheer numbers, the chain is the largest of its kind in the world.

Franchise Highlights

Began operating: 1964
Began franchising: 1967
Outlets currently open: 166
Initial franchise fee: Min $4,000
Max. $11,000

Monthly royalty: 8%
Advertising fee: 1%
Training program: 1 week
Term: 10 years

Tunex

Industry experience:	★★★	*Franchising experience:*	★★★
Financial strength:	★★★	*Training & services:*	★★★★
Fees & royalties:	★★★	*Satisfied franchisees:*	★★★

Tunex, Inc.
556 E. 2100 South
Salt Lake City, Utah 84106
(801) 486-8133

Since Tunex began franchising in 1975, the company has experienced moderate but consistent growth, opening an average of six outlets per year through 1983. Tunex recently stepped up its recruitment program and is now expanding throughout the west coast and Ohio Valley.

The Franchise: The Tunex franchisee operates a retail automobile electronic diagnosis and tune-up center, offering a wide range of related maintenance and repair services, from ignition systems to fuel systems. The typical outlet operates six service bays and employs a full-time staff of four mechanics.

Franchisee Profile: Previous mechanical or technical experience is not a prerequisite, but demonstrated mechanical aptitude and business know-how are beneficial. The company is not actively seeking absentee owners, but will consider granting area franchises to develop large territories.

Projected Earnings: On request, the franchisor will provide prospective franchisees with a written statement of the profit levels that a typical outlet might be able to achieve.

Franchisor's Services: Tunex conducts a ten-day training program at the company's learning center in Salt Lake City. The franchisee must pay travel and lodging expenses to attend the program. The curriculum includes engine diagnosis procedures, fuel and electrical system repairs, and business administration. An additional week of on-the-job instruction is provided at an operating Tunex outlet.

The franchisor will participate in selecting a site for the business, negotiating a lease for the premises, and planning construction and improvements. Ongoing support is provided by a field consultant in periodic visits to the franchisee's shop. Tunex operates a centralized purchasing system, enabling franchisees to order parts and equipment at competitive wholesale prices. The franchisor plans and monitor's each outlet's inventory level, to avert critical shortages.

Initial Investment: The total investment ranges from $65,000 to $70,000, including the initial franchise fee, lease deposits, improvements, tools, equipment, and an initial supply of parts. Tunex will not directly finance any part of the investment, but the franchisor will help qualified franchisees obtain financial assistance from a third party.

Advertising: Tunex franchisees contribute ten percent of gross monthly revenues to a co-op ad fund, which the franchisor uses to conduct regional and local campaigns and design promotional materials.

Contract Highlights: The term of the franchise is ten years, the industry average. On expiration, the contract is renewable for an additional term, if neither party is in violation of any material provisions. The franchisee receives a protected territory in which Tunex will not sell or open a competing outlet while the contract is in force. Subfranchising rights are available under a separate agreement.

Fees and Royalties: The initial fee of $19,000 is slightly high, but not unreasonable in view of the company's recent track record. The six percent monthly royalty is moderate, but including the ten percent advertising contribution, the total royalty burden is 16 percent of gross monthly revenues of the outlet.

Summary: Despite high advertising fees, Tunex is one of the most affordable franchise opportunities in the auto tune-up trade. By stressing quality rather than price, the company has established a reputation for dependable performance and carved out a solid niche in a highly competitive market.

Franchise Highlights

Began operating: 1972	**Monthly royalty: 6%**
Began franchising: 1975	**Advertising fee: 10%**
Outlets currently open: 130	**Training program: 2 weeks**
Initial franchise fee: $19,000	**Term: 10 years**

Ugly Duckling Rent-A-Car

Industry experience:	★★★	*Franchising experience:*	★★★
Financial strength:	★★★	*Training & services:*	★★★
Fees & royalties:	★★★★	*Satisfied franchisees:*	★★★★

Ugly Duckling Rent-A-Car
6375 E. Tanque Verde Road
Tucson, Arizona 85715
(602) 528-1584

Headquartered in Tucson, Arizona, Ugly Duckling Rent-A-Car has enjoyed a respectable growth rate of nearly 70 new outlets per year, since selling its first franchise in early 1979. One of the first national chains to rent used cars at discount rates, the franchisor is currently offering franchise locations throughout the United States and Canada, as well as in selected overseas markets.

The Franchise: The Ugly Duckling franchisee conducts an automobile rental business, using 'pre-owned' vehicles and operated under the franchisor's trademarks. A typical outlet offers a broad range of used passenger automobiles for rent, from economy cars to standard size sedans. The franchisee's fleet must be clean and in good running condition.

Franchisee profile: Some prior experience in the automobile rental business is preferred, but not mandatory. Absentee ownership is specifically probihited. The company focuses on applicants who will operate and manage the franchise business themselves.

Projected Earnings: Ugly Duckling does not currently make any statement or claim of projected earnings of a franchise outlet.

Franchisor's Services: The franchisor conducts a training program in three to four days at the company's headquarters in Tucson. An Ugly Duckling consultant assists with selecting a site for the operation and acquiring a rental fleet. After the agency has opened for business, an area manager pays a visit to the outlet to inspect the operation and provide on-site troubleshooting as required. The franchisor organizes annual conventions where franchisees share their experiences and receive continuing education.

Initial Investment: Depending on the location of the outlet and the size of the rental fleet, the total investment may be from $2,500 and up.

Advertising: The franchisor offers promotional materials, such as fliers and logo designs, and conducts periodic advertising campaigns on behalf of Ugly Duckling outlets. Franchisees contribute one percent of their gross monthly revenues to the ad fund.

Contract Highlights: The franchise agreement has no definite term. Ugly Duckling designates an exclusive territory for the outlet, promising not to sell or open other outlets within the protected area while the contract is in force.

Fees and Royalties: Both the initial franchise fee and the monthly royalty are moderate for the industry, although the initial fee may vary.

Summary: Ugly Duckling is an established used-car rental franchisor with a good base of outlets and a respectable track record. The low investment and unique market niche offer a viable avenue for entering a competitive field dominated by a handful of industry giants.

Franchise Highlights

Began operating: 1978	**Monthly royalty: 6%**
Began franchising: 1979	**Advertising fee: 1%**
Outlets currently open: 500	**Training program: 4 days**
Initial franchise fee: Min $1,500	**Term: None**

Western Auto Supply

Industry experience:	★★★★	*Franchising experience:*	★★★★
Financial strength:	★★★★	*Training & services:*	★★★
Fees & royalties:	★★★★	*Satisfied franchisees:*	★★★★

Western Auto Supply Company
2107 Grand Avenue
Kansas City, Missouri 64108
(816) 346-4015

Western Auto Supply is one of the oldest and best known auto parts suppliers in North America. Founded in 1909, the company has franchised roughly 2,500 outlets since 1935, opening nearly 80 new outlets every year. Fewer than a tenth of the company's 2,700 Western Auto stores are company-owned.

The Franchise: The franchisee operates a retail automobile parts business, under the trade name Western Auto Supply. A typical outlet is located in a retail strip center or a standalone site in a commercial or light industrial area, with a staff of two full-time and three part-time employees. The franchisee sells a broad range of auto parts, accessories, and home and recreational products. The primary customers of the outlet are individual consumers and automobile owners, but service stations, auto repair centers, and other auto parts suppliers are also potential customers.

Franchisee Profile: Prior experience in auto parts or general merchandising is preferred, but not mandatory. The company will consider absentee owners, as well as prospective franchisees who will own and operate the business full-time. Area franchises are not presently available.

Franchisor's Services: Western Auto conducts a one-week training program at the company's headquarters in Kansas City, Missouri. Attendees are resonsible for their own travel and lodging expenses. The franchisor participates in selecting a site for the auto parts store, negotiating a lease for the premises, and planning the store's layout. Franchisees also receive help with planning Grand Opening activities and in-store promotions. A Western Auto representative peridoically visits each store to inspect the operation and provide on-site assistance as required.

The franchisor carefully plans and monitors the franchisee's inventory. A centralized purchasing system enables franchisees to take advantage of wholesale discounts based on the consolidated inventory requirements all Western Auto stores.

Initial Investment: New franchisees should be prepared to invest a minimum of $75,000. The total investment includes lease deposits, improvements, fixtures, and an opening inventory of auto parts and other retail merchandise. Western Auto may finance a portion of the investment, based on the franchisee's creditworthiness and financial needs.

Advertising: The franchisor conducts national, regional, and local advertising campaigns on hebalf of all Western Auto franchises and company-owned stores. At present, there is no mandatory advertising royalty.

Contract Highlights: The franchise does not have a definite term. The franchisee does not receive a protected territory and has no specific expansion rights. Although absentee ownership is permitted, the franchise agreement does not grant subfranchising rights of any kind.

Fees and royalties: Western Auto franchisees do not pay any initial franchise fee or monthly royalties. However, the franchisor derives profits from the sale of merchandise to franchisees.

Summary: Western Auto receives high marks for outstanding name recognition, an affordable investment, the availability of financial assistance, an expansive network, and an exceptional support program.

Franchise Highlights

Began operating: 1909
Began franchising: 1935
Outlets currently open: 2,700
Initial franchise fee: None
Monthly royalty: None
Advertising fee: None
Training program: 1 week
Term: None

Ziebart

Industry experience:	★ ★ ★ ★	*Franchising experience:*	★ ★ ★ ★
Financial strength:	★ ★ ★	*Training & services:*	★ ★ ★ ★
Fees & royalties:	★ ★ ★	*Satisfied franchisees:*	★ ★ ★ ★

Ziebart Corporation
1290 E. Maple Road
Troy, Michigan 48099
(313) 588-4100

One of the oldest names in automobile rustproofing, the Ziebart trademark now appears on a wide range of car chemicals and accessories, from air conditioning products to sunroofs. The company has been franchising since 1962, with more than 600 franchise outlets and nearly 30 company-owned stores reportedly in operation today. Ziebart Corporation operates its own chemical company, allowing the company to expand from selling only rustproofing chemicals and services to such vertical products as exterior paint glaze, interior fabric protection, and radiator coolants. The company also markets its own line of auto trim accessories, including splash guards, sunroof modules, and pinstripe material.

The Franchise: The Ziebart franchisee sells automobile rustproofing, paint and fabric protection, and air conditioning chemicals and services, as well as trim accessories, to the general public. A typical outlet is a 6,000 sq. ft. facility with five full-time and two part-time employees. The franchisee is obligated to purchase equipment and merchandise from the franchisor or a supplier designated by Ziebart.

Franchisee Profile: Prior experience in automobile rustproofing or reconditioning is considered helpful, but is not mandatory.

Projected Earnings: Zierbart does not currently make any claims regarding projected earnings of anticipated profits of a franchise outlet.

Franchisor's Services: The franchisor provides three weeks of intensive training at Troy, Michigan. Franchisees must pay for their own travel and lodging. The curriculum includes one week of chemistry background and hands-on experience in rust prevention techniques, one week of exterior protection methods, and a final week devoted to management and operations. An additional week of on-the-job training is provided at the franchisee's place of business. Field representatives train both the franchisee and the franchisee's staff. An optional course on air conditioning and radiator service is available for an add-on tuition.

Ongoing telephone communications and periodic visitations by both a sales specialist and a technical expert are part of the Ziebart franchisee support program. National franchisee conferences are held annually. The company also operates a toll- free purchasing line and a centralized, computer-based billing system.

Initial investment: The initial investment ranges from $50,000 to $60,000, including the initial franchise fee, fixtures, equipment, and supplies. Ziebart Corporation does not presently offer direct financial assistance to franchisees.

Advertising: Ziebart conducts an aggressive co-op advertising program on behalf of franchisees. The franchisor supplies ad slicks for newspaper and magazine campaigns, radio and television commercials, public relations aids, and approved sign designs.

Contract Highlights: The franchisor does not designate an exclusive territory for the outlet. In addition to attending the mandatory training program, franchisees are obligated to purchase equipment and supplies from Ziebart Corporation and/or its stipulated suppliers.

Fees and Royalties: The eight percent franchise royalty is average for the industry, but adding in the five percent advertising fee, the total royalty burden is 13 percent of the gross revenues of the outlet.

Summary: Ziebart is a solid franchisor with ample experience in both auto rustproofing and franchising. The chain is backed by a progressive management team and a strong base of franchisees and dealers.

Franchise Highlights

Began operating: 1954
Began franchising: 1962
Outlets currently open: 600
Initial franchise fee: $15,000

Monthly royalty: 8%
Advertising fee: 5%
Training program: 3 weeks
Term: 10 years

Business Services

It was once widely believed that the rise of corporate conglomerates spelled doom for the small, independently owned business. The entrepreneurial 80s shattered that notion. There are more than 17 million small businesses in America today, and the success rate of new enterprises has doubled over the last decade. One reason for the revitalization of the small-time operator is a boom in services that support the independent business owner. Firms offering accounting, counseling, recruiting, and communications services equip today's small business with many resources that once only a large company could afford.

Poor financial management is one of the major causes of small business failure. Franchise systems marketing centralized accounting, record keeping, and financial services often supplant the need for in-house finance departments, at substantial savings to clients. Overall, franchisors in this sector experienced a ten percent growth rate between 1986 and 1987.

According to the Department of Commerce, temporary personnel services constitute one of the fastest growing segments of the economy, accounting for a $6 billion industry that is expanding at an annual rate of 20 percent. Executive recruiting is also a prominent trend in the employment trade. Since 1970, the industry focus has shifted gradually from the applicant to the employer. Personnel agencies fill 20 percent of the nation's job openings, recruiting 4 million applicants per year. Increasing job specialization has affected the personnel agency, as well, creating a new tier of service businesses that cater exclusively to such fields as health care and electronics.

The rise of the so-called instant-printing or quick-copy trade brought the cost of professional printing services within the reach of every small business. The printing industry is the fifth largest, accounting for $7 billion in annual sales, with more than half represented by instant-printing shops. Franchisors in this field are expanding at an annual rate of 25 percent. The most dramatic growth among business-service franchises over the last decade was experienced by the new breed of specialty 'business boutiques,' offering such support services as mail-box rentals, packaging, and freight forwarding.

AAA Employment

Industry experience:	★ ★ ★ ★	*Franchising experience:*	★ ★
Financial strength:	★ ★ ★	*Training & services:*	★ ★ ★
Fees & royalties:	★ ★ ★	*Satisfied franchisees:*	★ ★ ★ ★

AAA Employment
5533 Central Avenue
St. Petersburg, Florida 33710
(813) 343-3044

Founded in 1957, AAA Employment is arguably the largest privately owned employment agency in the United States, with more than 130 offices, most of them company-operated. Since the company began franchising in 177, a little more than 30 independently owned franchise outlets have opened their doors under the AAA sign.

The Franchise: The franchisee conducts an employment agency, recruiting and placing job candidates and doing business under the trade name AAA Employment. A typical outlet places individuals in all types of positions, from domestic to executive, from part-time to full-time, or from temporary to permanent. Applicants pay their own placement fees, equivalent to two weeks' salary — a low rate by industry standards. The fact that the service provides free employee recruitment to businesses encourages participation by employers.

Franchisee Profile: A background in personnel recruitment, placement, or administration is helpful, but not mandatory. Basic business, administrative, and communications skills take priority over experience.

Projected Earnings: On request, AAA will furnish prospective franchisees with a written statement of the projected earnings of a typical or average outlet.

Franchisor's Services: The franchisor provides a training program from two to four weeks in length, at the company's headquarters in St. Petersburg, Florida. Attendees are responsible for their own travel and lodging expenses. The curriculum includes all aspects of the business, including payroll, advertising, budget administration, tax rates, and bookkeeping principles. Franchisees receive copies of the confidential AAA operating manual, containing the franchisor's standardized policies and procedures.

The franchisor will assist with selecting a site for the outlet and negotiating a lease for the premises. When the agency is open, an AAA field representative will visit the franchisee's office periodically, to inspect the operation and offer on-site guidance. AAA publishes a weekly franchisee newsletter and conducts semi-annual seminars and workshops to keep franchisees abreast of industry developments and employment trends.

Initial Investment: New AAA franchisees should be prepared to invest from $13,000 to $35,000 to establish the business. The amount includes the initial fee, lease deposits, furnishings, and equipment. The franchisor may offer financial assistance to qualified franchisees.

Advertising:AAA franchisees do not pay a separate advertising royalty. The franchisor supplies franchisees with ad slicks, commercials, and promotional materials for local advertising efforts.

Contract Highlights: The term of the franchise is ten years. On expiration, the contract may be renewed for one or more additional years, at the franchisee's option. The franchisee receives a protected territory for the duration of the agreement. AAA will not sell another franchise or open a company-operated employment agency in the franchisee's territory while the franchise agreement is in force. The franchisee may purchase more than franchise or open multiple outlets, but has no subfranchising rights whatsoever.

Fees and Royalties: The initial franchise fee ranges from $4,000 to $15,000 — low to moderate for the industry. By itself, the ten percent monthly royalty tends toward the high end of the spectrum. But considering the franchisor does not exact an advertising royalty, the overall royalty burden is moderate.

Summary: The AAA franchise is characterized by an affordable initial investment and moderate royalties, backed by the resources of an industry leader. Prospective franchisees should bear in mind that three fourths of the AAA Employment agencies operating today are company-owned. The franchisor's operating manual and support program receive high marks from existing franchisees.

Franchise Highlights

Began operating: 1957
Began franchising: 1977
Outlets currently open: 130
Initial franchise fee: Min $4,000
Max. $15,000

Monthly royalty: 10%
Advertising fee: None
Training program: 2-4 weeks
Term: 10 years

Alphagraphics

Industry experience:	★ ★ ★ ★	*Franchising experience:*	★ ★ ★ ★
Financial strength:	★ ★ ★	*Training & services:*	★ ★ ★
Fees & royalties:	★ ★ ★	*Satisfied franchisees:*	★ ★ ★ ★

Alphagraphics Printshops of the Future
845 East Broadway
Tucson, Arizona 85719
(800) 528-4885

Alphagraphics has sold 200 'print shops of the future' since the company began franchising in 1980, opening an average of 30 outlets every year. In addition to conventional duplication and printing equipment, the firm's franchise shops also use Apple Macintosh computers and software to handle customer needs. The company is currently seeking new franchisees in most U.S. and Canadian markets, as well as Europe and Asia.

The Franchise: The franchisee operates a retail printing center specializing in duplicating services, offset printing, and desktop publishing services, under the trade name Alphagraphics. A typical outlet is situated in a retail strip center, business park, or other suitable commercial site, with a staff of four full-time and two part-time employees. Franchisees offer duplicating and offset printing services, self-service desktop publishing with personal computers and laser graphics, and related document collating, drilling, and binding services.

Franchisee Profile: A background in the quick-print or copy business is beneficial, but not mandatory. Absentee ownership is prohibited. A typical Alphagraphics franchisee is a former middle-management executive or sales professional with keen entrepreneurial incentive and a high level of self-esteem.

Projected Earnings: A statement of projected earnings was not available at press time.

Franchisor's Services: The franchisor provides a two-week training program at the company's headquarters in Tucson, Arizona. Attendees are responsible for their own travel and lodging expenses. The curriculum includes equipment operation, store procedures, marketing, customer relations, employee administration, and financial.

The franchisor will assist with selecting a site for the outlet and negotiating a lease for the premises. After the outlet has opened for business, an Alphagraphics representative will visit the outlet periodically, to offer guidance and troubleshooting. Other ongoing services include field seminars and a franchisee newsletter.

Initial Investment: New Alphagraphics franchisees should be prepared to invest around $264,000 to establish the business. The amount includes the initial franchise fee, lease deposits, site improvements, equipment purchases, and an initial inventory of computer, copy machine, printing, and bindery supplies. Alphagraphics does not offer direct financial assistance to franchisees.

Advertising: Alphagraphics franchisees contribute one percent of gross monthly revenues for advertising. The franchisor supplies franchisees with point-of-sale materials, pre-prepared advertising designs, and tools for conducting local ad campaigns.

Contract Highlights: The term of the franchise is 20 years. The contract may be renewed at the franchisee's option. The franchisee receives an exclusive territory in conjunction with the franchise.

Fees and Royalties: The initial franchise fee of $45,000 is high for the industry. Including the monthly franchise royalty and advertising fee, the total royalty burden is from four to percent of gross sales.

Summary: The Alphagraphics franchise is characterized by an upscale image, growing name recognition, and a diverse service mix with a high-tech motif. An existing franchisee cautions that long hours, persistent management attention, and dedication to hard work are essential to success.

Franchise Highlights

Began operating: 1970
Began franchising: 1980
Outlets currently open: 200
Initial franchise fee: $45,000

Monthly royalty: 3% to 8%
Advertising fee: 1%
Training program: 3 weeks
Term: 20 years

Audit Controls

Industry experience:	★ ★	*Franchising experience:*	★ ★
Financial strength:	★ ★	*Training & services:*	★
Fees & royalties:	★ ★ ★ ★	*Satisfied franchisees:*	★ ★ ★

Audit Controls, Inc.
87 Northeast 44th Street
Ft. Lauderdale, Florida 33334
(305) 491-3275

Founded in 1960, Audit Controls has an estimated 160 franchisees throughout the United States, providing at no-cost collection service to businesses with accounts receivable problems. Although the Audit Controls system is not a business-format franchise in the pure strict sense, the company maintains one of the largest credit collection networks in the country.

The Franchise: The franchisee conducts a collection service under the trade name Audit Controls. The outlet derives profits from fees exacted from client accounts. Customers of the outlet include businesses and institutions requiring the services of a collection bureau.

Franchisee Profile: Franchisees should be in the credit collection business or have some experience in the field, to be successful. Audit Controls does not require any particular qualifications of prospective franchisees, but the franchisor's support services are limited.

Projected Earnings: No information is available regarding the average or projected earnings of an Audit Controls franchise.

Franchisor's Services: The franchisor supplies Audit Controls franchisees with predesigned materials for operating an effective credit collection bureau, including a set of standardized correspondence with demonstrated effectiveness in the collection of past-due accounts. Franchisees also receive direct-mail advertising materials and a mailing list of potential clients furnished on adhesive labels.

The franchise program does not include any special training or field support services.

Initial Investment: Audit Controls franchisees purchase a startup kit for $250. Other startup costs depend on the site and staff size. An outlet with two full-time employees in a modest commercial or industrial complex might require an investment of from $5,000 to $10,000, including business permits, lease deposits, insurance, and working capital. The franchisor does not offer any direct financial assistance to franchisees.

Advertising: Franchisees receive a brochure and mailing list with which to cultivate an initial client base. There are no advertising royalties or fees.

Contract Highlights: The term of the franchise is one year, with an option to renew for an additional year, at the franchisee's option. The franchisee does not receive an exclusive territory. Area franchises are not available.

Fees and Royalties: Other than the initial purchase of the Audit Controls startup kit, there are no franchise fees or royalties connected with the franchise.

Summary: The Audit Controls franchise provides an entry-level opportunity for would-be entrepreneurs with little working capital. The business demands a high level of personal industriousness, tenacity, and verbal communication skills. Aside from the start-up kit, Audit Controls does not provide an extensive support package, so the onus of success is primarily on the franchisee.

Franchise Highlights

Began operating: 1960
Began franchising: 1965
Outlets currently open: 180
Initial franchise fee: None
Monthly royalty: None
Advertising fee: None
Training program: None
Term: 1 year

Bryant Bureau

Industry experience:	★ ★ ★ ★	*Franchising experience:*	★ ★ ★
Financial strength:	★ ★ ★	*Training & services:*	★ ★ ★
Fees & royalties:	★ ★ ★	*Satisfied franchisees:*	★ ★ ★ ★

Bryant Bureau
4000 South Tamiami Trail
Sarasota, Florida 33581
(800) 237-9497

Founded in 1976, the Bryant Bureau is a subsidiary of Snelling and Snelling, the largest employment referral organization in North America. Since the company began franchising in 1976, the Bryant Bureau has opened more than 31 offices specializing in executive recruitment and placement.

The Franchise: The franchisee conducts an executive recruitment business, operated under the trade name Bryant Bureau. A typical outlet is situated in a commercial complex, with a staff of three to seven full-time employees. Franchisees specialize in finding executives to fill existing job openings and locating positions for executive candidates. Customers of the franchise business include employers in fields such as oil and gas, finance, marketing, and data processing.

Franchisee Profile: The company is seeking prospective franchisees who are adept at telephone sales and enjoy working with people. The ideal franchisee is someone who is sincerely interested in helping people pursue their careers and exploit their full potential.

Projected Earnings: The franchisor does not provide a statement of projected earnings.

Franchisor's Services: The franchisor provides a two-week training program at the company's headquarters in Sarasota, Florida. Attendees are responsible for their own travel and lodging expenses. Franchisees receive copies of the franchisor's confidential manuals for the director and staff of the employment office. An additional ten days of on-the-job training take place at the franchisee's site.

The franchisor will assist with selecting the location of the outlet and negotiating a lease for the premises. The startup package includes a videotape recorder and an initial inventory of business supplies. A marketing consultant helps kick off the outlet's initial client recruitment campaign.

When the business is operational, a field representative will visit the outlet periodically to offer guidance and troubleshooting. Ongoing seminars are held at various regional sites, usually at no charge to attendees. The company stresses the importance of employee recognition and awards. An insurance and benefits package is available at group rates for the franchisee's employees.

Initial Investment: The initial investment is estimated at from $40,000 to $80,000, depending on the location and size of the outlet. The total includes the initial franchise fee, lease deposits, equipment purchases, and working capital requirements. The franchisee may make a $15,000 cash down payment on the initial franchise fee, with the balance plus interest to be paid in installments.

Advertising: All franchisees contribute one percent of gross monthly revenues for advertising. The franchisor conducts regional campaigns on behalf of Bryant Bureau outlets. Target media include newspapers, magazines, and direct mail.

Contract Highlights: The franchisee does not receive a protected territory. The contract does not have a definite term, in effect, granting lifetime rights to the franchisee.

Fees and Royalties: The initial franchise fee ranges as high as $29,500. The seven percent monthly royalty, added to the one percent advertising royalty, exacts a total royalty bite of eight percent of gross revenues of the outlet.

Summary: A young but aggressive franchise program operated by an experienced industry giant, the Bryant Bureau offers the advantages of a solid support program, comprehensive training, and a reasonable likelihood of growth.

Franchise Highlights

Began operating: 1976
Began franchising: 1977
Outlets currently open: 31
Initial franchise fee: Min $18,500
Max. $29,500

Monthly royalty: 7%
Advertising fee: 1%
Training program: 2 weeks
Term: None

CAS/CBS

Industry experience:	★ ★ ★ ★	*Franchising experience:*	★ ★ ★ ★
Financial strength:	★ ★ ★	*Training & services:*	★ ★ ★
Fees & royalties:	★ ★ ★	*Satisfied franchisees:*	★ ★ ★ ★

Comprehensive Accounting Service/
Comprehensive Business Service
2111 Comprehensive Drive
Aurora, Illinois 60505
(800) 323-9000

Comprehensive Accounting Service/Comprehensive Business Service (CAS/CBS) has been providing commercial and industrial accounts with systematic accounting and bookkeeping services since 1949. Today, all of the company's 400-plus accounting offices are franchises.

The Franchise: The franchisee conducts a public accounting practice, catering to business clients and operating under the trade name Comprehensive Accounting Service or Comprehensive Business Service. Customers of the franchise business include corporations, small businesses, attorneys, medical practices, and self-employed individuals.

Franchisee Profile: CAS/CBS franchisees must possess an accredited accounting degree and be licensed to practice accounting in their respective localities. Absentee ownership is prohibited by the franchise agreement.

Projected Earnings: The franchisor does furnish prospective franchisees with a written statement of projected earnings.

Franchisor's Services: The franchisor provides a five-week training program at the company's headquarters in Aurora, Illinois. While there is no tuition for the program, the cost of travel, lodging, and meals is borne by the franchisee. The curriculum includes the CAS/CBS accounting system, client recruiting techniques, rates and billing, and general business practices.

Franchisees receive detailed operating manuals documenting the CAS/CBS system from startup to marketing. A field representative will visit the franchisee's offices periodically, to provide ongoing assistance in running the business and troubleshooting client problems. CAS/CBS conducts frequent seminars and workshops to keep franchisees abreast of new techniques and trends. A toll-free hotline puts franchise owners and their staffs in touch with company accounting and operations experts.

Initial Investment: The CAS/CBS franchisee typically invests $50,000 to establish the business. The amount includes lease deposits, equipment, supplies, and initial working capital. The franchisor has a financial assistance program for qualified franchisees.

Advertising: CAS/CBS franchisees do not pay a separate advertising royalty. The franchisor plans and oversees promotional campaigns on behalf of franchisees, and also supplies supplies ad slicks, commercials, sales literature, and public relations aids for local advertising efforts.

Contract Highlights: The term of the franchise is 15 years. The contract may be renewed for an additional term, if the franchisee is in compliance with all material provisions. The franchisee receives a protected territory for the duration of the agreement. The franchise may not be sold or assigned except with the franchisor's written permission. The assignee must be fully qualified to operate the business and must complete the CAS/CBS training program at his or her own expense.

Fees and Royalties: The initial franchise fee of $20,000 is moderate for an accounting service franchise of this stature. The royalty varies, depending on the client potential of the territory.

Summary: CAS/CBS is the second largest chain of independent public accounting practices in North America. Franchisees benefit from an outstanding training program, solid name recognition, and the backing of an industry leader. The 15-year term is 50 percent longer than the industry average, providing ample opportunity to develop the business and realize a return. The franchisor is currently seeking new franchisees in all areas of the continental U.S.

Franchise Highlights

Began operating: 1949
Began franchising: 1965
Outlets currently open: 420
Initial franchise fee: $20,000

Advertising fee: None
Training program: 5 weeks
Term: 15 years

Dunhill Personnel

Industry experience: ★★★★ *Franchising experience:* ★★★★
Financial strength: ★★★ *Training & services:* ★★★
Fees & royalties: ★★★ *Satisfied franchisees:* ★★★★

Dunhill Personnel System, Inc.
One Old Country Road
Carle Place, New York 11514
(516) 741-5081

Founded in 1951, Dunhill Personnel specializes in recruiting and placing executives, managers, and office personnel. The company offers three levels of franchise: Full Service, including all types of placement; Temporary Services; and Office Personnel. Since the company began franchising in 1961, more than 300 Dunhill offices began operating — all but six owned by independent franchisees. The heart of the Dunhill program is the use of a nationwide computer network to match applicants with job opportunities from coast to coast.

The Franchise: The franchisee conducts a white-collar personnel recruitment and placement business, under the trade name Dunhill Personnel. A typical outlet is situated in a contemporary office complex or commercial building, with from five to seven full-time employees. The outlet uses computer data to search for specialized applicants and positions. Customers of the franchise business include individuals searching for management and clerical positions, as well as employers with suitable job openings.

Franchisee Profile: A background in personnel recruitment or administration is not required. The company is not actively seeking absentee owners.

Projected Earnings: Dunhill does not provide a statement of projected earnings.

Franchisor's Services: Dunhill conducts a two-week training program at the company's headquarters in New York. Franchisees are responsible for their own travel and lodging expenses in connection with the training program. Three days of pre-opening assistance are provided at the franchisee's place of business.

The franchisee is responsible for selecting the location and acquiring the premises. Ongoing assistance is provided by an area field representative in periodic visits to the outlet. To take advantage of the franchisor's computerized referral system, the National Exchange System (NES), franchisees are encouraged - but not required - to purchase hardware and software. Besides the NES, a customized billing program is also available to franchisees at additional cost.

Initial Investment: The total investment ranges from $17,000 to $140,000, depending on the service level, location and size of the outlet, and equipment purchased. The amount also includes lease deposits, furnishings, data processing equipment, software, supplies, and working capital. Dunhill does not offer any form of direct financial assistance to franchisees.

Advertising: Dunhill franchisees contribute between one half and one percent of gross monthly revenues to the franchisor's ad fund. The franchisor uses this fund to conduct national and regional campaigns on behalf of all Dunhill offices. Target media include business journals, newspapers, magazines, and radio. The franchisor also supplies franchisees with ad slicks, commercials, and promotional materials for use in local advertising efforts.

Contract Highlights: The term of the franchise is five years, renewable for five more years at the franchisee's option. The franchisee receives no area or subfranchising rights under the agreement. The franchise may not be sold or transferred to another party except with the franchisor's written consent. Dunhill derives a profit from the sale of equipment and supplies to the franchisee, but the franchisee is free to purchase these items from other suppliers, as well.

Fees and Royalties: The initial franchise fee ranges from $15,000 to $25,000. The monthly royalty ranges from two percent to seven percent. Including the advertising royalty, the total royalty bite is from two and a half to eight percent of gross monthly revenues.

Summary: Dunhill projects an upscale corporate image, with high-tech overtones, emulating the clientele that the business strives to serve. Existing franchisees rate the franchisor's training program as above average to excellent.

Franchise Highlights

Began operating: 1952
Began franchising: 1961
Outlets currently open: 300
Initial franchise fee: Min $15,000
Max. $25,000

Monthly royalty: 7%
Advertising fee: 1%
Training program: 2 weeks
Term: 10 years

General Business Services

Industry experience:	★★★	*Franchising experience:*	★★★★
Financial strength:	★★★	*Training & services:*	★★★★
Fees & royalties:	★★★	*Satisfied franchisees:*	★★★★

General Business Services
20271 Goldenrod Lane
Germantown, Maryland 20874
(800) 638-7940

General Business Services (GBS) is arguably the world's largest accounting support organization, with more than 750 offices, all owned by independent franchisees. The company was launched in 1962 by a former small business operator, Bernard Browning. GBS has opened an average of 50 outlets every year. The heart of the business is a standardized system for organizing tax and accounting records, but the franchisor styles itself as a full-service consulting resource for the small business operator.

The Franchise: The franchisee conducts a bookkeeping/accounting service catering to small business owners and self-employed individuals and operating under the trade name General Business Services (GBS). Franchisees offer counseling on business organization and record keeping, tax planning, and general accounting support services.

Franchisee Profile: No special qualifications are required, but prospective franchisees should possess basic business and communications skills.

Projected Earnings: The franchisor does not provide a statement of projected earnings.

Franchisor's Services: The franchisor provides a three-week training program at the company's headquarters in Germantown, Maryland. Attendees are responsible for their own travel and lodging expenses, but the tuition is included in the initial franchise fee. An additional five days of on-site assistance and on-the-job training are provided at the franchisee's place of business.

The franchisee is responsible for acquiring suitable office premises from which to conduct the business. When the office is operational, a GBS representative will visit the outlet periodically to offer ongoing guidance and assistance. GBS publishes a newsletter for franchisees and conducts seminars to keep franchisees abreast of industry trends and developments. A toll-free hotline provides franchisees with access to the franchisor's technical and operations consultants.

Initial Investment: New GBS franchisees invest about $30,000 to establish their businesses. The amount includes the initial franchise fee, lease deposits, office equipment, business forms, supplies, and miscellaneous start-up costs. The franchisor does not offer any direct financial assistance to franchisees.

Advertising: GBS franchisees do not pay any advertising royalty. The franchisor conducts national and regional campaigns on behalf of franchisees. Franchisees also receive prepared advertising materials, including ad slicks, commercials, sales literature, and public relations aids.

Contract Highlights: The term of the franchise is five years, with an option to renew at the franchisee's option. The GBS outlet may not be sold or assigned except with the franchisor's consent.

Fees and Royalties: The initial franchise fee of $21,500 is on the high side, but not unreasonable, in light of the franchisor's stature as an industry leader. The seven percent monthly royalty is moderate for a franchise in this field.

Summary: The GBS franchise is characterized by a large base of outlets, strong name recognition in most U.S. markets, and the competitive benefits of an industry giant.

Franchise Highlights

Began operating: 1962
Began franchising: 1962
Outlets currently open: 750
Initial franchise fee: $21,500
Monthly royalty: 7%
Advertising fee: None
Training program: 3 weeks
Term: 5 years

H & R Block

Industry experience:	★ ★ ★ ★	*Franchising experience:*	★ ★ ★ ★
Financial strength:	★ ★ ★ ★	*Training & services:*	★ ★ ★
Fees & royalties:	★ ★ ★	*Satisfied franchisees:*	★ ★ ★ ★

H & R Block, Inc.
4410 Main Street
Kansas City, Missouri 64111
(816) 753-6900

Founded in 1946, H & R Block is one of the most expansive franchise chains of any kind in the world. Among tax preparation services, the company is the undisputed leader, with more than 7,000 outlets in the U.S., Canada, and overseas.

The Franchise: The franchisee operates a tax preparation service, using the trade name H & R Block. A typical franchise is operated in conjunction with a related business, such as an accounting, bookkeeping, or real estate office.

Franchisor's Services: H & R Block provides training in accounting, personnel administration, marketing and sales at a site near the franchisee's location. Each franchisee receives a copy of the confidential H & R Block operations manuals, which documents the policies and procedures of the tax preparation service. A field consultant is available to offer ongoing advice and troubleshooting. The franchisor provides all the basic forms and supplies required to conduct the business.

Initial Investment: The capital requirement is estimated at between $2,000 to $5,000. The franchisor does not offer any direct financial assistance to franchisees.

Fees and Royalties: The initial franchise fee ranges from $600 to $1,200, but is refundable. The ongoing royalty is calculated at 50 percent of gross sales from tax preparation service, for sales of $5,000 or less. A 30 percent royalty applies to amounts in excess of $5,000.

Summary: The H & R Block franchise is characterized by widespread name recognition, national advertising support, and strong seasonal demand for the franchisee's services. The market received an impetus from the 1987 Tax Reform Law, which introduced a host of new intricacies in tax planning and preparation.

Franchise Highlights

Began operating: 1946
Began franchising: 1958
Outlets currently open: 7,400
Initial franchise fee: Min. $600
Max. $1,200

Monthly royalty: Varies
Advertising fee: None
Training program: Varies
Term: 5 years

Insty-Prints

Industry experience:	★★★★	*Franchising experience:*	★★★★
Financial strength:	★★★	*Training & services:*	★★★
Fees & royalties:	★★★	*Satisfied franchisees:*	★★★★

Insty-Prints Printing Centers
1215 Marshall Street NE
Minneapolis, Minnesota 55413
(612) 379-0039

Founded in 1965, Insty-Prints has established 360 instant-print shops since the company began franchising in 1965, opening an average of 17 outlets every year. The company is currently seeking new franchisees in most U.S. markets.

The Franchise: The franchisee operates a retail quick-print shop, under the trade name Insty-Prints. A typical outlet is situated in a retail strip center, business park, or commercial building, with a staff of two full-time and two part-time employees. Franchisees offer instant printing and document duplication service.

Franchisee Profile: A background in the printing trade is beneficial, but not mandatory. Absentee ownership is discouraged.

Projected Earnings: A statement of projected earnings was not available at press time.

Franchisor's Services: The franchisor provides a four-week training program at the company's headquarters in Minneapolis. Attendees are responsible for their own travel and lodging expenses. The curriculum includes shop operations, personnel recruitment, marketing, customer assistance, inventory planning, and business administration.

The franchisor will assist with selecting a site for the outlet and negotiating a lease for the premises. After the outlet has opened for business, a Insty-Prints representative will visit the outlet periodically, to offer guidance and troubleshooting. Other ongoing services include a confidential operations manual, a franchise newsletter, and unlimited telephone consultations with company operations experts.

Initial Investment: New Insty-Prints franchisees should be prepared to invest $75,000 to establish the business. The amount includes the initial franchise fee, lease deposits, site improvements, equipment purchases, and an initial inventory of papers, inks, and duplicating supplies. Insty-Prints does not offer direct financial assistance to franchisees.

Advertising: Insty-Prints franchisees contribute one and a half percent of gross monthly revenues for advertising. The franchisor supplies franchisees with sales literature, ad designs, commercials, and public relations tools.

Contract Highlights: The term of the franchise is 15 years. The contract may be renewed at the franchisee's option. The franchisee receives an exclusive territory in conjunction with the franchise.

Fees and Royalties: The initial franchise fee of $33,500 is high for the industry. Including the monthly franchise royalty and advertising fee, the total royalty burden is less than seven percent of gross sales.

Summary: The Insty-Prints franchise is characterized by an ample base of outlets, spreading name recognition, and a ready-to-go business format in a trade supported by consistent market demand.

Franchise Highlights

Began operating: 1965	**Monthly royalty: 3% to 4.5%**
Began franchising: 1965	**Advertising fee: 2%**
Outlets currently open: 360	**Training program: 4 weeks**
Initial franchise fee: $33,500	**Term: 15 years**

Kwik-Kopy

Industry experience:	★ ★ ★	*Franchising experience:*	★ ★ ★ ★
Financial strength:	★ ★ ★	*Training & services:*	★ ★ ★ ★
Fees & royalties:	★ ★ ★ ★	*Satisfied franchisees:*	★ ★ ★ ★

Kwik-Kopy Corporation
P.O. Box 777
Cypress, Texas 77429-0777
(713) 373-3535

The quick-print business first began to flourish in the early 1970s, as America underwent a dramatic transformation into an 'information society.' Unlike conventional printing establishments, which utilize a time-consuming technique involving expensive metal printing plates, the quick-print shop uses a low-cost disposable medium to reproduce printed images. Kwik-Kopy started its franchise printing business in 1967 and has since become the largest quick-print service in the world. The company operates more than a thousand franchises in 42 states and four continents.

The Franchise: The Kwik-Kopy franchisee conducts an instant printing shop, focusing on quick-print services and photocopies. A typical outlet has three full-time employees, producing business cards, stationery, forms, and other printed materials. The franchisee utilizes state-of-the-art typesetting, camera, and press equipment.

Franchisee Profile: Printing experience is not a necessity. Qualified press operators are hired by the franchisee. A wide range of entrepreneurs currently own Kwik-Kopy franchises, including individuals from both blue-collar and white-collar trades.

Projected Earnings: Based on the parent company's reported annual sales, the average gross revenues of a Kwik-Kopy outlet are about $170,000 before expenses.

Franchisor's Services: Kwik-Kopy employs a staff of more than 100 industry professionals to help franchisees learn and perform their trade. A franchise representative helps the franchisee acquire a suitable site by researching area demographics and assisting in lease negotiations. On occasion, Kwik-Kopy may buy or lease the site itself and sublease the premises to the franchisee.

The Kwik-Kopy training program teaches franchisees the standardized procedures for managing a Kwik-Kopy instant print shop, covering accounting, employee relations, marketing, and advertising. Franchisees must travel to company headquarters in Cypress, Texas for the three-week program.

The franchisor provides on-site assistance starting a week before the outlet opens. Careful attention is paid to the franchisee's operations in the first month after opening. Kwik-Kopy operates a central purchasing system for paper, inks, and other printing supplies, passing along wholesale price discounts to the franchisee. The franchisor also helps plan and monitor the franchisee's supply levels to avert shortages.

Franchisees attend regional meetings and continuing education seminars to keep abreast of current printing techniques and industry trends. Kwik-Kopy also publishes a newsletter for franchisees.

Initial Investment: The total investment is estimated at about $125,000, including the initial franchise fee, lease deposits, site improvements, equipment, and inventory. The franchisor will carry up to three-fourths of the franchise fee for ten years at simple interest. Printing equipment can be leased from Kwik-Kopy for up to eight years.

Advertising: The company and franchisee share advertising costs through a co-op advertising program, based on funding from franchisee advertising royalties. Kwik-Kopy provides the new franchise with a special opening promotional package.

Fees and Royalties: The initial license fee of $42,000 is steep in comparison to other businesses. in the field. However, the company offers the option of a cash discount or partial financing. The monthly franchise royalty varies from four percent on gross sales up to $5,000 to as much as eight percent on gross sales above $10,000.

Contract Highlights: The term of the franchise is 25 years. Franchisees are granted exclusive rights to a territory and, while they may expand within this territory, they are not allowed to subfranchise. Kwik-Kopy is not currently seeking absentee owners, area franchisees, or subfranchisors.

Summary: Kwik-Kopy is an attractive franchise for entrepreneurs who envision a family-run business. The franchise is characterized by moderate overhead, few employees, and reasonable hours. Franchisees benefit from a manageable capital investment and a flexible royalty structure.

Franchise Highlights

Began operating: 1967
Began franchising: 1967
Outlets currently open: 1000
Initial franchise fee: $42,000

Monthly royalty: 4% to 8%
Advertising fee: 2%
Training program: 3 weeks
Term: 25 years

Mail Boxes Etc. USA

Industry experience: ★ ★ *Franchising experience:* ★ ★
Financial strength: ★ ★ ★ *Training & services:* ★ ★ ★
Fees & royalties: ★ ★ ★ *Satisfied franchisees:* ★ ★ ★

Mail Boxes Etc. USA, Inc.
5555 Oberlin Drive
San Diego, California 92121
(619) 452-1553

Mail Boxes Etc. USA successfully capitalized on the entrepreneurial movement of the early to mid 1980s, by providing basic support services to very small businesses and self-employed individuals. Founded in 1980, the chain has expanded to nearly 500 outlets over 20 states, with the heaviest concentration in California.

The Franchise: The franchisee operates a business services office, providing clients with a central address, telephone answering, and general secretarial services. Franchise stores receive a license to use the Mail Boxes Etc. USA trade name. A typical outlet is situated in a strip center, business park, or commercial building with a staff of two full-time and one part- time employees. Franchisees rent mailboxes, dispatch package shipments, and provide telephone answering, word processing, and related services to small business clients.

Franchisee Profile: A background in telephone answering or business services is beneficial, but not mandatory. Absentee ownership is not strictly prohibited. The franchisor will consider granting area franchises to develop large territories.

Franchisor's Services: The franchisor provides a two-week training program at the company's headquarters in San Diego. Attendees are responsible for their own travel and lodging expenses. An additional two weeks of on-the-job training take place at the franchisee's place of business.

On graduation, the franchisee receives a confidential operations manual containing the franchisor's policies and procedures. A field representative will visit the outlet periodically, to offer on-site guidance and management troubleshooting. The franchisor also publishes monthly franchisee newsletter and administers an information hotline.

Initial Investment: The total investment may range from $40,000 to $60,000, including lease deposits, improvements, equipment purchases, and supplies. The franchisor does not offer any direct financial assistance to franchisees.

Advertising: Franchisees contribute two percent of gross monthly revenues for advertising. The franchisor supplies prepared advertising materials, sales tools, price lists, and public relations aids.

Contract Highlights: The term of the franchise is ten years. The contract may be renewed for an additional term, providing the franchisee is in compliance with all material provisions. The franchisee receives a protected territory for the duration of the agreement. Area franchises are available under separate agreement.

Fees and Royalties: The initial franchise fee of $17,500 is somewhat high for the mail receiving sector, reflecting the company's stature as the leader of the pack. The total royalty obligation, including the franchise royalty and the monthly advertising fee, is seven percent of gross sales.

Summary: Mail Boxes Etc. USA almost singlehandedly created the mail receiving-package forwarding industry, which the chain continues to dominate today. Franchisees benefit from a steadily increasing market and an easy-to-operate business format requiring a moderate investment.

Franchise Highlights

Began operating: 1980	**Monthly royalty: 5%**
Began franchising: 1980	**Advertising fee: 2%**
Outlets currently open: 490	**Training program: 2 weeks**
Initial franchise fee: $17,500	**Term: 10 years**

Management Recruiters

Industry experience:	★★★★	*Franchising experience:*	★★★
Financial strength:	★★★	*Training & services:*	★★★★
Fees & royalties:	★★★	*Satisfied franchisees:*	★★★★

Management Recruiters, Inc.
1127 Euclid Avenue, Ste. 1400
Cleveland, Ohio 44115
(216) 696-1122

Founded in 1957, Management Recruiters has established more than 300 outlets since the company began franchising in 1965, opening an average of more than 15 new offices each year. As their trade name implies, Management Recruiters franchisees specialize in executive search, recruitment, and placement services, catering to middle management job candidates, as well as employers with executive openings.

The parent company, Management Recruiters International (MRI), operates three other subsidiaries specializing in different fields. Sales Consultants focuses on sales and marketing profesisonals, whereas Office Mates 5 recruits and places office and clerical personnel. The company's CompuSearch division is devoted exclusively to the data processing industry.

The Franchise: The Management Recruiters franchisee conducts a white-collar employment agency, specializing in middle management and executive positions in the $25,000 to $100,000 salary range. The agency accepts only candidates who are currently employed in appropriate management positions and have demonstrated track records. Recruitment fees are paid by the employer. A typical outlet is housed in an 800 sq. ft. commercial space in an office complex or park, with three full-time employee and one part-time.

Franchisee Profile: A background in executive recruitment or personnel placement is not required. A sales or management aptitude is beneficial.

Projected Earnings: On request, the franchisor will provide prospective franchisees with a written statement of projected earnings. A typical Management Recruiters outlet generates about $300,000 in annual revenues, with close to $100,000 in profit.

Franchisor's Services: The franchisor provides a comprehensive three-week training program at the company's headquarters in Cleveland. Attendees are responsible for their own travel and lodging expenses. The curriculum includes interviewing techniques, marketing, sales, accounting, and buisness administration. An additional three weeks of on-the-job training are provided at the franchisee's office.

An MRI field consultant will help establish and develop the business. After the outlet has opened, an area representative will visit the office periodically. The franchisor publishes a franchisee newsletter and conducts frequent seminars and workshops to keep franchisees abreast of industry developments and employment trends. All franchisees receive copies of the franchisor's confidential operating manual, containing policies, procedures, and guidelines for success.

Initial Investment: New franchisees should be prepared to invest from $22,000 to $35,000 to establish the business. The amount includes the initial franchise fee, lease deposits, equipment purchases, supplies, and miscellaneous expenses.

Initial Investment: The total investment is estimated between $30,000 and $50,000 — a moderate sum for a business with an earnings potential of $100,000 per year. The investment includes the initial franchise fee, lease deposits, business licenses, furnishings, and equipment. Partial financial assistance may be available to qualified franchisees.

Advertising: Management Recruiters franchisees contribute one percent of gross monthly revenues for advertising. The franchisor conducts promotional campaigns on behalf of franchisees, using newspapers, magazines, and radio. Management Recruiters also offers ad slicks, commercials, sales literature, and public relations aids.

Contract Highlights: The minimum franchise term is five years. On expiration, the contract may be renewed if the franchisee is in compliance with all material provisions. The franchisee receives an exclusive territory for as long as the contract is in effect. Absentee ownership is prohibited by the franchise agreement. The franchisee may open more than one outlet by paying an additional franchise fee for each, but does not receive any subfranchising rights within the designated territory.

Fees and Royalties: The maximum initial franchise fee of $25,000 is moderate for the industry. The five percent monthly royalty, added to the one half percent advertising royalty, exacts a total of just five and one half percent of gross revenues of the outlet — a light royalty burden by any standard.

Summary: MRI is arguably the largest executive recruiter in North America, with close to $200 million in annual revenues. The Management Recruiters franchise is characterized by a moderate investment, a manageable royalty structure, and one of the most thorough training programs in the executive recruiting field.

Franchise Highlights

Began operating: 1957
Began franchising: 1965
Outlets currently open: 330
Initial franchise fee: Min $17,000
Max. $25,000

Monthly royalty: 5%
Advertising fee: .5%
Training program: 3 weeks
Term: 5 years

Manpower Temporary Services

Industry experience:	★ ★ ★ ★	*Franchising experience:*	★ ★ ★ ★
Financial strength:	★ ★ ★	*Training & services:*	★ ★ ★
Fees & royalties:	★ ★ ★	*Satisfied franchisees:*	★ ★ ★ ★

Manpower, Inc.
5301 N. Ironwood Road
Milwaukee, Wisconsin 53201
(414) 961-1000

Elmer Winter and Aaron Sheinfield founded Manpower, Inc. in 1948, opening two offices simultaneously in Milwaukee and Chicago. After struggling for five years, their service-oriented temporary personnel business began to thrive. Today, Manpower is an international company with nearly 1,000 offices in 30 countries. Approximately 300 Manpower agencies operating in the United States are franchises.

The Franchise: The franchisee conducts a temporary personnel placement business, under the trade name Manpower. The franchisee places temporary help in all job categories, ranging from office workers and data processing operators to technical, industrial, and medical/dental specialists. A typical outlet is located in a suitable commercial building or office complex, with three or more full-time employees. Customers of the franchise business include individuals searching for job opportunities, as well as employers searching for qualified applicants.

Franchisee Profile: Prior business in the industry is not required. The company is not presently seeking absentee owners, but area franchises may be available.

Projected Earnings: The franchisor does not provide a statement of projected earnings.

Franchisor's Services: Franchisees receive preliminary training in three to four days at the company's headquarters in Milwaukee. The costs of travel, lodging, and meals are borne by attendees. The curriculum includes recruitment and interviewing techniques, client billing practices, and business administration. A field training specialist conducts an additional two to three days of on-site training at the franchisee's place of business.

Manpower operates a centralized purchasing program to enable franchisees to realize significant discounts from volume purchases of equipment and supplies. A monthly newsletter and a series of workshops keep franchisees abreast of employment trends and industry developments. When immediate assistance is required, company support personnel are accessible by telephone.

Initial Investment: The initial investment is estimated at approximately $50,000, including the initial franchise fee, lease deposits, equipment, furnishings, and supplies. The franchisor does not presently offer any direct financial assistance to franchisees.

Advertising: Manpower franchisees do not pay any monthly advertising royalty. The franchisor conducts national and regional campaigns on behalf of all Manpower offices. Target media include business journals, newspapers, magazines, and radio. Manpower supplies franchisees with ad slicks, radio commercials, fliers, and public relations materials.

Contract Highlights: The term of the franchise is five years. The contract may be renewed for an additional five-year term at the franchisee's option. Manpower franchisees do not receive exclusive territories. The contract may not be sold or assigned except with the franchisor's written permission.

Fees and Royalties: The initial franchise fee of $4,500 and the four percent monthly royalty are both low for the industry.

Summary: Manpower has a history of suspending its franchisee recruitment program periodically. When new franchises are available, they are offered at a low initial fee and royalty to encourage the rapid development of new markets.

Franchise Highlights

Began operating: 1948
Began franchising: 1974
Outlets currently open: 300
Initial franchise fee: $4,500
Monthly royalty: 4%
Advertising fee: None
Training program: 3 to 4 days
Term: 5 years

Marcoin Business Services

Industry experience: ★★★★
Financial strength: ★★★
Fees & royalties: ★★★
Franchising experience: ★★★★
Training & services: ★★★★
Satisfied franchisees: ★★★★

Marcoin Business Services
1924 Cliff Valley Way NE
Atlanta, Georgia 30329
(404) 325-1200

Founded in 1952, Marcoin Business Services started out by providing specialized accounting services to the petroleum industry. Today, the company operates a network of 150 franchised offices, making it one of the largest chains of its type in the nation. Marcoin franchisees offer a diversity of business services, ranging from bookkeeping to computer consulting. The company is currently seeking new franchisees in all U.S. markets.

The Franchise: The franchisee conducts an accounting/bookkeeping service, under the trade name Marcoin Business Services. Franchisees offer full-service bookkeeping, computer hardware and software services, tax preparation, and basic business consulting. Customers of the franchise business include corporations, small businesses, and self-employed individuals.

Franchisee Profile: A background in accounting or bookkeeping is preferred, but not mandatory. The company is seeking prospective franchisees who present a favorable business image and demonstrate basic organizational and communications skills.

Projected Earnings: Marcoin does not provide a statement of projected earnings.

Franchisor's Services: The franchisor provides a training program of three and a half weeks in duration at the company's headquarters in Atlanta. Attendees are responsible for their own travel and lodging expenses. The curriculum includes client recruitment and relations, accounting principles, tax rules and forms, computer hardware and software, company procedures, and general business administration.

When the office is open, a Marcoin field consultant will visit the site periodically to offer guidance and troubleshooting. Franchisees receive a standardized computer system, complete with client software and demonstration aids. Marcoin publishes a monthly franchisee newsletter and conducts frequent seminars and workshops to keep franchisees abreast of industry developments and trends. A toll-free hotline puts franchise owners and their staffs in touch with company technical and operations experts.

Initial Investment: New Marcoin franchisees should be prepared to invest from $50,000 to $90,000 to establish the business. The amount includes lease deposits, equipment purchases, supplies, forms, and working capital. Marcoin has a financial assistance program for qualified franchisees.

Advertising: All franchisees contribute one half of one percent of gross monthly revenues for advertising. The franchisor conducts national and regional campaigns on behalf of all Marcoin outlets. Target media include newspapers, magazines, and radio. In addition, Marcoin supplies franchisees with ad slicks, radio commercials, sales literature, and public relations aids.

Contract Highlights: The term of the franchise is 15 years. The contract may be renewed for an additional 15-year term, if the franchisee is in compliance with all material provisions. The franchisee receives a protected territory for the duration of the agreement.

Fees and Royalties: The initial franchise fee of $20,000 is moderate for the industry. The franchisee's royalty obligation is 6.5 percent of gross monthly revenues. Including the advertising fee, the total royalty bite is just seven percent.

Summary: Marcoin franchisees benefit from professional imaging, marketing support, and strong industry ties cultivated by the franchisor over the past decade.

Franchise Highlights

Began operating: 1952	**Monthly royalty: 6.5% plus $100 per month**
Began franchising: 1952	**Advertising fee: .5%**
Outlets currently open: 150	**Training program: 3.5 weeks**
Initial franchise fee: $20,000	**Term: 15 years**

Minuteman Press

Industry experience:	★ ★ ★	*Franchising experience:*	★ ★ ★
Financial strength:	★ ★ ★	*Training & services:*	★ ★ ★
Fees & royalties:	★ ★ ★	*Satisfied franchisees:*	★ ★ ★

Minuteman Press International
1640 New Highway
Farmingdale, New York 11735
(516) 249-1370

Minuteman Press based its early success on the emergence of the market for instant-printing services, opening its first company-owned shop in 1973. Since, the firm has attempted to set its franchise stores apart by taking on a full-service printing motif, offering offset printing, color reproduction, and bindery services, in addition to the usual photocopying and quick-print services offered by the competition.

The Franchise: The franchisee operates a contemporary, full-service printing shop, under the trade name Minuteman Press. A typical outlet is situated in a retail strip center, shopping mall, business park, or other suitable commercial space, offering a broad range of printing, binding, and document reproduction services.

Franchisee Profile: No special background or experience is required. The company prefers prospective franchisees who are willing to manage the business personally. Minuteman will consider granting area franchises to develop large territories.

Projected Earnings: A statement of projected earnings was not available at press time.

Franchisor's Services: Minuteman offers a two-week training program at the company's headquarters in Farmingdale, New York. Attendees are responsible for their own travel and lodging expenses. An additional week of hands-on training takes place at the franchisee's shop prior to opening.

The franchisor will assist with selecting a site for the outlet, negotiating a lease, and equipping the shop for opening. A Minuteman representative will visit the outlet periodically, to offer ongoing guidance and troubleshooting. The franchisor operates a centralized purchasing program for paper, inks, and related printing supplies. Minuteman also publishes a monthly franchisee newsletter and conducts field seminars to keep franchisees current of new printing techniques and industry developments.

Initial Investment: The total investment may range from $60,000 to $75,000, including lease deposits, site improvements, equipment purchases, and an initial inventory of printing supplies. A franchisee with an existing print shop may be able to convert to the franchise program for less. Financial assistance is available to qualified franchisees through a third party lender.

Advertising: Minuteman franchisees do not pay a separate royalty for advertising. The franchisor supplies franchisees with ad slicks, commercials, point-of-sale materials, and public relations tools.

Contract Highlights: The Minuteman franchise has a 25-year term, well above the industry-wide average. The franchisee does not receive a protected territory.

Fees and Royalties: The initial franchise fee of $22,500 is somewhat high for a print-shop franchise, reflecting, in part, the chain's stature as an industry leader. The franchisee's royalty obligation is a moderate six percent of gross sales.

Summary: Minuteman Press offers prospective franchisees upscale imaging, increasing name recognition, and the competitive benefits of a full-service printing operation.

Franchise Highlights

Began operating: 1973	**Monthly royalty: 6%**
Began franchising: 1975	**Advertising fee: None**
Outlets currently open: 500	**Training program: 2 weeks**
Initial franchise fee: $22,500	**Term: 25 years**

Norell Temporary Services

Industry experience:	★★★	*Franchising experience:*	★★★
Financial strength:	★★★	*Training & services:*	★★★
Fees & royalties:	★★★	*Satisfied franchisees:*	★★★★

Norell Temporary Services
3092 Piedmont Road NE
Atlanta, Georgia 30305
(800) 334-9694

Founded in 1961, Norell Temporary Services has enjoyed a 400 percent growth rate since 1977. Since the company sold its first franchise in 1967, more than 400 Norell offices have opened their doors, specializing in supplying temporary office, clerical, and data processing workers whose references have been thoroughly checked.

The Franchise: The franchisee conducts a temporary office personnel agency, doing business under the name Norell Temporary Services. The company's service objective is the ability to respond to a personnel request within 45 minutes.

Franchisee Profile: Franchisees are selected after three interviews at the company's headquarters in Atlanta. Although experience in temporary personnel services is not necessary, an aptitude for management or sales is beneficial. Norell stresses basic verbal communciations skills and a desire to work with people.

Projected Earnings: The franchisor does not provide a statement of projected earnings.

Franchisor's Services: The franchisor provides a one-week training program in Atlanta. The tuition for the program is included in the initial franchise fee, but the costs of travel, lodging, and meals are borne by the franchisee. The curriculum includes employee interviewing and screening techniques, marketing, customer relations, and client invoicing. According to a company spokesman, franchisees receive in excess of 200 hours of training every year, including refresher courses and continuing education workshops.

Prior to opening, a Norell representative will assist in setting up the office, hiring staff, and developing daily business procedures. After the office has opened for business, a district manager will visit the franchisee's office periodically to offer on-site guidance and troubleshooting. The company maintains a ratio of one district manager for every 12 franchisees. Norell has organized a consolidated purchasing program for supplies and equipment, helping franchisees earn discount pricing. The franchisor also publishes a franchisee newsletter and conducts seminars both at company headquarters and in the field. Field consultants are accessible by telephone as required.

Initial Investment: New Norell franchisees should be prepared to invest from $40,000 to $70,000 to establish the business. The amount includes lease deposits, equipment, and working capital. The franchisor does not offer any direct financial assistance to franchisees.

Advertising: Norell franchisees do not pay any monthly advertising royalty. The franchisor conducts advertising campaigns on behalf of all Norell outlets, three fourths of which are company owned. Franchisees also benefit from Norell's national accounts program, which supplies new outlets with presold clientele.

Contract Highlights: The term of the franchise is 15 years. The contract may be renewed for an additional year term, at the franchisee's option. Because Norell places a high value on the personal aptitudes and skills of each franchisee, the outlet may not be sold, transferred, or otherwise assigned without the franchisor's written consent. The assignee must meet the same qualifications as any other Norell franchise holder.

Fees and Royalties: Norell does not charge an initial franchise fee. The monthly royalty varies, depending on the value of the territory.

Summary: Norell is a high-growth entry in the temporary personnel field, with a ratio of three company-owned offices to every franchise outlet. Franchisees benefit from presold accounts, comprehensive training, and the co-operative benefits of a large organization.

Franchise Highlights

Began operating: 1961
Began franchising: 1967
Outlets currently open: 420
Initial franchise fee: None

Monthly royalty: Varies
Advertising fee: None
Training program: As required
Term: 15 years

Packy the Shipper

Industry experience:	★ ★ ★	*Franchising experience:*	★ ★
Financial strength:	★ ★ ★	*Training & services:*	★ ★ ★
Fees & royalties:	★ ★ ★	*Satisfied franchisees:*	★ ★ ★

Packy the Shipper
409 Main Street
Racine, Wisconsin 53403
(414) 633-9540

The Franchise: The franchisee operates a packaging and shipping service, using the trade name Packy the Shipper. A typical outlet is situated in a business park, commercial building, or strip center, with two full-time employees. Franchisees sell packing, boxing, wrapping, labeling, and package forwarding services to small businesses and the general public.

Franchisor's Services: Franchisees receive training in two weeks at the company's headquarters in Racine, Wisconsin. Pre-opening assistance is also provided at the franchisee's place of business. Each Packy the Shipper franchisee receives a set of manuals detailing the daily operation of the business. A field consultant provides ongoing operations assistance in periodic visits to the outlet. The franchisor also offers liability insurance and a profit-sharing program for franchise holders.

Initial Investment: The start-up investment may range from $1,500 to $3,000, depending on the size and location of the outlet. Packy the Shipper does not offer any direct financial assistance to franchisees.

Fees and Royalties: The initial franchise fee ranges from $995 to $1,295. The franchisor does not exact a monthly advertising fee, so the total royalty obligation is a moderate five percent of gross sales.

Summary: The Packy the Shipper franchise offers an easy-to-operate, low-overhead business format with a small capital requirement.

Franchise Highlights

Began operating: 1976
Began franchising: 1981
Outlets currently open: 1,400
Initial franchise fee: Min $995
Max. $1,295

Monthly royalty: 5%
Advertising fee: None
Training program: 2 weeks
Term: 5 years

Personnel Pool of America

Industry experience:	★ ★ ★ ★	*Franchising experience:*	★ ★ ★ ★
Financial strength:	★ ★ ★	*Training & services:*	★ ★ ★
Fees & royalties:	★ ★ ★ ★	*Satisfied franchisees:*	★ ★ ★ ★

Personnel Pool of America
303 S.E. 17th Street
Fort Lauderdale, Florida 33316
(800) 327-1396

Personnel Pool of America (PPA) is a subsidiary of H & R Block, one of the most prolific franchisors in North America. Founded in 1946, PPA has successfully established nearly 400 outlets since the company began franchising in 1956. The business has two divisions, one specializing in semi-skilled industrial personnel, the other specializing in medical personnel. The Medical Personnel Pool is presumably the largest temporary employment agency in the field of individual and institutional medical care in North America.

The Franchise: The franchisee conducts a personnel recruitment and temporary employment business, under the trade name Personnel Pool of America. The outlet supplies temporary workers to industry — primarily technical and semi-skilled workers, including clerks, word processing operators, paralegal specialists, and others. A related service, the Medical Personnel Pool, supplies nurses, physical therapists, and home care specialists, handling calls 24 hours a day, seven days a week. The franchisee may operate one service - or both - depending on the nature and size of the locality.

Franchisee Profile: Prior experience in the temporary personnel field is not required. The company is seeking prospective franchisees who have achieved personal career success; many of the company's established franchisees came from such fields as banking, engineering, accounting, and professional athletics.

Projected Earnings: The franchisor does furnish a written statement of projected earnings of a franchise outlet.

Franchisor's Services: The franchisor conducts a two-week training program for new franchisees at the company's headquarters in Fort Lauderdale. PPA takes care of the attendee's travel and lodging expenses. The curriculum covers operations, sales, and marketing, with hands-on exposure to a company-operated PPA office in Florida. An additional ten days of on-the-job training take place at the franchisee's place of business during the first four months after the outlet has opened.

The company provides an advertising budget to recruit personnel, an initial direct-mail marketing campaign, and a site selection guide to help new franchisees acquire suitable premises for the business. PPA provides ongoing consultation by phone or in person, and sells office equipment and supplies to franchisees.

Initial Investment: New franchisees should be prepared to invest from $100,000 to $200,000 to establish the business. The amount includes the initial fee, lease deposits, furnishings, improvements, equipment purchases, and working capital. The franchisor does not offer any direct financial assistance for the investment.

Advertising: PPA franchisees do not pay any monthly advertising royalty. The franchisor provides a direct-mail campaign allowance for initial advertising to recruit personnel.

Contract Highlights: The term of the franchise is five years. On expiration, the contract may be renewed for another five years, if the franchisee is in compliance with all material provisions. The franchisee does not receive a protected territory. The franchise may not be sold or transferred without the franchisor's consent.

Fees and Royalties: The initial franchise fee of $15,000 is moderate by industry standards. The five percent monthly royalty is low, particularly since PPA franchisees do not pay a separate royalty for advertising.

Summary: Personnel Pool of America is an experienced franchisor backed by the resources of an industry giant. Franchisees benefit from comprehensive training, low royalties, and a consistently high demand for temporary semi-skilled and medical personnel.

Franchise Highlights

Began operating: 1946	**Monthly royalty: 5%**
Began franchising: 1956	**Advertising fee: None**
Outlets currently open: 390	**Training program: 2 weeks**
Initial franchise fee: $15,000	**Term: 5 years**

PIP Postal Instant Press

Industry experience:	★★★★	*Franchising experience:*	★★★★
Financial strength:	★★★★	*Training & services:*	★★★★
Fees & royalties:	★★★	*Satisfied franchisees:*	★★★★

Postal Instant Press
8201 Beverly Blvd.
Los Angeles, California 90048
(800) 421-4634

PIP Postal Instant Press claims the title of the world's most prolific printing chain. The company's franchise program was launched in 1968 by then-CEO Bill LeVine, transforming a handful of instant printing shops into an industry giant. Even today, only five of the 1,000-plus PIP shops in operation remain company owned. The company's outlets shops are distributed throughout 48 U.S. states and in Canada, Great Britain, and Japan.

The Franchise: The franchisee operates an instant printing shop, under the trade name PIP Postal Instant Press. Instant printing, also called quick printing, involves the use of inexpensive, disposable plates to produce printed images speedily. In contrast, a conventional printer uses costly metal plates that are very time-consuming to prepare. Each outlet conforms to the franchisor's standard red, white, blue, and gray decor and uses state-of-the-art equipment specified by the company. Franchisees offer a wide range of instant-printing services, including business cards, stationery, resumes, and fliers. A typical outlet is located in a high density urban or suburban area in a strip center, business park, or light industrial building, with two full-time press operators.

Franchisee Profile: Experience in the printing trade is not required, but management ability and a high level of self-esteem are beneficial. Franchisees hire qualified press operators to handle the printing work.

Projected Earnings: According to the company's reported sales, the average revenues of a PIP outlet are about $200,000 per year, before expenses.

Franchise Services: The PIP training program is held for two weeks at the company's headquarters in Los Angeles. Attendees are responsible for their own travel and lodging expenses. The curriculum covers printing background, store procedures, technical operations, sales, and business administration. Before the new outlet opens, the company sends a representative to train the franchisee's staff. The franchisor also oversees the acquisition and installation of equipment, and assists with initial advertising efforts. PIP supplies an opening inventory of paper, inks, and other supplies. Ongoing inventory requirements are filled by company-approved sources at negotiated prices.

Initial investment: New franchisees should be able to handle an initial investment of about $90,000, including site acquisition, improvements, equipment, supplies, and working capital. PIP offers financing on $32,500 of the license fee at low interest rates.

Advertising: PIP's phenomenal success is attributable, in part, to its agressive advertising policies. The company offers advertising assistance to franchisees through a national co-op program to which each shop contributes one percent of gross monthly sales. The franchisor promotes the PIP name with television, radio, magazine, newspaper, and billboard advertising. Franchisees also receive a Yellow Page layout, videotape training aids, and public relations materials.

Fees and Royalties: The initial fee of $40,000 is high for a printing franchise, but is partially offset by low startup costs and the availability of financial assistance. To encourage multiple-unit ownership, PIP charges just $2,500 for additional outlets in the same territory. The six percent to eight percent franchise royalty is moderate. Including the advertising fee, the total royalty bite ranges from seven to nine percent.

Renewal and Assignment: The term of the PIP franchise is 20 years. The franchisee receives an exclusive territory for the franchise, with the option to open additional outlets at a reduced fee. The franchise may not be transferred or sold without the franchisor's consent.

Summary: PIP has done an excellent job with marketing and promotion, supplying its franchisees with solid name recognition and uniform imaging in a highly competitive market. The franchise is characterized by a moderate investment with relatively few risks, but persistent management attention and dedication to hard work are mandatory. PIP claims a 98 percent success rate among its franchisees.

Franchise Highlights

Began operating: 1965	**Monthly royalty: 6% to 8%**
Began franchising: 1968	**Advertising fee: 1%**
Outlets currently open: 1,000	**Training program: 2 weeks**
Initial franchise fee: $40,000	**Term: 20 years**

Sales Consultants International

Industry experience:	★ ★ ★ ★	*Franchising experience:*	★ ★ ★
Financial strength:	★ ★ ★	*Training & services:*	★ ★ ★ ★
Fees & royalties:	★ ★ ★	*Satisfied franchisees:*	★ ★ ★ ★

Sales Consultants International
1127 Euclid Avenue
Cleveland, Ohio 44115
(216) 696-1122

A division of Management Recruiters International, Inc., Sales Consultants was founded in 1957 to handle the recruitment and placement of upper- to mid- management personnel. Since the first franchise was sold in 1965, the company has established more than 120 offices in North America. Sales Consultants is actively seeking new franchisees in all areas of the U.S. and Canada.

The Franchise: The franchisee conducts an executive search, recruitment, and placement business, operating under the trade name Sales Consultants and specializing in sales and marketing professionals. A typical outlet is situated in an upscale commercial complex or light industrial center, with from three to five employees. Customers of the franchise business include both job candidates and employers.

Franchisee Profile: No special qualifications are required. The company evaluates prospective franchisees with respect to their industriousness, self-management aptitude, and verbal communications skills.

Projected Earnings: The franchisor does not furnish prospective franchisees with a written statement of projected earnings.

Franchisor's Services: Sales Consultants provides a three-week training program at the company's headquarters in Cleveland. Attendees are responsible for their own travel and lodging expenses. An additional three weeks of on-the-job training are provided at the franchisee's place of business.

The franchisor will assist with selecting a site for the business and acquiring equipment, furnishings, and telephones. Franchisees receive a videotape recorder and a set of 21 tapes for on-site training and review. Additional training tapes are available on request. The franchisor's area representative will inspect the outlet periodically and provide on-site guidance and troubleshooting. Sales Consultants operates a toll-free hotline to put franchisees in touch with corporate operations, marketing, and recruitment experts.

Initial Investment: New franchisees should be prepared to invest from $31,500 to $57,400 to establish and develop the business. The amount includes the initial fee, lease deposits, furnishings, and equipment purchases. The franchisor does not offer any direct financial assistance to franchisees.

Advertising: Sales Consultants franchisees contribute just one half of one percent of gross monthly revenues for advertising. The franchisor conducts national and regional campaigns, using business journals, magazines, and radio. The company supplies franchisees with ad slicks, promotional sale materials, and public relations aids.

Contract Highlights: The term of the franchise is five years, with an option to renew for another five years. The franchise may be sold or assigned to another party with the franchisor's consent, but absentee ownership is discouraged.

Fees and Royalties: The initial franchise fee ranges from $17,000 to $25,000, depending on the territory. The five percent monthly royalty is moderate for franchises in this category, especially in light of the fact that the advertising royalty is a mere one half of one percent.

Summary: The Sales Consultants franchise is characterized by a thorough training program, first-hand start-up assistance, and moderate but stable growth over the last two decades.

Franchise Highlights

Began operating: 1957
Began franchising: 1965
Outlets currently open: 125
Initial franchise fee: Min $16,000
Max. $25,000

Monthly royalty: 5%
Advertising fee: .5%
Training program: 3 weeks
Term: 5 years

Sir Speedy

Industry experience:	★ ★ ★	*Franchising experience:*	★ ★ ★
Financial strength:	★ ★ ★	*Training & services:*	★ ★ ★
Fees & royalties:	★ ★ ★	*Satisfied franchisees:*	★ ★ ★

Sir Speedy Printing Centers
23131 Verdugo Drive
Laguna Hills, California 92653
(800) 854-3321

Sir Speedy rode to success on the emergence of instant-printing technology, which catapulted the company into overnight prominence as an industry giant. Over the last two decades, the franchisor has opened an average of 35 shops every year, supplying small businesses, corporate accounts, and individual consumers with professional printing, duplication, and limited bindery services.

The Franchise: The franchisee conducts a retail printing business, specializing in quick-copy services, under the trade name Sir Speedy Printing Center. A typical outlet is situated in a retail strip center, business park, or commercial building, offering while-you-wait and overnight printing of stationery, business cards, forms, announcements, and other documents. Besides quick-print services, the franchisee may also derive income from bindery services, specialty advertising products, and lithographic printing subcontracted to commercial printers.

Franchisee Profile: A background in the printing trade is beneficial, but not mandatory. Absentee ownership is discouraged, but not strictly prohibited.

Projected Earnings: A statement of projected earnings was not available at press time.

Franchisor's Services: Sir Speedy franchisees attend a two-week orientation program at the company's upscale training center in Newport Beach, California. Attendees are responsible for their own travel and lodging expenses. The program is supplemented by two and a half weeks of on-site training for franchisees and their staffs.

The franchisor assists with site selection, lease negotiations, and shop construction. After the print shop has opened for business, a Sir Speedy field adviser will call on the franchisee periodically, to inspect the quality of the product and troubleshoot operations. The franchisor's centralized purchasing system enables franchisees to obtain equipment and supplies and competitive prices. Sir Speedy also promises to assist new franchise owners with the preparation of financial projections and budget analyses, and publishes a monthly newsletter for franchisees.

Initial Investment: The total investment is estimated at about $85,000 for a new shop, including lease deposits, site improvements, equipment purchases, and an initial inventory of papers, inks, and other printing supplies. Financial assistance may be available from a third party lender.

Advertising: Sir Speedy franchisees contribute two percent of gross monthly revenues for advertising. The franchisor conducts national and regional campaigns and supplies franchisees with ad slicks, radio and television commercials, point-of-sale materials, and public relations aids.

Contract Highlights: The Sir Speedy franchise has 20-year term, twice the national average. The contract is renewable without charge. The franchisee receives a protected territory for the duration of the agreement, but has no subfranchising rights whatsoever.

Fees and Royalties: The initial franchise fee of $17,500 is moderate for the quick-print industry. The franchisee's total royalty obligation, including the monthly franchise royalty and the advertising fee, is eight percent or less.

Summary: Sir Speedy franchises are heavily concentrated in the Sunbelt, with 90 outlets in California and 75 in Florida. The program offers increasing name recognition, a highly regarded training program, and a ready-to-run business format for rapidly entering a potentially lucrative business market.

Franchise Highlights

Began operating: 1968
Began franchising: 1968
Outlets currently open: 730
Initial franchise fee: $17,500
Monthly royalty: 4% to 6%
Advertising fee: 2%
Training program: 2 weeks
Term: 20 years

Snelling and Snelling

Industry experience:	★ ★ ★ ★	*Franchising experience:*	★ ★ ★ ★
Financial strength:	★ ★ ★ ★	*Training & services:*	★ ★ ★
Fees & royalties:	★ ★ ★	*Satisfied franchisees:*	★ ★ ★ ★

Snelling and Snelling
4000 South Tamiami Trail
Sarasota, Florida 33518
(813) 922-9616

Founded in Philadelphia in 1951 by Robert and Anne Snelling, the Snelling and Snelling organization is the largest employment agency in the world. The company places candidates in clerical, administration, engineering, technical, sales, marketing, and the gas and oil fields. The organization is known for its employee awards program which regularly recognizes personal achievement.

The Franchise: The franchisee conducts a personnel recruitment and employment referral agency, operating under the trade name Snelling and Snelling. A typical outlet is situated in a commercial building or office complex, with a staff of four full-time employees.

Franchisee Profile: A background in the employment referral or executive recruitment field is beneficial, but not mandatory.

Projected Earnings: The franchisor does not provide a statement of projected earnings.

Franchisor's Services: The franchisor provides a two-week training program at the company's headquarters in Sarasota, Florida. Attendees are responsible for their own travel and lodging expenses. The curriculum includes recruitment and interviewing techniques, evaluation and placement, public relations strategies, and business administration.

Additional on-site assistance is provided prior to opening. The company offers guidance on site selection, lease negotiation, and furnishings, and supplies franchisees with forms, stationery, and business cards. All franchisees receive copies of the Snelling and Snelling operating manuals and videotapes. When the business is operational, a field representative will visit the outlet periodically, to offer guidance and troubleshooting. Snelling and Snelling publishes a monthly franchisee newsletter and conducts frequent seminars and workshops to keep franchisees abreast of industry developments.

Initial Investment: The total investment may range from $25,000 to $80,000. The variables include lease deposits, furnishings, and working capital requirements. Snelling and Snelling will finance $14,500 of the initial franchise fee.

Advertising: Franchisees contribute one percent of gross monthly revenues for advertising. The franchisor conducts national and regional campaigns on behalf of all Snelling and Snelling offices. Target media include business journals, such as The Wall Street Journal and Business Week, and general interest publications, such as Reader's Digest, TV Guide, and Cosmopolitan. The franchisor also supplies franchisees with materials for local advertising campaigns and public relations efforts. A typical outlet spends about five percent of its gross revenues on local advertising.

Contract Highlights: The term of the franchise is 50 years. The franchisee does not receive an exclusive territory for the employment agency, but expansion in the area may be possible. The franchisee is personally responsible for managing the business. Area franchises are not presently available.

Fees and Royalties: The initial franchise fee of $29,500 is somewhat high for the industry, reflecting the franchisor's stature as an industry leader. The seven percent monthly royalty is a moderate price to pay for a sophisticated support package. Including the one percent advertising royalty, the total royalty bite is only eight percent of gross revenues of the outlet.

Summary: The Snelling and Snelling franchise is characterized by a moderate initial investment and manageable monthly royalties. Franchisees benefit from aggressive co-op advertising and the competitive benefits of one of the largest and most experienced organizations in the employment field.

Franchise Highlights

Began operating: 1951	**Monthly royalty: 7%**
Began franchising: 1955	**Advertising fee: 1%**
Outlets currently open: 445	**Training program: 2 weeks**
Initial franchise fee: $29,500	**Term: 50 years**

Tender Sender

Industry experience:	★★	*Franchising experience:*	★★
Financial strength:	★★★	*Training & services:*	★★★
Fees & royalties:	★★★	*Satisfied franchisees:*	★★★★

Tender Sender, Inc.
7370 SW Durham Road
Portland, Oregon 97224
(503) 684-1426

When Mike Hanna, a paper sales executive, was asked to transfer from his home in Oregon, he and his wife decided to go into business for themselves. The result was Tender Sender, a gift wrap and shipping service set up in a regional shopping mall. Within three years, they had five shops and 49 franchises and were looking for sites for another 125 franchises which had already been sold.

Most Tender Sender stores are permanent mall stores, but some are small kiosks in mall lobbies. A major factor in the franchisor's success is the outlet's ability to cooperate with and complement the services of other retailers in the mall.

The Franchise: The franchisee conducts a gift wrapping, packaging, and freight forwarding business, under the trade name Tender Sender. The outlet can be operated one employee, except during the holiday season. Franchisees purchase gift wrapping supplies from the franchisor and offer a variety of services to mall patrons, including on-site gift wrapping, with or without shipping. The outlet also sells gift wrapping containers and materials.

Franchisee Profile: No special training or experience is required.

Projected Earnings: The franchisor does not provide a statement of projected earnings.

Franchisor's Services: Tender Sender conducts a comprehensive five-day training program at the company's headquarters in Portland. Franchisees are responsible for their own travel and lodging expenses in connection with the training program. The franchisor sends a field consultant to assist with grand opening activities.

A Tender Sender representative also visits the outlet periodically, to offer guidance and troubleshooting. The franchisor operates a centralized purchasing program to enable franchisees to realize significant discounts from volume purchases of gift wrapping supplies. Tender Sender publishes a franchisee newsletter and conducts frequent seminars to keep franchisees abreast of new developments.

Initial Investment: The total investment ranges from $50,000 to $70,000 depending on the location and size of the outlet. The amount includes the initial franchisee fee, lease deposits, improvements, fixtures, and an initial inventory of gift wrapping packaging, and labeling supplies. Tender Sender does not offer any direct financial assistance to franchisees.

Advertising: Franchisees contribute two percent of gross monthly revenues for advertising. Contract Highlights: The term of the franchise is ten years. The contract may be renewed for an additional ten-year term, providing the franchisee is in compliance with all material provisions. The franchisee receives a protected territory for the duration of the agreement.

Fees and Royalties: The initial franchise fee of $20,000 is high for the packaging and shipping field. The five percent monthly royalty is low for franchises in general, but average for this field. Including the two percent advertising royalty, the total royalty bite is just seven percent of the gross monthly revenues of the outlet.

Summary: The Tender Sender franchise is characterized by rapid growth in an industry that only recently emerged to occupy a permanent niche in the seasonally influenced retail mall trade.

Franchise Highlights

Began operating: 1982	**Monthly royalty: 6%**
Began franchising: 1984	**Advertising fee: 2%**
Outlets currently open: 175	**Training program: 5 days**
Initial franchise fee: $20,000	**Term: 10 years**

UBI Business Brokers

Industry experience:	★★★	*Franchising experience:*	★★
Financial strength:	★★★	*Training & services:*	★★★
Fees & royalties:	★★★	*Satisfied franchisees:*	★★★

UBI Business Brokers, Inc.
727 South Main Street
Burbank, California 91506
(213) 843-7774

UBI Business Brokers was one of the first franchise organizations to capitalize on the frenzy of business sales, acquisitions, and mergers that typify the commercial atmosphere of the 1980s. Founded in 1969, the company established more than a hundred offices since it sold its first franchise in 1982, opening an average of over 20 outlets per year.

The Franchise: The franchisee conducts a brokerage operation for businesses for sale, operating under the trade name UBI Business Brokers. A typical outlet is situated in a commercial office building or industrial park, with a staff of from one to five full-time and two part-time employees. Customers of the franchise business include small business owners interested in selling all or part of their operations.

Franchisee Profile: A background in business, communications, finance, law, or a related field is required. UBI is looking for franchisees with the credibility and image that characterize a successful business analyst.

Projected Earnings: The franchisor does not provide a statement of projected earnings.

Franchisor's Services: The franchisor provides a ten-day training program at the company's headquarters in Burbank, California. Attendees are responsible for their own travel and lodging expenses. The curriculum includes client relations, marketing, advertising, management, and business record keeping. An additional week of on-the-job training is provided at the franchisee's place of business.

The franchisor will assist with selecting a site for the outlet and negotiating a lease for the premises. When the business is operational, a UBI business consultant will visit the outlet periodically, to offer on-site guidance and troubleshooting. The company operates a computerized referral system, called the Internal Multiple Listing Service (IMLS), which provides franchisees with access to coast-to-coast listings of business opportunities.

A proprietary UBI computer program, Analyx, assists franchisees with valuating businesses based on standard criteria and industry-wide averages. The franchisor also supplies franchisees with business forms, insurance, and confidential operating manuals.

Initial Investment: The total investment ranges from $50,000 to $75,000, including the initial franchise fee, lease deposits, equipment, supplies, and working capital. UBI does not offer any direct financial assistance to franchisees.

Advertising: UBI franchisees contribute two percent of their gross monthly revenues for advertising. The franchisor supplies franchisees with ad slicks, brochures, and audiovisual aids for promoting the outlet and recruiting clientele.

Contract Highlights: The term of the franchise is ten years. The contract may be renewed for an additional term, providing the franchisee is in compliance with all material provisions. The franchisee receives an exclusive territory in which UBI will not sell another franchise or open a company-owned outlet in competition with the franchisee's outlet. The franchisee is free to hire a qualified manager to run the operation.

Fees and Royalties: The initial franchise fee of $27,500 is slightly high for the industry, reflecting in part the franchisor's rapid growth rate over the last three years. The six percent monthly royalty, added to the two percent advertising royalty, exacts a total of just eight percent of gross revenues of the outlet.

Summary: The UBI franchise is characterized by good name recognition in major markets, a manageable royalty structure, and a thorough training program. The franchisor is currently seeking new franchisees in most U.S. regions, Europe, and Asia.

Franchise Highlights

Began operating: 1969	**Monthly royalty: 6%**
Began franchising: 1982	**Advertising fee: 2%**
Outlets currently open: 110	**Training program: 2 weeks**
Initial franchise fee: $27,500	**Term: 10 years**

Western Temporary Services

Industry experience:	★ ★ ★ ★	*Franchising experience:*	★ ★ ★ ★
Financial strength:	★ ★ ★	*Training & services:*	★ ★ ★
Fees & royalties:	★ ★ ★	*Satisfied franchisees:*	★ ★ ★ ★

Western Temporary Services, Inc.
P. O. Box 9280
Walnut Creek, California 94596
(800) USA-TEMP

Founded in 1948, Western Temporary has established nearly 400 outlets since the company sold its first franchise in 1960. The company handles a wide range of temporary personnel requirements, including clerical, medical, industrial, technical, marketing, and security workers - even Santa Clauses. Western Temporary places a high priority on image, maintaining strict standards among its 245 franchises and 145 company-operated offices.

The Franchise: The franchisee conducts a temporary personnel recruitment and placement agency, under the trade name Western Temporary Services. A typical outlet is situated in a commercial office complex or light industrial area, with a staff of five to seven full-time employees. The staff size and workload may vary depending on local market conditions. Representative customers include large companies such as Lockheed, IBM, General Dynamics, and General Electric.

Franchisee Profile: A background in personnel recruitment or temporary services is considered helpful, but not mandatory. Western Temporary is currently seeking prospective franchisees with general administrative and communication skills.

Projected Earnings: The franchisor does not provide a statement of projected earnings.

Franchisor's Services: Western Temporary conducts a one-week training program at the company's headquarters in Walnut Creek, California, just north of Oakland, plus and additional week of first-hand exposure to an operating outlet. Attendees are responsible for their own travel and lodging expenses. The curriculum includes employee interviewing techniques, evaluation and screening, job placement, and customer relations.

The franchisee is responsible for selecting a suitable location for the business, but Western Temporary will provide a representative to arrange and pay for telephones and plan an initial sales strategy for the outlet.

The franchisor handles invoicing and accounts receivable. Temporary personnel are paid directly by Western Temporary. Franchisees receive payment according to invoices submitted to the franchisor, which in effect finances the outlet's payroll and accounts receivable.

Initial Investment: The initial investment ranges from $10,000 to $80,000, including the initial fee, lease deposits, furnishings and equipment. Western Temporary does not offer any direct financial assistance to franchisees.

Advertising: Franchisees contribute eight percent of gross monthly revenues for advertising, to a maximum of $700 in any given month. The franchisor conducts national and regional campaigns on behalf of all [Franchise] outlets. Target media include trade journals, newspapers, and magazines. The franchisor also supplies press materials and ad slicks for local promotions.

Contract Highlights: The term of the franchise is five years. The contract may be renewed for an additional five years, at the franchisee's option. The franchisee receives a protected territory for the outlet.

Fees and Royalties: The initial franchise fee ranges from $2,500 to $15,000 based on the population of the franchisee's territory. Franchisees do not pay a monthly franchise royalty during the first six months after the office has opened for business. Thereafter, a variable royalty applies.

Summary: Western Temporary franchisees give the franchisor high marks for hands-on training and after-sale support. A growing base of outlets, an aggressive advertising program, and a light royalty burden encourage the new development of new outlets.

Franchise Highlights

Began operating: 1948
Began franchising: 1960
Outlets currently open: 390
Initial franchise fee: Min $2,500
Max. $15,000

Monthly royalty: Varies
Advertising fee: Varies
Training program: 2 weeks
Term: 5 years

Zarex

Industry experience:	★★★	*Franchising experience:*	★★
Financial strength:	★★★	*Training & services:*	★★★
Fees & royalties:	★★★	*Satisfied franchisees:*	★★★

Zarex Business Centres
21 St. Clair Avenue E., Suite 14
Toronto, Ontario, Canada M4T 1M1
(416) 968-0339

Founded in 1979, Toronto-based Zarex Business Centres offer a comprehensive range of business support services, with particular emphasis on franchise consulting and marketing programs.

The Franchise: The franchisee conducts a business consulting practice, under the trade name Zarex Business Centre. A typical outlet is situated in a commercial building, strip center, or industrial park, employing a staff of three full-time consultants. Franchisees offer counseling, planning and brokerage services in financial systems, mergers and acquisitions, franchise expansion programs, and market development. Customers of the franchise business include small business owners and corporations.

Franchisee Profile: A background in business management or consulting is considered beneficial, but not mandatory. The company is seeking franchisees who project a professional image and demonstrate solid communications skills. Absentee ownership is discouraged, but not specifically prohibited.

Franchisor's Services: Zarex franchisees receive two and a half weeks of training at the company's headquarters in Toronto, Ontario. Attendees are responsible for their own travel and lodging expenses.

Franchisees receive copies of a confidential operations manual and have access to company consultants for ongoing guidance and troubleshooting. Corporate experts are also available by telephone for consultation, as required.

Initial Investment: New Zarex franchisees should be prepared to invest around $50,000 to establish the business. The amount includes lease deposits, furnishings, equipment, and miscellaneous start-up expenses. Financial assistance is available to qualified franchisees from a third party lender.

Advertising: Zarex franchisees contribute two percent of their gross monthly revenues for advertising. The franchisor conducts ad camaigns on behalf of all Zarex outlets, and supplies franchisees with ad slicks, commercials, and public relations aids.

Fees and Royalties: The initial franchise fee of $30,000 is high for a franchise of this type. The six percent monthly royalty, added to the two percent advertising royalty, exacts a total of eight percent of gross revenues of the outlet.

Summary: The Zarex group is primarily known for its expertise in Canadian franchising. Franchisees benefit from positive imaging and personal support from a savy management team.

Franchise Highlights

Began operating: 1979	**Monthly royalty: 6%**
Began franchising: 1983	**Advertising fee: 2%**
Outlets currently open: 60	**Training program: 2.5 weeks**
Initial franchise fee: $30,000	**Term: 10 years**

Construction, Decoration, and Maintenance

Property services, including construction, decoration, and maintenance, constitute a $100 billion industry. High interest rates in the early to mid 1980s inspired a boom in build-yourself and modular housing. Firms that had been manufacturing precut homes began adding upscale designs reflecting contemporary architectural themes. Log homes also enjoyed renewed popularity among Post-War Baby Boomers keen on such features as passive insulation and durability. Consumers who in the 1960s were keen on alternative lifetsyles turned their attention in the 80s to alternative housing.

Other property service businesses also benefited from the maturing 'yuppie' generation. Franchisors in the lawn care, interior decoration, and carpet restoration trades experienced dramatic growth spurts from the early 70s to the mid 80s. One obvious appeal to franchises in this category is the fact that almost anyone can operate one of these businesses. Demand for the products and services tends to be steady, rather than explosive, but in most cases, investment and overhead are low.

Americlean

Industry experience: ★ *Franchising experience:* ★
Financial strength: ★ ★ ★ *Training & services:* ★ ★ ★
Fees & royalties: ★ ★ ★ *Satisfied franchisees:* ★ ★ ★ ★

Americlean Mobile Power Wash & Restoration
50 Sandoe Road
Gettysburg, Pennsylvania 17325
(800) 262-9278

Pennsylvania-based Americlean Mobile Power Wash & Restoration (not to be confused with another Americlean chain headquartered in Billings, Montana) was founded in 1985 by entrepreneur Stephen Wiley. The chian already has 100 outlets and, according to USA Today, ranks among 'Franchising's Best.'

The Franchise: The franchisee operates a mobile cleaning and restoration service for residences and commercial buildings, using the franchisor's standardized equipment package and trademarks. The main highlight of the business is a specially retrofitted truck. In addition to the mobile power and wash business, the franchisor also sells Ameri-Mobile Car Care franchises, which perform a similar service for automobiles. Americlean sells equipment and supplies to franchisees.

Franchisee Profile: No particular qualifications are required, but the franchisor looks for evidence of success in a prior business or field. Subfranchising is discouraged.

Projected Earnings: An estimate of projected earnings was not available at press time.

Franchisor's Services: Americlean conducts a 30-hour training course at the company's headquarters in Gettysburg, Pennsylvania. Each franchisee receives a set of operations manuals and has access to company technical experts via a toll-free hotline. The franchisor also publishes a franchisee newsletter and organized ongoing seminars and workshops.

Initial Investment: The total start-up investment is estimated at $31,000, including the initial fee and the franchisor's equipment package. Financial assistance is available from Americlean for qualified franchisees.

Fees and Royalties: The initial franchise fee of $15,000 is moderate for the building services industry. The franchisee's total royalty obligation is six percent of gross sales, including a four percent monthly franchise royalty and a two percent advertising fee.

Summary: The Americlean franchise offers an easy-to-operate business and a ready-to-go equipment package for entering a market with demonstrated customer demand. Area franchises are currently available.

Franchise Highlights

Began operating: 1985
Began franchising: 1985
Outlets currently open: 100
Initial franchise fee: $15,000
Monthly royalty: 4%
Advertising fee: 2%
Training program: 30 hours
Term: 5 years

Chem-Dry

Industry experience:	★ ★ ★	*Franchising experience:*	★ ★ ★
Financial strength:	★ ★ ★	*Training & services:*	★ ★
Fees & royalties:	★ ★ ★	*Satisfied franchisees:*	★ ★ ★ ★

Chem-Dry
3330 Cameron Park Drive, Ste. 700
Cameron Park, California 95682
U.S. (800) 841-6583
Calif. (800) 821-3240

Founded in 1975 by Robert Harris, Chem-Dry has experienced a stunning growth rate, opening more than 100 outlets every year of the company's existence.

The Franchise: The franchisee operates a commercial carpet, drapery and upholstery cleaning business, using the franchisor's standardized mobile cleaning system and trademarks. The heart of the business is a patented process based on chemical cleaners manufactured by the parent company, Harris Research, Inc. A typical franchisee starts out with one truck outfitted with cleaning equipment and enough chemicals to clean 84,000 sq. ft. of carpet.

Franchisee Profile: A background in carpet or upholstery cleaning is beneficial, but not mandatory.

Projected Earnings: A written statement of projected earnings was not available at press time.

Franchisor's Services: Chem-Dry conducts a two-day training seminar at the company's headquarters in Cameron Park, California, supplemented by a self-study program that franchisees can take at home. Each franchisee receives cleaning equipment, a standardized bookkeeping system, an ad kit, and an opening supply of the franchisor's private line of cleaning solutions.

Initial Investment: The initial investment is estimated at about $6,000, including the initial fee and the Chem-Dry start-up package. The franchisor does not offer any direct financial assistance to franchisees.

Fees and Royalties: The initial franchise fee of $3,600 is low for the trade. Franchisees pay a set monthly fee of $100 per month, regardless of gross sales levels.

Contract Highlights: The franchise agreement is renewable every five years, at the franchisee's option. The franchisor derives a profit from the sale of cleaning equipment and supplies to the franchisee.

Summary: The Chem-Dry franchise offers an easy-to-operate, low-overhead business format based on a mobile service concept with moderate start-up costs.

Franchise Highlights

Began operating: 1975
Began franchising: 1977
Outlets currently open: 1,100
Initial franchise fee: $6,500

Monthly royalty: $100 per month
Advertising fee: None
Training program: 2 days
Term: 5 years

Decorating Den

Industry experience:	★★★	*Franchising experience:*	★★★
Financial strength:	★★★	*Training & services:*	★★★
Fees & royalties:	★★★	*Satisfied franchisees:*	★★

Decorating Den Systems, Inc.
4630 Montgomery Avenue
Bethesda, Maryland 20814
(301) 652-6393

Founded in 1969, Decorating Den Systems has launched the careers of approximately 500 self-styled interior decorators since the company sold its first franchise in 1970. The heart of the Decorating Den franchise is a business format based on a mobile showroom stocked with carpet, upholstery, wallcovering, and drapery samples.

The Franchise: The franchisee conducts an interior decorating business, operated from a specially outfitted van, using the trade name Decorating Den. The van supplants the need for a retail showroom, enabling complete consultation and decorating services to be performed at the client's home or office. The business can be successfully conducted by the owner with or without additional employees.

Franchisee Profile: No previous background in interior decorating is required, but an intense desire to succeed in the business is essential.

Projected Earnings: The franchisor does not provide a statement of projected earnings.

Franchisor's Services: The franchisor participates first-hand in setting up the business, starting with a three-week training program at one of the company's regional training centers in Indianapolis or Dallas. The curriculum includes marketing and sales, business administration, interior decorating principles, and accounting systems. On-going training is provided in the franchisee's own territory as required.

The franchisor operates a toll-free hotline providing franchisees with access to company marketing and operations experts. Frequent conferences and seminars keep franchisees abreast of current techniques and products. Franchisees benefit from discounts on materials and supplies, made possible through the company's centralized purchasing system.

Initial Investment: The initial investment ranges from $22,000 to $32,000. The franchisor offers a lease plan on the specially equipped Decorating Den van, but otherwise, does not offer any direct financial assistance to franchisees.

Advertising: Franchisees contribute two percent of gross monthly revenues for advertising.

Contract Highlights: The term of the franchise is five years. The contract may be renewed for an additional five-year term, at the franchisee's option. The franchisee receives a protected territory in conjunction with the franchise. The owner is obligated to participate full-time in the management of the business.

Fees and Royalties: The initial franchise fee ranges from $12,000 to $19,000 — moderate to high for a franchise of this type. The 11 percent monthly royalty plus the two percent advertising royalty create a total royalty bite of 13 percent of gross revenues.

Disputes and Litigation: The company has recently been involved in ligitation with franchisees in Washington, D.C. and Phoenix, Arizona. One litigant is attempting to organize a class-action suit against the franchisor. At publishing time, neither dispute had been resolved.

Summary: Decorating Den offers a unique marketing concept and a moderate investment. The company's growth rate is testimony to the concept's widespead appeal. The presence of litigation is not necessarily a warning signal, but prospective franchisees would benefit from hearing both sides of the dispute before executing a franchise agreement.

Franchise Highlights

Began operating: 1969
Began franchising: 1970
Outlets currently open: 500
Initial franchise fee: Min $12,000
Max. $19,000

Monthly royalty: 11%
Advertising fee: 2%
Training program: 2 weeks
Term: 10 years

Four Seasons Greenhouses

Industry experience:	★★★	*Franchising experience:*	★★
Financial strength:	★★★	*Training & services:*	★★★
Fees & royalties:	★★★	*Satisfied franchisees:*	★★★★

Four Seasons Greenhouses
5005 Veterans Memorial Highway
Holbrook, New York 11741
(800) 521-0179

Since Four Seasons sold its first greenhouse in 1975, the company has expanded into 300 outlets in the U.S. and Canada. All but five are franchises. The franchising program is still young (Four Seasons sold its first franchise in 1984) but the system has matured rapidly, establishing an average of 100 new outlets every year.

Four Seasons claims credit for 'single handedly molding the entire greenhouse/solarium industry as it exists today.' The company first sold greenhouse kits by mail, then later began setting up dealer showrooms with protected territories. Today, the franchise system generates more than $125 million in gross annual sales.

The Franchise: The franchisee conducts a home improvement and remodeling business specializing in glass structures for residential and commercial applications. The outlet operates under the trade name Four Seasons Greenhouse Design and Remodeling, with a general manager/sales manager and a construction manager. The franchisee typically fills the role of general manager and sales executive, while a construction manager oversees greenhouse installations performed by local subcontractors. The average showroom is located in 1,500 to 3,000 sq. ft. of commercial space on a main traffic artery, in proximity to furniture stores, appliance dealers, lumber yards, or similar durable goods retailers. The market for the franchisee's products includes new homes, townhouses, and condominiums; remodeled residences; and new or remodeled restaurants, hotels, nursing homes, and commercial buildings.

About 90 percent of the greenhouses and solariums sold by the franchisee are accompanied by complete installation, with the remainder sold as kits or parts. Franchisees are encouraged to stock other remodeling products, such as skylights, windows, hot tubs, and ceramic tiles.

Franchisee Profile: Prospective franchisees should possess a background or aptitude in residential construction or a related craft. The franchisor is currently seeking franchisees who are 'sales oriented' and 'business minded,' with verbal communications skills and entrepreneurial enthusiasm.

Projected Earnings: The franchisor will furnish prospective franchisees with a written statement of projected earnings. The average volume for a Four Seasons outlet is about $637,000 per year, before deducting operating expenses and the cost of goods.

Franchisor's Services: The franchisor conducts a two-week training program at the company's headquarters in Holbrook, New York. The tuition is included in the franchise fee, but attendees are responsible for their own travel and lodging expenses. The curriculum includes greenhouse design and installation, marketing and sales, and business management. An additional week of on-the-job training is provided in the franchisee's own territory.

When the outlet is open for business, a field consultant periodically visits the franchisee to provide advice and troubleshooting. Four Seasons publishes a newsletter and organizes annual conventions to keep franchisees abreast of new developments.

Initial Investment: The total investment may range from $30,000 to $100,000, depending on the location and size of the outlet. The franchisor estimates the franchisee's initial investment as follows:

	Low	High
Initial franchise fee	$10,000	20,000
Displays & inventory	10,000	20,000
Lease deposits	1,000	13,500
Improvements & signs	2,000	23,000
Utilities & insurance	1,000	3,500
Working capital	6,000	20,000
Total	30,000	100,000

The low breakdown is based on the minimum investment for a 'mini-franchise' designed for rural areas. The high breakdown is based on the maximum investment for a full franchise with a fully developed showroom and inventory.

Four Seasons does not offer direct financial assistance, but creditworthy franchisees may qualify for financing from CIT Financial Services, or another third party lender.

Advertising: Four Seasons franchisees do not pay an advertising royalty per se. The franchisor applies 7.5 percent of the company's own sales revenues toward advertising. Five percent is rebated to the franchisee to fund local newspaper and television campaigns. The remainder is applied to national advertising on behalf of all Four Seasons franchisees. The franchisor estimates that it spends more then $3 million annually to promote its franchisees.

Franchisees also receive customer leads from pre-sold national accounts, including numerous restaurant and lodging chains.

Contract Highlights: The term of the franchise is ten years. The contract may be renewed for an additional ten-year term, if the franchisee is not in violation of any material provisions. The franchisee receives a protected territory based on a population of 250,000.

Fees and Royalties: The initial franchise fee ranges from $10,000 to $20,000, depending on the size of the outlet. The low figure applies to a 'mini-franchise' designed for rural areas and involving fewer showroom and inventory requirements. Four Seasons does not charge franchisees any royalty on sales of greenhouse products purchased from the franchisor. A 2.5 percent royalty applies to other products.

Summary: The Four Seasons franchise is characterized by a sophisticated marketing system run by a professional organization. Franchisees benefit from a flexible investment, a manageable royalty structure, and pre-sold commercial accounts.

Franchise Highlights

Began operating: 1978	**Monthly royalty: Varies**
Began franchising: 1984	**Advertising fee: None**
Outlets currently open: 300	**Training program: 2 weeks**
Initial franchise fee: Min $10,000 **Max. $20,000**	**Term: 10 years**

Jani-King

Industry experience:	★ ★ ★	*Franchising experience:*	★ ★ ★
Financial strength:	★ ★ ★ ★	*Training & services:*	★ ★ ★ ★
Fees & royalties:	★ ★ ★ ★	*Satisfied franchisees:*	★ ★ ★ ★

Jani-King International, Inc.
4950 Keller Spring Suite 190
Dallas, Texas 75248
(214) 991-0900

According to the Department of Labor, the demand for janitorial labor falls third on the list of national priorities — one reason for the phenomenal growth of Jani-King, one of the fastest growing franchise businesses in North America. Established in 1969, Jani-King began franchising in 1974, opening 1,150 outlets in 13 years. Today, the franchise network generates more than $15 million in sales each year, making Jani-King the largest grossing janitorial firm on the continent.

The Franchise: The franchisee operates a commercial cleaning service for business and industrial clients, doing business under the trade name Jani-King. Most of the outlet's customers are recruited under long-term contracts. A typical outlet operates from a central office, using standardized procedures and equipment authorized by the franchisor. The franchisee utilizes state-of-the-art equipment and modern chemical cleaners, as well as the time-honored formula of mop, broom, and elbow grease.

To conserve on expenses during the financially crucial start-up period, the company permits new franchisees to operate the custodial service without any additional employees, often on a part-time basis. As the business grows and new employees are added, the franchisee gradually assumes a management role.

Franchisee Profile: Jani-King franchisees come from varied backgrounds. Most assume active roles in the janitorial service at the outset. The franchisee and all employees of the outlet must be bonded and insured.

Projected Earnings: Franchisees who perform the janitorial work themselves report profits as high as 70 percent of gross billings. When employee payrolls are added to the overhead, the margin drops to around 35 percent. Client contracts reportedly range from $100 to as much as $100,000 per month. The franchisor assures that a new franchisee will gross a minimum of $1,000 per month in the first fiscal quarter.

Franchisor Services: Jani-King provides new franchisees with pre-sold accounts, averaging from $1,000 to $2,500 per month in value. Customer payments are made directly to the franchisor, who deducts franchise royalties and passes along the balance to franchisees. Franchisees are trained at the company's headquarters in Dallas, Texas, receiving hands-on instruction on industrial cleaning techniques and equipment. The curriculum also covers the business business aspects of running a Jani-King franchise, including accounting systems, personnel administration, and marketing techniques.

The training program varies from 20 hours for an 'associate' franchisee to two weeks for area franchisees. The costs of travel, lodging, and meals are borne by the franchisee. Semiannual franchisee conventions and quarterly seminars provide a forum for continuing education and communications. The company publishes a newsletter and monthly product updates to keep franchisees abreast of current trends and developments.

Investment Breakdown: The total investment may range from $34,000 to $51,500. Financing is available with a minimum cash down payment of $4,000.

Advertising: The advertising royalty is currently set at one half of one percent. Franchisees receive ad slicks for newspaper and magazine campaigns, Yellow Pages advertising, and public relations aids. Brochures, catalogs, and pre-recorded radio spots are presumably available at nominal cost.

Fees and Royalties: The initial franchise fee and monthly royalties vary, based on the location of the outlet and the range of contract services provided. The maximum franchise fee is $16,500 with a ten percent monthly royalty, for which a monthly return of $2,500 is guaranteed from pre-sold accounts.

Summary: Jani-King International ranked number 11 in a recent Venture magazine listing of the 100 best U.S. franchises. One reason for the franchise's phenomenal growth record is its low startup costs and low initial overhead. For the hard-working entrepreneur with little capital to invest, Jani-King may represent a viable entry-level opportunity to start a successful business from the ground floor.

Franchise Highlights

Began operating: 1969
Began franchising: 1974
Outlets currently open: 1,150
Initial franchise fee: Min. $10,000
Max. $16,500

Monthly royalty: Min. 7%
Max. 10%
Advertising fee: 0.5%
Training program: 20 to 40 hours
Term: 10 years

Lawn Doctor, Inc.

Industry experience:	★★★★	*Franchising experience:*	★★★★
Financial strength:	★★★	*Training & services:*	★★★
Fees & royalties:	★★★★	*Satisfied franchisees:*	★★★

Lawn Doctor
142 Highway 34
Matawan, New Jersey 07747
(800) 631-5660

Anyone who has tried to start and maintain a lawn knows that a soft green carpet represents a culmination of struggle against crabgrass, dandelions, gophers, moles, poor soil conditions, and tricky irrigation systems. Lawn Doctor first began caring for lawns in 1967. Today, the company boasts 300 franchises in 28 states, mostly in the East.

The Franchise: A Lawn Doctor franchise provides complete lawn installation and planning service, including seeding, soil nutrition, irrigation, and the application of safe chemicals to control weeds and pests. An integral part of the business is the patented Lawn Doctor Turf Tamer, a machine that facilitates the tedious process of applying chemicals and sprays.

Franchisees do not need to operate from a business site, but must purchase or lease equipment, chemicals, a company vehicle, and a Turf Tamer. A typical outlet has a staff of two full-time and two part-time employees.

Franchisor Profile: Experience in lawn care or a related field, such as landscaping or gardening, is helpful but not necessary.

Projected Earnings: Lawn Doctor will supply prospective franchisees with an Earnings Claim Document prior to the first personal meeting.

Franchisor Services: A company liaison is assigned to each new franchisee during the first year in which the outlet is open. A tuition-free training program is held in East Windsor, New Jersey. The two-week seminar teaches franchisees the company's business format, lawn care systems, methods, and operating procedures, background agronomy, and effective marketing strategies. Franchisees pay their own travel and lodging expenses to attend the training program.

Some equipment and supplies are provided as part of the franchise package.

Advertising: The franchisor administers a co-op advertising program partially funded by the monthly franchise royalty fees.

Fees and Royalties: The initial franchise fee of $26,500 is high for the industry.

Contract Highlights: The franchise term is 20 years. The franchisee receive exclusive rights to a territory, but is not allowed to expand or subfranchise. The franchise may not be sold or transferred without the franchisor's consent.

offering kit home sales, construction, and finishing to the general public. Customers are free to do any or all of the construction themselves.

Franchisee Profile: Prior experience in residential sales or construction is not required. Absentee ownership is discouraged, though not strictly prohibited.

Projected Earnings: Based on the company's reported annual sales, the average gross revenues of a Lindal franchisee are about $75,000 before expenses.

Franchisor's Services: Lindal franchisees receive four days of training at the company's headquarters in Seattle, Washington. Attendees are responsible for their own travel and lodging expenses. The curriculum includes marketing and sales, construction engineering, financing, and business management.

Franchisees receive a confidential operating manual, a separate marketing guide, an ample supply of promotional materials, and point-of-sale displays. Lindal operates a toll-free hotline for franchisees requiring immediate assistance, and publishes a weekly newsletter. A field representative visits each franchise location periodically to offer advice and guidance.

Lindal Cedar Homes designs, mills, and manufactures the kits marketed by franchisees to the public. Two standard types of home construction are offered: conventional-wall exteriors over post-and-beam framing, and solid stacked cedar sidewalls. Sunspace kits are also available.

Initial Investment: Franchisees should be prepared to invest from $5,000 to $200,000 to open the business. The actual amount depends on the inventory level. The franchisor does not offer any direct financial assistance to franchisees.

Advertising: Lindal outlets do not pay a monthly advertising royalty, but a co-op program is available to reimburse franchisees for the cost of local ad campaigns using approved materials and media. The franchisor supplies Yellow Pages ad designs, slicks for newspaper and magazine advertisements, and radio and television commercials.

Summary: The main appeal of the Lawn Doctor franchise is its low investment and minimal overhead. According to an inside source, the key to success is locating a suitable suburban market with proper zoning and an absence of competition.

Franchise Highlights

Began operating: 1967	**Monthly royalty: 10%**
Began franchising: 1969	**Advertising fee: 5%**
Outlets currently open: 300	**Training program: 2 weeks**
Initial franchise fee: $26,500	**Term: 20 years**

Lincoln Log Homes

Industry experience:	★★★	*Franchising experience:*	★★
Financial strength:	★★★	*Training & services:*	★★
Fees & royalties:	★★★★	*Satisfied franchisees:*	★★★

Lincoln Log Homes
6000 Lumber Lane
Kannapolis, North Carolina 28081
(704) 932-6151

Like the toy logs of the same name, Lincoln Log Homes are assembled from modular kits using specially sized and treated logs with interlocking corners. Lincoln Log Homes, a subsidiary of Log Systems, Inc., is represented by more than 550 franchised dealerships in all U.S. states. Founded in 1978, the company has recruited an average of 60 new dealers ever year, riding the crest of contemporary demand for affordable housing and alternative lifestyles.

The Franchise: The Lincoln Log franchisee conducts a home sales and construction business, specializing in log houses assembled from modular kits. A typical outlet is housed in a model Lincoln Log home. The franchisee may employ a full-time or part-time construction staff, or use the services of independent contractors to assemble and finish the modular log homes. The dealership may also derive profits from the sale of solar heating and cooling systems and home improvement accessories.

Franchisee Profile: A background in residential construction is recommended. Besides individual dealerships, area franchises are also available.

Projected Earnings: Franchisees realize an average profit of $4,000 on each Lincoln Log home kit sold. A Lincoln Log dealer averaging two kit sales per month would generate $96,000 per year in profits, excluding billings for labor or accessories.

Franchisor's Services: The franchisor provides a two-day training seminar at the company's headquarters in Kannapolis, North Carolina. Attendees are responsible for their own travel and lodging expenses. The agenda includes classes on kit construction, marketing, advertising, and sales.

For a fee, Lincoln Log will construct the franchisee's model kit home. Franchisees receive complete architectural plans and construction specifications. When the business is operational, a field representative will periodically visit the outlet to provide ongoing consultation and advice. The franchisor also operates a toll-free hotline and publishes a monthly newsletter. All franchisees receive a confidential dealer operations manual containing the franchisor's standardized policies, specifications, and procedures.

Initial Investment: New Lincoln Log dealers should be prepared to invest from $10,000 to $75,000 to establish the business. The amount includes the purchase and construction of a model Lincoln Log home, materials, and an inventory of log home kits. The franchisor does not offer any direct financial assistance to franchisees.

Advertising: Lincoln Log franchisees do not pay an advertising royalty. The franchisor supplies franchisees with customer referrals generated from national advertising in do-it-yourself periodicals.

Contract Highlights: The franchisee receives a protected territory based on population. The average territory embraces a population of approximately 100,000. The franchisee must purchase at least one Lincoln Log Homes kit to start the business. The franchisor derives profits from the sale of kits and supplies to franchisees for resale.

Fees and Royalties: Lincoln Log dealers do not pay any initial franchise fee other than the cost of purchasing the model home kit.

Summary: Though not a true business-format franchise in the classical sense, a Lincoln Log Homes dealership offers a unique opportunity in low-cost residential sales and construction, with a moderate startup investment.

Franchise Highlights

Began operating: 1978	**Monthly royalty: None**
Began franchising: 1978	**Advertising fee: None**
Outlets currently open: 560	**Training program: 2 days**
Initial franchise fee: None	**Term: None**

Lindal Cedar Homes

Industry experience:	★ ★ ★ ★	*Franchising experience:*	★ ★ ★
Financial strength:	★ ★ ★	*Training & services:*	★ ★ ★
Fees & royalties:	★ ★ ★ ★	*Satisfied franchisees:*	★ ★ ★ ★

Lindal Cedar Homes
P. O. Box 24426
Seattle, Washington 98124
(206) 725-0900

Founded in 1945, Lindal Cedar Homes has established more than 300 outlets in the United States and Canada since the company sold its first franchise in 1968. The business was built on the concept of a compact, precut cedar home kit utilizing contemporary architecture and preassembled modules. All components are cut to size and shipped to franchisees' inventories or direct to the customer's building site.

The Franchise: The franchisee conducts a new home sales and construction business, based on modular kits for upscale residential structures, operating under the trade name Lindal Cedar Homes. Each kit is manufactured from Western red cedar throughout, sawn and kiln-dried in the franchisor's own lumber mills in Vancouver, Washington. Even the window frames, beams, and posts are solid cedar. A typical franchise outlet is housed in a 1,700 sq. ft. model Lindal Cedar Home or a suitable retail or commercial site, with two full-time and two part-time employees,

Contract Highlights: The term of the franchise is one year. The contract may be renewed each year, as long as both parties are in agreement. The franchisee is obligated to purchase cedar home kits from Lindal and to sell only the franchisor's line of construction materials. The owner of the outlet may not engage in any business which directly competes with the Lindal Cedar Homes operation.

Fees and Royalties: Lindal franchisees do not pay an initial fee or ongoing royalties. The company derives profits from the sale of home kits to franchisees.

Summary: Lindal Cedar Homes franchisees benefit from a solid base of outlets, a thorough advertising support program, and a low initial investment. The owner-built home market has increased by 30 percent since 1980.

Franchise Highlights

Began operating: 1945	**Monthly royalty: None**
Began franchising: 1962	**Advertising fee: None**
Outlets currently open: 320	**Training program: 4 weeks**
Initial franchise fee: None	**Term: 1 year**

The Maids International

Industry experience:	★★★	*Franchising experience:*	★★★
Financial strength:	★★	*Training & services:*	★★★★
Fees & royalties:	★★★	*Satisfied franchisees:*	★★★

Maids International, Inc.
5015 Underwood Ave.
Omaha, Nebraska 68132
(800) 843-6243

The Maids International prides itself on professional, scientific interior home maintenance services. The company advertises a four-person housecleaning system developed from time and motion studies, the use of standardized modern equipment, and expert application of safe and efficient chemicals.

Today, The Maids International boasts more than 250 outlets, all franchises, in 16 states and selected overseas territories. The company is currently seeking prospective franchisees in all U.S. markets and in Canada.

The Franchise: The franchisee offers complete housecleaning services, including special projects for floors, upholstery, carpets, and kitchen appliances, operating under the trade name The Maids International. A typical outlet has a 700 sq. ft. office facility and employs one full-time employee to supervise the efforts of twelve part-time housecleaners.

The franchise site requires space for storage and maintenance of cleaning equipment and company-trademarked vans. The franchisee is encouraged to use a computerized accounting system, especially designed for The Maids International outlets.

Franchisees are obligated to purchase a comprehensive insurance policy covering liability for theft and property damage, as part of the franchise package.

Franchisor Profile: The Maids International notes that many franchisees are retired professionals or business entrepeneurs with little or no related experience. New franchisees are trained in all aspects of the business. Multiple unit ownership is common.

Projected Earnings: A statement of projected earnings is not available.

Franchisor Services: The franchisor supplies two months of training, most of which takes place at the franchisee's site. The franchise owner and management staff spend three weeks in Omaha, Nebraska, where company instructors conduct workshops in personnel relations, marketing and promotion, and computerized management systems. Videotaped training is also available.

The franchisor markets equipment, supplies, and company vans to franchisees.

Initial Investment: The franchisee's initial investment is estimated as follows:

Initial franchise fee	$11,500
Equipment	3,500
Miscellaneous startup costs	20,000
Total	35,000

The franchisor may assist with obtaining financial assistance from a third party lender.

Advertising: The company administers a cooperative advertising program funded by franchisee ad royalties.

Fees and Royalties: The intial franchise fee of $11,500 is moderate for the industry. Franchisees who purchase rights to more than one outlet pay a reduced fee for each additional franchise. Monthly royalty payments decrease as sales increase. Payments typically fluctuate between five and seven percent of gross monthly revenues.

Contract Highlights: The term of the franchise is five years, half the industry average. The franchisee receives an exclusive territory with expansion rights. Absentee ownership is not prohibited. Area franchises are available by special arrangement.

Summary: The demand for professional housecleaning services has increased in proportion to the number of households in which both spouses work outside the home. Maids International has invested considerable effort in creating efficient service techniques, modern business practices, and an effective advertising program.

Franchise Highlights

Began operating: 1979
Began franchising: 1980
Outlets currently open: 250
Initial franchise fee: $11,500
Monthly royalty: Min. 7%
Max. 9%

Advertising fee: 2%
Training program: 3 weeks
Term: 5 years

Mr. Build

Industry experience:	★★	*Franchising experience:*	★★★
Financial strength:	★★★	*Training & services:*	★★
Fees & royalties:	★★★★	*Satisfied franchisees:*	★★★★

Mr. Build International
One Univac Lane, Ste. 402
Windsor, Connecticut 06095
(203) 285-0766

Mr. Build International has recruited more than 600 franchisees since the company was founded in 1981 - representing a growth rate of nearly a hundred new outlets per year. The company is currently seeking new franchisees in the U.S., Canada, and Japan.

The Franchise: The franchisee conducts a home improvement and construction business, operating under the trade name Mr. Build. A typical outlet performs one or more contracting services, such as plumbing, electrical, roofing, construction or maintenance.

Franchisee Profile: The typical Mr. Build franchisee is a qualified contractor in a construction trade. Multiple unit ownership is common, and area franchises are also available.

Projected Earnings: The franchisor does not furnish prospective franchisees with a written statement of projected earnings.

Franchisor's Services: The franchisor conducts a one-day training program during the company's annual franchisee conference. The tuition is included in the initial franchise fee, but airfare and hotel costs must be borne by the franchisee. Regional seminars and refresher courses are conducted periodically. The training programs focus on business administration, marketing, sales, and personnel development.

The franchisor assists with acquiring vehicles, purchasing supplies, and hiring qualified employees. In addition, business and employee insurance plans are available through the franchise organization. When the business is operational, Mr. Build supports franchisees with a technical newsletter, bulletins, market reports, and a centralized purchasing system.

Initial Investment: New franchisees should be prepared to invest around $20,000 to establish and equip the business. The investment amount includes deposits, equipment purchases, signs, office supplies, and uniforms. The franchisor offers financial assistance to creditworthy franchisees.

Advertising: Mr. Build franchisees contribute $300 per month for advertising. The franchisor supplies ad slicks for newspaper and magazine campaigns, preprinted brochures, radio and TV commercials, and public relations aids. Negatives for full-color ads are available at additional cost.

Contract Highlights: The term of the franchise is five years. The contract may be renewed for an additional five years at the franchisee's option. The franchisee does not receive an exclusive territory, but an area franchise may be negotiated under a separate agreement. The contract stipulates that the franchisee must use the franchisor's approved logo, advertising designs, and uniform specifications.

Fees and Royalties: The initial franchise fee ranges from $6,000 to $10,000, depending on the market and type of outlet. The monthly royalty varies from one outlet to another.

Summary: Mr. Build is the largest franchisor in the construction trade, offering franchisees the benefits of consolidated purchasing power, a uniform image, and a ready-made vehicle for entering the marketplace.

Franchise Highlights

Began operating: 1981
Began franchising: 1981
Outlets currently open: 650
Initial franchise fee: Min $6,000
Max. $10,000

Monthly royalty: Varies
Advertising fee: $300 per month
Training program: 1 day
Term: 5 years

Rainbow International

Industry experience:	★★★★	*Franchising experience:*	★★★
Financial strength:	★★★★	*Training & services:*	★★★
Fees & royalties:	★★★★	*Satisfied franchisees:*	★★★★

Rainbow International Carpet Dyeing and Cleaning Co.
P.O. Box 3164
Waco, Texas 76707
(800) 433-3322

The Rainbow International Carpet Dyeing and Cleaning Company is a high-volume business devoted to restoring carpets, upholstery, and draperies. The company has been refurbishing floors and furniture since 1975. In 1981, the owners set out to sell franchises, and in the first five years, growth has been nothing short of phenomenal. During a period of near-frantic expansion, Rainbow has successfully opened more than a thousand outlets, only six of which are company-owned. Today, the franchisor boasts the largest carpet cleaning chain in North America.

Rainbow International is registered in California, Illinois, Indiana, Maryland, Michigan, Maine, New York, Virginia, Washington, and Wisconsin.

The Franchise: The franchisee operates a retail carpet and upholstery renovation business, under the trade name Rainbow International Carpet Dyeing and Cleaning Company. A typical outlet performs cleaning, dyeing, water and fire restoration at the customer's home or office. The franchisor supplies cleaning chemicals and equipment, but franchisees are free to purchase supplies from any vendor that meets Rainbow's quality and delivery standards.

Franchisee Profile: Previous business or chemical cleaning experience is helpful but not necessary

Franchisor Services: The company holds a one-week mandatory training program in Waco, Texas, where the new franchisee is introduced to the company's standardized restoration methods. The curriculum also covers business procedures, marketing and sales, and personnel administration.

On-site assistance is available from Rainbow field representatives. The franchisor also operates a toll-free hotline providing access to company technical and operations experts.

Initial Investment: The initial cash investment is estimated at $10,000. The franchisee should also have an additional $10,000 in working capital.

Advertising: Rainbow franchisees do not pay any monthly advertising royalty.

Contract Highlights: The term of the franchise is 20 years. The franchisee receives an exclusive territory in conjunction with the franchise, but has no expansion or subfranchising rights. The franchise may not be transferred or sold without the franchisor's consent. The franchisee is obligated to participate full-time in the management of the business.

Fees and Royalties: The $15,000 initial franchise fee and seven percent monthly royalty are moderate by industry standards.

Summary: Rainbow International is a young company with exceptional growth potential. Low start-up costs and a reasonable royalty bite encourage the development of new outlets. Rainbow enjoys a high level of satisfaction among established franchisees.

Franchise Highlights

Began operating: 1975
Began franchising: 1981
Outlets currently open: 1000
Initial franchise fee: $15,000

Monthly royalty: 7%
Advertising fee:
None Training program: 1 week
Term: 20 years

Rainsoft

Industry experience:	★ ★ ★ ★	*Franchising experience:*	★ ★ ★
Financial strength:	★ ★ ★	*Training & services:*	★ ★ ★
Fees & royalties:	★ ★ ★ ★	*Satisfied franchisees:*	★ ★ ★

Rainsoft Water Conditioning Company
2080 East Lunt Avenue
Elk Grove Village, Illinois 60007
(312) 437-9400

The Franchise: The franchisee purchases a territory in which to sell and service the franchisor's private line of water conditioning equipment and supplies. The Rainsoft trademark may be used in conjunction with the franchisee's business. A typical outlet markets water softeners, tanks, filtering systems, and chemicals to residential customers and businesses in the franchise territory.

Franchisee Profile: A background in route sales is beneficial. Prior experience in the water conditioning trade is not required.

Projected Earnings: A written statement of projected earnings was not available at press time.

Franchisor's Services: Rainsoft conducts a one-week training program at the company's headquarters in Elk Grove Village, Illinois. An additional one to three weeks of on-site training are provided at the franchisee's place of business. The franchisor also supplies a set of technical and business operations manuals governing sales, equipment installation, service, and business management. A field consultant provides ongoing management assistance in periodic visits to the outlet.

Initial Investment: The total start-up investment may range as high as $50,000, including equipment purchases, supplies, and working capital. The franchisor does not offer any direct financial assistance to franchisees.

Fees and Royalties: The initial franchise fee ranges from $4,000 to $7,000, depending on the territory. Rainsoft franchisees do not pay any ongoing fees or royalties.

Contract highlights: The Rainsoft franchise does not have a definite term. The franchisee, in effect, receives lifetime rights to the franchisee as long as he wishes to service the territory. The franchisor derives a profit from the distribution of water conditioning equipment, supplies, and chemicals to franchisees for lease or sale.

Summary: Rainsoft has consistently adapted its marketing strategy and image to cope with changing attitudes about water conditioning and health. Once a primarily rural business, the water conditioning trade today is equally strong in suburban markets where public concern about water purity is at an unsurpassed high.

Franchise Highlights

Began operating: 1953
Began franchising: 1968
Outlets currently open: 300
Initial franchise fee: Min $4,000
Max. $7,000
Monthly royalty: None
Advertising fee: None
Training program: 1 week
Term: None

Educational Services

In the popular conception of the American Dream, the key to advancement is education. Services ranging from preschool development centers to adult vocational training schools generate $3.1 billion in annual revenues. Franchisors have engaged in personal education since Arthur Murray opened his first dance studio. Today, franchised schools teach everything from truck driving to speed reading.

A great deal of recent publicity has been devoted to declining test scores in the public schools. Nervousness about the quality of the nation's education system (and its educators) inspired a new type of franchise devoted to alternative and supplemental learning. The Learning Game was the first franchisor to market a system to teach children with problems keeping up in school. The company is no longer recruiting new franchisees, but others, including Sylvan Learning Corporation and SMI International, continue to offer individualized instruction to school children of varying grade levels.

According to the U.S. Department of Commerce, franchises specializing in educational services of all types are growing at a rate of 11 percent per year, generating more than $850 million in annual revenues.

Arthur Murray School of Dancing

Industry experience:	★★★★	*Franchising experience:*	★★★★
Financial strength:	★★★	*Training & services:*	★★★
Fees & royalties:	★★★	*Satisfied franchisees:*	★★★★

Arthur Murray Franchised Schools of Dancing
1077 Ponce de Leon Boulevard
Coral Gables, Florida 33134
(305) 445-9645

Dance schools were among the first business formats to be franchised, and Arthur Murray, the popular maven of ballroom dancing, was the industry pioneer. The first Arthur Murray dance studio opened in 1912, but it was 27 years later before independent dance instructors were able to capitalize on the Arthur Murray name. Over the century, franchisees have managed to remain competitive by adapting to changing dance and social trends — teaching everything from the Charleston to the Twist. Throughout, the primary focus remained — and continues to remain — on ballroom dancing.

The Franchise: The franchisee operates a dance instruction studio, specializing in ballroom dance steps and doing business under the trade name Arthur Murray School of Dancing.

Franchisee Profile: A background in dance instruction is beneficial, but not mandatory.

Franchisor's Services: Training programs are held at one of the company's operating dance schools, or the company's headquarters in Coral Gables, Florida. Attendees are responsible for their own travel and lodging expenses.

Franchisees receive a confidential manual detailing the daily operation, promotion, and management of the dance studio. An Arthur Murray field representative will visit the studio periodically, to offer ongoing training and operations assistance. A monthly franchisee newsletter keeps studio owners abreast of dance trends, company developments, and new techniques.

Initial Investment: The total investment may range fromn $25,000 to $75,000, including the initial franchise fee, lease deposits, decorations and furnishings, and miscellaneous startup expenses. The franchisor does not offer any direct financial assistance to franchisees.

Advertising: Arthur Murray franchisees do not pay a separate royalty for advertising.

Contract Highlights: The franchise is renewable every three years, by mutual agreement of the franchisor and franchisee. The franchisee receives a protected territory as long as the contract is in force.

Fees and Royalties: Arthur Murray does not charge any initial franchise fee to open a new dancing school. Monthly franchise royalties range from five to eight percent of gross revenues.

Summary: The Arthur Murray system is a pioneering franchise with excellent name recognition and an enduring track record. The program is characterized by a low-to-moderate startup investment, a manageable royalty structure, and consistent consumer demand.

Franchise Highlights

Began operating: 1912	**Monthly royalty: 5% to 8%**
Began franchising: 1938	**Advertising fee: None**
Outlets currently open: 200	**Training program: Varies**
Initial franchise fee: None	**Term: 3 years**

Gymboree Corporation

Industry experience: ★ ★ ★ *Franchising experience:* ★ ★ ★
Financial strength: ★ ★ ★ *Training & services:* ★ ★ ★ ★
Fees & royalties: ★ ★ ★ *Satisfied franchisees:* ★ ★ ★ ★

Gymboree Corporation
872 Hinkely Road
Burlingame, CA. 94010
(415) 692-8080

Gymboree founder Joan Barnes had a keen interest in the psychomotor and emotional development of infants, toddlers, and preschoolers. In the mid 1970s, a myriad of parenting books began to examine the stages of child development, prompting American mothers to feel the need to be involved first-hand in early childhood play. Thus, in an environment designed to promote self-confidence and self-esteem, Gymboree was born, catering to parents and children alike. Barnes opened her first exercise center for children nine years ago in a San Francisco suburb.

Usually located in rented churches, synagogues, or community centers, Gymboree centers house colorful play equipment such as balance beams, slides, mats, trampolines, and parachutes. Structured exercise, games, and singing are led by trained Gymboree personnel. In this setting, a group of from ten to twenty parent-child pairs experience self-discovery, relationship building, and community sharing. A Gymboree spokesman estimates that at least 35,000 children participate in the program today.

The franchise: The Gymboree center may be situated in any rented community space at least 1,800 sq. ft. in size and where the specially designed exercise equipment can be conveniently stored and assembled on-site. Once or twice a week, in 45-minute session, children from three months to four years old limber up with light exercises. On miniature jungle gyms and trampolines, they bounce, slide, climb, chant, and sing to disco, folk, and Latin rhythms. The outlet offers three group levels of ascending age and sophistication: Babygym, Gymboree One, and Gymgrad. Each Classe lasts 12 weeks, at an average tuition of $50 per attendee.

Franchise Profile: A typical Gymboree franchisee is an interested parent with a background in business. Previous experience in preschool education business is helpful but not necessary. Franchisees do not have to be certified teachers, but absentee ownership is not allowed.

Projected Earnings: Gymboree does not furnish a written projected earnings statement.

Franchisor's Services: A mandatory training program is held in nine days in Burlingame, California. The tuition is included in the initial franchise fee, but attendees are responsible for travel, lodging, and meals. Field representatives provide five days of on-site training and assistance prior to opening.

Gymboree provides franchisees with a set of site guidelines, but does not actively participate in selecting a location or negotiating a rental agreement. The franchisee must purchase a standardized equipment package from the franchsior. Equipment costs range from $7,000 to $9,000. Daily operating procedures are documented in the confidential Gymboree franchise manual.

A field consultant provides on-site assistance in semi-annual visitations during the first year of operation. Franchisee conferences are held annually.

Initial Investment: The franchisee's investment is estimated between $25,385 and $32,465, excluding working capital. Partial financial assistance is available from Gymboree.

Advertising: A number of records, cassettes, and books marketed under the Gymboree trademark are produced and advertised by major manufacturers. In addition, a syndicated 'Gymboree' newspaper column appears in most major markets. The franchisor recently instituted a cooperative ad program, to which franchisees contribute two percent of their gross monthly income from the business. Gymboree conducts national and regional campaigns, using television, newspapers, and magazines.

Fees and Royalties: The initial franchise fee ranges from $7,000 to $14,000, depending on the size of the facility. Franchisees interested in opening more than one center may purchase additional franchises at a discount. The total royalty bite, including the franchise royalty and co-op advertising fee, is eight percent of gross sales. However, Gymboree is a low overhead business with a simple, standardized operating format.

Contract Highlights: The Gymboree franchise has a term of ten years — the industry average. On expiration, the contract may be renewed for an additional ten-year term, without payment of a renewal fee. The franchisee receives an exclusive territory, but has no subfranchising rights whatsoever. Area franchises are available only outside the U.S.

Summary: Gymboree's current popularity has elicited glowing reviews in such periodicals as Newsweek, Ms., Time, and The Wall Street Journal. Besides favorable publicity, the Baby Boom of the late 1970s and the current popularity of non-traditional parenting practices contribute to the program's short-term viability. Franchisees benefit from a small investment, low overhead, and an easy-to-operate business.

Franchise Highlights

Began operating: 1976	**Monthly royalty: 6%**
Began franchising: 1979	**Advertising fee: 2%**
Outlets currently open: 320	**Training program: 9 days**
Initial franchise fee: $14,000	**Term: 10 years**

John Robert Powers

Industry experience:	★★★★	*Franchising experience:*	★★★★
Financial strength:	★★★	*Training & services:*	★★★
Fees & royalties:	★★★	*Satisfied franchisees:*	★★★

John Robert Powers
9 Newberry Street
Boston, Massachusetts
(617) 267-8781

Since the first John Powers Finishing School opened in 1923, the firm's name has grown into one of the oldest and most recognizable in the private education sector. Today, the John Powers chain prepares thousands of young women and men for careers in modeling, fashion, and other media-related fields. The company has continually modified its course offerings in response to the demands of emerging job markets, taking on such diverisified curricula as flight attendant training and interior decoration.

The Franchise: The franchisee operates a private career preparation school, under the trade name John Robert Powers. A typical school conducts curricula in modeling, self-improvement, and finishing; acting, drama, and makeup; fashion merchandising; interior design; and flight attendant training. Both day and evening classes are offered.

Franchisee Profile: A background in vocational education is beneficial, but not mandatory. The company is seeking prospective franchisees with adminstrative and financial aptitudes. Absentee ownership is not prohibited.

Franchisor's Services: JRP provides a three-week training program at the company's headquarters in the Boston area. Attendees are responsible for their own travel and lodging expenses.

On graduation, the franchisees receives a set of comprehensive operations manuals and student materials. Ongoing training and guidance are provided by a field adviser in periodic visits to the franchisee's school. JRP operates a centralized purchasing program to supply franchised schools with student aids and study materials. The franchisor publishes a monthly franchisee newsletter and conducts periodic workshops to keep franchisees abreast of job market trends and new curriculum materials. A toll-free hotline puts school owners and their staffs in touch with company technical and operations experts.

Initial Investment: New school owners should be prepared to invest up to $100,000. A franchisee with an existing school may be able to convert to the franchise program for less. The franchisor does not offer any direct financial assistance to franchisees.

Advertising: All JRP franchisees contribute a set fee of $150 per month for for advertising. The franchisor supplies ad slicks, commercials, student recruitment materials, and public relations aids.

Contract Highlights: The JRP franchise has an indefinite term, granting the school owner lifetime rights to the franchise. The franchisee may receive an exclusive territory.

Fees and Royalties: The initial franchise fee ranges from $10,000 to $25,000. The monthly franchise royalty is a hefty ten percent, exlcuding advertising fees.

Summary: The John Robert Powers franchise offers the benefits of solid name recognition, upscale imaging, and a ready-made format for entering the potentially lucrative private education field.

Franchise Highlights

Began operating: 1923
Began franchising: 1950
Outlets currently open: 90
Initial franchise fee: Min $10,000
Max. $25,000

Monthly royalty: 10%
Advertising fee: $150 per month
Training program: 3 weeks
Term: None

Sylvan Learning Corporation

Industry experience:	★★★★	*Franchising experience:*	★★★★
Financial strength:	★★★	*Training & services:*	★★★★
Fees & royalties:	★★★	*Satisfied franchisees:*	★★★★

Sylvan Learning Corporation
10777 Main Street, #204
Bellevue Washington
(206) 453-1119

Sylvan Learning Corporation operates a chain of 'teaching stores' that tutor children in reading and math in the after-school hours. The company was recently acquired by Kinder-Care, a diversified company specializing in kiddie-oriented industries, including life insurance, books, and apparel for children.

The Sylvan concept evolved in 1979 in answer to a rising demand for supplemental learning resources for children of elementary-school age. Sylvan features both remediation and enrichment in mathematics and reading. Intensive diagnostic intake testing is used to determine appropriate curriculum levels and to detect potential learning disabilities. Students are typically enrolled for two individualized tutorial sessions per week over a course of 18 weeks. A merit system of positive rewards is used to motivate achievement. For students who complete the program, Sylvan promises a forward leap in grade level competency of one to one and a half years.

The Franchise: The franchisee operates a learning center using the franchisor's standardized program and techniques and doing business under the trade name Sylvan Learning Center. Students receive individualized instruction and a customized curriculum from qualified educators. The educational service is realistically affordable to middle-class parents. The majority of the center's students are elementary school age, but adults with remedial learning problems are also welcome. A typical learning center is located in a 700 to 1,600 sq. ft. space in a medical/dental building or other suitable professional office in a middle class community with a population of at least 25,000. Two full-time educators and qualified part-time instructors are required to operate the centers.

Franchisee Profile: The franchisor gives preference to qualified educators.

Projected Earnings: Sylvan does not furnish a written statement of projected earnings.

Franchisor's Services: New franchisees undergo a two week training program in Bellevue, Washington, to become familiar with the curriculum. Franchisee training also includes the business and marketing aspects of the Sylvan system. The franchisor assists with securing financing from a third party lender, selecting a site for the learning center, and negotiating a lease for the premises. The company also takes an active role in planning and designing the facility.

Sylvan field representatives spend up to three weeks on-site prior to opening, helping with staff hiring and training, and overseeing the planning and execution of advertising programs. The franchisor also acts as a supplier for educational materials, forms, promotional packages, and furnishings. Periodic visits from a regional advisor provide the opportunity for ongoing guidance after the learning center has opened. Sylvan also publishes a franchisee newsletter and organizes annual conferences.

Initial Investment: The franchisee's initial investment is estimated as follows:

	Low	High
Initial fee	20,000	30,000
Lease deposits	750	3,000
Materials & equipment	12,800	14,100
Furnishings & supplies	2,500	6,100
Computer equipment	2,800	2,800
Grand Opening expenses	2,000	8,000
Working capital	8,000	35,000
Miscellaneous	2,500	8,000
Total	51,350	107,000

Sylvan does not offer any form of direct financial assistance to franchisees.

Advertising: The francisor competes directly with the Sylvan Learning Center. The franchise is accompanied by an exclusive territory.

Summary: Sylvan Learning Centers cater to the perception that the modern educational system is not doing quite enough to educate American children. The franchise offers a moderate invesment, excellent credentials, and a unique opportunity in educational services.

Franchise Highlights

Began operating: 1979
Began franchising: 1981
Outlets currently open: 136
Initial franchise fee: Min. 20,000
Max. 30,000

Monthly royalty: 8% - 10%
Advertising fee: 4%
Training program: 2 weeks in Bellevue, Washington
Term: 5 years

Electronics, Video, and Appliance Franchises

In the electronics field, computer retailing is second only to the lucrative video equipment sales and rental industry. Nearly 3.5 million personal computers are sold each year, generating over $12 billion in revenues. When the first computer shop opened in July, 1976, the chairman of IBM predicted computers would never be successfully sold in retail stores. 'It's a pretty screwball idea,' he told a Business Week editor. Computerland defied that prediction by opening an average of 60 new stores per year over the next decade, creating and dominating an entirely new retail industry. Today, more than 70 percent of all computers sold in America are vended by retail outlets, according to an estimate by Computer Dealer magazine.

Computerland's success was not overlooked by the competition, nor by industry potentate IBM. In 1980, a host of new franchisors entered the computer field, flooding the market with retail sites. Two years later, IBM introduced its own personal computer to be sold at retail.

The phenomenal rise of the personal computer industry was matched by an equally stunning downswing in the fall of 1985, when two thirds of the nation's computer retailers closed their doors. By the end of the year, six Boston-area Computerland outlets had gone under, despite brisk Christmas sales, and General Microcomputer, a 22-store chain with more than $70 million in annual sales, filed for bankruptcy. Franchisors who had started out with a flourish, including MicroAge, Byte Shops, and The Computer Store, Inc., suddenly retrenched or went out of business altogether. In the wake of these disastrous events, profits at IBM and Apple began to plunge. The industry gradually regained its footing, largely through the massive restructuring of marketing channels and significant technological changes in the product. The surviving franchisors are pursuing a more cautious but optimistic growth course.

But the peaks and valleys of the computer industry pale in comparison to the vast horizons of the video boom. In 1986, approximately 12.5 million VCRs were sold, most of them for household use. Nearly 60 percent of all U.S. homes that have at least one TV also have a VCR. The total number of U.S. households will increase by 7 million, to a total of 94 million, by 1991. Personal disposable income will increase about three percent per year, creating a continually increasing market for VCRs and related products.

Adventureland

Industry experience:	★★	*Franchising experience:*	★★
Financial strength:	★★★	*Training & services:*	★★
Fees & royalties:	★★★	*Satisfied franchisees:*	★★★★

Adventureland International Corp.
4516 South 700 East, Ste. 260
Salt Lake City, Utah 84107
(801) 266-9679

Brent Smith and Martin Ehman started Adventureland in 1981, as a hobby for their wives. The enterprising soup salesmen were more concerned with wholesome entertainment than obscene profits. Their videocassette rental business bluntly refused to handle any X-rated movies, disdaining an estimated 20 percent of the trade. Such lofty moralism did not blunt their growth, which transformed a $20,000 investment into a $50 million small business empire.

In 1986, when Adventureland International Corp. acquired Video Biz - its second largest competitor - Smith's and Ehman's wholesome hobby instantly became the largest home video chain in America.

The Franchise: The franchisee operates a videocassette rental business under the trade name Adventureland. A typical outlet is situated in a retail strip center or shopping mall, with two full-time employees and four part-time employees.

Franchisee Profile: Prospective franchisees must be capable of demonstrating a minimum net worth of $100,000 and enjoy working with people. A background in retail business is beneficial, but not mandatory.

Franchisor's Services: Adventureland conducts a one-week training program in Salt Lake City. Additional training and pre-opening assistance are provided at the franchisee's place of business.

The franchisor provides a confidential operating manual detailing the operation of the business. An Adventureland adviser will visit the franchisee's store periodically, to offer managerial assistance, as required. The franchisor operates a centralized purchasing system to supply franchisees' videocassette inventories.

Initial Investment: The total start-up investment is estimated at between $70,000 and $120,000, including lease deposits, fixtures, equipment purchases, business supplies, and an inventory of videocassettes. The franchisor does not offer any direct financial assistance to franchisees.

Advertising: Adventureland franchisees pay three percent of their gross monthly revenues for advertising. The franchisor conducts ongoing advertising campaigns on behalf of its franchise stores.

Contract Highlights: The Adventureland franchise has a ten-year term, renewable for an additional term at the franchisee's option. The franchisee is obligated to comply with the franchisor's standards regarding the selection and rental of videocassettes.

Fees and Royalties: The initial franchise fee of $15,500 is moderate for the industry. The franchisee's total royalty obligation, including the monthly franchise fee and the advertising fee, is less than eight percent of gross sales.

Summary: Brand loyalty is virtually nonexistant in the home video trade, and — though lucrative — the market is besieged by fierce competition. The Adventureland franchise offers a standardized vehicle for rapidly entering the market, with the organizational benefits of an industry leader.

Franchise Highlights

Began operating: 1981	**Monthly royalty: 4.5%**
Began franchising: 1982	**Advertising fee: 3%**
Outlets currently open: 790	**Training program: 1 week**
Initial franchise fee: $15,500	**Term: 10 years**

Celluland

Industry experience:	★	*Franchising experience:*	★
Financial strength:	★ ★	*Training & services:*	★ ★ ★ ★
Fees & royalties:	★ ★ ★	*Satisfied franchisees:*	★ ★ ★

Celluland
5812 Miramar Road
San Diego, California 92121
(619) 455-1600

Celluland was among the first retailers to capitalize on the emergence of cellular telephone technology, literally packing telecommunications into the cars and briefcases of the American work force.

The Franchise: The franchisee conducts a mobile telephone equipment and service business, operated under the trade name Celluland. Besides selling cellular telephones, franchisees may also qualify individually to provide local-area telephone network service in their respective territories, under a separate license from regional cellular telphone carriers.

Franchisee Profile: A background in retail sales or marketing is preferred, but not mandatory. The company is seeking prospective franchisees who have strong business and financial qualifications. Absentee ownership is not strictly prohibited.

Projected Earnings: A statement of projected earnings was not available at press time.

Franchisor's Services: Celluland conducts a comprehensive six-week training program at the company's headquarters in San Diego. The tuition is included in the initial fee, but attendees are responsible for their own travel and lodging expenses. An additional week of on-the-job training is provided in the franchisee's own territory.

Franchisees receive copies of the confidential Celluland franchise manual, which documents the franchisor's operating standards and specifications. The company will select the site for the mobile telephone center and oversee the design and construction of the facility. When the business is operational, a Celluland field adviser visits each outlet periodically, to offer on-site guidance. The franchisor operates a centralized purchasing program to supply franchisees with equipment and supplies merchandise at competitive wholesale prices. Celluland also publishes a monthly franchisee newsletter to keep franchisees abreast of industry developments and new products. A toll-free franchise hotline provides ongoing access to company technical and operations experts.

Initial Investment: New Celluland franchisees should be prepared to invest from $125,000 to $175,000 to establish the business. The amount includes lease deposits, site improvements, signs, equipment purchases, initial inventory, and miscellaneous start-up costs. The franchisor does not offer any direct financial assistance to franchisees.

Advertising: Celluland franchisees contribute one percent of their gross monthly revenues for advertising. The franchisor conducts regional campaigns, using newspapers, magazines, radio, and television. For promoting their own stores, franchisees receive ad designs, commercials, sales literature, displays, and public relations tools.

Contract Highlights: The term of the franchise is ten years. On expiration, the contract may be renewed for an additional term, providing the franchisee is in compliance with all material provisions. The franchisee receives an exclusive territory for the duration of the agreement.

Fees and Royalties: The initial franchise fee of $25,000 is high for a small franchise network — reflecting the franchisor's investment in start-up assistance and training. The total royalty obligation, including the franchise royalty and the advertising fee, is a moderate six percent of gross revenues of the outlet.

Summary: Celluland is a young franchisor in an emerging, future-oriented market, offering a ground-floor opportunity with the potential for explosive growth.

Franchise Highlights

Began operating: 1985
Began franchising: 1986
Outlets currently open: 20
Initial franchise fee: $25,000
Monthly royalty: 5%
Advertising fee: 1%
Training program: 6 weeks
Term: 10 years

Colortyme

Industry experience:	★ ★ ★	*Franchising experience:*	★ ★ ★
Financial strength:	★ ★ ★	*Training & services:*	★ ★
Fees & royalties:	★ ★ ★ ★	*Satisfied franchisees:*	★ ★ ★

Colortyme
P. O. Box 1781
Athens, Texas 75751
(214) 675-9291

Colortyme was founded in 1978, as a subsidiary of TV-appliance franchise king Curtis Mathes. A year later, the company was purchased by its founding father, Willie Talley, an early advocate of the rent-to-own concept. Colortyme has established 540 TV and appliance rental outlets since the company began franchising in 1980, representing a growth rate of nearly 80 outlets per year. The company is currently seeking new franchisees in all U.S. and Canadian markets.

The Franchise: The franchisee operates a television and appliance rental business, under the trade name Colortyme. A typical outlet is situated in a strip center, shopping mall, or other suitable retail site, with a staff of two full-time and five part-time employees. Franchisees offer a broad selection of televisions, videotape systems, and home appliances for rent or lease.

Franchisee Profile: A background in business or retail merchandising is beneficial, but not mandatory. Absentee ownership is not specifically prohibited.

Projected Earnings: The average volume of a Colortyme outlet is reportedly about $600,000 before expenses. Average pre-tax profits are around $120,000.

Franchisor's Services: The franchisor conducts a five-week training program at the company's headquarters in Athens, Texas. Attendees are responsible for their own travel and lodging expenses. The curriculum includes marketing, customer relations, sales procedures, inventory control, purchasing, and accounting.

A Colortyme field representative helps select a site and oversees the development of the store. When the business is open, he visits each outlet periodically to offer on-site guidance. Franchisees receive a confidential business operating manual, employee training, and a franchisee newsletter.

Initial Investment: New Colortyme franchisees should be prepared to invest $76,000 to establish the business. The amount includes the initial franchise fee, fixtures, signs, and an initial inventory of rental merchandise. Colortyme does not offer any form of direct financial assistance to franchisees.

Advertising: Colortyme franchisees contribute one percent of gross monthly revenues for advertising. The franchisor supplies franchisees with a marketing manual, sales tools, preprepared advertising materials, and point-of-sale aids.

Contract Highlights: The term of the franchise is five years. The contract may be renewed at the franchisee's option. The franchisee does not receive an exclusive territory in conjunction with the franchise.

Fees and Royalties: The initial franchise fee of $6,000 is low for the industry. Including the monthly franchise royalty and advertising fee, the total royalty burden is a moderate five percent of gross sales.

Summary: The Colortyme franchise is characterized by an easily operated business format catering to a consistently strong market for TV and appliance rentals.

Franchise Highlights

Began operating: 1978	**Monthly royalty: 3%**
Began franchising: 1980	**Advertising fee: 1%**
Outlets currently open: 540	**Training program: 5 weeks**
Initial franchise fee: $6,000	**Term: 5 years**

Computerland

Industry experience:	★★★★	*Franchising experience:*	★★★
Financial strength:	★★★	*Training & services:*	★★★
Fees & royalties:	★★★	*Satisfied franchisees:*	★★★

Computerland Corporation
30985 Santana St.
Hayward, California 94544
(415) 487-5000

Few franchises in the electronics field have received as much publicity, both positive and adverse, as Computerland, one of the original Cinderella success stories of the high-tech revolution of the late 1970s. The company launched its franchising program in 1976, amid grandiose forecasts in such publications as *Fortune* and *Business Week*. Despite a history of ownership disputes, management turmoil, and lawsuits, Computerland is still the largest and most recognizable chain of retail computer stores, with 600 outlets worldwide.

The Franchise: The Computerland franchisee operates a retail computer store, typically 1,500 to 2,400 fq. ft. in size, in a strip center, shopping mall, or free-standing retail site. A qualified franchisee sells computer hardware from IBM, Apple, Compaq, NEC, Epson, and other manufacturers. Although their emphasis is on hardware, Computerland stores also sell some software, books, and related services, such as customer education classes and warranty service. Franchisees must qualify individually to sell some product lines, including Apple and IBM. The outlet's customers include small businesses, corporate accounts, financial institutions, schools, and consumers.

Franchisee Profile: Computerland seeks prospective franchisees with some experience in computers or data processing. A common trait of existing franchisees is a background in management or marketing in an electronics-related field.

Projected Earnings: Based on suggested retail prices, a typical franchisee's net revenues average about 40 percent of gross sales. An outlet that grosses $500,000 might expect to net about $200,000. One franchisee reports pre-tax profits of eight percent of gross sales. He also estimates that his store must generate at least $360,000 to break even.

Franchisor's Services: Computerland conducts a mandatory training program in nine days at the franchisor's headquarters in Hayward, California. The franchisee is responsible for travel and lodging expenses. The curriculum covers computer background, purchasing, inventory control, marketing, advertising, and business administration.

Computerland supplies franchisees with guidelines for the layout and decor of the computer store and participates in grand opening activities. A field advisor provides ongoing assistance in periodic visits to the outlet. The franchisor also operates a centralized purchasing system to enable franchisees to take advantage of favorable wholesale prices and delivery terms.

Initial Investment: The total investment may range from $200,000 to $450,000. The amount includes the initial fee, site acquisition, the design and construction of improvements, fixtures and office equipment, an opening inventory of computer hardware and software, and working capital. Computerland does not offer any form of direct financial assistance to franchisees.

Advertising: Computerland conducts national advertising campaigns on behalf of all Computerland franchisees. The franchisor also provides an ad kit for planning and administering local advertising programs.

Fees and Royalties: The initial franchise fee varies with location. The high estimate is based on a store in one of the top ten U.S. markets; the low estimate, on a store in a small town or suburb. Besides the franchise fee, Computerland also charges a 'Store Design and Implementation Fee' of $10,000 to cover the cost of site selection assistance, the franchise training program, illuminated signs, and on-site help from a representative of the franchise company.

Disputes and Litigation: When Computerland first began franchising, it did not charge a separate royalty for advertising. In 1980, the company tried to force established franchisees to begin paying a co-op ad royalty in addition to the standard franchise royalty. Many of the company's franchisees went to court to avoid paying the surcharge.

The franchisor was also in the headlines over a stock dispute involving a former employee who insisted he had a verbal option to purchase Computerland stock at a guaranteed price. The option eventually ended up in the hands of an investment group, who succeeded in enforcing the option.

Contract Highlights: The term of the franchise is ten years. On expiration, the franchise may be renewed, at the franchisee's option. A renewal fee may apply. The franchise may not be sold, assigned, or otherwise transferred by the franchisee without the franchisor's consent. In the eventuality of an approved assignment, the new owner must pay a $4,000 transfer fee.

Summary: In its ten-year history, Computerland has undergone more than its share of litigation problems and managerial instability. In the industry downswing of 1985-86, a fourth of the company's outlets closed their doors or dropped out of the franchise program. Today, Computerland - and the computer industry - have apparently regrouped. With revitalized management and strong name recognition, the company remains the distant leader in retail computer sales. Because of the firm's widespread growth, new franchises may be difficult to acquire.

Franchise Highlights

Began operating: 1976	**Monthly royalty: 8%**
Began franchising: 1976	**Advertising fee: 1%**
Outlets currently open: 600	**Training program: 9 days**
Initial franchise fee: Min. $15,000 Max. 75,000	**Term: 10 years**

Curtis Mathes

Industry experience:	★ ★ ★ ★	*Franchising experience:*	★ ★
Financial strength:	★ ★ ★	*Training & services:*	★ ★ ★
Fees & royalties:	★ ★ ★	*Satisfied franchisees:*	★ ★ ★

Curtis Mathes
1411 Greenway Drive
Irving, Texas 75083
(214) 550-8050

Curtis Mathes operates the nation's oldest and most prolific chain of home entertainment stores. Founded in 1920, the company has more than 600 outlets across the U.S. today. All but 15 are independently owned franchises.

The Franchise: The franchisee operates a retail store specializing in home entertainment appliances and doing business under the trade name Curtis Mathes. A typical outlet is situated in a strip center, shopping mall, or other suitable retail site, offering the franchisor's private line of televisions, videotape equipment, and stereo systems. Franchisees purchase their store inventories from Curtis Mathes and participate in the company's limited four-year warranty program.

Franchisee Profile: A background in electronics is not required. The company is currently seeking franchisees with demonstratable career success, preferably in business or management. Applicants should demonstrate strong motivation and a willingness to learn.

Projected Earnings: Curtis Mathes franchisor does not provide a statement of projected earnings.

Franchisor's Services: The franchisor conducts a three-week training program at the company's headquarters in Irving, Texas, near Dallas-Ft. Worth. Franchisees must pay for their own travel and lodging expenses. An additional week of on-the-job training takes place at the franchisee's store prior to opening.

Curtis Mathes helps select a site for the store and negotiate a lease for the premises. When the business is open, a field representative will call on the store to provide ongoing assistance with operations and inventory. The franchisor's centralized purchasing program streamlines reorders and customer warranty service. The franchisor publishes a newsletter for franchisees and organizes offers ongoing seminars and workshops. A telephone hotline puts store owners in touch with key support and service personnel at franchise headquarters.

Initial Investment: New Curtis Mathes franchisees should be prepared to invest between $70,000 and $175,000, depending on the location and size of the outlet and the opening inventory level. The amount includes lease deposits, site improvements, equipment purchases, inventory, and working capital. The franchisor may finance part of the investment, including the cost of equipment and inventory.

Advertising: Curtis Mathes franchisees pay six percent of gross monthly sales for advertising. The franchisor conducts aggressive national ad campaigns, using television, radio, newspapers, and magazines. Franchisees also receive an ongoing supply of ad slicks, commercials, point-of-sale materials, and public relations aids for use in local promotions.

Contract Highlights: The franchise is renewable every year, by agreement of both franchisor and franchisee. The franchisee receives a protected territory for as long as the contract is in effect. The franchisee may not operate another business in direct competition with the Curtis Mathes outlet, but is free to open other stores in the territory.

Fees and Royalties: Apart from the six percent ad fee, Curtis Mathes franchisees do not pay a separate franchise royalty. The initial franchise fee of $15,000 is average for the retail trade.

Summary: The Curtis Mathes franchise offers strong brand identification in a lucrative market, plus the competitive advantages of the company's exclusive four-year limited product warranty.

Franchise Highlights

Began operating: 1920	**Monthly royalty: None**
Began franchising: 1982	**Advertising fee: 6%**
Outlets currently open: 620	**Training program: 3 weeks**
Initial franchise fee: $25,000	**Term: 1 year**

Entre

Industry experience:	★★★	*Franchising experience:*	★★
Financial strength:	★★★	*Training & services:*	★★★
Fees & royalties:	★★★	*Satisfied franchisees:*	★★★★

Entre Computer Centers
1951 Kidwell Drive
Vienna, Virginia 22180
(703) 556-0800

Founded in 1981, Entre has established nearly 300 retail computer stores since the company began franchising, opening an average of 60 new outlets each year.

The Franchise: The franchisee operates a retail store specializing in computer hardware and software and doing business under the trade name Entre Computer Center. The outlet uses a counseling approach to computer sales, employing trained consultants to analyze customer needs, before offering specific combinations of hardware and software.

Franchisee Profile: A background in the computer field not required. The company currently stresses management ability and sales aptitude.

Projected Earnings: Based on the company's reported annual sales, the average gross revenues of an Entre outlet are approximately $1.4 million, before subtracting the cost of goods and operating expenses. This figure does not take into account individual variables such as outlet location, size or inventory level, and is not based on any projected earnings claim furnished by the franchisor.

Franchisor's Services: Entre conducts a training program in one to three weeks at the company's headquarters in Vienna, Virginia. The tuition is included in the initial franchise fee, but the costs of travel, lodging, and meals are borne by the franchisee. The curriculum focuses on management, sales, product knowledge, and technical background.

Entre helps select a site for the computer store, negotiate a lease, and develop the facility. Purchasing assistance is available at additional cost. The franchisor sends a field representative to the outlet periodically, to offer additional on-site guidance. The franchisor constantly researches the market and identifies product lines for inclusion in franchisee inventories. Company advisors are available by phone whenever required.

Initial Investment: Prospective franchisees should be prepared to invest from $150,000 to $850,000 to establish a new store. The amount includes lease deposits, improvements, fixtures, business equipment, inventory, and working capital. Entre does not offer any form of direct financial assistance to franchisees.

Advertising: Entre franchisees contribute one half of one percent of gross monthly sales to the franchisor's advertising fund. Entre supplies ad slicks for newspaper and magazine campaigns, radio commercials, sales literature, and public relations materials.

Contract Highlights: The term of the franchise is ten years, renewable for another ten years at the franchisee's option. The franchisee receives a protected territory for the store. The outlet must be open for business within six months after the franchise agreement has been signed.

Fees and Royalties: The initial franchise fee of $40,000 is typical for the computer field, but high for the general retail industry. The 5.5 percent monthly royalty and one half percent ad fee are both moderate.

Summary: Second only to Computerland in total number of outlets, Entre Computer Centers is the largest chain still actively seeking new franchisees in this field. The franchise offers industry training, positive imaging, and a ready-made format for establishing a foothold in a highly competitive market.

Franchise Highlights

Began operating: 1981	**Monthly royalty: 5.5%**
Began franchising: 1982	**Advertising fee: .5%**
Outlets currently open: 290	**Training program: 3 weeks**
Initial franchise fee: $40,000	**Term: 10 years**

MicroAge

Industry experience:	★ ★ ★	*Franchising experience:*	★ ★ ★
Financial strength:	★ ★ ★	*Training & services:*	★ ★ ★
Fees & royalties:	★ ★ ★	*Satisfied franchisees:*	★ ★ ★ ★

MicroAge Computer Stores
2308 S. 55th Street
Tempe, Arizona 85282
(602) 968-3168

MicroAge founders Alan Hald and Jeff McKeever opened their first computer store in 1976, in a dry riverbed outside the university town of Tempe, Arizona. A year later, they were riding the wave of the Computer Revolution and began opening sites in upscale shopping centers in Phoenix, Tucson, and Dallas. By 1979, the industrious partners were also operating a computer mail-order business and a wholesale warehouse. They began franchising in 1980, taking on the industry leader, Computerland, in head-to-head competition.

Apparently, the company's resources became too diluted by its diverse operations and, in 1982, MicroAge filed for bankrupcty. Since, the revamped organization has successfully struggled back to solvency. Today, MicroAge boasts 160 outlets, and its stock is traded over the counter on the public exchange.

The Franchise: The franchisee operates a retail store specializing in computer hardware and software, and doing business under the trade name MicroAge Computer Store. A typical outlet is situated in a 3,500 sq. ft. retail facility, a staff of six to 20 full-time employees. Franchisees offer computer hardware manufactured by IBM, Apple, AT&T, and others, as well as some software and training services. The store owner must qualify individually to sell some product lines. The outlet's customers include business owners, managers, and consumers.

In addition to personal computers and small business systems, the franchisee may also offer integrated voice-and-data equipment and wide area network services.

Franchisee Profile: A background in the electronics or computer industry is preferred. Absentee ownership is prohibited. Existing computer dealers are also considered.

Projected Earnings: Based on the company's reported annual sales, the average gross of a MicroAge Computer Store is about $1.6 million, before expenses. This figure does not take into account individual variables, such as outlet location, size, or inventory level, and is not based on any projected earnings claim furnished by the franchisor.

Franchisor's Services: The franchisor conducts a training program in two to three weeks at the MicroAge Learning Center in Tempe, Arizona, just south of Phoenix. Attendees are responsible for their own travel and lodging expenses. The curriculum covers computer background, store operations, business administration, finance, marketing and advertising. Additional training and assistance may be provided at the franchisee's place of business.

The franchisor will assist with selecting a site for the outlet and negotiating a lease for the premises. When the store is open, a MicroAge representative will visit the outlet periodically, to inspect the operation and offer on-site troubleshooting. The franchisor operates a centralized purchasing system and works closely with vendors to assure favorable pricing and delivery for franchisees. MicroAge also publishes a franchisee newsletter and offers continuing education via the company's own satellite TV channel. A toll-free hotline provides access to technical and operations experts.

Initial Investment: The initial investment ranges from $200,000 to $500,000. The amount includes lease deposits, site improvements, equipment purchases, inventory, and miscellaneous startup costs. A lower investment is required for a 'conversion' franchisee with an established store. The franchisor does not offer any direct financial assistance to franchisees.

Advertising: MicroAge franchisees contribute one percent of their gross monthly revenues for advertising. The franchisor conducts national and regional campaigns on behalf of all MicroAge outlets, using newspapers, magazines, radio, and television. The franchisor also supplies ad slicks, radio and television commercials, point-of-sale materials, and public relations aids.

Contract Highlights: The MicroAge franchise has a ten-year term. On expiration, the contract may be renewed for an additional term, at the franchisee's option. The franchisee receives a protected territory for the duration of the agreement.

Fees and Royalties: The initial franchise fee of $30,000 is high for a chain of this size, but low for the computer field. The six percent monthly royalty is moderate. Including the one percent advertising royalty, the total royalty bite is only seven percent of gross sales.

Summary: Despite the company's past financial woes, MicroAge has re-established a stable growth course, prompting renewed optimism among its management. The franchisor receives high marks for comprehensive training and keen personal support.

Franchise Highlights

Began operating: 1976	**Monthly royalty: 6%**
Began franchising: 1980	**Advertising fee: 1%**
Outlets currently open: 160	**Training program: 3 weeks**
Initial franchise fee: $30,000	**Term: 10 years**

Food Service Franchises

Fast food, long associated with junk food, has undergone a cultural transition in response to changing consumer appetites. Since 1980, increasing public health consciousness and industry competition prompted experimentation with everything from taco salads to low-calorie cheeseburgers. But on the heels of lagging growth, most chains have adopted a 'back-to-basics' philosophy in the hope of recapturing bygone glory days. According to industry observers, the fast-food trade isn't exactly ailing; it is simply growing at a more moderate rate than previously. Current sales are estimated at about $120 billion per year, representing an annual growth rate of about six percent. The largest chains continue to outpace the field.

Pepsico is the largest franchisor of food service establishments, with 14,000 Kentucky Fried Chicken, Taco Bell, and Pizza Hut outlets. McDonald's is second in domestic outlets, but first in international expansion. McDonald's U.S. sales are about $4.6 billion per year, with another $1.3 billion generated by its 2,000-plus overseas restaurants. McDonald's primary competition in the perennial 'Burger Wars' are Wendy's International and Burger King, which is no longer recruiting franchisees.

To some degree, the industry has been altered by the trend for 'healthy' food. Just as a sporty car is not exactly a sports car, healthy food is not quite health food. But the resemblance is close enough to have prompted a boom in fast-food chains that promise all-natural, low-fat ingredients. On the other end of the spectrum, franchisors catering to consumers' sweet tooths have also enjoyed above-average expansion. Upscale ice cream parlors and chocolate chip cookie companies are examples.

Overall, fast-food is a cyclical industry, typified by alternating periods of sluggish growth and rapid sales. Menu prices, which used to increase by eight to ten percent per year, have tended to smooth out in recent years, pinching profits across the board. Nevertheless, the overall food service industry may be expected to continue expanding in a reasonably favorable economic environment.

A & W Great Food Restaurant

Industry experience: ★★★★ *Franchising experience:* ★★★★
Financial strength: ★★★★ *Training & services:* ★★★
Fees & royalties: ★★★ *Satisfied franchisees:* ★★★

A & W Restaurants, Inc.
One Park Lane Boulevarde, 500 East
Dearborn, Michigan 48126
(313) 271-9300

A & W has been associated with root beer since the turn of the century, and the restaurant chain of the same name is one of the oldest franchise networks in America. The company oversees more than 500 outlets worldwide — all but ten owned by independent franchisees.

The Franchise: The franchisee operates a family-oriented fast-food restaurant, under the trade name A & W Great Food Restaurant. Supplementing sales of A & W's famous private brand of root beer is a bevy of traditional fast-food fare, such as hamburgers, chicken, salads, and french fried potatoes.

Franchisee Profile: A background in food and beverage management is beneficial, but not mandatory.

Franchisor's Services: A & W provides two weeks of centralized training at the company's headquarters in Dearborn, Michigan, or at a designated regional site. Franchisees must bear the cost of travel, lodging, and meals. An additional two weeks of training take place at the franchisee's restaurant.

The A & W manual documents the franchisor's strictly enforced standards for food preparation, sanitation, and management of the outlet. A field representative will inspect the restaurant periodically and offer operational assistance. A & W publishes a franchisee newsletter to keep franchisees informed of new products, consumer trends, and franchise developments.

Initial Investment: The total start-up investment is estimated at $150,000, including site acquisition, construction, equipment purchases, restaurant supplies, and miscellaneous start-up expenses. A & W does not offer any direct financial assistance to franchisees.

Advertising: A & W franchisees pay four percent of their gross monthly revenues for advertising. In return, the franchisor provides conducts national ad campaigns and supplies franchisees with designs, commercials, and point-of-sale aids.

Contract Highlights: The A & W franchise has a 20-year term, renewable for an additional term at the franchisee's option. There is no fee to renew the franchise agreement. The franchisee agrees to sell the A & W brand of root beer and to purchase all supplies and foodstuffs in accordance with the franchisor's specifications. The contract does not restrict the franchisee from owning another food and beverage establishment.

Fees and Royalties: The initial franchise fee begins at $10,000, about average for a fast-food restaurant. The franchisee's total royalty obligation, including the monthly franchise fee and the advertising fee, is eight percent of gross sales.

Summary: The A & W franchise offers exceptional name recognition, competent training, and a loyal base of root beer-guzzling consumers.

Franchise Highlights

Began operating: 1919
Began franchising: 1925
Outlets currently open: 525
Initial franchise fee: Min $10,000
Monthly royalty: 4%
Advertising fee: 4%
Training program: 1 weeks
Term: 20 years

Arby's

Industry experience: ★★★★
Financial strength: ★★★★
Fees & royalties: ★★★
Franchising experience: ★★★★
Training & services: ★★★★
Satisfied franchisees: ★★★

Arby's, Inc.
3495 Piedmont Rd.
Ten Piedmont Center, Suite 700
Atlanta, Georgia 30305-1796
(404) 262-2729

Consistently ranked among the top ten fast-food franchises, Arby's Inc. enjoys a solid niche of the market with its famous roast beef sandwiches. In 1987, system-wide sales exceeded $1 billion. The company is currently working to upgrade its image and expand its reach.

The Franchise: A typical Arby's outlet is located in a well-trafficked urban area, serving over-the-counter packaged meals and with both on-premises dining and take-out facilities. A classic Arby's meal features a roast beef sandwich, crisp french fried potatoes, and a Jamocha shake. The limited menu also offers other sandwich selections, hamburgers, home-style fried potatoes, a salad bar, and an assortment of soft drinks.

Franchisee Profile: Fast-food or restaurant experience is beneficial, but not mandatory. The company prefers to sell multi-unit franchise packages, which are available at discounted fees.

Franchisor Services: The company conducts a comprehensive four-week training program for new franchisees in Atlanta, Georgia. Using a combination of classroom and hands-on instruction, Arby's trainers provide franchisees with a thorough understanding of all facets of the food-service establishment. Ongoing seminars are offered monthly at various regional locations. The franchisor's training programs are offered without charge, but the franchisee must pay for travel and lodging.

To insure consistency and quality to the benefit of all Arby's franchisees, the company enforces strict standards concerning site selection and development, including the purchase of equipment and supplies. Most supplies may be purchased through the company's cooperative distributor, ARCORP, presumably at competitive prices. Only the franchisor's approved suppliers may be used to fill the restaurant's ongoing needs.

Initial Investment: Prospective franchisees must be capable of handling a minimum cash investment of $100,000. The estimated cost of startup operations for the first year runs from $235,000 to $304. The amount includes the initial franchise fee, lease deposits, construction, equipment, fixtures, furnishings, supplies, and working capital. Arby's does not offer any form of direct financial assistance to franchisees.

Advertising: The company recently made a substantial investment in national advertising to boost the Arby's image. To support the franchisor's campaigns, franchisees contribute 4.2 percent of gross sales to the Arby's ad fund. Franchisees also participate in local co-op ad programs and promotions.

Fees and Royalties: The initial franchise fee for a single unit is $32,000. Additional units are available for $20,000, encouraging multi-unit ownership. The monthly royalty payment is based on three percent of gross revenues, moderate by industry standards. Including the advertising contribution, the total royalty bite is less than eight percent.

Summary: Arby's appears to be healthy at a point where many fast-food chains are struggling to carve out niches in a competitive marketplace with lagging growth. Franchisees benefit from aggressive advertising, solid name recognition, and a new healthy-cuisine image.

Franchise Highlights

Began operating: 1964
Began franchising: 1965
Outlets currently open: 1,500
Initial franchise fee: Min. $20,000
Max. $32,000

Monthly royalty: 3%
Advertising fee: 4.2%
Training program: 4 weeks
Term: 20 years

Baskin-Robbins Ice Cream Company

Industry experience:	★★★★	*Franchising experience:*	★★★★
Financial strength:	★★★★	*Training & services:*	★★★
Fees & royalties:	★★★★	*Satisfied franchisees:*	★★★

Baskin-Robbins Ice Cream Company
31 Baskin-Robbins Place
Glendale, California 91201
(818) 956 - 0031

Resting on its laurels as the bastion of American scooped ice cream, Baskin-Robbins has been slow to acknowledge competition from the new, richer-flavored, superpremium ice cream companies. In the mid 1980s, the parent company, Allied Lytons, launched a new campaign to perk the organization's softening sales. Baskin-Robbins ice cream parlors now offer richer, creamier, higher-priced flavors and sell a diversity of cones and toppings. For the first time, outlets also sell prepackaged sorbets.

The Franchise: The franchisee operates a retail ice cream parlor, under the trade name Baskin-Robins, selling the franchisor's private brand of ice cream. A typical outlet is located in a 900 sq. ft. retail space in a shopping mall, strip center, or freestanding site, in a high-traffic urban area. The recognizable pink and brown trademark promises a choice of 31 ice cream flavors. Recent offerings range from Pralines n' Cream to such trendy attractions as Baseball Crunch, Mississippi Mud, and Pink Bubblegum. The new superpremium line includes such esoteric flavors as Grand Marnier, Raspberry Truffle, and Cappuccino Chip. In total, the company boasts 550 different flavors, rotated throughout the chain at two-month intervals. Beside over-the-counter ice cream sales, the franchisee may also derive income from the sale of toppings, accessories, and ice cream-filled cakes.

Franchisee Profile: The company looks for applicants with previous business experience and good management potential. Absentee ownership is allowed, as long as the person who will manage the store meets the franchisor's standards.

Projected Earnings: According to an independent source, a Baskin-Robbins store can do as well as $200,000 per year in gross revenues. The estimate is not an average based on the company's annual reported sales, and is not based on any projected earnings statement supplied by the franchisor.

Franchisor Services: Baskin-Robbins conducts a two-week training program in Glendale, California, where the new franchisee learns all facets of operating an ice cream parlor. A district manager is present just prior to and during the opening of the outlet. Ongoing support is available from field advisors who visit each ice cream parlor periodically. Franchisees are kept up-to-date with new products and marketing developments and are encouraged to attend national and regional seminars.

Initial Investment: The franchisee's initial investment is estimated at about $145,000, including lease deposits, site improvements, equipment, fixtures, signs, and working capital. Franchisees must demonstrate liquid assets of at least $60,000.

Advertising: Baskin-Robbins recently initiated an aggressive national advertising campaign to upgrade the company's image. In the past, Baskin-Robbins franchises were not required to contribute advertising fees, but the present franchise agreement calls for a monthly contribution of three percent of gross sales.

Fees and Royalties: There is no initial license fee for a Baskin-Robbins franchise. Franchisees pay just one half of one percent of gross monthly revenues in franchise royalties. Including the ad fee, the total royalty bite is less than five percent.

Disputes and Litigation: In 1982, Baskin-Robbins was sued by a group of franchisees who argued that they were being illegally forced to buy only the franchisor's private brand of ice cream. The court ruled in favor of Baskin-Robbins, affirming the right of a franchisor to license outlets strictly for the purpose of distributing its own products.

Summary: The Baskin-Robbins franchise is a popular family business, characterized by a low-risk investment and a strong, traditional company.

Franchise Highlights

Began operating: 1945
Began franchising: 1948
Outlets currently open: 3,300
Initial franchise fee: None

Monthly royalty: 0.5%
Advertising fee: 3%
Training program: 2 weeks
Term: 5 years

Ben & Jerry's Ice Cream

Industry experience:	★★	*Franchising experience:*	★
Financial strength:	★★★	*Training & services:*	★★
Fees & royalties:	★★★	*Satisfied franchisees:*	★★★

Ben & Jerry's Ice Cream
Route 100
P.O. Box 240
Waterbury, Vermont 05676
(802) 224-5641

Since 1983, sales of Ben & Jerry's rich, buttery ice cream have increased by an average of 20 percent. Encouraged by early success, Ben & Jerry's is ambitiously soliciting franchise expansion on the East Coast, southern California and Chicago.

The Franchise: A typical Ben & Jerry's ice cream shop is located in a high-traffic suburban area, with a motif designed to attract an upscale clientele. The decor emphasizes the nostalgic and natural quality of the franchisor's 'old-fashioned' ice cream. The franchisee must purchase all of the the 34 flavors from Ben & Jerry's. Others supplies and equipment may be purchased through the company or from an approved supplier.

Franchisee Profile: Prospective franchisees are screened on the basis of past business experience, enthusiasm, and entrepreneurial potential.

Franchisor Services: The company provides one week of training at the company's headquarters in Vermont, where new franchisees get the inside scoop on the ice cream shop business. Before the outlet opens, company representatives spend five days on-site assisting with start-up activities. The company provides a continuing update service to keep franchisees abreast of new products and developments.

Advertising: Franchisees participate in regional co-op programs and pay four percent of their gross monthly revenues to the franchisor's ad fund.

Fees and Royalties: The initial license fee for a Ben & Jerry's franchise is $15,000. Franchisees need $80,000 in cash to start a new ice cream shop, plus about $100,000 in working capital for the first year of operation. The franchisor derives profits from the sale of its ice cream to the franchisee, alleviating the outlet of franchise royalties.

Summary: Ben & Jerry's is a comfortable franchise opportunity for the small, independent entrepreneur, requiring little expertise and a moderate cash investment. Market trends suggest a cautious but favorable outlook for ice cream shops that cater to middle and upper-middle class connoiseurs.

Franchise Highlights

Began operating: 1978
Began franchising: 1981
Outlets currently open: 16
Initial franchise fee: $15,000
Monthly royalty: None
Advertising fee: 4%
Training program: 1 week
Term: 10 years

Benihana of Tokyo

Industry experience:	★★★	*Franchising experience:*	★
Financial strength:	★★★	*Training & services:*	★★★★
Fees & royalties:	★★	*Satisfied franchisees:*	★★★

Benihana of Tokyo
P.O. Box 020210
Miami, Florida 33102-0210
(305) 593-0770

Rocky Aoki's Benihana of Toykyo steakhouses serve Japanese cuisine with great ebullience and an authentic flair. The modest size of the chain is more a reflection of the capital investment than the restaurant's consumer appeal. All but seven of the 48 Benihana outlets in operation today are independently owned franchises.

The Franchise: The franchisee operates a full-service restaurant specializing in Japanese cuisine and doing business under the trade name Benihana of Tokyo. Food quality, preparation, and service adhere closely to the franchisor's motif. Meals are served in the traditional Japanese style, with customers seated around communal habachi tables. Trained chefs prepare and cook entrees before their customers' eyes, as kimonoed waitress serve sidedishes, emulating both the ambience and repast of Old Japan.

Franchisee Profile: Prospective franchisees must demonstrate knowledge and experience in the food and beverage industry. Absentee ownership is not prohibited. The focus of company's current expansion program is the Midwest.

Franchisor Services: Much of Benihana's success relies on the attention the franchisor devotes to franchisee training. The initial training program consists of 12 weeks at an operating Benihana restaurant, where franchisees study food preparation, personnel relations, cost control proceduress, and financial administration. Additional training programs are offered for chefs. The franchisee is responsible for travel expenses and wages.

Benihana field advisors participate in site selection, loan negotiation, site construction, and opening activities. After the restaurant has opened for business, a franchise representative visits the outlet periodically to inspect the operation and offer on-site assistance.

Initial Investment: The initial investment is estimated at $375,000, including site acquisition, construction, equipment, fixtures, furnishings, decor, and staff training. The franchisor does not offer any direct financial assistance to franchisees. According to an independent source, the total working capital requirement to sustain the business until it begins to turn a profit may be as high as $1 million.

Advertising: Benihana franchisees contribute one half of one percent of gross monthly sales for advertising. The franchisor supplies art for Yellow Page, newspaper, and magazine ads. Radio and television commercials are also available for local campaigns conducted at the franchisee's expense.

Fees and Royalties: The initial franchise fee is a hefty $50,000. Including the five percent franchise royalty, the total royalty burden is less than six percent.

Summary: The Benihana organization is typified by moderate growth and a unique restaurant format with strong consumer appeal. The initial fee and cash investment are steep, but once the business begins to turn a profit, a manageable royalty structure maximizes the owner's long-term return.

Franchise Highlights

Began operating: 1964
Began franchising: 1970
Outlets currently open: 48
Initial franchise fee: $50,000
Monthly royalty: 5%
Advertising fee: 0.5%
Training program: 12 weeks
Term: 15 years

Bob's Big Boy

Industry experience: ★★★★ *Franchising experience:* ★★★★
Financial strength: ★★★★ *Training & services:* ★★★★
Fees & royalties: ★★★ *Satisfied franchisees:* ★★★★

Bob's Big Boy
1 Marriott Drive
Washington, DC 20058
(301) 897-7863

A few years ago, Marriott Corporation, the parent company of the 1,000-plus Bob's Big Boy chain, held a nationwide election among the restaurant's patrons to decide whether to retire the company's cherubic, red-bibbed advertising symbol. Big Boy's devilish smile and rosy cheeks had already been enshrined in the Advertising Symbol Hall of Fame. By popular demand, the Big Boy character stayed, which is more than one can say about Howard Johnson's, another Marriott subsidiary. The company is currently converting all its roadside Ho-Jo coffee shops to Bob's Big Boys. Even so, Marriott is actively seeking new Big Boy franchisees in most U.S. and Canadian markets.

The Franchise: The franchisee operates a family-oriented restaurant with a coffee-shop mofit, under the trade name Bob's Big Boy. The Bob's drive-ins of the 1950s have given way to fully enclosed dining facilities, featuring a selection of basic American entrees, in addition to the original Big Boy double decker hamburger on which the company's original success was based. Today's Bob's Big Boy restaurants are contemporary, upscale establishments catering to families and singles of all demographic and age groups.

Franchisee Profile: A background in food and beverage management is beneficial, but not mandatory.

Projected Earnings: A written statement of projected earnings was not available at press time.

Franchisor's Services: Marriott conducts a comprehensive six-week training program for Big Boy franchisees at a designated company-owned site. Additional training and grand opening assistance are provided at the franchisee's restaurant. Franchisees receive site selection assistance, a marketing kit, and a confidential operations manual.

A Marriott representative visits the restaurant periodically to inspect the outlet and offer ongoing management support. The franchisor continually modifies the menu to reflect changing consumer trends identified by the Marriott market research team.

Initial Investment: The total start-up investment for a new restaurant starts at $100,000. Including working capital to sustain the business until it becomes profitable, the cash requirement may range as high as $1 million. The franchisor does not offer any direct financial assistance to franchisees.

Fees and Royalties: The initial franchise fee of $25,000 is commensurate with the chain's stature and maturity. The franchisee's total royalty obligation, including the monthly franchise fee and the advertising fee, is seven percent of gross sales.

Summary: Bob's Big Boy is a pioneer in both the coffee-shop sector and the franchise industry, with a track record of adapting successfully to often-radical shifts in consumer dining trends. The parent company, Marriott, is both a major influence in the lodging industry and the second largest food-service operator in the world.

Franchise Highlights

Began operating: 1936
Began franchising: 1946
Outlets currently open: 1,000
Initial franchise fee: $25,000
Monthly royalty: 3%
Advertising fee: 4%
Training program: 6 weeks
Term: 20 years

Bojangles

Industry experience:	★ ★ ★	*Franchising experience:*	★ ★
Financial strength:	★ ★ ★	*Training & services:*	★ ★ ★ ★
Fees & royalties:	★ ★ ★	*Satisfied franchisees:*	★ ★ ★ ★

Bojangles Corporation
P. O. Box 240239
Charlotte, North Carolina 28224
(704) 527-2675

When Horn and Hardart Company bought the privately-owned Bojangles chain in 1982, the North Carolina company was already operating 52 restaurants. Since, the number of outlets has grown to 380, fewer than half of which are company-owned. The organization's sales volume has grown with equal vim, catapulting Bojangles to fourth place among the nation's fried chicken franchises.

The Franchise: The franchisee conducts a fast-food restaurant specializing in Cajun-style chicken and doing business under the trade name Bojangles. Bojangles restaurants combine an upscale, sit-down dining motif with the convenience of take-out and drive-through facilities. The menu is designed with the competition in mind, featuring Cajun-style chicken, rice and biscuits, hamburger sandwiches, and french fried potatoes, all prepared 'home-style.' The breakfast menu accounts for 35 percent of the restaurant's average revenues.

Franchisee Profile: A background in food and beverage service is not required. The company is seeking prospective franchisees who have managerial talent and are capable of handling the investment.

Projected Earnings: An estimate of projected earnings was not available at press time.

Franchisor's Services: The franchisor provides a comprehensive six-week training program, including two weeks at the company's headquarters in Charlotte, North Carolina and four weeks at an operating Bojangles restaurant. Attendees are responsible for their own travel and lodging expenses.

Bojangles field representatives provide on-site assistance prior to opening. Franchisees are required to attend quarterly training seminars to keep abreast of industry developments and new techniques.

Initial Investment: Bojangles franchisees should be prepared to invest a minimum of $120,000 to open a new restaurant. The amount includes site acquisition, construction, improvements, equipment purchases, and an initial inventory of restaurant supplies. Including working capital to sustain the business until it becomes profitable, the total capital requirement may run as high as $700,000 or more.

Advertising: Bojangles franchisees contribute a hefty five percent of gross monthly revenues for advertising. The franchisor conducts regional campaigns on behalf of franchisees, using newspapers, radio, and television. Franchisees also receive point-of-sale materials and public relations aids.

Contract Highlights: The term of the franchise is 20 years. The contract may be renewed for an additional year term, providing the franchisee is in compliance with all material provisions. The franchise may not be sold, assigned, or transferred without the franchisor's written consent.

Fees and Royalties: The initial franchise fee of $25,000 is at the high end of the fast-food spectrum. The four percent monthly royalty, added to the five percent advertising royalty, exacts a total of nine percent of gross revenues of the outlet, slightly higher than average for the industry.

Summary: The Bojangles franchise is characterized by rapid growth, moderate but increasing name recognition, savy management, and one of the most thorough training programs of its kind.

Franchise Highlights

Began operating: 1977
Began franchising: 1979
Outlets currently open: 380
Initial franchise fee: Min $25,000
Max. $35,000

Monthly royalty: 4%
Advertising fee: 5%
Training program: 6 weeks
Term: 20 years

Carl's Jr.

Industry experience: ★★★★ *Franchising experience:* ★
Financial strength: ★★★ *Training & services:* ★★★
Fees & royalties: ★★ *Satisfied franchisees:* ★★★

Carl Karcher Enterprises
1200 N. Harbor Boulevard
Anaheim, California 92801
(714) 774-5796

Karl Karcher, with over 30 years experience in chain-operated food service, today finds his Carls Jr. restaurants serving hamburgers to a new generation of fast-food devotees. The California burger maestro already had 300 company-owned outlets, when he began franchising in 1984. At present, more than 100 of the Carl's Jr. restaurants operating under the smiling yellow-star logo are owned by independent franchisees.

The Franchise: The franchisee conducts a limited-menu restaurant, specializing in hamburgers, specialty sandwiches, and salads, and doing business under the trade name Carl's Jr. Entrees range from traditional-style 'Star' and 'Super Star' burgers, to barbecued chicken with smoked hickory sauce. The menu also features such contemporary offerings as batter-fried zuccini and, for sit-down patrons, a well-stocked salad bar.

A typical outlet is situated in a retail shopping mall, strip center, or freestanding restaurant facility. In comparative market studies, Carl's Jr. consistently ranks near the top in consumer acceptance among fast-food outlets specializing in hamburger sandwiches.

Franchisee Profile: A background in the food and beverage business is helpful, but not mandatory. The company is seeking prospective franchisees with demonstrated business ability and keen entrepreneurial ambition. Absentee ownership is not prohibited, in the case of multiple-unit franchises.

Projected Earnings: A statement of projected earnings was not available at press time.

Franchisor's Services: Carl's Jr. provides a comprehensive training program, including one week at the company's headquarters in Anaheim, California. Attendees are responsible for their own travel and lodging expenses. Additional hands-on training is provided at an operating restaurant. The franchisor will assist with selecting a site for the outlet, overseeing construction and improvements, training employees, and planning Grand Opening promotions. When the retaurant is open for business, a Carl's Jr. representative will visit the outlet periodically, to offer ongoing guidance and troubleshooting.

Initial Investment: New Carl's Jr. franchisees should be prepared to handle a cash investment of $175,000 to open the restaurant. The amount includes the initial fee, site acquisition and improvements, equipment purchases, and miscellaneous start-up costs. The franchisor does not offer any direct financial assistance to franchisees.

Advertising: Carl's Jr. franchisees contribute four percent of their gross monthly revenues for advertising. The franchisor conducts national and regional campaigns on behalf of all outlets, using newspapers, radio, and television. Franchisees receive ad slicks, radio and television commercials, and point-of-sale materials.

Contract Highlights: The Carl's Jr. franchise has a 20-year term. On expiration, the contract may be renewed for an additional term, providing the franchisee is not in violation of any material provisions. The restaurant may not be sold or assigned to any other party, without the franchisor's approval.

Fees and Royalties: The $35,000 initial franchise fee is somewhat high for the industry. The three to four percent monthly royalty, added to the four percent advertising royalty, represents a total royalty burden of seven to eight percent of gross sales — about average for a well developed fast-food chain.

Summary: The Carl's Jr. franchise offers the competitive benefits of a rapidly growing organization with steadily increasing name recognition. Franchisees benefit from hands-on training, keen personal support, and favorable consumer acceptance.

Franchise Highlights

Began operating: 1956
Began franchising: 1984
Outlets currently open: 480
Initial franchise fee: $35,000
Monthly royalty: 3% to 4%
Advertising fee: 4%
Training program: 1 weeks
Term: 20 years

Church's Fried Chicken

Industry experience:	★ ★ ★ ★	*Franchising experience:*	★ ★ ★ ★
Financial strength:	★ ★	*Training & services:*	★ ★ ★ ★
Fees & royalties:	★ ★ ★	*Satisfied franchisees:*	★ ★ ★

Church's Fried Chicken, Inc.
P.O. Box 001
San Antonio, Texas 78284
(512) 735-9392

Church's has been serving its popular version of Southern fried chicken for more than 35 years. The 1960s and early 1970s were particularly profitable for the company, as its franchise organization swelled to over 1,000 outlets. But in 1986, Church's was thrown into turmoil by dramatic increases in poultry prices and the fact that most outlets were located in the economically troubled South. After a period of retrenchment, the company is currently pursuing a stable growth course. Only 20 percent of the 1,500 Church's Fried Chicken restaurants in the U.S., Canada, and 50 foreign countries are franchises.

The Franchise: The franchisee operates a quick-service restaurant specializing in fried chicken and doing business under the trade name Church's Fried Chicken. A typical outlet is located in a high-traffic inner-city area, cateirng to a a predominately blue-collar clientele. The outlet's 'back to basics' menu features a limited selection of large-portion, moderately-priced fried chicken entrees.

Franchisee Profile: Previous restaurant experience is preferred but not required. The franchisor is currently emphasizing the need for active management participation.

Projected Earnings: The franchisor will provide a written statement of projected earnings to prospective franchisees prior to the personal interview.

Franchisor Services: The company's franchising experience has made Church's sensitive to the franchisee's need for information and support. Franchisees are required to adhere strictly to the franchisor's site selection and construction standards.

A five-week training course in San Antonio, Texas includes two weeks of hands-on experience at an operating Church's outlet. The curriculum presumably covers all phases of restaurant operation, from sanitation to bookkeeping. The franchisor offers ongoing assistance with purchasing, inventory control, and accounting systems.

Initial Investment: Prospective franchisees should be prepared to invest between $100,000 and $200,000 to open a new restaurant. Church's does not offer direct financial assistance to franchisees on any part of the initial investment.

Fees and Royalties: The initial license fee is $15,000. The total royalty bite, including the monthly franchise royalty and the ongoing advertising fee, is ten percent of the gross sales of the restaurant.

Summary: As Church's regroups following the financial slump of 1986, co-founder David Bamberger is still in charge, advocating his old ideas with renewed energy — among them, a simplified menu, lower prices, and a return to active management.

Franchise Highlights

Began operating: 1952
Began franchising: 1952
Outlets currently open: 1,000
Initial franchise fee: $15,000
Monthly royalty: 5%
Advertising fee: 5%
Training program: 5 weeks
Term: 15 years

Dairy Queen

Industry experience:	★★★★	*Franchising experience:*	★★★★
Financial strength:	★★★★	*Training & services:*	★★★
Fees & royalties:	★★★★	*Satisfied franchisees:*	★★★

International Dairy Queen
5701 Green Valley Drive
Minneapolis, Minnesota 55437
(612) 830-0327

Dairy Queen sold its first soft-cream cone with a curly tip more than 35 years ago. Despite changing times and volatile consumer loyalties, the giant dessert franchise is still a formidable contender for the American sweet tooth. The company has successfully preserved its time-honored image, while quietly responding to new marketing demands. Although, Dairy Queen still offers its special low-fat ice cream, it has long-since enlarged its dessert menu. Some of the newer franchises offer non-dessert fast-foods. With 4,800 outlets worldwide, the company continues to seek new franchisees in most major markets.

The Franchise: International Dairy Queen outlets vary in size and indoor seating capacity, but most are free-standing establishments with convenient parking and efficient over-the-counter or window-ordering service. The company's blue and white trademark is most familiar in the Sunbelt, promising a refreshing selection of ice cream, cones, shakes, sundaes, parfaits, frozen drinks, and the 'Blizzard,' a candy and ice cream drink. At a Dairy Queen/Brazier, customers can order complete meals, in addition to dessert.

Franchisee Profile: Experience in restaurant management is helpful, but not mandatory.

Franchisor Services: Franchisees are trained in Minneapolis, Minnesota, receiving classroom instruction and hands-on observation at an operating Dairy Queen outlet. The curriculum covers personnel management, marketing techniques, food preparation, equipment operation, and sanitation. There is no cost for the training program, but travel and lodging expenses must be borne by the franchisee.

The company provides specifications for site selection and construction. For a fee, Dairy Queen will acquire a site and oversee the development of the restaurant. A week of on-site assistance is provided just before and during the grand opening.

All equipment and supplies must be purchased through the company's authorized vendors. A Dairy Queen affiliate offers a financing plan on restaurant equipment.

Fees and Royalties: The franchisee pays $30,000 for the franchise license, with the option of company financing over a five-year period. The franchisor exacts a four percent monthly franchise royalty.

Summary: International Dairy Queen offers the security of 35 years of successful franchise experience and a trade name recognized by virtually every child in America. The company predicts that outlet sales will increase system-wide.

Franchise Highlights

Began operating: 1940
Began franchising: 1944
Outlets currently open: 4,800
Initial franchise fee: $30,000
Monthly royalty: 4%
Advertising fee: 3% to 5%
Term: None

David's Cookies

Industry experience:	★★★	*Franchising experience:*	★★
Financial strength:	★★★	*Training & services:*	★★★
Fees & royalties:	★★★	*Satisfied franchisees:*	★★★★

David's Specialty Food Products
12 East 42nd Street
New York, NY 10017
(212) 682-0210

After graduating simultaneously from law college and cooking school, David Liederman set out for central France, where he caught on as a cook in a three-star restaurant. Three years later, he was back home in New York, writing a Nouvelle Cuisine cookbook. Chasing a dream of financial independence, he started a private sauce business and opened his own restaurant, the Manhattan Market. He opened his first cookie shop in 1979, to the rave reviews of New York food critics.

Today, Liederman is arguably the nation's cookie king, with nearly 200 outlets and $20 million in annual sales. His product and franchise, both named David's Cookies, have unquestionably benefited from his French-chef training and the fact that he uses only genuine Swiss chocolate from Lindt & Sprungli in Switzerland.

The Franchise: The franchisee conducts a retail baked goods business, specializing in chocolate chip cookies prepared with the franchisor's 'secret' dough, and doing business under the trade name David's Cookies. A typical outlet is situated in a suburban shopping mall, retail strip center, or an urban area with dense foot traffic. Besides a selection of soft, chewy chocolate chip cookies made from chemical-free ingredients, the store also offers a private line of David's ice cream, yoghurt, brownies, and beverages.

Franchisee Profile: Prospective franchisees need not be experienced bakers. Rather, the company focuses on business and management aptitudes.

Projected Earnings: Based on the company's annual sales, the average volume of a David's Cookies outlet is about $110,000 per year, before expenses. This figure does not take into consideration individual variables such as location or size of the outlet, and is not based on any projected earnings statement furnished by the franchisor. Pre-tax profits may range between ten and twenty percent.

Franchisor's Services: David's Cookies franchisees attend a training session at company headquarters in New York, where they receive hands-on experience in an operating cookie shop. The store's goods are baked from premade doughs supplied by the franchisor's manufacturing affiliates. The cooking takes place in specially designed, computerized ovens. Franchisees are obligated to purchase all equipment and supplies from David's Cookies and/or its designated vendors.

Initial Investment: New franchisees should be prepared to invest about $125,000. The total amount includes initial franchise fee, lease deposits, site improvements, equipment purchases, supplies, and working capital. The franchisor does not offer any direct financial assistance to franchisees.

Advertising: David's Cookies does not charge any monthly advertising fee. The primary marketing thrust is at the point of sale, where customers are ostensibly lured by the aroma of freshly baked cookies and brownies.

Fees and Royalties: The initial franchise fee of $25,000 is high for the fast-food industry, but franchisees do not pay a monthly franchise royalty. The franchisor derives profits from the sale of dough and supplies to franchisees.

Summary: Annual sales as high as $500,000 have been reported by some outlets. However, the company is currently focusing on small shops with a diversified product line. In the last five years, numerous competitors have taken bites from the $3 billion retail cookie market, creating an atmosphere of intense competition. David's Cookies ranks near the top of the field in both number of outlets and per-unit profitability.

Franchise Highlights

Began operating: 1979
Began franchising: 1983
Outlets currently open: 190
Initial franchise fee: $25,000

Monthly royalty: None
Advertising fee: None
Training program: Varies

Denny's

Industry experience:	★ ★ ★ ★	*Franchising experience:*	★ ★ ★
Financial strength:	★ ★ ★ ★	*Training & services:*	★ ★ ★
Fees & royalties:	★ ★ ★	*Satisfied franchisees:*	★ ★ ★

Dennys', Inc.
16700 Valley View Avenue
La Mirada, California
(714) 739-8100

Denny's is one of the largest roadside restaurant chains in the country, with more than 1,200 company-owned outlets. The company began first began offering franchises to independent restaurateurs in 1984.

The Franchise: The franchisee operates a family-style restaurant, under the trade name Denny's. A typical outlet is situated in a 3,500 sq. ft. free-standing site with ample visibility from a high-traffic thoroughfare or intersection. The menu features a wide selection of coffee-shop meals and entrees, including breakfast, lunch, dinner, and special promotional fare.

Franchisee Profile: Denny's awards preference to prospective franchisees with a background in the food and beverage trade. The company is seeking prospective franchisees with strong financial credentials.

Projected Earnings: A statement of projected earnings was not available at press time.

Franchisor's Services: Denny's franchisees receive training at the company's headquarters in La Mirada, California, near Los Angeles. Attendees are responsible for their own travel and lodging expenses. The program includes three days of on-site training.

Initial Investment: The total investment may range as high as $750,000, including site acquisition, construction, fixtures, equipment purchases, signs, supplies, and working capital. Direct financial assistance is available to qualified franchisees.

Advertising: Denny's franchisees pay an advertising fee equal to two percent of their gross monthly revenues. The franchisor conducts aggressive national and regional campaigns on behalf of all Denny's company-owned and franchised outlets. Target media include radio, television, and newspaper. Franchisees also receive support with local ad campaigns.

Contract Highlights: The Denny's franchise has a term of 20 years — twice the national average. On expiration, the contract may be renewed if the franchisee is in compliance with all material provisions. The franchise may not be sold, transfered, or otherwise assigned to another party without the franchisor's express consent.

Fees and Royalties: The initial franchise fee of $35,000 is high for the food-service industry, but the franchisee's total royalty obligation is a moderate six percent of gross revenues.

Summary: Denny's franchisees enjoy the name recognition and competitive benefits of one of the largest restaurant chains in North America. Foremost among these values are an aggressive advertising program and thorough industry training.

Franchise Highlights

Began operating: 1953
Began franchising: 1984
Outlets currently open: 1,300
Initial franchise fee: $35,000
Monthly royalty: 4%
Advertising fee: 2%
Training program: As required
Term: 20 years

D'Lites

Industry experience: ★★★
Financial strength: ★★
Fees & royalties: ★★★
Franchising experience: ★★
Training & services: ★★★
Satisfied franchisees: ★★

D'Lites of America, Inc.
6075 The Corners Parkway
Suite 200
Norcross, Georgia 30092
(404) 448-0654

Douglas N. Sheley opened the first D'Lites restaurant in Atlanta, Georgia in 1981. Specializing in 'lite' versions of mainstream American fast-food, his idea was to offer standard culinary fare with reduced fat and cholestorol. For example, D'Lites boasts a hamburger that contains five to 19 percent less cholesterol than the average fast-food burger and is served on a high-fiber bun with 25 percent fewer calories. The first fast-food hamburger franchise to specialize in healthful meals, the company grew overnight to number 100 franchises in 19 states scattered throughout the Midwest and southeastern Sunbelt.

The Franchise: D'Lites restaurants are designed to attract an upscale clientele. The cedar decor is light and airy, with indoor and outdoor dining on wooden tables and chairs, accented by an abundance of green plants and windows. The menu features classic American cuisine prepared with reduced calories. A typical meal might consist of a low-cal cheeseburger, baked potato, and a sugar-free soft drink. The outlet also offers more esoteric items, such as pita-bread vegetarian sandwichs and frozen yoghurt desserts.

Franchisee Profile: Prospective franchisees must have some previous experience in restaurant operations. Multiple-unit ownership is encouraged.

Projected Earnings: A statement of projected earnings was not available at press time.

Franchisor's Services: The company requires that new franchisees and two managers from each franchise outlet attend a six-week training program at the company's headquarters in Atlanta, Georgia. The curriculum covers food preparation, financial controls, market analysis, and promotional techniques.

The franchisee may choose from four possible outlet designs. All supplies and equipment may be purchased from either D'Lite's contracted distributors or other vendors that meet the franchisor's specifications and standards. Franchisees are eligible for purchasing discounts through D'Lites' national account purchasing system.

Initial Investment: The company requires that prospective franchisees be able to document at least $150,000 in liquid assets. Estimated capital expenditures for the first year range from $740,000 to $1,000,000. D'Lites does not offer any direct financial assistance to franchisees.

Advertising: In the past, D'Lites franchisees were obligated to spend four percent of their gross monthly revenues on local advertising campaigns. In a recent policy switch, the franchisor instituted a one percent ad royalty to fund a new national advertising program.

Fees and Royalties: The initial franchise fee is $15,000, plus another $20,000 for each franchise purchased. The minimum purchase is four outlets. In an attempt to boost morale among franchisees, D'Lites recently lowered the monthly royalty from four percent to two percent.

Disputes and Litigation: In 1986, a number of franchisees voiced complaints over company funds spent to 'bail out insiders.' The franchisor had bought back failing franchises owned by past D'Lite president Doug Sheley and his brother Darrel. The outlets were repurchased at their original cost, even though their market value had ostensibly declined. The total buyback amounted to nearly $3 million.

Summary: The company's current expansion focus is on multiple-unit ownership. According to an independent source, a new franchisee should be prepared to sustain the business with working capital for a period of three to five years.

Franchise Highlights

Began operating: 1981
Began franchising: 1982
Outlets currently open: 100
Initial franchise fee: $35,000
Monthly royalty: 2%
Advertising fee: 1%
Training program: 6 weeks
Term: 20 years

Domino's Pizza

Industry experience:	★ ★ ★	*Franchising experience:*	★ ★ ★
Financial strength:	★ ★ ★ ★	*Training & services:*	★ ★ ★
Fees & royalties:	★ ★ ★	*Satisfied franchisees:*	★ ★ ★ ★

Domino's Pizza, Inc.
Prairie House, Domino's Farms
30 Frank Lloyd Wright Drive
P.O. Box 997
Ann Arbor, Michigan 48104-0997
(313) 668-6055

Thomas Monaghan was an architecture student at the University of Michigan, when he scraped together $900 to buy a pizza restaurant named Dominick's, near the Michigan campus. His funds were so sparse, he had to sleep on a pizza table in the back of the restaurant. Today, 20 years later, he heads the largest pizza home-delivery operation in the world. He attributes his phenomenal success to finding the right niche in the competitive pizza market — free home delivery. The road wasn't been entirely free of pitfalls for Monaghan; he faced bankruptcy on four different occasions. At one point, he was involved in a multimillion dollar lawsuit over the Domino trade name. Yet, Domino's sales have been increasing at an annual rate of 40 percent since 1978, and his franchise system has bulged to 2,800 outlets in 48 states. Monaghan's goal is 5,000 franchises.

The Franchise: The franchisee operates a pizza delivery service, under the trade name Domino's Pizza. A typical outlet is situated in a moderate-rent site with low overhead. Pizzas are prepared in two sizes with a variety of toppings. Franchisees guarantee their customers 30-minute delivery. The product is kept warm inside delivery vehicles with specially installed ovens.

Franchisee Profile: The company looks for prospective franchisees with enthusiastic entrepreneurial qualities and a sound financial record. Many of the company's existing franchisees started out as delivery drivers. The average age of a Domino's franchisee is 23.

Projected Earnings: According to one source, a typical Domino's franchisee generates about $8,000 per week in gross revenues. Net profits are said to average about 15 percent.

Franchisor Services: A training program is held in Ann Arbor, Michigan, where new franchisees receive instruction in pizza preparation, inventory control, accounting, promotion, and management. Part of the training takes place in a local Domino's outlet.

Before the business opens, a Domino's representative will handle the the new franchise's promotional and advertising campaigns. The company supplies guidelines and assistance in site acquisition and construction, and provides specialized equipment and signs. Ongoing supplies must be purchased from distributors that meet the franchisor's standards and specifications.

Initial Investment: The minimum cash requirement is $60,000. The total capital investment could run as high as $135,000.

Advertising: Domino's franchisees contribute two percent of their gross weekly sales for advertising. The franchisor actively promotes the company in national television campaigns. Monaghan's personal eccentricities account for at least part of the franchise's widespread publicity. Monaghan purchased the Detroit Tigers in 1984 and later constructed a 'Leaning Tower of Pizza' as part of his Ann Arbor headquarters.

Fees and Royalties: The initial franchise fee ranges from $1,300 to $3,250. An additional 'grand opening' deposit of $3,000 is required for the first outlet. The monthly royalty is paid weekly, based on 5.5 percent of the gross sales of the outlet.

Disputes and Litigation: In 1980, Domino's was sued by Amstar Corporation, which claimed that the franchisor was infringing on the trademark of Domino-brand sugar. The court ruled in favor of Domino's pizza, determining that the similarity is unlikely to cause confusion between the two products.

Summary: Since 1970, the demand for pizza has grown faster than any other segment of the fast-food market. Domino's offers a low-overhead business format with a modest startup investment.

Franchise Highlights

Began operating: 1960
Began franchising: 1967
Outlets currently open: 2,800
Initial franchise fee: Min. $1,300
Max. $3,250

Monthly royalty: 5.5%
Advertising fee: 3%
Term: 10 years

Dunkin' Donuts

Industry experience:	★★★★	*Franchising experience:*	★★★★
Financial strength:	★★★★	*Training & services:*	★★★★
Fees & royalties:	★★★	*Satisfied franchisees:*	★★★★

Dunkin' Donuts of America, Inc.
P.O. Box 317
Randolph, MA 02368
(617) 961-4000

Meticulous quality control, marketing expertise, and creative advertising have made Dunkin' Donuts a favorite fast-food stop for millions of sweet-toothed Americans. Dunkin' Donuts first hung out its orange and raspberry sign in 1950, making it a franchise trademark in 1956. Today, the company operates more than a thousand donut shops in 39 states.

The Franchise: The franchisee operates a fast-food service specializing in donuts and coffee, and doing business under the trade Dunkin' Donuts. A typical outlet has four full-time and eight part-time employees and is open for business 24 hours a day. Dunkin' Donuts has carefully cultivated a standardized image in both building design and product. Outlets sell donuts, coffee, and bakery items selected by the franchisor's market research team. Each shop makes its own bakery goods from ingredients that undergo rigorous quality control inspection. All products sold by the outlet must be approved by the franchisor.

Franchisee Profile: Qualified applicants need not be experienced bakers or business entrepreneurs.

Franchisor's Services: A four-week training program in Saint Paul, Minnesota provides comprehensive instruction in the daily operation of a Dunkin' Donuts restaurant. The curriculum covers marketing, inventory control, purchasing, employee relations, and production methods.

Regional representatives provide on-site training and guidance, from Grand Opening to staff hiring. Dunkin' Donuts employs more than a thousand consultants to administer and support franchise operations.

Initial Investment: The total cash investment is estimated at between $110,000 and $544,000, including the initial franchise fee, site acquisition, improvements, fixtures, equipment, supplies, and miscellaneous startup costs. Dunkin' Donuts has a financial assistance program for qualified franchisees.

Fees and Royalties: The initial franchise license runs between $20,000 and $40,000, depending upon the location and size of the outlet. Monthly royalty payments are moderate — an ongoing franchise royalty of 4.9 percent, plus five percent for advertising.

Summary: The Dunkin' Donuts franchise offers the administrative and marketing sophistication of one of the most experienced franchisors in the donut/coffee shop trade. The initial investment is steep, but the franchise fees and royalties are reasonable for an organization of this stature. The company's focus on quality and standardization maintains a high level of uniformity and positive imaging througout the franchise system. On the opposite side of that coin, franchisees must be prepared to sacrifice some measure of independence in return for the competitive benefits.

Franchise Highlights

Began operating: 1950
Began franchising: 1956
Outlets currently open: 1,350
Initial franchise fee: Min. $30,000
Max. $40,000

Monthly royalty: 4.5%
Advertising fee: 4%
Training program: 6 weeks
Term: 20 years

Everything Yoghurt

Industry experience:	★ ★ ★	*Franchising experience:*	★ ★
Financial strength:	★ ★ ★	*Training & services:*	★ ★ ★
Fees & royalties:	★ ★ ★ ★	*Satisfied franchisees:*	★ ★ ★

Everything Yoghurt
304 Port Richmond Ave.
Staton Island, New York 10302
(718) 816-7800

Of the numerous yoghurt restaurants built on the wave of the 1970s health-food mania, Everything Yoghurt is arguably the most competitive today. As the number of outlets approaches 100, the company is pursuing expansion from its predominately Eastern base to the Midwest and West.

The Franchise: The franchisee operates a fast-food stand specializing in yoghurt products, and doing business under the trade name Everything Yoghurt. A typical outlet is located in a shopping mall or retail strip center and features frozen yoghurt, desserts, and drinks, as well as a full-scale dinner menu. Entrees include salads, vegetable dishes, quiches, and pasta, all prepared with yoghurt. EY's Chef Salad is a chicken salad mixed with various fresh greens and marinated in a mustard and poppy seed dressing. A yoghurt snack bar designed to attract mall shoppers is also available.

Franchisee Profile: Prior food and beverage experience is considered beneficial but not mandatory.

Franchisor Services: The franchisor conducts a seven-day training program at an operating Everything Yoghurt outlet. Prior to opening, a company representative supervises site selection, outlet design, and construction. Some equipment and most food supplies must be purchased from the franchisor's designated vendors. Franchisees receive copies of the confidential Everything Yoghurt operations manual, containing the franchisor's documented policies and procedures.

Initial Investment: The total investment is estimated at from $125,000 to $175,000, including the initial franchise fee, lease deposits, site improvements, fixtures, equipment, and supplies. EY does not offer any form of direct financial assistance to franchisees.

Advertising: EY franchisees contribute one percent of their gross sales for advertising. The ad contributions are pooled to fund radio, television, and newspaper campaigns.

Fees and Royalties: The intial franchise fee is $25,000, decidedly high for both fast-food restaurants and yoghurt franchises. An additional $5,000 fee applies for a Bananas mall kiosk purchased in conjunction with an Everything Yoghurt franchise. The franchise for a standalone Bananas kiosk is $15,000. The five percent monthly royalty and one percent advertising contribution are both moderate.

Summary: It would appear that two important factors have enabled Everything Yoghurt to compete favorably in a market burgeoning with contenders: the fact that its restaurants offer full meal service, in addition to the standard yoghurt fare, and an emphasis on dining room decor and food presentation.

Franchise Highlights

Began operating: 1976	**Monthly royalty: 5%**
Began franchising: 1982	**Advertising fee: None**
Outlets currently open: 100	**Training program: 7 days**
Initial franchise fee: $20,000	**Term: 10 years**

Gelato Classico Italian Ice Cream

Industry experience:	★★★	*Franchising experience:*	★★
Financial strength:	★★	*Training & services:*	★★
Fees & royalties:	★★★	*Satisfied franchisees:*	★★★★

Gelato Classico Italian Ice Cream
369 Pine St., Suite 90
San Francisco, California 94104
(415) 433-3111

Gelato Classico Italian Ice Cream caters to the American appetite for rich, premium, buttery-tasting ice cream. A San Francisco favorite for more than a decade, Gelato's special blend combines a creamy texture with a subtle Italian taste, in an esoteric range of gourmet flavors.

The Franchise: The franchisee operates a retail ice cream parlor, marketing the franchisor's private brand of ice cream. The outlet does business under the trade name Gelato Classico Italian Ice Cream. A typical parlor is less than 1,000 sq. ft. in size, tastefully decorated to attract an upscale clientele. Twenty different ice cream flavors may be offered at any given time, including such purported delicacies as Coppa Mista, (a rich blend of natural vanilla, chocolate, and pistachio), Joseph Saint-Almond, Banana Walnut, and Crema di Limone. Besides ice cream, most outlets also serve expresso coffee, tea, and soft drinks.

Franchisee Profile: Previous experience in the restaurant business is considered helpful, but not mandatory. The company is actively seeking new franchisees in the eastern U.S., Hawaii, Canada, and the Far East.

Franchisor Services: The franchisor provides a one-week training program in San Francisco, California. The tuition for the program is included in the initial franchise fee, but the franchisee is responsible for travel and lodging expenses.

The franchisee is responsible for selecting, securing, and building out the site, in accordance with the franchisor's specifications and standards. A confidential operations manual documents policies and procedures for efficiently running the business. A field adviser visits each Gelato store periodically to inspect the site and offer counsel, as required.

Initial Investment: New franchisees should be prepared to invest between $100,000 and $150,000 to open a new parlor. The amount includes site acquisition, improvements, fixtures, equipment, signs, opening inventory, and working capital. Gelato offers financial assistance to qualified franchisees.

Advertising: At press time, there was no monthly advertising fee, although the franchisor suggests that future plans include a national ad campaign that might require imposition of a two percent monthly ad royalty. Franchisees are responsible for their own promotions. The franchisor supplies guidelines and examples of newspaper and Yellow Pages ads.

Fees and Royalties: The initial franchise fee of $25,000 is high for the industry, but Gelato franchisees do not pay any monthly royalties. The franchisor derives profits from the sale of ice cream.

Summary: Gelato is a young but aggressive franchise organization catering to the upscale market for premium-brand ice cream. The franchisor offers training, inventory support, and an easy-to-operate business motif.

Franchise Highlights

Began operating: 1976
Began franchising: 1982
Outlets currently open: 35
Initial franchise fee: $25,000
Monthly royalty: None
Advertising fee: 1% to 2%
Training program: 1 week
Term: 10 years

Hardee's Food Systems, Inc.

Industry experience: ★ ★ ★ ★ *Franchising experience:* ★ ★ ★ ★
Financial strength: ★ ★ ★ ★ *Training & services:* ★ ★ ★
Fees & royalties: ★ ★ ★ ★ *Satisfied franchisees:* ★ ★ ★ ★

Hardee's Food Systems, Inc.
1233 N. Church St
Rocky Mount, North Carolina
27802 (919) 977-2000

Nick and Bayo Boddie are the offspring of a North Carolina tobacco farmer who lost his land in the Depression era. Together with an old high school buddy, the two brothers built the first Hardee's restaurant in Rocky Mount in 1960, selling 15-cent charcoal-broiled hamburgers. The charcoal broiling part was the idea of a restaurateur named Wilbur Hardee, who had sold the concept to the Boddie boys and their parnter, Jim Gardner.

Today, Hardee's Food Systems, Inc. is currently working hard to satiate a big appetite for expansion. The company was purchased by a Canadian conglomerate, Imasco Ltd., in 1981. With a fresh cash infusion, Hardee's purchased the 650-unit Burger Chef chain from General Foods Corp. in 1982. Since then, the company has expanded rapidly to 2,800 franchise restaurants in 40 states and nine foreign countries. Hardee's plans to add another 300 restaurants every year, moving into new territory in Texas, Ohio, New York, Pennsylvania, Louisiana, Michigan, and Colorado.

The Franchise: The franchise operates a fast-food restaurant specializing in hamburgers and sandwiches, with a moderate seating capacity, drive-through ordering and take-out service. Most franchises are located in small blue-collar towns; a majority of Hardee's outlets are situated in the southeastern states.

The menu reflects a successful reconciliation of economic and marketing goals, by limiting selection size to maintain cost effectiveness, while offering enough diversity to satisfy the tastes of today's fast-food consumer. Hot Ham 'N' Cheese sandwiches and Mushroom 'N' Swiss Burgers share the bill with more traditional fare like 'plain' hamburgers and Hardee's own Big Roast Beef Sandwich. Some outlets also offer a breakfast menu.

Franchisee Profile: Hardee's prefers to sell multi-unit franchise packages, but will consider licensing single units to qualified owner/operators. Ten-outlet packages are common. The largest franchisee, Boddie-Noel Enterprises, owns 208 outlets in five states.

Projected Earnings: According to the company's reported sales, the average volume of a Hardee's outlet is about $800,000 per year, before deducting operating expenses.

Franchisor Services: Hardee's strives to allow franchisees a measure of entrepreneurial freedom, within the constraints of the franchisor's operating standards and guidelines. For instance, construction materials must adhere to the franchisor's specifications, but the franchisee may exercise personal creativity in designing and decorating the interior. Hardee's does require that franchisees purchase most of their foodstuffs from the company's distribution affiliate, Fast Food Merchandisers, Inc.

Franchisees receive training in four weeks at a regional center, undergoing both hands-on and classroom instruction in all facets of restaurant management. Company representatives lend their expertise during the crucial period startup period. A Hardee's field advisor visits the restaurant periodically to offer ongoing guidance.

Initial Investment: A prospective franchisee must have at least $150,000 in liquid assets. The total startup requirement is estimated at between $633,000 and $1.22 million. The investment is broken down as follows:

	Low	High
Initial franchise fee	$15,000	15,000
Land	150,000	400,000
Construction	185,000	270,000
Improvements	60,000	250,000
Equipment	197,400	250,700
Miscellaneous	25,000	35,000
Total	632,900	1,220,700

Advertising: To support the company's expansion program, the company is planning an aggressive national ad campaign. Hardee's franchisees contribute five percent of their gross monthly sales for advertising.

Fees and Royalties: The intitial franchise fee is $15,000. The four percent monthly franchise royalty is moderate for the fast-food trade. Including the advertising fee, the total royalty bite is nine percent of gross monthly revenues.

Summary: Hardee's game plan is to transform its small town appeal into a big city image. Franchisees benefit from ample name recognition and the competitive benefits of an expansive network of established franchisees.

Franchise Highlights

Began operating: 1960
Began franchising: 1962
Outlets currently open: 2,800
Initial franchise fee: $15,000

Monthly royalty: 3.5% to 4%
Advertising fee: 5%
Training program: 4 weeks
Term: 20 years

Hickory Farms of Ohio

Industry experience:	★★★★	*Franchising experience:*	★★★★
Financial strength:	★★★	*Training & services:*	★★★★
Fees & royalties:	★★★	*Satisfied franchisees:*	★★★★

Hickory Farms of Ohio, Inc.
P.O. Box 219
Maumee, Ohio 43537
(419) 893-7611

Hickory Farms of Ohio, Inc., a subsidiary of General Host Corporation, has been selling its specialty foods since 1926. The company began franchising in 1960, but still owns and operates slightly more than half of the Hickory Farms retail stores open today. Gradual changes in American taste spurred demand for Hickory Farms products, providing an impetus for franchise expansion. The company is currently seeking new franchisees in most areas of the U.S. and Canada.

The Franchise: The franchisee operates a retail food store focusing on three product categories: specialty, traditional, and gift foods. The outlet is allowed some flexibility in marketing, but any food items sold by a Hickory Farms retail store must meet with the franchisor's appoval. The franchisee offers a selection of known and exotic cheeses, meats, crackers, old-fashioned candies, nuts, fruit preserves, and beef-stick sausage.

A typical outlet is located in a shopping mall or retail strip center, with a staff of 15 full-time and ten part-time employees. The store is decorated to project an ambience of country harvest time. During the Christmas holiday season, Hickory Farms erects temporary sales kiosks to market an extended line of gift packages. Kiosks may be operated from a franchise outlet or as a short-term franchise at a reduced fee.

The Franchisee Profile: The company places no restrictions on applicants with regard to background or experience. However, some related experience in food merchandising is helpful.

Franchisor's Services: In most instances, franchises choose their sites from a selection of locations pre-developed by Hickory Farms. The franchisee who opts to develop a new retail store will receive assistance with site selection, lease negotiation, interior buildout, and decoration.

The franchise training program takes place in Maumee, Ohio. Hickory Farms picks up the tab for travel expenses and lodging. The one-week program covers retail operations, inventory planning, food merchandising, business management, and advertising. An additional week of on-site training coincides with the store opening.

A field representative visits each store to provide periodic on-site assistance. The franchisor's central purchasing system supplies the franchisee with a controlled inventory of products at competitive prices.

Initial Investment: New franchisees should be able to handle a cash investment of $215,000. Including working capital requirements, a new startup may run as high as $327,000. Hickory Farms does not offer any form of financial assistance to franchisees.

Advertising: Hickory Farms operates a national advertising co-op funded by franchisee monthly royalty contributions. As part of the program, each franchisee is required to conduct a nine-week specialized advertising campaign on opening.

Fees and Royalties: The initial franchise fee of $20,000 covers all opening support services. The six percent monthly franchise royalty, added to the six percent advertising royalty, exacts a total of 12 percent of the gross revenues of the outlet.

Contract Highlights: The contact term is ten years. The franchisee receives an exclusive territory for the business, guaranteeing that no other Hickory Farms store will be opened in within the designated boundaries while the contract is in effect. However, the franchisee receives no area or subfranchising rights whatsoever. Absentee ownership is prohibited; the individual who is awarded the franchise is personally responsible for managing the business.

Summary: Hickory Farms of Ohio is a well-established retailer riding the crest of increased popular demand for specialty foods. The franchise organization has enjoyed steady growth, enabling the company to increase its support services to franchisees.

Franchise Highlights

Began operating: 1926	**Monthly royalty: 6%**
Began franchising: 1960	**Advertising fee: 6%**
Outlets currently open: 570	**Training program: 1 week**
Initial franchise fee: $20,000	**Term: Variable**

Jack in the Box

Industry experience:	★ ★ ★ ★	*Franchising experience:*	★ ★
Financial strength:	★ ★ ★ ★	*Training & services:*	★ ★ ★
Fees & royalties:	★ ★ ★ ★	*Satisfied franchisees:*	★ ★ ★

Foodmaker Inc.
P.O. Box 783
San Diego, California 92112
(619) 571-2288

Jack in the Box, the fifth largest hamburger chain in the United States, opened its first fast-food restaurant 35 years ago, but did not begin selling franchises until the early 1980s. Since 1951, the chain has proliferated throughout the western U.S., with 750 company-operated units and 100 franchises.

The Franchise: The franchisee operates a fast-food restaurant characterized by a limited menu and drive-through facilities, doing business under the trade name Jack in the Box. The franchisor stresses the importance of market research in the fast-food trade. Jack in the Box restaurants cater to young working adults — the segment of the population that most frequently patronizes fast-food establishments. The menu reflects the changing tastes of the American public, offering tacos, chicken sandwiches, salads, and specialty meals, in addition to the time-honored fare of hamburgers and fries.

Franchisee Profile: Jack in the Box does not restrict applicants to those with restaurant experience, but the franchisor considers previous business experience to be important. A franchisee must live within an hour's commute time of the prospective site. Partnerships are considered.

Franchisor's Services: Jack in the Box field consultants assist with selecting a site for the restaurant and supervise construction. Outlets must adhere to a standardized building standard and decor package. Existing Jack in the Box outlets may be leased from the company at favorable terms.

A mandatory six-week training program is held at the Foodmaker Management Institute in San Diego, California. New franchisees are taught all aspects of operating a Jack in the Box restaurant. The training covers food preparation, personnel relations, marketing analysis, accounting, inventory control, and advertising and promotion.

The franchisor's ongoing services include central purchasing, inventory assistance, brochures, and a franchisee hotline. A Jack in the Box field representative inspects each franchise outlet periodically to verify compliance with the company's operating procedures and performance standards.

Initial Investment: Franchisees must invest from $190,000 to $3090,000 to establish a new restaurant. Jack in the Box does not offer direct financial assistance but will help the franchisee obtain a loan from a third party lender.

Advertising: Franchisees contribute four percent of gross monthly sales to fund advertising. Outlets benefit from extensive national advertising campaigns, including regional television commercials, newspaper ads, and special promotions.

Fees and Royalties: The initial franchise fee is $25,000. The monthly royalty starts out at two percent of gross monthly sales, rising to four percent after two years.

Contract Highlights: The term of the franchise is 20 years. The franchisee receives a protected terrritory. Expansion and subfranchising rights are available under a separate agreement. The company expects the franchisee to actively participate in the operation of the restaurant. The outlet must be operated in strict compliance with the franchisor's operating procedures, quality standards, and product specifications. The franchise cannot be sold or transferred without the franchisor's consent. The purchaser must meet all the qualifications of a Jack in the Box franchisee and assume all the obligations, duties, and responsibilities stipulated by the franchise agreement.

Summary: Jack-in-the-Box is one of the most recognizable names in fast-food service and, including company-operated and franchise restaurants, holds a significant share of the market. Jack in the Box only recently opened its doors to franchisees and plans an aggressive expansion program aimed at establishing independently owned outlets, backed by the company's trademarks and resources.

Franchise Highlights

Began operating: 1951
Began franchising: 1982
Outlets currently open: 850
Initial franchise fee: $25,000
Monthly royalty: 2% to 4%
Advertising fee: 4%
Training program: 8 weeks
Term: 20 years

Kentucky Fried Chicken

Industry experience:	★ ★ ★ ★	*Franchising experience:*	★ ★ ★ ★
Financial strength:	★ ★ ★ ★	*Training & services:*	★ ★ ★ ★
Fees & royalties:	★ ★ ★	*Satisfied franchisees:*	★ ★ ★ ★

Kentucky Fried Chicken
1441 Gardiner Lane
Louisville, Kentucky 40218
(502) 456-8300

The world's largest Kentucky Fried Chicken restaurant opened recently in Beijing, China, on a corner of Tian An Men Square, within view of the Gate of Heavenly Peace. At the Grand Opening ceremonies, the three-story, 500-seat fast-food establishment was heralded as 'the start of the new China.' Faithfully reproducing the atmosphere, decor, and menu of more than 9,000 other Kentucky Fried Chicken outlets worldwide, the new Beijing restaurant bears witness — for better or worse — to the phenomenal cultural influence of franchising on the modern world.

Since Colonel Harland Sanders served up his first golden-fried drumstick in 1939, Kentucky Fried Chicken has become one of the most recognizable names in food service. Colonel Sanders began franchising in 1952, opening an average of nearly 200 restaurants every year in North America alone. Three fourths of the Kentucky Fried Chicken eateries operating in the United States today are franchised outlets. The company is presently owned by Pepsico, which also operates 7,500 Taco Bell and Pizza Hut outlets. New Kentucky Fried Chicken franchises in North America are hard to come by, but the company still accepts applications from minority entrepreneurs, and from others wishing to be considered when existing sites may be offered for resale in the future.

The Franchise: The franchisee operates a retail fast-food restaurant specializing in chicken presumably prepared according to Colonel Sander's original secret recipe. The outlet does business under the registered trade name Kentucky Fried Chicken. All restaurants adhere closely to the franchisor's designs and specifications for layout, decor, quality of ingredients, and food preparation. The franchisee purchases supplies from the franchisor's designated vendors.

Franchisee Profile: A background in fast-food retailing or related business experience is preferred. Applicants must normally demonstrate liquid assets of at least $125,000 and a net worth of $350,000 or more. Absentee ownership is prohibited. The company considers only prospective franchisees who are willing to assume personal responsibility for managing the business. Kentucky Fried Chicken has an excellent track record in supporting minority members who want to own their own restaurants.

Projected Earnings: According to one source, Kentucky Fried Chicken considers any franchise successful if it earns $500,000 per year. Some existing outlets have reported annual earnings as high as $1 to $2 million. These figures are not based on any written projected earnings claim furnished by the franchisor.

Franchisor's Services: Kentucky Fried Chicken franchisor provides an intensive three-week training program at the company's headquarters in Louisville, Kentucky. The tuition is included in the initial franchise fee, but attendees are responsible for most of their own travel expenses. The company contributes $75 per person for lodging and meals, for a maximum of two attendees. The curriculum covers every aspect of operating a Kentucky Fried outlet, from sanitary systems to bookkeeping. An employee training program is available at additional cost.

A franchise representative will visit the restaurant periodically, to inspect the outlet and offer ongoing guidance and troubleshooting. Kentucky Fried Chicken operates a centralized purchasing system for supplies and equipment, and works closely with the company's designated vendors to assure favorable pricing and delivery for franchisees. The franchisor publishes a monthly franchisee newsletter and conducts frequent seminars and workshops. The company's rigid performance standards for food preparation, sanitation, and daily operations are documented in a confidential franchise manual.

Initial Investment: New franchisees should be prepared to handle an investment of $360,000 or more. The total includes the initial franchise fee, site acquisition and construction, fixtures and equipment, supplies, miscellaneous start-up costs, and working capital. Kentucky Fried Chicken does not offer any direct financial assistance to franchisees.

Advertising: Franchisees contribute between two and five percent of gross monthly revenues for advertising. The franchisor conducts widespread national, regional, and local campaigns on behal of all Kentucky Fried Chicken restaurants, using television, radio, newspapers, magazines, and direct mail.

Contract Highlights: The term of the franchise is 20 years — twice the national average. The franchisee is required to personally manage the outlet. Supplies must be purchased from the franchisor's designated vendors. The restaurant may not be sold, transferred, or assigned by the franchisee.

Fees and Royalties: The initial franchise fee usually ranges between $20,000 and $50,000 - not unreasonable for a franchise of this stature and maturity. The four percent monthly royalty is moderate, but including the five percent advertising fee, the total royalty bite is nine percent of gross sales.

Disputes and Litigation: In a famous 1977 court case, Kentucky Fried Chicken was sued by a packaging distributor who claimed that the franchisor had no right to restrict franchisees from buying supplies from any vendor of their own choosing. The court ruled in favor of the franchisor's right to approve the suppliers from whom franchisees purchase supplies.

Summary: Pepsico is currently the largest franchisor in the fast-food industry, with more than 15,000 Kentucky Fried Chicken, Taco Bell, and Pizza Hut outlets. A Kentucky Fried Chicken restaurant is one of the most coveted franchises in the world. Franchisees benefit from superior brand identification, high-profile advertising, thorough training, and the competitive benefits of an industry giant. The company deserves high marks for its recent expansion program aimed at recruiting new minority franchisees.

Franchise Highlights

Began operating: 1930
Began franchising: 1956
Outlets currently open: 9,300
Initial franchise fee: Min. $20,000
Max. $50,000

Monthly royalty: 4%
Advertising fee: 5%
Training program: 3 weeks
Term: 20 years

Long John Silver's

Industry experience: ★ ★ ★ ★ *Franchising experience:* ★ ★ ★ ★
Financial strength: ★ ★ ★ ★ *Training & services:* ★ ★ ★
Fees & royalties: ★ ★ ★ *Satisfied franchisees:* ★ ★ ★

Long John Silver's, Inc.
P.O. Box 11988
Lexington, Kentucky 40579
(606) 268-2000

Styled after an old English fish and chips shop, Long John Silver's restaurants feature an assortment of marine regale to diners in 37 states. The popularity of this 18-year-old subsidiary of Jerrico, Inc. is evidenced by the company's 1,300 outlets in major U.S. markets, Canada, and six foreign countries. The franchisor is currently seeking new franchisees in all U.S. regions.

The Franchise: The franchisee operates a fast-food restaurant specializing in seafood prepared in accordance with the franchisor's specifications and standards, and doing business under the trade name Long John Silver's Seafood Shoppes. An average outlet is located in a 2,650 site in a shopping mall, strip center, or office building, with 15 full-time and five part-time employees. A typical meal at Long John Silver's is a crispy, breaded fish fillet served on a sesame roll, with a side order of french fried potaotes and cole slaw. The menu also features fried shrimp, clams, oysters and scallops. A state-of-the-art food preparation system utilizes computers for timing and inventory control.

Franchisor Profile: Previous experience in the food and beverage industry is beneficial, but not mandatory.

Franchisor Services: The initial training program is divided into two parts. First, the franchisee is required to attend instructional seminars at the company headquarters in Lexington, Kentucky, to learn the basics of restaurant management. The curriculum includes the operation of the franchisor's proprietary computer system. The second part of the training program takes place at the franchisee's site, where Long John Silver's consultants go over the franchisor's daily operating procedures. The company's management training program is accredited by the American Council on Education.

The advisory team remains on-site through the grand opening, assisting with the recruitment and hiring of personnel, staff training, and promotional activities. The ongoing support package includes optimized bookkeeping and inventory systems and periodic assistance from a field consultant. The franchisor operates a centralized purchasing program for franchisees.

Initial Investment: The prospective franchisee must be able to handle an investment of $380,000 to $630,000 including the initial franchise fee, site acquisition, fixtures, and equipment. A net worth of at least $300,000 is required.

Advertising: Long John Silver's franchisees pay a monthly advertising fee of five percent of gross monthly sales. The franchisor supplies ad slicks for newspaper campaigns, television and radio commercials, and public relations materials.

Fees and Royalties: The initial franchise fee is $15,000, moderate for the fast-food industry. Including the four percent franchise royalty and the five percent advertising fee, the total royalty burden is nine percent of gross monthly sales.

Summary: Long John Silver's receives high marks for its managerial training program.

Franchise Highlights

Began operating: 1969
Began franchising: 1970
Outlets currently open: 1,380
Initial franchise fee: $15,000
Monthly royalty: 4%
Advertising fee: 5%
Term: 25 years

McDonald's

Industry experience:	★ ★ ★ ★	*Franchising experience:*	★ ★ ★ ★
Financial strength:	★ ★ ★ ★	*Training & services:*	★ ★ ★ ★
Fees & royalties:	★ ★ ★	*Satisfied franchisees:*	★ ★ ★ ★

McDonald's
McDonald's Plaza
Oakbrook, Illinois 6052
(312) 575-6196

Ray Kroc was a milkshake-machine salesman in 1954, when he called on a drive-in hamburger stand in San Bernadino, California to find out why the owners had ordered eight of his machines. There, he found Mac and Dick MacDonald, turning out 15-cent hamburgers with assembly-line efficiency. The MacDonald boys weren't as excited about expanding the business as Kroc, who bought the development rights for a small consideration.

Today, Ray Kroc's McDonald's hamburger empire is the world's second largest food service chain, outnumbered only by soft-drink conglomerate Pepsico, which operates Kentucky Fried Chicken, Taco Bell, and Pizza Hut. With annual sales approaching $10 billion, 9,000 McDonald's restaurants currently lead the pack in the bitterly fought 'Hamburger Wars' for the loyalties of the eat-and-run set. With the most desirable locations already claimed, the company's primary expansion efforts are currently aimed at overseas markets.

The Franchise: The franchisee conducts a retail fast-food restaurant, specializing in hamburgers and a selection of limited-menu items, and doing business under the trade name McDonald's.

Franchisee Profile: A background in food service is not mandatory. Business aptitude, personal ambition, and motivation are more important that past experience in the restaurant trade. Absentee ownership is prohibited.

Projected Earnings: Based on the company's reported annual sales, the average volume of a McDonald's outlet is about $1.05 million per year before expenses. This figure does not take into account individual variables such as location or size, and is not based on any earnings claim furnished by the franchisor. McDonald's will provide prospective franchisees with a written statement of projected earnings prior to the personal interview.

Franchisor's Services: The franchisor provides a comprehensive training program which includes from four to eight weeks at the Hamburger University in Oak Brook, Illinois, an upscale suburb of Chicago. Attendees are responsible for their own travel and lodging expenses. Prospective franchisees must successfully complete the training program before being considered for a franchise.

New outlets are typically acquired and constructed by the franchisor, to assure exact compliance with the company's standards and specifications. However, most franchises currently available in the United States are for established outlets. A McDonald's field representative visits every restaurant periodically, to inspect the operation and offer on-site guidance. The operates a centralized purchasing program and offers frequent retraining seminars and continuing education workshops in conjunction with Hamburger U.

Initial Investment: New McDonald's franchisees should be prepared to invest from $325,000 to $385,500 to establish a new restaurant. The amount includes the initial franchise fee, lease deposits, site improvements, equipment purchases, signs, furnishings, decor, cash register, and miscellaneous startup costs. In some cases, the franchisor may lease an existing site to a new franchisee, lowering the initial cash requirement to around $65,000. McDonald's does not offer any direct financial assistance to franchisees.

Advertising: McDonald's franchisees contribute four percent of their of gross monthly sales for advertising. The franchisor conducts high-profile national and regional campaigns on behalf of all McDonald's outlets, using television, radio, newspapers, magazines, and direct mail. The company's advertising reach and effectiveness are among the highest of all U.S. advertisers.

Contract Highlights: The term of the franchise is 20 years. The contract may be renewed for an additional year term, by mutual agreement of franchisor and franchisee.

Fees and Royalties: The initial franchise fee for a new outlet is $22,500, placing a high value on name recognition and goodwill. However, when outlets are resold by their existing owners, the asking price may vary significantly. The 12 percent monthly royalty, added to the four percent advertising royalty, creates a total royalty burden of 16 percent of gross monthly sales.

Disputes and litigation: Some history of litigation is inevitable in any organization with 9,000 independent contractors. But none of the company's past lawsuits have seriously tarnished the image or reputation of the golden arched franchisor. In a recent case, a restaurant owner who had been a McDonald's franchisee for 14 years stopped paying franchise royalties, but continued operating the restaurant. The franchisor sued to terminate the franchise and recover back fees. The franchisee's lawyers claimed that McDonald's was harassing the franchisee and engaging in antitrust activity. The court sided with the franchisor, empowering McDonald's to take possession of the restaurant and recover all of the unpaid royalties. In 1983, an Illinois court also ruled in favor of the franchisor for terminating a franchisee who had failed to comply with McDonald's standards for quality, service, and cleanliness. Not only did the franchisee lose the lawsuit, but he was also held liable for the franchisor's legal fees and expenses. The outlets in question, which happen to be located in Paris, are now called O'Kitch.

Summary: For at least two decades, a McDonald's hamburger restaurant has been the most coveted franchise in America. But today's fast-food market is characterized by intense competition and lagging growth, prompting frequent changes in marketing strategy among the industry leaders. McDonald's is a favorite business among minority entrepreneurs.

Franchise Highlights

Began operating: 1955
Began franchising: 1955
Outlets currently open: 9,000
Initial franchise fee: $22,500
Monthly royalty: 12%
Training program: 4 weeks
Term: 20 years

Mister Donut of America, Inc.

Industry experience:	★★★★	*Franchising experience:*	★★★★
Financial strength:	★★★	*Training & services:*	★★★★
Fees & royalties:	★★★	*Satisfied franchisees:*	★★★

Mister Donut of America, Inc.
Multifoods Tower
Box 2945
Minneapolis, Minnesota 55402
(800) 328-8304, Ext. 3477

A subsidiary of Multifoods Corporation, Mister Donut maintains a high profile in the competive fast-food donut market. The third-largest donut chain in the United States, Mister Donut is second in average sales volume per outlet. The company plans to continue expanding throughout the U.S. and Canada, hoping to open 80 new units every year.

The Franchise: The franchisee operates a retail coffee shop, specializing in donuts, using the trade name Mister Donut. Freshly ground coffee and other beverages supplement the outlet's selection of 55 varieties of donuts and bakery goods. Donuts and bakery items are sold over the counter, served to sit-down patrons in indoor booths, and supplied to drive-up and take-out customers. A typical outlet is located in a well-traveled area, in close proximity to a school, church, or retail shopping mall. The coffee shop itself may be situated in a freestanding site, strip center, or mall facility. Bakery goods and coffee are prepared at the franchisee's shop according to the franchisor's standardized procedures, and using approved ingredients.

Franchisee Profile: No prior experience in food service or coffee shop management is required.

Franchisor's Services: The franchisor takes an active part in the initial development of the new franchise, from site selection to opening. To assure standardization in outlet design, company representatives offer advice and approval during the building process. A four-week training program is held at company headquarters in St. Paul, Minnesota. The cost of the training is included in the initial franchise fee, but travel expenses must be handled by the franchisee. The program covers all aspects of store management, including purchasing, baking, quality control, customer service, personnel relations, and cost analysis. Company representatives assist in Grand Opening activities and are available on a continuing basis as needed.

Initial Investment: The new franchisee may expect to spend at least $60,000 in initial cash investment. The total investment for the first year ranges from $150,000 to $300,000. The franchisor may be willing to offset some initial expense by financing the purchase of restaurant equipment and fixtures.

Advertising: The franchisor supplies franchisees with pre-prepared promotional materials and operates a cooperative advertising program. Mister Donut franchisees contribute four percent of gross sales for advertising support.

Fees and Royalties: The initial license fee is $15,000 — moderate for a donut shop. The monthly royalties on gross revenues are calculated at 5.4 percent. Advertising royalties are a moderate three percent of gross sales.

Summary: Mister Donut franchisees benefit from the franchisor's name, highly developed operating methods, and standardized motif.

Franchise Highlights

Began operating: 1955	**Monthly royalty: 5.4%**
Began franchising: 1956	**Advertising fee: 3%**
Outlets currently open: 700	**Training program: 4 weeks**
Initial franchise fee: $15,000	**Term: 20 years**

Orange Julius

Industry experience:	★ ★ ★ ★	*Franchising experience:*	★ ★ ★
Financial strength:	★ ★ ★	*Training & services:*	★ ★ ★
Fees & royalties:	★ ★ ★	*Satisfied franchisees:*	★ ★ ★

Orange Julius of America
2850 Ocean Park Blvd., Suite 200
Santa Monica, CA 90405
(800) 421-7127

The worldwide Orange Julius chain rose to prominence like the foam on its frothy, patented orange juice recipe of the same name. Founded in 1926, the pioneering fast-food and beverage operation sold its first franchise in 1963, and today boasts nearly 800 outlets throughout the United States and Canada, and in 30 foreign countries.

The Franchise: The franchisee operates a specialty fast-food and beverage restaurant, under the trade name Orange Julius. A typical outlet is located in a retail shopping mall or retail strip center, easily noticed by an orange-lighted decor featuring displays of fresh oranges and the company's famous 'red devil' trademark. Outlets range in size from a small, open juice bar to a free-standing restaurant offering hamburgers, hot dogs, and specialty sandwiches. All Orange Julius outlets serve a varied assortment of real fruit juice drinks.

Franchisee Profile: Previous food-service management experience is not required. Prospective franchisees should demonstrate personal ambition, self-management, and the willingness to learn.

Projected Earnings: A projected earnings claim is not available.

Franchisor's Services: Orange Julius sites are often sold or leased as turnkey operations. The franchisee who opts to develop a new establishment receives assistance in all phases of development from company consultants.

New franchisees attend a ten-day training program at a regional training center, learning — among other things — the secret Orange Julius formula. The curriculum also covers inventory control, accounting, personel relations, marketing and advertising. Franchisees are responsible for their own travel and lodging expenses in connection with the training program.

At the franchisee's site, Orange Julius consultants spend time training the new staff and helping to prepare the outlet for opening. The company maintains a full-time staff of 48 representatives to handle franchise support. A team of field inspectors visits each outlet periodically to assure compliance with the company's high standards of quality, cleanliness, and performance.

Initial Investment: The total investment is estimated between $110,000 and $160,000, including site acquisition, construction and improvements, fixtures, equipment, business permits, insurance, and working capital.

Advertising: Orange Julius franchisees do not pay a monthly advertising royalty. Instead, they are required to invest one percent of total monthly sales in local advertising.

Fees and Royalties: The initial franchise fee is $18,000. The monthly royalty is six percent of gross sales, moderate for the fast-food industry.

Summary: Orange Julius markets a unique food product that enjoys renewed popularity among an increasingly health-conscious consumer population. According to an existing franchisee, location is the key to profitability in the business. A moderate investment, low royalties, and excellent name recognition bolster the odds of success.

Franchise Highlights

Began operating: 1926
Began franchising: 1963
Outlets currently open: 790
Initial franchise fee: $18,000
Monthly royalty: 6%
Advertising fee:
None Training program: 10 days
Term: 10 years

Pizza Hut

Industry experience:	★★★★	*Franchising experience:*	★★★★
Financial strength:	★★★★	*Training & services:*	★★★★
Fees & royalties:	★★★	*Satisfied franchisees:*	★★★★

Pizza Hut
P.O. Box 428
Wichita, Kansas 67201
(316) 681-9000

The Pizza Hut chain is owned by Pepsico, which became the world's largest fast-food restaurateur when it also acquired Kentucky Fried Chicken and Taco Bell. A little less than half of the nearly 6,000 Pizza Huts around the world are operated by independent franchisees. At the present, the most viable avenue to obtaining a franchise is by acquiring an established outlet.

The Franchise: The franchisee operates a fast-food restaurant specializing in Italian-style cuisine, under the trade name Pizza Hut. Besides freshly prepared pizza, the menu also features specialty sandwiches, salads, and pasta.

Franchisee Profile: Pizza Hut franchisees must possess strong business and financial credentials.

Franchisor's Services: The franchisor provides a five-week training program at the company's headquarters in Wichita, Kansas. The curriculum covers food preparation, restaurant santitation, marketing, customer service, food and beverage cost control, and outlet management. Additional on-the-job training and grand opening assistance are provided at the franchisee's place of business.

Pizza Hut field representatives visit each franchise outlet periodically, to inspect the restaurant and offer ongoing guidance. Franchisees receive copies of the confidential Pizza Hut franchise manual, which details the daily operation and management of the restaurant. The franchisor updates the manual as required and publishes a newsletter to inform franchisees of new trends, techniques, and industry developments.

Initial Investment: The initial investment varies, depending on the size and location of the outlet. The franchisor does not offer any direct financial assistance to franchisees.

Advertising: Pizza Hut franchisees pay an advertising royalty which the franchisor uses to fund national, regional, and co-op ad campaigns. The amount of the royalty varies.

Summary: Pizza Hut is not actively seeking new franchisees, but occasionally, established outlets become available for resale or lease.

Franchise Highlights

Began operating: 1958
Began franchising: 1959
Outlets currently open: 5,600
Initial franchise fee: $15,000
Monthly royalty: Varies
Advertising fee: Varies
Training program: 5 weeks
Term: Varies

Ponderosa Steakhouses

Industry experience:	★ ★ ★ ★	*Franchising experience:*	★ ★ ★
Financial strength:	★ ★ ★ ★	*Training & services:*	★ ★
Fees & royalties:	★ ★ ★	*Satisfied franchisees:*	★ ★ ★

Ponderosa, Inc.
P.O. Box 578
Dayton, Ohio 45401
(800) 543-9670

Ponderosa opened its first steakhouse in Indiana in 1965, based on the premise of quick service, a moderately-priced steakhouse menu, and a comfortable, family-oriented ambience. The limited menu and buffet-style service made the restaurant a natural prototype for franchising. Today, Ponderosa oversees a chain of 650 restaurants, about a third of which are franchise outlets. The company is currently seeking new franchisees in the United States, Canada, and Great Britain.

The franchise: The franchisee operates a family-style restaurant featuring a limited menu and a buffet-style motif, under the trade name Ponderosa Steakhouse. A typical outlet has seating for 200 patrons, who order menu selections at a self-service counter and receive their meals at their tables from uniformed waiters and waitresses. The outlet's design and decor are based on strictly enforced standards. Besides steak, the menu offers chicken, seafood, and pork entrees, supplemented by a salad and dessert bar.

Franchisee Profile: Prior experience in food service management is not required. According to a franchise representative, the company is seeking prospective franchisees who have basic financial and business qualifications, and take pride in personal accomplishment.

Projected Earnings: A projected earnings claim is not available.

Franchisor's Services: The franchisor conducts a comprehensive four-week training program at the company's headquarters in Dayton, Ohio. The tuition is included in the initial franchise fee, but the costs of travel, lodging, and meals must be borne by the franchisee. The curriculum covers restaurant management, food and beverage cost controls, daily operating procedures, service policies, marketing, and advertising.

Ponderosa supplies a start-up kit containing guidelines for site selection, building design, and equipment acquisition. The franchisor sells restaurant fixtures and equipment at competitive prices, but franchisees are free to purchase these items from any approved supplier. The equipment must comply with Ponderosa's specifications. Before the outlet opens for business, the restaurant staff receives on-site training from a team of operations experts.

An area representative visits each steakhouse periodically to inspect the operation and offer on-site assistance. Ponderosa publishes a franchisee newsletter and offers continuing education at company workshops and in the form of videotape instruction.

Initial Investment: The total investment is estimated at $125,000 or more, including the initial franchise fee, site acquisition, construction, fixtures, equipment, supplies, and miscellaneous start-up costs. Franchisees must be capable of documenting a minimum of $125,000 in liquid assets. Ponderosa does not offer any form of direct financial assistance to franchisees.

Advertising: Franchisees contribute one half of one percent to a co-op ad fund, which the franchisor uses to conduct advertising campaigns on behalf of all Ponderosa Steakhouses. Target media include television, radio, and newspapers.

Fees and Royalties: The initial franchise fee of $25,000 is average for a franchise of this stature in the family-style restaurant field. The four percent monthly royalty is low. Including the one half percent advertising fee, the total royalty bite is a mere four and a half percent.

Summary: The Ponderosa Steakhouse franchise features a popular self-service restaurant motif with the drawing power of a moderately priced menu. Franchisees benefit from favorable imaging, low royalties, and comprehensive training.

Franchise Highlights

Began operating: 1965
Began franchising: 1966
Outlets currently open: 650
Initial franchise fee: $15,000

Monthly royalty: 4%
Advertising fee: 4%
Training program: 4 weeks
Term: 20 years

Popeye's Famous Fried Chicken & Biscuits

Industry experience:	★★★	*Franchising experience:*	★★
Financial strength:	★★★★	*Training & services:*	★★★
Fees & royalties:	★★★	*Satisfied franchisees:*	★★★

Popeye's Famous Fried Chicken & Biscuits
One Popeye Plaza
1333 S. Clearview Parkway
Jefferson, Louisiana 70121
(504) 733-4300

Alvin Copeland was working in a grocery market in New Orleans when his brother Gilbert launched a small chain of donut franchises. Alvin quit his job and set out to learn the restaurant trade. After working the business for five years, he decided that donuts were chicken feed and the real dough was in fried chicken. Copeland tried and failed with two different chicken restaurants, before he finally hit it big with Popeye's Mighty Good Fried Chicken. He named the restaurant after Popeye Doyle, the main character in the movie The French Connection. Later, he obtained the right to use the cartoon image of the brawling, spinach-guzzling Popeye the Sailor.

When Copeland opened his second restaurant in 1972, he changed the name to Popeye's Famous Fried Chicken. Today, Copeland's Popeye's is one of the most successful fried chicken chains in North America. Besides his 680 company-owned and franchised outlets, Copeland also owns a famous restaurant in New Orleans that bears his name.

The Franchise: The franchisee operates a fast-food restaurant, specializing in fried chicken prepared according to the franchisor's recipe and specifications, and doing business under the trade name Popeye's Famous Fried Chicken & Biscuits. The company's red-roofed buildings range in size from small take-out stands to larger sit-down restaurants with complete decor packages. Geared for volume as well as convenience, most Popeye's outlets incorporate drive-through windows to supplement enclosed dining facilities. The menu features Cajun-style chicken sold by the bucket or by the piece, with spicily prepared orders of rice, red beans, home-style biscuits, and other options. Newer outlets also feature expanded menus and salad bars.

Franchisee Profile: Previous experience in the food and beverage industry is not required. Multi-unit ownership is encouraged.

Projected Earnings: According to one source, a Popeye's restaurant can gross from $2,000 to $5,000 per week. Based on such performance, a typical outlet might generate between $104,000 and $260,000 in gross annual sales. Including 112 company-owned outlets, the system-wide average volume is a stunning $625,000, before expenses.

Franchisor's Services: The franchisor provides a comprehensive six-week training program at the company's headquarters in Jefferson, Louisiana, near New Orleans. Attendees are responsible for their own travel and lodging expenses. The curriculum covers sanitation systems, food preparation, marketing, bookkeeping, restaurant maintenance, and daily operating procedures.

A special consulting team provides on-site support during site preparation, assisting with the hiring and training of employees Franchisees are reponsible for selecting their own sites and overseeing construction. The franchisor offers 20 optional site design packages for varying start-up budgets and local market conditions.

After the restaurant has opened, a Popeye's representative will visit the outlet periodically, to offer on-site guidance. system for equipment and supplies. Franchisees receive a confidential operations manual that is updated periodically during the 20-year term of the franchise. A toll-free hotline provides access to company operations and marketing consultants.

Initial Investment: New Popeye's franchisees should be prepared to invest a minimum of $250,000 to establish the business. The amount includes the initial franchise fee, site acquisition, construction and improvements, equipment purchases, and restaurant supplies. The franchisor does not offer any direct financial assistance to franchisees.

Advertising: Popeye's franchisees contribute three percent of gross monthly revenues for advertising.

Contract Highlights: The term of the Popeye's franchise is 20 years, twice the national average for franchises. The contract may be renewed for an additional year term, providing the franchisee is in compliance with all material provisions. The franchisee receives a protected territory for the duration of the agreement.

Fees and Royalties: Popeye's franchises its restaurants five at a time. The total licensing fee is $65,000, including $25,000 for the first outlet and options to open four additional outlets at $10,000 each. The total royalty burden, including both the monthly franchise royalty and the advertising fee, is a moderate eight percent of gross sales.

Summary: Popeye's goal is to open 1,400 outlets, putting the franchise system on an equal footing with its closest competitor, Church's. The Popeye's product is set apart by its Cajun-style preparation, and the franchise program is equally distinctive for its unique, mandatory multi-unit ownership plan.

Franchise Highlights

Began operating: 1972
Began franchising: 1976
Outlets currently open: 680
Initial franchise fee: $25,000
Monthly royalty: 5%
Advertising fee: 3%
Training program: 6 weeks
Term: 20 years

Rax

Industry experience:	★★★	*Franchising experience:*	★★★
Financial strength:	★★★	*Training & services:*	★★★★
Fees & royalties:	★★★	*Satisfied franchisees:*	★★★

Rax Restaurants, Inc.
1266 Dublin Rd.
Columbus, Ohio 43215
(614) 486-3669

The objective of Rax Restaurants of Columbus, Ohio is to combine fast-food service with a nutritionally sound product and a comfortable dining ambience. The Rax menu features entrees that meet American Heart Association dietary criteria. In the early 1980s, the franchise gained considerable popularity with middle-aged consumers, by addressing growing public concern over nutrition and chloresterol. But in recent years, Rax has begun to feel the heat from industry competition, as other fast-food chains edge into the market with new menus designed to attract the same customers. Partially in response to this threat, the company is aggressively expanding in all U.S. markets.

The Franchise: Rax Restaurants are predominately freestanding establishments with seating for about 100 customers. The standardized Rax decor features stucco and tile exteriors of soft pastels, accented by plum-colored awnings. The interior esthetics focus on textured furniture and solid wood tables. The Rax menu offers a selection of hot and cold sandwiches featuring roast beef, turkey, chicken, and ham; baked potatoes with various stuffings; and a multi-vegetable salad bar. Special items are available for diners on low-salt diets.

Franchisee Profile: The company requires that applicants have past experience or training in restaurant management and operation.

Projected Earnings: Based on the company's reported annual sales, the average volume of a Rax outlet is about $627,000 per year before expenses, with pre-tax profits of around five percent.

Franchisor's Services: Franchisees and their key staff members attend a five-week training course at a regional site in Ohio, Florida, or Missouri. Two weeks of classroom instruction focus on restaurant management and financial controls. Attendees spend the remaining three weeks at an operating Rax Restaurant, receiving hands-on experience in all phases of restaurant operations.

A Rax representative consults with new franchisees on site selection, lease negotiation, and equipment purchasing, and assists with pre-opening activites. Rax franchisees are obligated to purchase equipment and supplies from the franchisor's approved distributors.

Initial Investment: The franchisor estimates the franchisee's initial investment at between $625,000 and $725,000. The following breakdown illustrates a typical Rax startup:

Land	$175,000
Building	211,500
Site improvements	80,000
Equipment	170,500
Working capital	50,000
Total	687,000

The above breakdown is based on low estimates for the cost of land, construction, and equipment, and excludes an optional breakfast bar package.

Advertising: Rax franchisees contribute four percent of their gross monthly revenues for advertising. The franchisor conducts aggressive regional campaigns, using television and radio, in markets where its outlets are operating.

Fees and Royalties: The franchise license fee of $25,000 is somewhat high for the food service industry, but not unreasonable in light of the franchisor's track record. Rax requires a four percent franchise royalty; including the advertising fee, the total royalty bite is a moderate eight percent of gross sales.

Summary: Rax is an up-and-coming franchisor with a vision of changing public attitudes toward food and nutrition. According to an existing franchisee, the key to succeeding in the business is finding the right market and location. Although the franchisor provides some guidelines, the franchisee bears the responsibility for securing a site and constructing the restaurant.

Franchise Highlights

Began operating: 1978	**Monthly royalty: 4%**
Began franchising: 1978	**Advertising fee: 4%**
Outlets currently open: 500	**Training program: 5 weeks**
Initial franchise fee: $25,000	**Term: 20 years**

Round Table Pizza

Industry experience:	★ ★ ★ ★	*Franchising experience:*	★ ★ ★ ★
Financial strength:	★ ★ ★ ★	*Training & services:*	★ ★ ★ ★
Fees & royalties:	★ ★ ★ ★	*Satisfied franchisees:*	★ ★ ★ ★

Round Table Franchise Corporation
601 Montgomery St., 5th Floor
San Francisco, California 94111
(415) 392-7500

Round Table Pizza, the home of 'The Last Honest Pizza', is arguably the largest chain of pizza restaurants in the West. The company's success is built on the premise of an authentic product prepared with fresh ingredients and a home-style sauce that is prepared daily on the premises.

The Franchise: The franchisee operates a pizza restaurant with a standardized exertior and interior design, under the trade name Round Table Pizza. A typical outlet is housed in approximately 3,000 sq. ft. of space in a suitable retail center or standalone site, with a staff of four full-time and 14 part-time employees. Pizzas are prepared from with a variety of meat, vegetable, seafood, or fruit toppings. The menu includes sandwiches, a salad bar, and Italian specialties such as 'Camelot Calzones' and 'Pizzatatos' (baked potatoes with pizza filling). The outlet may also derive profits from the sale of wine, beer, and soft drinks.

The Franchisee Profile: Experience in hotel and restaurant management is helpful, but not mandatory.

Projected Earnings: A projected earnings claim is not available. Based on the company's reported sales, the average income of a Round Table outlet is about $500,000 per year, before expenses.

The Franchisor's Services: Round Table closely supervises the design and construction of the franchisee's restaurant, to assure compliance with the franchisor's standards and specifications. On request, the company will help select the site and negotiate a lease. The franchisor operates its own supply company which offers restaurant fixtures, equipment, and supplies to franchisees without profit.

A four-week training program in Pacifica, California provides thorough instruction on all phases of the business, from sauce preparation to employee supervison. The curriculum includes hands-on experience in an operating Round Table Pizza restaurant. At the franchisee's own restaurant, Round Table consultants assist with the hiring and training of staff, the installation of equipment, and grand opening promotions.

After the restaurant has opened, an area manager visits the outlet periodically to inspect the operation and offer on-site assistance.

Initial Investment: The estimated total working capital needed to open a Round Table outlet ranges from $280,000 to $300,000. The estimate includes the initial franchise fee, site acquisition, construction, fixtures, equipment, supplies, and miscellaneous startup expenses. Round Table does not offer any form of direct financial assistance to franchisees.

Advertising: New Round Table franchisees contribute from one to three percent of their gross monthly revenues to a co-op ad fund. The franchisor uses this pool to conduct aggressive advertising campaigns on behalf of all Round Table Pizza restaurants. Target media include television, radio, newspapers, and special promotions.

Fees and Royalties: The initial franchise fee of $20,000 is reasonable for an organization of this stature. Round Table exacts a mere four percent royalty of gross sales. Including the three percent advertising fee, the total royalty obligation is just seven percent.

Contract Highlights: The term of the franchise is 15 years. The franchise must manage the outlet in close compliance with the franchisor's operating procedures and performance standards. The restaurant may not be sold without the franchisor's consent; in the event of an approved sale, the purchaser must be fully qualified to own and operate a Round Table franchise.

Summary: The Round Table franchise is characterized by outstanding name recognition, aggressive advertising, and consistent market demand. As with other restaurants of this type, the initial investment is steep, but the franchisor eases the franchisee's debt burden with low royalties. Satisfaction among existing franchisees is high.

Franchise Highlights

Began operating: 1959
Began franchising: 1962
Outlets currently open: 481
Initial franchise fee: Min. $20,000

Monthly royalty: 4%
Advertising fee: 3%
Training program: 4 weeks
Term: 15 years

Roy Rodgers Restaurant

Industry experience: ★ ★ ★ *Franchising experience:* ★ ★
Financial strength: ★ ★ ★ ★ *Training & services:* ★ ★ ★
Fees & royalties: ★ ★ ★ *Satisfied franchisees:* ★ ★ ★

Roy Rodgers Restaurants
One Marriott Drive
Washington, D.C. 20058
(301) 897-1487

The restaurant chain that bears the name of the retired singing cowboy is actually a subsidiary of Marriott Corporation, the world's second largest hotelier. Founded in the late Sixties, the franchisor has opened an average of nearly 30 outlets per year. Over the last two decades, the company has experienced varying degrees of success. Once devoted primarily to roast beef, today's Roy Rodgers menu also features such traditional fast-food fare as fried chicken and hamburgers.

The Franchise: The franchisee operates a retail fast-food restaurant using the Roy Rodgers trademark. A typical outlet serves hot sandwiches prepared with roast beef or ham and cheese, chicken, french fried potatoes, and salads.

Franchisee Profile: A background in food and beverage management is preferred. Absentee ownership is prohibited.

Franchisor's Services: Roy Rodgers Restaurants conducts a comprehensive training program at the company's headquarters in Maryland, or at a designated regional site. Pre-opening assistance is provided by a field consultant at the franchisee's restaurant.

The Roy Rodgers manual details the franchisor's policies and procedures for streamlining daily operations. An area representative inspects each restaurant periodically and offers ongoing guidance.

Initial Investment: The total start-up investment ranges from $750,000 to $1 million, including site acquisition, construction, equipment purchases, signs, furnishings, decor, restaurant supplies, and working capital. The franchisor does not offer any direct financial assistance to franchisees.

Advertising: Roy Rodgers franchisees pay four percent of their gross monthly revenues for advertising.

Contract Highlights: The Roy Rodgers franchise has a 20-year term, renewable for an additional term at the franchisee's option. The franchise may not be sold, transferred, or otherwise assigned except to a fully qualified buyer who meets the standard criteria for a Roy Rodgers franchisee.

Fees and Royalties: The initial franchise fee of $25,000 is on the high side, reflecting the organization's growth and maturity. The franchisee's total royalty obligation, including the monthly franchise royalty and the advertising fee, is a moderate eight percent of gross sales.

Summary: Roy Rodgers franchisees benefit from widespread name recognition, thorough hands-on training, and the management support of an industry giant.

Franchise Highlights

Began operating: 1968
Began franchising: 1968
Outlets currently open: 550
Initial franchise fee: $25,000
Monthly royalty: 4%
Advertising fee: 4%
Training program: 10 weeks
Term: 20 years

Sbarro

Industry experience:	★ ★ ★	*Franchising experience:*	★ ★
Financial strength:	★ ★ ★	*Training & services:*	★ ★ ★
Fees & royalties:	★ ★	*Satisfied franchisees:*	★ ★ ★

Sbarro, Inc.
763 Larkfield Rd.
Commack, New York 11725
(516) 864-0200

Sbarro, a New York Italian-style cafeteria that opened in 1977, exploded from $4 million in sales in 1981 to $40 million in 1985. The restaurant owes its phenomenal success to the lure of southern Italian dishes served at the point of sale in high-traffic shopping malls. The business's most powerful sales tool is the spicy aroma that draws passing shoppers into the eatery. The company's management feels so strongly about this principle that it hesitates to open freestanding facilities. Sbarro currently oversees 150 outlets, roughly a third of which are franchised restaurants. The company is presently pursuing a path of ambitious expansion, seeking new franchisees in all major U.S. markets.

The Franchise: The franchisee operates a cafeteria-style food service business, specializing in Italian cuisine, and doing business under the trade name Sbarro. A typical Sbarro cafeteria is located in a 1,500 to 3,000 sq. ft. retail space in a shopping mall or strip center, with from six to 27 employees and seating capacity for 60 to 100 customers. Each outlet is distinguished by its decorative display of hanging salamis and cheeses. Diners choose from a buffet of pizza, pasta, sandwiches, salads, and desserts, including a Sbarro specialty cheesecake.

Franchisee Profile: Previous experience or training in the food and beverage industry is desirable. Multiple-unit ownership is encouraged.

Franchisor's Services: The company conducts an extensive, five-week training program at company headquarters in Commack, New York. The program covers food preparation, personnel management, accounting, and promotional techniques. Trainees have an opportunity to work in various capacities at an operating Sbarro restaurant as an essential part of the training experience. Company staff offer active support during pre-opening activities. All supplies and equipment must be purchased from an approved distributor. Purchasing through the company distributor is available at discount rates.

Initial Investment: The total capital investment to start a Sbarro franchise ranges from $250,000 to $500,000.

Advertising: Sbarro franchisees pay three percent of gross monthly sales for advertising.

Fees and Royalties: The initial franchise fee is $35,000, for a single outlet. The franchisee must demonstrate a minimum of $108,500 in liquid cash assets to qualify for the license. The monthly franchise royalty is five percent. Including the three-percent advertising fee, the total royalty burden is eight percent of gross monthly sales, about average for a mall-based food service franchise.

Summary: A young franchisor, Sbarro has a ten-year track record that includes periods of stunning success. According to some sources, the company is reluctant to grant new franchises, preferring instead to expand the number of company-owned outlets. At present, the most viable entry into the Sbarro chain is by purchasing the rights to open several outlets.

Franchise Highlights

Began operating: 1977
Began franchising: 1977
Outlets currently open: 150
Initial franchise fee: $35,000
Monthly royalty: 5%
Advertising fee: 3%
Training program: 5 weeks
Term: 15 years

Sonic

Industry experience:	★ ★ ★ ★	*Franchising experience:*	★ ★ ★
Financial strength:	★ ★ ★	*Training & services:*	★ ★ ★
Fees & royalties:	★ ★ ★ ★	*Satisfied franchisees:*	★ ★ ★

Sonic Industies, Inc.
6800 North Bryant
Oklahoma City, Oklahoma 73121
(405) 478-0731

Sonic continues the old-fashioned tradition of the Great American Drive-In, with a distinctive 1950s flair. Originally called Top Hat, Sonic is a popular fast-food franchise in the rural Sunbelt. The company is currently encouraging expansion in Alabama, Georgia, Tennessee, Kentucky, South Carolina, and California.

The Franchise: A typical Sonic outlet requires about 20,000 square feet of land, with the restaurant itself housed on 1,150 square feet. Customers place their order through an intercom system, and 'car hops' deliver fast-food classics, such as hamburger sandwiches, onion rings, and Coney-Island-style hot dogs, to waiting customers. Recently, the company has included enclosed seating in the design of newer outlets to accomodate clientele who prefer indoor dining.

Franchisor Profile: The company does not require any previous experience in the food industry. The franchisee may hire a manager to run the operation. Sonic encourages the purchase of regional franchises but is willing to sell rights to individual outlets.

Franchisor's Services: Sonic conducts a two-week training program at its corporate headquarters in Okahoma City. Attendees study inventory control, accounting, marketing, promotion, sanitation, and, personnel management. The curriculum also focuses on topics specific to Sonic restaurants, including food preparation and equipment operation. One attendee (the franchisee or his designated manager) may undergo the training program at no charge, but the franchisee must pay for all travel-related expenses. An additional week of hands-on training takes place at the franchisee's drive-in restaurant.

Sonic representatives assist with site selection and construction, working with local contractors to assure compliance with the franchisor's standards and specifications. All equipment must meet company specifications, but may be purchased either from the franchisor or from independent vendors. Franchisees who opt to purchase equipment from Sonic may qualify for company financing.

The company provides franchisees and their managers with copies of Sonic's confidential operating manual, and publishes a newsletter to keep franchisees abreast of industry and company developments.

Initial Investment: The capital investment is estimated between $45,000 and $60,000. Other than credit on purchases of equipment and supplies offered by the franchisor, Sonic does not offer any form of direct financial assistance to franchisees.

Advertising: Three percent of the franchisee's monthly sales must be set aside for advertising. A portion of this royalty must be for local promotions. Many Sonic franchisees participate in local and regional co-op campaigns, sharing the cost of newspaper, radio, and TV advertising.

Fees and Royalties: The initial franchise fee of $7,500 is low for the fast-food industry. Franchise royalties increase with monthly sales. Sonic franchisees pay just one percent of their gross revenues, until the outlet achieves $10,000 in monthly sales. Thereafter, royalty payments are incremented by one-half percent for each additional $10,000 generated by the restaurant each month.

Summary: The Sonic franchise is characterized by a low initial investment, a manageable royalty structure, and the novelty of the drive-in restaurant in an era of drive-through services.

Franchise Highlights

Began operating: 1953
Began franchising: 1975
Outlets currently open: 950
Initial franchise fee: $7,500
Monthly royalty: Graduated
Advertising fee: 1.5%
Term: 15 years

SUBWAY Sandwiches & Salads

Industry experience:	★★★★	*Franchising experience:*	★★★
Financial strength:	★★★	*Training & services:*	★★★
Fees & royalties:	★★★★	*Satisfied franchisees:*	★★★★

SUBWAY Sandwiches and Salads
25 High Street
Milford, Connecticut 06460
U.S. (800) 243-9741
Conn. (800) 222-4610

In 1965, 17-year-old Fred DeLuca was looking around for ways to finance his college education. He discussed the problem with his friend, a nuclear physicist named Peter Buck, who came up with the idea of starting a small sandwich shop in their home town, Bridgeport, Connecticut. There was only one hitch: DeLuca didn't have any money. Buck wrote out a check for $1,000, and Pete's Submarine Sandwiches was born. The partners later came up with the more urbane trade name SUBWAY Sandwiches and Salads.

The first sandwich shop was a miserable failure. DeLuca's only form of advertising was standing on the street corner accosting passing motorists with fliers. Finally, the two owners decided their only hope was opening a second shop to improve the business's visibility. The tactic worked, and their company — which they named Doctor's Associates, Inc. — has never stopped growing since.

Today, DeLuca's and Buck's brainchild is the most rapidly expanding fast-food chain in North America, with a stunning, 56 percent annual growth rate.

The Franchise: The franchisee operates a fast-food restaurant specializing in 'submarine' sandwiches, and doing business under the trade name SUBWAY Sandwiches and Salads. A typical outlet occupies 300 sq. ft. to 800 sq. ft. of retail space in a shopping mall, strip center, or freestanding facility with two or more employees and seating for 25 customers. The decor is centered around historical photos of the New York subway system.

SUBWAY's objective is to offer high-quality fast food to customers at low overhead to franchisees. A typical menu includes at least 15 varieties of the traditional Eastern submarine sandwich, based on a combination of meats, cheeses, and vegetables on a long Italian roll. Depending on the location, the price of a SUBWAY sandwich ranges from under three dollars to around five dollars. Franchisees are encouraged to adapt the menu to reflect local tastes and cultural influences. SUBWAY salads are prepared with the same ingredients as sandwiches. Since neither require cooking, preparation costs are kept at a minimum.

Franchisee Profile: Franchisees come from varied backgrounds. Most have had little or no previous restaurant experience. Multiple unit ownership and/or expansion is common.

Franchisor Services: A two-week training program at SUBWAY's headquarters in Milford, Connecticut combines classroom instruction with hands-on experience to familiarize new franchisees with all facets of operating a SUBWAY outlet. The program is tuition-free, but franchisees must pay for travel, lodging, and meals.

A SUBWAY development agent spends a week at the franchisee's restaurant prior to opening. The franchisor operates a centralized purchasing system to enable franchisees to take advantage of wholesale discounts on restaurant fixtures and equipment. Alternatively, a new franchisee may lease equipment to reduce the initial cash requirement. SUBWAY franchisees are obligated to purchase supplies only from the franchisor's approved vendors.

Initial Investment: The capital required to establish a new SUBWAY restaurant ranges between $29,900 and $59,900. The investment is broken as follows:

	Low	Moderate	High
Initial franchise fee	7,500	7,500	7,500
Lease deposits	$1,500	2,500	5,000
Improvements	11,000	17,000	30,000
Equipment deposits	1,000	1,000	1,000
Signs	800	1,500	3,000
Inventory	2,100	2,100	2,100
Miscellaneous	6,000	8,300	11,300
Total	29,900	39,900	59,900

SUBWAY does not offer any form of direct financial assistance to franchisees, but offers an equipment leasing plan. The above breakdown assumes an equipment lease deposit of $1,000; the total capital requirement for major equipment is about $21,000 higher.

Advertising: SUBWAY franchisees are required to pay two and one half percent of gross sales into a regional co-op advertising fund. The fund is administered by a Board of Directors comprised solely of SUBWAY franchisees.

Fees and Royalties: The initial franchise fee is $7,500 for a single outlet — about half the average franchise fee for a specialty sandwich restaurant. A franchisee who opts to open more than one outlet may obtain additional franchises for $1,000 each. The eight percent royalty is paid weekly. Including the advertising fee, the total royalty bite is 10.5 percent of gross sales.

Summary: SUBWAY Sandwiches and Salads has enjoyed a phenomenal growth rate over the last four years, exploding from 130 outlets in 1983 to nearly 2,000 today. In 1986, system-wide revenues increased by a healthy nine percent. Encouraged by its success, the company plans to double the number of existing franchises by 1990. Franchisees benefit from a low initial investment, true co-op advertising, and a manageable overhead.

Franchise Highlights

Began operating: 1965
Began franchising: 1975
Outlets currently open: 1,800
Initial franchise fee: $7,500
Monthly royalty: 8% per week
Advertising fee: 2.5%
Training program: 2 weeks
Term: 20 years

Swensen's

Industry experience: ★★★★ *Franchising experience:* ★★★★
Financial strength: ★★★★ *Training & services:* ★★★★
Fees & royalties: ★★★★ *Satisfied franchisees:* ★★★★

Swensen's Ice Cream Company
2408 E. Arizona
Biltmore Circle
Phoenix, Arizona 85064
(602) 995-1130

Earl Swensen served up his first scoop of ice cream in 1948; his famous Swensen's Ice Cream Factory is still a familiar landmark in San Francisco, near the top of Russian Hill. Forty years and 400 franchises later, Swensen's ice cream parlors and restaurants continue to feature a traditional turn-of-the-century decor and a wholesome soup-and-sandwich menu. The ice cream is churned from fresh cream right on the premises, presumably in strict adherence to Earl's original recipe.

The franchisor boasts locations in all 50 U.S. states, Canada, and 60 foreign countries.

The Franchise: The franchisee operates a family-style ice cream parlor under the trade name Swensen's Ice Cream Company. The outlet features a nostalgic ambience derived from an antique American motif, with such touches as marble counters, brass fixtures, and Tiffany lamps. The territory must have a minimum population of 50,000 within a three-mile radius of the restaurant. The franchisee is required to construct the outlet in close compliance with the franchisor's designs and specifications. Only Swensen's proprietary ice cream can be sold at the restaurant.

Franchisee Profile: Experience in business and/or the food and beverage industry is preferred.

Franchisor's Services: A team of Swensen's consultants provides guidance in site selection and construction, equipment acquisition, and pre-opening activitiers.

The franchisor conducts a comprehensive four-week training program in Phoenix, Arizona, at the company's appropriately named 'Sundae School'. The curriculum includes first-hand exposure to an operating ice cream parlor. An additional week or more of training takes place at the franchisee's restaurant.

Swensen's operates a centralized purchasing system offering supplies and foodstuffs at competitive prices. The franchisor plans and monitors each franchisee's inventory to avert potential shortages of critical ingredients. Swensen's also publishes a franchisee newsletter and conducts frequent seminars to keep franchisees abreast of industry developments and product innovations.

Initial Investment: The total capital required to open a full-service Swensen's restaurant ranges from $390,000 to $520,000. The investment amount includes the initial franchise fee, site acquisition and construction, fixtures, equipment, supplies, and miscellaneous start-up expenses.

Advertising: Swensen's franchisee are obligated to contribute one percent of their gross monthly sales to a co-op ad fund. The franchisor uses these ad royalties to conduct national and regional ad campaigns. Franchisees also receive prepared advertising materials for use in local promotions.

Fees and Royalties: The initial franchise of $25,000 is about average for the industry. The five and a half percent monthly royalty is moderate. Including the one percent advertising contribution, the total royalty bite is just seven and a half percent.

Contract Highlights: The term of the franchise is 20 years, twice the national average. The franchisee receives an exclusive territory, with the guarantee that no other Swensen's outlets will be established within the boundaries during the term of the franchise.

Summary: Arguably the world's largest chain of ice cream parlors, Swensen's is an established franchisor with solid name recognition and the reputation of an industry leader. The initial investment is steep, but the franchisee's ongoing royalty burden is moderate.

Franchise Highlights

Began operating: 1948
Began franchising: 1963
Outlets currently open: 400
Initial franchise fee: Min. 25,000
Max. 30,000
Monthly royalty: 5.5%
Advertising fee: 1% to 3%
Training Program: 3 weeks
Term: 20 years

T.J. Cinnamons

Industry experience:	★	*Franchising experience:*	★
Financial strength:	★ ★ ★	*Training & services:*	★ ★ ★
Fees & royalties:	★ ★ ★	*Satisfied franchisees:*	★ ★ ★

T.J. Cinnamons Gourmet Bakeries
300 W. 47th Street
Kansas City, Missouri 64112
(316) 931-9341

T.J. Cinnamons has been on a roll since 1985, when the company opened its first gourmet bakery shop. The company's expansion program is devoted exclusively to area franchising.

The Franchise: The franchisee operates a retail baked goods store, specializing in cinnamon rolls and doing business under the trade name T.J. Cinnamons. A typical outlet is situated in a 800 sq. ft. retail space in a high-traffic shopping mall or strip center.

Franchisee Profile: No special qualifications are required to run a store, other than personal ambition and the dedication to succeed.

Projected Earnings: T.J. Cinnamons shops reportedly generate from $250,000 to $300,000 in gross revenues, before deducting inventory costs and operating expenses.

Franchisor's Services: T.J. Cinnamons offers a 12-day training program at the company's headquarters in Kansas City, Missouri. Four additional days of training and grand opening assistance are provided at the franchisee's shop.

The business is detailed in the T.J. Cinnamons operations manual. Franchisees receive ongoing assistance from an area representative.

Initial Investment: The total start-up investment may range from $79,100 to as much as $130,400, including lease deposits, site improvements, equipment purchases, signs, supplies, and miscellaneous expenses. The franchisor does not offer any direct financial assistance to franchisees.

Fees and Royalties: The initial franchise fee of $15,000 is moderate for a specialty baked goods outlet. The franchisee's total royalty obligation is nine percent of gross sales, including a five percent monthly franchise royalty and a four percent advertising fee.

Summary: The T.J. Cinnamons franchise is characterized by a rapidly growing chain and a unique product with demonstrated popular acceptance. Only area franchises may be purchased directly from the franchisor. Individual outlets are marketed by established area franchisees.

Franchise Highlights

Began operating: 1985	**Monthly royalty: 5%**
Began franchising: 1985	**Advertising fee: 4%**
Outlets currently open: 100	**Training program: 12 days**
Initial franchise fee: $15,000	**Term: Varies**

Taco Bell

Industry experience:	★ ★ ★	*Franchising experience:*	★ ★ ★
Financial strength:	★ ★ ★ ★	*Training & services:*	★ ★ ★ ★
Fees & royalties:	★ ★ ★	*Satisfied franchisees:*	★ ★ ★ ★

Taco Bell Corporation
1801 Royal Lane
Irvine, California 92714
(714) 863-4595

When Pepsico Inc. bought the Taco Bell chain in 1978, the competitive soft drink franchisor was well on the road to becoming the world's largest fast-food franchisor as well. Pepsico immediately invested $200 million to upgrade the image of the nation's largest Mexican food retailer. Now, CEO John E. Martin plans to double the number of Taco Bell outlets by 1992, with an aggressive expansion program focusing on the northeastern U.S.

The chain's controversial logo, which depicted a sleepy Mexican lounging under an oversized sombrero, was replaced with a new, upscale, illuminated mission bell. But if, in the past, the company had problems with its image, it never had a similar experience with its product, which consistently earns high marks in independent tests for nutritious content and consumer satisfaction. Perhaps more than any other fast-food phenomenon from the 1960s, Taco Bell still retains the impact of flavor and freshness that characterized the original product.

The Franchise: The franchisee conducts a retail fast-food business, specializing in Mexican cuisine and operated under the trade name Taco Bell. A typical outlet offers seating for 40 to 60 patrons, with a menu featuring tacos, burritos, and specialty entrees prepared with the franchisor's standardized ingredients. Newer outlets incorporate drive-through windows and serve up such experimental offerings as seafood tacos and grilled chicken with salsa.

Franchisee Profile: A background in food and beverage service is preferred, but not mandatory.

Projected Earnings: The average volume of a Taco Bell outlet is reportedly around $600,000 per year before expenses. The new larger outlets are designed to generate as much as $1 million in gross annual sales, although no such sales levels are assured for a prospective franchisee.

Franchisor's Services: The franchisor provides a four-week training program at the company's headquarters in Irvine, California, in the Los Angeles area. Attendees are responsible for their own travel and lodging expenses. Franchisees also receive from one to weeks of on-the-job training at their own restaurants.

Taco Bell field consultants visit each restaurant periodically, to inspect the facility and provide on-site guidance. The franchisor administers strict food purchasing and preparation standards to assure consistency in the final product.

Initial Investment: The total capital investment required to open a new Taco Bell restaurant is about $100,000. The amount includes site acquisition, construction, equipment purchases, signs, and restaurant supplies. Taco Bell does not offer any direct financial assistance to franchisees.

Advertising: Taco Bell franchisees contribute four and one half percent of their gross monthly revenues for advertising. The franchisor conducts aggressive national and regional promotions on behalf of all company-owned and franchised Taco Bell outlets, including high-profile television and radio campaigns.

Contract Highlights: The term of the franchise is 20 years. The contract may be renewed for an additional year term, providing the franchisee is in compliance with all material provisions.

Fees and Royalties: The initial franchise fee of $35,000 is high for the food-service industry, reflecting the chain's stature as the largest of its type in the world. The franchisee's total royalty burden is ten percent of gross sales.

Summary: Taco Bell, Kentucky Fried Chicken, and Pizza Hut are all part of the Pepsico fast-food empire, offering franchisees the competitive advantages of the world's largest restaurateur. Franchisees benefit from superior name recognition, comprehensive training, and demonstrated consumer acceptance.

Franchise Highlights

Began operating: 1962
Began franchising: 1965
Outlets currently open: 2,540
Initial franchise fee: $35,000
Monthly royalty: 5%
Advertising fee: 5%
Training program: 6 weeks
Term: 20 years

Taco John's

Industry experience:	★ ★ ★	*Franchising experience:*	★ ★ ★
Financial strength:	★ ★ ★	*Training & services:*	★ ★ ★
Fees & royalties:	★ ★ ★	*Satisfied franchisees:*	★ ★ ★

Taco John's International
808 West 20th Street
Cheyenne. Wyoming 82001
(307) 635-0101

The Franchise: The franchisee operates a retail fast-food restaurant, specializing in Mexican-style cuisine, and doing business under the trade name Taco John's. A typical outlet is situated in a 1,600 sq. ft. commercial space in a retail strip center or freestanding facility, with six full-time and six part-time employees.

Franchisee Profile: A background in food and beverage management is beneficial, but not mandatory. Absentee ownership, though discouraged, is not strictly prohibited.

Projected Earnings: Based on the company's annual sales figures, the average volume of a Taco John's outlet is about $255,000 per year, before expenses. The franchisor estimates that a franchisee can earn net profits of from 20 to 30 percent. Thus, a restaurant that grosses $240,000 per year might expect to show pre-tax profits between $48,000 and $72,000.

Franchisor's Services: Taco John's franchisees must successfully complete a three-week training program at the company's headquarters in Cheyenne, Wyoming. Ten days of additional training and grand opening assistance are also provided at the franchisee's restaurant site.

The franchisor will help identify a site for the outlet, negotiate a lease, and design the layout. Each franchisee receives a set of comprehensive operations manuals containing standardized policies and procedures for running a successful fast-food restaurant. A Taco John's representative provides ongoing assistance with management and operations in periodic visits to the outlet. The franchisor also publishes a franchisee newsletter and organizes biannual conventions.

Initial Investment: The total start-up investment may run as high as $350,000, including site acquisition, improvements, equipment purchases, restaurant supplies, signs, and working capital. Taco John's does not offer any direct financial assistance to franchisees.

Advertising: Taco John's franchisees pay two percent of their gross monthly sales for advertising. The franchisor supplies Yellow Pages and newspaper ad designs, commercials, and point-of-sale aids.

Fees and Royalties: The initial franchise fee of $16,500 is about average for the trade. The franchisee's total royalty obligation, including the monthly franchise fee and the advertising fee, is a moderate six percent of gross sales.

Summary: The Taco John's franchise offers a competitive vehicle for entering the fast-food business with a popular, Mexican-style motif that piggybacks the success of industry arch rival Taco Bell.

Franchise Highlights

Began operating: 1969
Began franchising: 1969
Outlets currently open: 425
Initial franchise fee: $16,500
Monthly royalty: 4%
Advertising fee: 2%
Training program: 3 weeks
Term: 20 years

Tastee-Freez

Industry experience:	★ ★ ★ ★	*Franchising experience:*	★ ★ ★ ★
Financial strength:	★ ★ ★	*Training & services:*	★ ★
Fees & royalties:	★ ★ ★ ★	*Satisfied franchisees:*	★ ★ ★

Tastee-Freez International, Inc.
8345 Hall Rd.
P.O. Box 162
Utica, Michigan 48087
(313) 739-5520

In recent years, Tastee-Freez has undergone a rigorous transformation from a soft ice cream vendor to a diversified, gourmet ice cream store. Company management is currently attempting to revitalize a chain that faces strong competition in a fluctuating market.

Tastee-Freez outlets are located in 38 states, with none of the approximately 650 fast food eateries owned by the parent company. Currently a subsidiary of DeNovo Corporation, Tastee Freez has been scooping ice cream since 1950.

The Franchise: The new Tastee-Freez image sports a shingled 'heritage' look, with patriotic red, white, and blue trim. In addition to soft ice-cream cones, the outlet offers a selection of gourmet ice creams made with 14 percent butterfat in avant-garde flavors, and the 'Freezee,' a sweetened fruit and ice-cream drink. Some Tastee-Freez restaurants also offer more substantial options, such as hamburger sandwiches and french fried potatoess. A typical outlet operates with three full-time and eight part-time employees.

Franchisee Profile: A background in the food and beverage industry is beneficial, but not mandatory. Tastee Freez franchisees have varied backgrounds. The company is not currently seeking absentee owners.

Franchisor Services: New franchisees spend two days at the company's College of Ice Cream Knowledge in Michigan. The cost of the seminar is not included in the initial franchise fee. For a separate fee, a field consultant will assist with grand opening activities. The optional startup program includes familiarizing franchisees with the use of company equipment, ice cream production, and restaurant management procedures.

Company technicai and operations experts are available by phone as required.

Initial Investment: The minimum cash requirement ranges from $20,000 to $75,000 depending upon the location and size of the outlet. The total investment, including site acquisition, construction, fixtures, equipment, and supplies, may run as high as $225,000.

Advertising: Tastee-Freez conducts frequent national advertising campaigns and special promotions in markets where the company's outlets are located. Franchisees contribute one percent of their gross monthly sales to support the franchisor's advertising efforts.

Fees and Royalties: The initial franchise fee of $10,000 is moderate for the specialty ice cream sector. The company exacts a low 4.5 precent monthly royalty. Including the advertising fee, the total royalty bite is less than six percent.

Contract Highlights: The franchisee executes a ten-year contract with a five-year renewal option. The contract gives the franchisee exclusive territorial rights. Area franchises are available under a separate agreement.

Summary: Recent changes in decor and cuisine promise to revive the company's image and popularity. The Tastee-Freez franchise offers a flexibile investment, a manageable royalty structure, and a new upscale motif catering to an expanded segment of the contemporary fast-food market.

Franchise Highlights

Began operating: 1950	**Monthly royalty: 4.25%**
Began franchising: 1950	**Advertising fee: 1%**
Outlets currently open: 650	**Training program: 2 days**
Initial franchise fee: $10,000	**Term: 10 years**

Togo's Eatery

Industry experience:	★ ★ ★	*Franchising experience:*	★ ★ ★
Financial strength:	★ ★ ★	*Training & services:*	★ ★ ★
Fees & royalties:	★ ★ ★	*Satisfied franchisees:*	★ ★ ★ ★

Togo's Eatery
900 East Campbell Avenue
Campbell, California 95008
(408) 377-1754

Togo's Eatery offers a delicatessen-style fast-food motif in an appealing ambience. The menu features a wide selection of specialty sandwiches and salads prepared in ample portions before the customer's eyes.

The Franchise: The franchisee operates a fast-food restaurant specializing in delicatessen sandwiches, salads, and beverages, and doing business under the trade name Togo's Eatery. A typical outlet is situated in a retail strip center with two full-time and up to 18 part-time employees.

Franchisee Profile: A background in the food and beverage business is beneficial, but not mandatory. Absentee ownership, though discouraged, is not strictly prohibited. The franchisor will consider granting area franchises to develop large territories or regions.

Franchisor's Services: Togo's conducts a two-week training program at the company's headquarters in Campbell, California, east of Los Angeles. Additional training and grand opening assistance are staged at the franchisee's restaurant.

The Togo's manual details standards for food preparation and service, as well as daily operating procedures. A field adviser visits each outlet periodically, to inspect and troubleshoot the restaurant. Togo's publishes a franchisee newsletter to keep franchisees abreast of new products, trends, and industry developments.

Initial Investment: The total start-up investment may range from $100,000 to $150,000, including the initial franchise fee, lease deposits, site improvements, equipment purchases, supplies, and miscellaneous start-up expenses. The franchisor does not offer any direct financial assistance to franchisees.

Advertising: Togo's franchisees pay two percent of their gross monthly revenues for advertising. In return, the franchisor provides ad designs, commercials, and public relations tools.

Contract Highlights: The Togo's franchise has a ten-year term, renewable for an additional term at the franchisee's option. The franchisee receives a protected territory for as long as the contract remains in effect. The franchise may not be sold, transferred, or otherwise assigned except to a fully qualified buyer who meets the standard criteria for a Togo's franchisee.

Fees and Royalties: The initial franchise fee ranges from a minimum of $10,000 to as high as $25,000. The franchisee's total royalty obligation, including the monthly franchise fee and the advertising fee, is a moderate seven percent of gross sales.

Summary: The Togo's franchise offers an appealing restaurant format and a product mix that is exceptionally popular with both white- and blue-collar lunch crowds. The franchisor is currently seeking new franchisees in the western U.S.

Franchise Highlights

Began operating: 1972
Began franchising: 1977
Outlets currently open: 100
Initial franchise fee: Min $10,000
Max. $25,000

Monthly royalty: 5%
Advertising fee: 2%
Training program: 2 weeks
Term: 10 years

Wendy's

Industry experience:	★ ★ ★ ★	*Franchising experience:*	★ ★ ★ ★
Financial strength:	★ ★ ★ ★	*Training & services:*	★ ★ ★ ★
Fees & royalties:	★ ★ ★	*Satisfied franchisees:*	★ ★ ★

Wendy's International, Inc.
P.O. Box 256
Dublin, Ohio 43017
(614) 764-3100

Fortune, Forbes, and The Wall Street Journal all use the same phrase to describe competition among the top four hamburger chains: The Burger Wars. Before Wendy's Old Fashioned Hamburgers burst on the scene in the late 1960s, there were no Burger Wars: There was only McDonald's and after that, everybody else. McDonald's marketing maven Ray Kroc had built an empire on the premise of assembly-line efficiency and uniform consistency. It was the idea of Wendy's founder R. David Thomas to build a franchise system that marketed cooked-to-order hamburgers without skimping on content or condiments. In the decade that followed, the Wendy's chain lept to worldwide prominence, prompting a new era of fierce competition for the fast-food consumer. Today, with 3,500 outlets in the United States, Canada, and more than 30 foreign countries, Wendy's International ranks third in the Burger Wars, but Number One in consumer taste tests.

The Franchise: The franchisee operates a limited-menu restaurant, specializing in hamburgers and other selected menu items, and doing business under the trade name Wendy's Old Fashioned Hamburgers. The Wendy's hamburger is characterized by generous proportions and preparation by broiling. Franchisees may also offer Texas-style chili, chicken sandwiches, various specialty salads, and potatoes with a variety of toppings. A typical outlet is located in approximately 2,600 sq. ft. of space in a shopping mall, strip center, office building, or free-standing site, with four full-time and 30 part-time employees. The interior design features wood lattice dividers, ample use of plants, and a comfortable, airy ambience.

Franchisee Profile: Previous restaurant experience is preferred. The company insists on active ownership and requires that the franchisee live within fifty miles of the franchise. Recently, the company has begun granting single-unit franchises, but generally encourages area franchising or multiple-unit ownership.

Franchisor Services: New franchisees receive 14 weeks of training at Wendy's Management Institute in Dublin, Ohio. Company representatives actively participate in site selection and lease or purchase negotiations. The franchisor provides design specifications and supervises the construction of the new unit. Before the restaurant opens, Wendy's advisors help recruit and hire personnel, plan promotional campaigns, and oversee the installation of food preparation equipment.

Franchisee conventions are held annually, and continuing education seminars are available every quarter.

Initial Investment: The initial investment is estimated at around $200,000, including the initial franchisee, site acquisition, improvements, fixtures, equipment, supplies, signs, and miscellaneous startup costs. Wendy's does not offer any direct financial assistance to franchisees.

Advertising: Franchisees contribute four percent of their gross monthly revenues to the franchisor's ad fund. Wendy's has invested heavily in television and radio advertising to keep abreast with competition. Franchisees may also take advantage of local and regional co-op programs to conduct local campaigns.

Fees and Royalties: The initial franchise fee is $25,000, reflecting a high value placed on name recognition and goodwill. The monthly franchise royalty is eight percent, also high for the industry. Including the advertising fee, the total royalty bite is 12 percent of the gross monthly revenues of the outlet.

Summary: Wendy's stresses local ownership by motivated entrepreneurs with proven track records of success.

Franchise Highlights

Began operating: 1969	**Monthly royalty: 4%**
Began franchising: 1971	**Advertising fee: 4%**
Outlets currently open: 3,500	**Training program: 14 weeks**
Initial franchise fee: $25,000	**Term: 20 years**

Der Wienerschnitzel

Industry experience:	★ ★ ★	*Franchising experience:*	★ ★ ★
Financial strength:	★ ★ ★	*Training & services:*	★ ★ ★ ★
Fees & royalties:	★ ★ ★	*Satisfied franchisees:*	★ ★ ★

Der Wienerschnitzel International
4440 Von Karman Avenue
Newport Beach, California 92660
(714) 752-5800

The first Der Wienerschnitzel opened in California in 1964, with a uniquely diversified hot-dog menu and a convenient, drive-through motif. Over the last two decades, the company's red caped doggie logo has flown over more than 275 outlets, most of them in the west. Fewer than a third the Der Wienerschnitzel restaurants operating today are company-owned, with the rest run by franchisees.

The Franchise: The franchisee operates a retail fast-food restaurant specializing in hot dog sandwiches and doing business under the trade name Der Wienerschnitzel. A typical outlet is a drive-through facility supplemented by enclosed or patio seating for 20 patrons. The restaurant's menu features a selection of hot dogs, including Polish-style sausage sandwiches, served with chili or cheese toppings; traditional hamburger sandwiches; and chicken.

Franchisee Profile: A background in food and beverage management is beneficial, but not mandatory.

Projected Earnings: A written statement of projected earnings was not available at press time.

Franchisor's Services: Der Wienerschnitzel conducts a comprehensive six-week training program for franchisees at the company's headquarters in Newport Beach, California. Another two weeks of training take place at the franchisee's restaurant. Each franchisee receives a set of operations and marketing manuals detailing advertising strategies, business administration, and daily restaurant operations. A Wienerschnitzel representative oversees pre-opening activities and provides ongoing management assistance in periodic visits to the outlet.

Initial Investment: The total start-up investment is estimated at between $100,000 and $400,000, including site acquisition, improvements, equipment purchases, restaurant supplies, and working capital. Der Wienerschnitzel does not offer any direct financial assistance to franchisees.

Fees and Royalties: The initial franchise fee ranges from $10,000 to $30,000, moderate to high for a franchise of this stature. The franchisee's total royalty obligation, including the monthly franchise fee and the advertising fee, is nine percent of gross sales.

Summary: The Der Wienerschnitzel franchise offers good name recognition, a thorough hands-on training process, and the competitive advantages of an established chain.

Franchise Highlights

Began operating: 1964
Began franchising: 1965
Outlets currently open: 275
Initial franchise fee: Min $10,000
Max. $30,000
Monthly royalty: 5%
Advertising fee: 4%
Training program: 6 weeks
Term: Varies

Winchell's Donut House

Industry experience:	★★★★	*Franchising experience:*	★
Financial strength:	★★★★	*Training & services:*	★★★
Fees & royalties:	★★★	*Satisfied franchisees:*	★★★

Winchell's Donut House
16424 Valley View Avenue
La Mirada, California 90637
(714) 670-5300

Winchell's has been spelling the word 'doughnut' as 'donut' for so long that most English dictionaries now recognize both spellings as correct. One of the oldest haunts of hungry law officers, Winchell's has been serving up donuts and coffee since 1948. The company only recently began offering franchises to independent owner/operators. Less than five percent of the chain's 750-plus donut shops are franchise operations.

The Franchise: The franchisee operates a retail fast-food restaurant, specializing in donuts and doing business under the Winchell's Donut House trademark.

Franchisee Profile: A background in food and beverage management is beneficial, but not mandatory. Absentee ownership is prohibited.

Projected Earnings: An estimate of the franchisee's projected earnings was not available at press time.

Franchisor's Services: Winchell's offers six weeks of training at the company's headquarters in La Mirada, California. The curriculum covers food preparation and service, sanitation, personnel administration, restaurant operation, and business procedures. A field specialist assists with pre-opening activities.

A set of operations manuals provide a blueprint for operating and managing the restaurant. Ongoing assistance is available from an area representative during periodic visits to the outlet.

Initial Investment: The total start-up investment ranges from $130,000 to $180,000, including site acquisition, improvements, equipment purchases, furnishings, signs, restaurant supplies, and miscellaneous expenses. Winchell's does not offer any direct financial assistance to franchisees.

Fees and Royalties: The initial franchise fee of $30,000 is high for the trade, but not unreasonable for an organization of this stature. The franchisee's total royalty obligation, including the monthly franchise fee and the advertising fee, is eight percent of gross sales.

Summary: The Winchell's franchise offers good name recognition, comprehensive training, and the competitive benefits of an industry leader. In the donut trade, only Dunkin' Donuts has more outlets.

Franchise Highlights

Began operating: 1948	**Monthly royalty: 5%**
Began franchising: 1985	**Advertising fee: 3%**
Outlets currently open: 770	**Training program: 6 weeks**
Initial franchise fee: $30,000	**Term: 20 years**

Zack's Famous Frozen Yogurt

Industry experience:	★ ★ ★	*Franchising experience:*	★ ★ ★
Financial strength:	★ ★ ★	*Training & services:*	★ ★ ★
Fees & royalties:	★ ★ ★	*Satisfied franchisees:*	★ ★ ★

Zack's Famous Frozen Yogurt
P. O. Box 8522
Metairie, Louisiana 70011
(504) 836-7080

Founded in 1977, Zack's was one of the earliest yoghurt vendors to capitalize on the sensational popularity of frozen desserts served up in shopping malls and department stores. With 120 outlets coast to coast, Zack's boasts the third largest frozen-yoghurt chain in North America. More than 90 percent of the firm's yoghurt stands are owned by independent franchisees. Zack's current expansion plans include Canada, as well as undeveloped U.S. markets.

The Franchise: The franchisee conducts a retail fast-food business, specializing in items prepared with frozen yoghurt and operating under the trade name Zack's Famous Frozen Yogurt. A typical outlet is situated in a regional shopping mall, strip center, or other suitable commercial site, employing a staff of full-time and five part-time employees. Franchisees offer a broad selection of over-the-counter frozen-dessert items, designed to mimick popular ice-cream concoctions, including yoghurt cones, shakes, and sundaes.

Franchisee Profile: A background in the food and beverage industry is beneficial, but not mandatory. Absentee ownership is not prohibited, as long as the franchisee hires a qualified manager to oversee the operation.

Projected Earnings: The average gross revenues of a Zack's outlet are about $170,000 per year, before expenses. Net profits average about $35,000 per outlet.

Franchisor's Services: The franchisor provides a one-week training program at an operating Zack's outlet. Attendees are responsible for their own travel and lodging expenses. The curriculum covers product preparation, storage, sanitation, promotion, and daily operations. An additional three weeks of on-the-job training take place at the franchisee's outlet.

The management and operation of the yoghurt stand are documented in a confidential franchise operations manual. After the stand has opened for business, a Zack's field consultant will visit the outlet periodically, to offer assistance with operations and promotion. The franchisor publishes a franchisee newsletter and conducts ongoing workshops to keep franchisees abreast of new developments and products. A toll-free hotline puts franchisees in touch with Zack's technical and operations experts.

Initial Investment: New Zack's franchisees should be prepared to invest from $100,600 to $117,200 to establish the business. The amount includes lease deposits, site improvements, equipment purchases, initial inventory, advertising, training, and miscellaneous start-up expenses. The franchisor does not offer any direct financial assistance to franchisees.

Advertising: Zack's franchisees contribute three percent of gross monthly revenues for advertising. The franchisor supplies promotional materials, signs, commercials, and direct-mail advertising. Partial reimbursement for ongoing advertising expenses may be available under the franchisor's co-op ad program.

Contract Highlights: The term of the franchise is 20 years. The contract may be renewed for an additional term, by agreement of both parties. The franchisee does not receive a protected territory for the franchise.

Fees and Royalties: The initial franchise fee of $18,000 is moderate for the industry. The five percent monthly royalty, added to the three percent advertising royalty, exacts a total royalty bite of eight percent of gross sales.

Summary: The Zack's franchise offers a ready-made business motif based on a high-profile mall concept with established customer demand. Franchisees benefit from an experienced management team, co-op advertising support, and the competitive benefits of a solid organization that has demonstrated consistent growth for more than a decade.

Franchise Highlights

Began operating: 1977
Began franchising: 1977
Outlets currently open: 120
Initial franchise fee: $18,000

Monthly royalty: 5%
Advertising fee: 3%
Training program: 1 week
Term: 20 years

Lodging Franchises

For the third time in the twentieth century, the hotel industry is undergoing a building spree. Lured by changes in the tax laws that discourage other types of real estate investment, entrepreneurs have infused more than $30 billion to build new lodging establishments over the last decade. As a result, the total number of hotel rooms in America is expanding by four percent every year.

The upstart in this growth picture is the budget motel. A traditional hotel is located on premium property and derives income not only from room sales, but also food and beverage sales, conventions services, and banquets. In contrast, a budget motel eschews expensive roadside real estate and sells nothing but room space. Most budget motels have neither bell hops nor telephones or televisions in the rooms. By eliminating the expenses of running a restaurant, cocktail lounge, and bell service, the motel manages to turn a profit while charging rates 20 to 60 percent lower than a traditional hotel.

About 60 percent of an average hotel's revenues are generated by rooms, with 34 percent emanating from food and beverage service. Ninety seven percent of a budget hotel's income is from room sales. But the average pretax earnings of a budget hotel are 24 percent of gross sales, compared to the 5.1 pretax percent profit of other hotels. Budget motels also constitute the fast growing sector of the $36 billion hotel industry, with chains such as Days Inn, Quality Inn, and La Quinta expanding at a rate of 15 percent per year.

The current building spree has a potential downside. More rooms mean more vacancies, unless business travel increases at an equivalent pace. Some observers predict an industry-wide rate war, which would harm independent operators more than the major chains.

Days Inn

Industry experience:	★★★	*Franchising experience:*	★★★
Financial strength:	★★★	*Training & services:*	★★★
Fees & royalties:	★★★	*Satisfied franchisees:*	★★★★

Days Inns of America
2751 Buford Highway NE
Atlanta, Georgia 30324
(404) 728-4145

Days Inn was the brainchild of Atlanta real estate developer Cecil B. Day, who started out with a group of six no-frills motels. One of Day's key executives, Richard Kessler, happened to be in Florida when he noticed a flurry of construction activity in the Orlando area. The company moved quickly to open new outlets nearby, sowing the seeds for the seventh largest lodging organization in the United States. Today, Days Inn is the major host to visitors to America's number one tourist attraction — Disney World — with 18 motels in Orlando and 50 others throughout Florida. In total, the chain has 450 outlets in 42 states, the District of Columbia, and Canada. Cecil Day died in 1978, but Kessler went on to become the chain's chief executive.

In 1984, the chain was purchased by Reliance Capital, an investment group headed by New York financier Saul Steinberg. Steinberg, who paid about $20,000 per room, resold the chain to a second group at a profit of $10,000 per room. The new syndicator, Integrated Resources, then peddled Days Inn to individual investors. Meanwhile, Steinberg's group continues to operate the chain under a management contract.

The Franchise: The franchisee operates a limited-service lodging establishment under the trade name Days Inn. A typical outlet offers clean, comfortable accommodations without frills, at an average room rate of about $35, a 20 to 60 percent savings over rates at commercial- or executive-class hotels. To reduce the franchisee's investment and overhead, the motel is normally constructed on low- or moderately-priced land, without food or beverage service, meeting facilities, or a swimming pool. The outlet's primary source of revenues is room sales.

Franchisee Profile: A background in hospitality management is preferred. Absentee ownership is permitted.

Projected Earnings: The franchisor does not provide a statement of projected earnings.

Franchisor's Services: The franchisor conducts a two-week program in Atlanta. Attendees are responsible for their own travel and lodging expenses. Two days of on-site training are also included in the program.

The franchisor will supply guidelines for selecting a site, planning layout and construction, and acquiring equipment and furnishings. A Days Inn representative will visit the hotel periodically to offer ongoing guidance. Franchisees receive copies of the confidential Days Inn operating manual, documenting the franchisor's policies and procedures for running the budget motel.

Initial Investment: The initial investment is estimated at around $500,000, including site acquisition, construction, fixtures, equipment, and miscellaneous startup costs. According to an independent source, the cost per room may average around $30,000, depending on location. The franchisor does not offer any direct financial assistance to franchisees.

Advertising: Days Inn motel operators do not pay a separate royalty for advertising. The franchisor conducts national and regional campaigns on behalf of all Days Inn outlets, using travel magazines, hotel directories, and radio. The franchisor also supplies Yellow Page ads, slicks, and commercials for use in local campaigns conducted at the franchisee's expense. Days Inn operates its own national reservation network and is also represented in the computer systems of major airlines and travel agencies.

Contract Highlights: For a new motel, the franchise term is 20 years. The franchisee receives a protected territory for the duration of the agreement.

Fees and Royalties: The initial franchise fee varies, depending on the location and size of the motel. The 6.5 percent monthly royalty is average for the hospitality industry.

Summary: Over the last decade, Days Inn earned a reputation as one of the fastest-growing and most profitable lodging chains in America. The budget motel trade is considerably more competitive today, and the market may be nearing saturation. The Days Inn franchise still offers the erstwhile budget-hotelier a ready-made format with a proven track record of success.

Franchise Highlights

Began operating: 1970	**Monthly royalty: 6.5%**
Began franchising: 1971	**Advertising fee: None**
Outlets currently open: 450	**Training program: 2 weeks**
Initial franchise fee: Varies	**Term: 20 years**

Econo Lodge

Industry experience:	★ ★ ★	*Franchising experience:*	★ ★ ★
Financial strength:	★ ★ ★	*Training & services:*	★ ★ ★
Fees & royalties:	★ ★ ★	*Satisfied franchisees:*	★ ★ ★

Econo Lodges of America
6135 Park Road, Ste. 200
Charlotte, North Carolina 28210
(704) 554-0088

'Spend the night, not a fortune' is the slogan that blinks down on motorists from the marquees of Econo Lodge outlets. Founded in 1969, the chain has grown to more than 420 budget motels in less than two decades.

The Franchise: The franchisee operates a roadside motor inn, based on the franchisor's specifications, designs, and trademark. A typical outlet has 100 rooms and offers clean, attractively furnished accommodations at competitive rates. Econo Lodge properties do not offer food and beverage service.

Franchisee Profile: A background in hospitality management is beneficial, but not mandatory.

Projected Earnings: An estimate of projected earnings was not available at press time.

Franchisor's Services: Econo Lodge franchisees receive training in one to three weeks at the company's headquarters in Charlotte, North Carolina. A team of start-up specialists spends time at the franchisee's site, assisting with planning, layout, construction, equipment purchases, and furnishings. A set of operations manuals documents the franchisor's standards and specifications for operating the budget motel. Field representatives inspect the site periodically and offer ongoing management assistance.

Initial Investment: The total start-up investment is estimated at from $250,000 to $2.5 million, including land, construction, equipment purchases, supplies, and miscellaneous expenses. The franchisor does not offer any direct financial assistance to franchisees.

Fees and Royalties: The initial franchise fee of $20,000 is moderate for the lodging industry. The franchisee's total royalty obligation, including the monthly franchise fee and the advertising fee, is less than seven percent of gross sales.

Summary: Econo Lodge, primarily concentrated in the southeast, is one of the fastest growing lodging chains in North America. The franchisor is currently seeking new franchisees in most U.S. and Canadian markets.

Franchise Highlights

Began operating: 1969	**Monthly royalty: 4%**
Began franchising: 1969	**Advertising fee: 2.5%**
Outlets currently open: 420	**Training program: 3 weeks**
Initial franchise fee: $20,000	**Term: 5 years**

Friendship Inns

Industry experience:	★ ★ ★	*Franchising experience:*	★
Financial strength:	★ ★ ★	*Training & services:*	★ ★ ★
Fees & royalties:	★ ★ ★	*Satisfied franchisees:*	★ ★ ★

Friendship Inns International
2627 Paterson Plank Road
North Bergen, New Jersey 07047
(201) 863-3443

Friendship Inns was formerly a referral organization made up of 380 independent hotel operators who paid annual dues to participate in a low-key, national promotion program. Hotelier Al Olshan acquired the trade name rights in 1985 and set out to convert member hotels to full-fledged franchise operations.

The Franchise: Converted franchisees participate in a national reservation system and operate under the Friendship Inn trademark. The properties must comply with the franchisor's standards for sanitation, appearance, and maintenance.

Franchisee Profile: A typical Friendship Inn franchisee previously owned and operated an independent lodging establishment. The chain's emphasis is on full-service, mid-market hotels, rather than executive-class or budget lodging.

Projected Earnings: An estimate of average volume or earnings was not available at press time.

Franchisor's Services: Friendship Inns administers a national, toll-free reservation system and promotes franchisees to travel agencies and tour operators. The franchisor has committed 30 percent of franchise royalties to advertising, in an attempt to heighten name recognition and upgrade the chain's image.

Initial Investment: The investment is estimated at about $12,600, including the initial fee and minor, miscellaneous expenses. The franchisor does not offer any direct financial assistance to franchisees.

Fees and Royalties: The initial franchise fee of $12,500 is low for a lodging franchise. The franchisee's royalty obligation is calculated at the rate of 49 cents per room per day. For example, a 100-room hotel might pay $1,470 in royalties in a 30-day month. There is no separate advertising fee.

Summary: The Friendship Inn franchise program offers a low-investment vehicle for adding national advertising and uniform imaging to the established, independent lodging establishment.

Franchise Highlights

Began operating: 1960
Began franchising: 1985
Outlets currently open: 90
Initial franchise fee: $12,500
Monthly royalty: Varies
Advertising fee: None
Term: 10 years

Hilton Inn

Industry experience:	★ ★ ★ ★	*Franchising experience:*	★ ★ ★ ★
Financial strength:	★ ★ ★ ★	*Training & services:*	★ ★ ★ ★
Fees & royalties:	★ ★ ★	*Satisfied franchisees:*	★ ★ ★ ★

Hilton Inns
P. O. Box 5567
Beverly Hills, California 90210
(213) 205-4407

Franchises account for approximately 55 percent of Hilton's total hotel rooms. Since 1972, franchisees have added 39,000 additional rooms to the prestigious lodging chain. Besides franchising, Hilton also offers a management leaseback program under which the company sells part of its equity in an existing hotel, but continues to manage the property for a percentage of room revenues and gross profits.

Barron Hilton, the second oldest son of the company's late founder, Conrad Hilton, convinced his father 21 years ago to sell Hilton's international hotels. Hilton International has changed hands twice, but still competes directly with Hilton Inns.

The Franchise: The franchisee operates an executive-class lodging establishment catering to business travelers, under the trade name Hilton Inn. A typical outlet has approximately 170 rooms, designed, constructed, and furnished according to the franchisor's specifications and standards. The franchisee produces revenues from room sales, banquets, food and beverage service, meetings, and conventions.

Franchisee Profile: A background in hotel management is required. Absentee ownership is permitted.

Franchisor's Services: Franchisees receive comprehensive training on all aspects of running a Hilton Inn, at the franchisor's training center in Beverly Hills and at the franchisee's own site. The franchisor supplies guidelines for site layout, construction, decor, and furnishings.

When the hotel is operational, a Hilton representative will inspect the outlet periodically and offer on-site guidance and troubleshooting.

Initial Investment: The total investment, including working capital, may range as high as $6 million, including the cost of land, construction, furnishings, decor, equipment, supplies, and miscellaneous start-up expenses.

Advertising: Hilton franchisees do not pay a separate royalty for advertising. The franchisor operates a toll-free reservation system and is represented in major airline and travel agency reservation computers.

Fees and Royalties: The initial franchise fee ranges from $25,000 to $60,000 — average for an executive-class hotel. The five percent monthly royalty is moderate.

Summary: The Hilton Inns franchise offers a prestigious name and the management support of one of the world's most influential lodging chains. As an indication of the company's performance, Forbes magazine once rated Hilton's stock first in long-term performance among all publicly held hotel corporations.

Franchise Highlights

Began operating: 1947
Began franchising: 1965
Outlets currently open: 350
Initial franchise fee: Min. $25,000
Max. $60,000

Monthly royalty: 5%
Advertising fee: None
Training program: Varies
Term: 20 years

Holiday Inn

Industry experience:	★★★★	*Franchising experience:*	★★★★
Financial strength:	★★★★	*Training & services:*	★★★★
Fees & royalties:	★★★	*Satisfied franchisees:*	★★★★

Holiday Inn
3796 Lamar Avenue
Memphis, Tennessee 38195
(901) 362-4663

The first pulsating pink and white Holiday Inn sign cast its neon arrow into the night sky in 1952. Thirty years later, the company replaced the classic relic of Fifties garishness with the more stately sign that adorns the inns today. Though its roadside image may have changed, Holiday Inn is still the world's largest hotel operator, with more than 1,600 lodging establishments. Since 1984, the company has pursued an aggressive system-wide campaign to upgrade both its image and standards, pruning inefficient franchises and company-operated hotels. Nearly 90 percent of the Holiday Inns in the United States are independently owned franchises.

The franchise: The Holiday Inn franchisee operates an upscale lodging establishment catering to vacationing family units and business travelers. A typical outlet has 184 rooms in a four to six story structure on a 3.5 acre site, with 45 full-time and 12 part-time employees. Depending on the size and investment, representative facilities include a restaurant, cocktail lounge, swimming pool, and meeting rooms. In addition to room revenues, franchisees also derive income from food and beverage sales, banquets, and convention services. Both midrise and vertical (highrise) prototypes are available.

Franchisee Profile: A background in hotel management or operations is mandatory. Absentee ownership is allowed, as long as a qualified director will manage the operation.

Projected Earnings: A typical Holiday Inn generates between $2 and $5 million in gross annual revenues.

Franchisor's Services: The franchisor provides an intensive two-week training program at the Holiday Inn University in Memphis. Attendees are responsible for their own travel and lodging expenses. The curriculum includes hotel organization, daily operations, food and beverage control, back office systems, marketing, promotion, and personnel administration.

The various departments of the outlet will be inspected regularly by franchise representatives to assure compliance with Holiday Inn standards and specifications. The company's field advisors work closely with franchisees to troubleshoot problems and maximize efficiency.

Use of a computerized reservation system, called Holidex, is available at a fee of $4.20 per room per month.

Initial Investment: The initial investment ranges from $49,400 per room for a midrise hotel to $67.000 per room based on the vertical prototype. The amount includes land financing, legal fees, site construction, furnishings, fixtures, and equipment. The franchisor does not offer any direct financial assistance to franchisees.

Advertising: Holiday Inn franchisees contribute two percent of gross monthly revenues for advertising. The franchisor conducts aggressive national ad campaigns, using television, radio, newspapers, and magazines. Franchisees also receive referrals from the franchisor's national reservation system. Holiday Inn is also represented in major travel agency and airline computer networks.

Fees and Royalties: The initial franchise fee is $300 per room. The minimum fee for any hotel is $30,000. Including the franchise royalty and advertising fee, the total royalty burden is a moderate six percent of gross revenues.

Summary: The Holiday Inn franchise offers excellent name recognition, a thorough start-up package, and some of the most sophisticated marketing, reservation, and management systems in the lodging industry. The franchisor estimates that 96 percent of the nation's travelers have stayed at least one night in a Holiday Inn.

Franchise Highlights

Began operating: 1952
Began franchising: 1954
Outlets currently open: 1,650
Initial franchise fee: Min. $30,000
Monthly royalty: 4%
Advertising fee: 1.5%
Training program: 2 weeks

Park Inn

Industry experience:	★★	*Franchising experience:*	★★
Financial strength:	★★★	*Training & services:*	★★
Fees & royalties:	★★★	*Satisfied franchisees:*	★★★★

Park Inns International
4441 W. Airport Freeway
Irving, Texas 75062
(214) 258-8507

The Park Inn concept was the brainchild of hotelier Robert L. Brock, who bought one of the first Holiday Inn franchises in 1955. Brock later founded the Showbiz Pizza chain. Combining his hotel and franchise experience, he opened the first Park Inn International in February, 1986. The chain already as 30 outlets, offering existing hotels the opportunity to convert to a national franchise system.

The Franchise: Hotels that opt to convert to Park Inns International receive a protected territory for the term of the agreement — 15 years. The new franchisee is not required to invest in any new construction or property alterations. The franchisor offers an optional Park Dome package incorporating such recreational facilities as a swimming pool, whirlpool, and open cocktail lounge.

Franchisee Profile: A typical Park Inn franchisee has owned and operated an existing hotel prior to converting to the franchise system.

Projected Earnings: An estimate of projected earnings was not available at press time.

Franchisor's Services: Park Inns offers the advertising, purchasing, and communications benefits of a franchise organization, combined with the entrepeneurial freedom of an independent hotel operator. The system includes former franchisees of other lodging franchises. Franchisees are required to honor the franchisor's policies and standards, which include rules governing landscaping and maintenance.

Initial Investment: The investment is estimated at from $54,000 to $7 million. The franchisor does not offer any direct financial assistance to franchisees.

Fees and Royalties: The initial franchise fee ranges from $4,500 to $22,500 — low to moderate for a lodging franchise. The franchisee's total royalty obligation, including the 2.9 percent monthly franchise royalty and the one percent advertising fee, is under four percent of gross revenues.

Summary: The Park Inn franchise offers a protected territory, low royalties, and positive imaging.

Franchise Highlights

Began operating: 1986
Began franchising: 1986
Outlets currently open: 30
Initial franchise fee: Min $4,500
Max. $22,500

Monthly royalty: 2.9%
Advertising fee: 1%
Term: 15 years

Quality Inns, Comfort Inns, Clarion Resorts

Industry experience:	★★★★	*Franchising experience:*	★★★★
Financial strength:	★★★★	*Training & services:*	★★★★
Fees & royalties:	★★★	*Satisfied franchisees:*	★★★★

Quality Inns
10750 Columbus Pike
Silver Springs, Maryland 20901
(301) 236-5080

In the wake of the budget motel boom of the mid 1960s, the Quality Inns/Comfort Inns chain emerged as a legitimate contender for the industry leadership. A moderate investment, low overhead, and new financial advantages under the 1987 Tax Reform Law prompted a recent growth spurt in the development of new motels.

The Franchise: The franchisee operates a budget motel under the trade name Quality Inn, Comfort Inn, or Clarion. A typical outlet is situated on low-to-moderately priced property, accessible from a major thoroughfare, offering clean, attractively furnished accommodations at competitive rates. Quality Inns and Comfort Inns eschew such conventional hotel amenities as bell service, expansive lobbies, and food and beverage operations, whereas a typical Clarion resort offers a full range of hotel services.

Franchisor's Services: The franchisor provides two days of training at corporate headquarters in Silver Spring, Maryland, near Washington, D.C., and additional training and pre-opening assistance at the franchisee's outlet. Each franchisee receives a set of comprehensive operations manuals detailing the management, finance, and daily operation of the business. A field consultant provides ongoing management assistance in periodic visits to the lodging establishment.

Initial Investment: The total investment starts at around $275,000. Actual start-up costs vary significantly, depending on the type, size, and location of the property.

Fees and Royalties: The initial franchise fee of $25,000 is moderate for a budget motel. The franchisee's total royalty obligation, including the monthly franchise fee and the advertising fee, is a low five percent of gross sales.

Summary: Quality Inns, Comfort Inns, and Clarion resorts are well represented by travel agents and major airline reservationists. Franchisees benefit from good name recognition, positive imaging, and a profitable operating motif.

Franchise Highlights

Began operating: 1941
Began franchising: 1941
Outlets currently open: 750
Initial franchise fee: $25,000
Monthly royalty: 4%
Advertising fee: 1%
Training program: 2 days
Term: 20 years

Ramada Inn

Industry experience:	★★★★	*Franchising experience:*	★★★★
Financial strength:	★★★	*Training & services:*	★★★
Fees & royalties:	★★★	*Satisfied franchisees:*	★★★

Ramada Inn System
3838 East Van Buren
Phoenix, Arizona 85008
(602) 273-4000

Ramada Inn derives approximately half of its income from its Tropicana casino hotels in Las Vegas and Atlantic City. But Ramada is not the only major lodging chain that has managed to stay afloat by catering to the public fascination with gambling and lotteries. Industry leaders Hilton and Marriott also operate gambling casinos to bolster system-wide earnings to the benefit of independent franchise operators.

CEO Richard Snell's current expansion plans include the establishment of new, upscale hotels capable of commanding higher room rates and attracting lucrative convention business. With close to 100,000 rooms in 570 properties, Ramada is the third largest hotel operator in the world.

The Franchise: The franchisee operates a tourist-class motor inn, under the trade name Ramada Inn. Besides the company's bread-and-butter hotels, Ramada also offers a posh, higher-class motif under the trade name Renaissance Inns. Ramada properties offer full-service hotel accommodations with coffee shops, restaurants, swimming pools, banquet rooms, and convention facilities.

Franchisor's Services: Ramada Inn trains franchisees at its headquarters in Phoenix, Arizona and at the franchisee's site. The franchisor also conducts continuing education seminars for franchisees and key members of their management staffs.

The confidential Ramada Inns operations manual provides an operational blueprint for planning, operating, and managing the lodging establishment in compliance with the franchisor's standards and specifications. An area representative provides periodic on-site guidance.

Fees and Royalties: The initial franchise fee varies, depending on the location and size of the motor inn. The total royalty obligation, including the monthly franchise fee and the advertising fee, is less than seven percent of gross sales.

Litigation and Disputes: In the case of Ramada Inns vs. Gadsden Motel Company, the franchisor terminated a franchisee involuntarily for failing to comply with the franchisor's standards for quality and service. Ramada ordered the franchisee to cease using the franchisor's trademarks, but the franchisee refused to take down the sign. A federal court ruled in favor of the franchisor, granting damages not only for unpaid royalties but also for infringing on the Ramada trademark.

Summary: In the past, Ramada Inn outlets have been typified by highly variable operating standards. The company is currently striving to enhance its repuation with new upscale hotels featuring an executive-class image. The franchise program offers good name recognition, competent training, and the management attention of an experienced support staff.

Franchise Highlights

Began operating: 1954
Began franchising: 1959
Outlets currently open: 570
Initial franchise fee: Varies
Monthly royalty: 3%
Advertising fee: 3.5%
Training program: Varies
Term: 20 years

Rodeway Inn

Industry experience:	★ ★ ★	*Franchising experience:*	★ ★ ★
Financial strength:	★ ★ ★	*Training & services:*	★ ★ ★
Fees & royalties:	★ ★ ★	*Satisfied franchisees:*	★ ★ ★

Rodeway Inns International
8585 N. Stemmons Freeway, Ste. 400-S
Dallas, Texas 75247
(800) 345-3453

The first Rodeway Inn opened in 1961 and, since that time, the company has opened more than 150 mid-market hotels.

The Franchise: The franchisee operates a full-service lodging establishment in the medium rate category, under the trade name Rodeway Inn. A typical outlet has 100 rooms and a swimming pool, and offers modest food and beverage service on the same premises. The franchisor licenses new franchisees, as well as existing hotels interested in converting to the franchise program.

Franchisee Profile: A background in hospitality management is beneficial, but not mandatory. The prospective franchisee must be capable of demonstrating a net worth of at least $1.5 million, with $750,000 in liquid assets.

Projected Earnings: An estimate of the franchisee's projected earnings was not available at press time.

Franchisor's Services: A Rodeway Inns development team provides on-site assistance prior to opening. Franchisees participate in the franchisor's national reservation system and are represented in major travel agency and airline systems. A field manager periodically inspects each hotel and offers on-site troubleshooting.

Initial Investment: The total start-up investment for a new hotel may range as high as $3 million, including the cost of land, construction, equipment, furnishings, signs, landscaping, and miscellaneous expenses. Rodeway Inns does not offer any direct financial assistance to franchisees.

Fees and Royalties: The initial franchise fee of $15,000 is moderate for a major hotel chain. The franchisee's total royalty obligation, including the monthly franchise fee and the advertising fee, is just four percent of gross revenues.

Summary: The Rodeway Inns franchise is characterized by increasing name recognition, on-site training, and a competitive rate structure.

Franchise Highlights

Began operating: 1961
Began franchising: 1961
Outlets currently open: 160
Initial franchise fee: $15,000
Monthly royalty: 3%
Advertising fee: 1%
Term: 10 years

Sheraton Inns

Industry experience:	★★★★	*Franchising experience:*	★★★★
Financial strength:	★★★★	*Training & services:*	★★★★
Fees & royalties:	★★★	*Satisfied franchisees:*	★★★★

Sheraton Inns
60 State Street
Boston, Massachusetts
(617) 367-5300

Founded in 1937, Sheraton Inns today operates a worldwide chain of 500 executive-class hotels and tourist resorts, 70 percent of which are owned by independent franchisees. A subsidiary of ITT Corporation, Sheraton enjoys annual franchise revenues of $800 million. In recent years, the company has undertaken a system-wide effort to upgrade the operating standards and image of its franchised properties.

The Franchise: The franchisee operates an upscale lodging establishment designed, constructed, and managed according to the franchisor's specifications, and doing business under the trade name Sheraton Inn. A typical outlet has 100 rooms with a restaurant, cocktail lounge, banquet facilities, meeting rooms and swimming pool. Larger resort properties may include additional facilities, such as multiple restaurants and/or a golf course. Franchisees derive revenues from room sales, food and beverage sales, convention services, and banquets. Customers of the franchise business include business travelers, conventions, resort patrons, and vacationing families.

Franchisee Profile: A background in the hospitality industry is preferred, but absentee ownership is permitted.

Projected Earnings: Based on the company's reported annual earnings, the average revenues of a Sheraton hotel are about $2.4 million, before deducting expenses and royalties. The average net profit per hotel is about $118,000 — approximately five percent of gross sales.

Franchisor's Services: The franchisor provides a five-day training program for the hotel's management staff and participates in grand opening activities. Sheraton helps plan, build, and decorate the establishment and recruit a qualified director.

A Sheraton field representative will inspect the hotel periodically and hold meetings with the franchisee's key management personnel. The franchisor operates a centralized purchasing program for supplies and equipment, much of which is marketed by Sheraton under its own trademark. The company's field advisers are accessible by phone as required.

Initial Investment: According to independent sources, the cost of constructing a new Sheraton hotel may range from $45,000 to $70,000 per room, depending on location and type. The estimate does not include the initial franchise fee, and is not based on any projection furnished by the franchisor. Sheraton does not offer any direct financial assistance to franchisees.

Advertising: Sheraton hotels participate in co-op programs to fund newspaper, magazine, radio, and Yellow Page advertising. Referrals are also provided from the franchisor's national toll- free reservation system. Sheraton works closely with major airlines, travel agencies, and tour operators to create new and repeat business for franchisees, as well as company-operated hotels. Apart from the franchise royalty, Sheraton franchisees do not pay a separate ad fee.

Contract Highlights: The Sheraton franchise agreement has a term of ten years. On expiration, the contract may be renewed for an additional term, if the franchisee is not in violation of any material provisions. The franchisee receives a protected territory for the duration of the agreement.

Fees and Royalties: The initial franchise fee is $30,000 for a hotel with up to 100 rooms. A surcharge of $150 per room applies for larger establishments. The five percent monthly royalty is moderate for the hospitality industry.

Summary: The Sheraton chain offers positive imaging and a sophisticated client recruitment system. Once characterized by variable standards, the franchisor is currently pursuing a program of building only executive-class and premium resort establishments.

Franchise Highlights

Began operating: 1937
Began franchising: 1962
Outlets currently open: 500
Initial franchise fee: $30,000
Monthly royalty: 5%
Advertising fee: None
Training program: 5 days
Term: 10 years

Super 8

Industry experience:	★ ★ ★	*Franchising experience:*	★ ★ ★
Financial strength:	★ ★ ★	*Training & services:*	★ ★ ★
Fees & royalties:	★ ★ ★	*Satisfied franchisees:*	★ ★ ★ ★

Super 8 Motels, Inc.
P. O. Box 4090
Aberdeen, South Dakota 57401
(605) 225-2272

Founded in 1974 in the wake of the budget motel boom of the late 1960s, Super 8 has expanded to over 400 sites across the U.S. and Canada. Although increasing operating costs and a weaker dollar have banished the original $18.88 room rate, the chain still retains its reputation for clean, comfortable accommodations at bottom-dollar prices.

The Franchise: The franchisee operates an economy-class lodging establishment under the trade name Super 8. A typical outlet offers full-size, attractively furnished rooms with limited hotel services, at highly competitive rates. Super 8 outlets are distinctive among budget motels for equipping rooms with color televisions and direct-dial telephone service.

Franchisee Profile: A background in hospitality management is beneficial, but not mandatory.

Projected Earnings: A projected earnings statement was not available at press time.

Franchisor's Services: Super 8 offers a three-week training program in Aberdeen, South Dakota. Additional training and grand opening assistance are provided at the franchisee's site. The franchisor provides a set of comprehensive operations manuals, ongoing assistance from an area manager, and telephone access to corporate operations experts.

Initial Investment: The total start-up investment is estimated at from $150,000 to $500,000, including land, construction, equipment, furnishings, signage, supplies, and miscellaneous expenses. Super 8 does not offer any direct financial assistance to franchisees.

Fees and Royalties: The initial franchise fee of $20,000 is moderate for a lodging chain of this stature. Super 8 franchisees pay an ongoing franchise royalty of 4 percent of room revenues, plus an additional two percent for advertising.

Summary: The Super 8 franchise offers a moderate initial investment (by lodging industry standards), a successful operating format, and ample name recognition.

Franchise Highlights

Began operating: 1974	**Monthly royalty: 4%**
Began franchising: 1974	**Advertising fee: 2%**
Outlets currently open: 430	**Training program: 3 weeks**
Initial franchise fee: $20,000	**Term: 20 years**

Travelodge

Industry experience:	★★★★	*Franchising experience:*	★★★★
Financial strength:	★★★	*Training & services:*	★★★
Fees & royalties:	★★★	*Satisfied franchisees:*	★★★

Travelodge
1973 Friendship Drive
El Cajon, California 92041
(619) 448-1884

In its 40-year history, Travelodge has suffered episodes of economic turmoil and problems with its image, but under the aegis of British leisure conglomerate Trusthouse Forte, promises to revitalize its system of 290 outlets, which extend from Florida to Fiji.

The Franchise: The franchisee operates a mid-market lodging establishment under the trade name Travelodge. A typical outlet provides comfortable accommodations with color televisions and in-room telephone service at competitive rates.

Franchisee Profile: Travelodge is currently seeking prospective franchisees with experience in hospitality management and/or hotel development.

Projected Earnings: An estimate of the franchisee's projected earnings was not available at press time.

Franchisor's Services: Travelodge provides a one-week training program in El Cajon, California prior to opening. Additional training takes place at the franchisee's hotel periodically. The franchisee receives a set of operations manuals, on-site grand opening assistance, and ongoing marketing support. The franchisor operates a worldwide reservation system and is tied into the automated hotel databases used by travel agents and airlines. Field consultants offer management support in regular visits to the franchisee's hotel.

Initial Investment: The start-up investment ranges from $500,000, including land and construction costs, equipment, furnishings, signs, supplies, and working capital. Travelodge does not offer any direct financial assistance to franchisees.

Fees and Royalties: The minimum franchise fee is $15,000, moderate for the industry. The franchisee's total royalty obligation, including the monthly franchise fee and the advertising fee, is seven percent of gross sales.

Summary: The Travelodge franchise offers strong, worldwide name recognition and outstanding advertising support in an increasingly competitive market.

Franchise Highlights

Began operating: 1947	**Monthly royalty: 3%**
Began franchising: 1966	**Advertising fee: 4%**
Outlets currently open: 290	**Training program: 1 week**
Initial franchise fee: Min. $15,000	**Term: 10 years**

Personal Services

Franchising has long been a favorite expansion strategy in the personal services industry. Hairstyling and beauty salons became popular weekly haunts of American housewives in the 1950s. The casual fashion trend of the 1960s dealt a severe blow to the industry, but as the Post-War Baby Boomers came of age, a new generation of unisex haircutting establishments took over the industry. Hair care today is a thriving $13 billion industry.

Besides being fashion-conscious, Americans are also more fitness-conscious than before. Revitalizing the careers of aging actresses, the exercise craze also catapulted ordinary people into multimillionaires. The list of the world's 20 largest franchise organizations include two fitness busineses — Jazzercise and Diet Center, Inc. With one of every ten Americans on some kind of diet at any given time, the nation spends more than $35 billion annually on diet and fitness.

The Barbers

Industry experience: ★★★★ *Franchising experience:* ★★★
Financial strength: ★★★ *Training & services:* ★★★
Fees & royalties: ★★★ *Satisfied franchisees:* ★★★★

Barbers Hairstyling For Men and Women
300 Industrial Boulevard NE
Maples, Minnesota 55413
(612) 331-8500

The Barbers Hairstyling For Men and Women has successfully established 150 franchised and company-owned outlets based on its standardized business format and hairstyling system. Today, the franchise organization offers the benefit of a steady growth record accompanied by increasing name recognition.

The Franchise: The franchisee conducts a retail hairstyling business for men and women, under the trade name The Barbers Hairstyling for Men & Women. A typical outlet is situated in a strip center, shopping mall, or other suitable retail site, employing up to ten full-time and five part-time hairstylists. Franchisees offer haircutting and styling services and sell hair care merchandise to the general public.

Franchisee Profile: A hairstyling background or license is not mandatory, although some prior experience is helpful. The franchisee does not have to participate full-time in the management of the outlet, providing that a qualified manager is on the payroll.

Projected Earnings: The franchisor does not furnish a statement of projected earnings to prospective franchisees.

Franchisor's Services: The Barbers conducts a training program from one to two weeks in length at the company's headquarters in Minnesota. Franchisees must pay for their own travel and lodging expenses. An additional two days of on-the-job training take place at the franchisee's salon.

The franchisor will assist with selecting a site for the outlet and negotiating a lease for the premises. In addition, a field representative will help plan construction and improvements before the site opens. When the salon is open for business, an area manager visits the outlet periodically to provide ongoing consultation. The support package also includes franchisee workshops and seminars, advertising assistance, and a newsletter.

Initial Investment: New franchisees should be prepared to invest from $10,000 to $150,000 to establish the business, depending on location and size. The amount includes lease deposits, site improvements, equipment purchases, and an initial inventory of hair care products for resale. The franchisor does not offer any direct financial assistance to franchisees.

Advertising: Franchisees contribute from one percent to five percent of gross monthly revenues for advertising. The franchisor conducts national and regional campaigns on behalf of franchisees.

Contract Highlights: The term of the franchise is 15 years. The contract may be renewed for an additional five years, if the franchisee is in compliance with all material provisions. There is no fee to renew the franchise agreement. The franchisee does not receive an exclusive territory.

Fees and Royalties: The initial franchise fee ranges from $6,000 to $12,000; both figures are moderate for the industry. The five percent monthly royalty, combined with an advertising contribution of one to five percent are lower than the norm.

Summary: The Barbers franchise has enjoyed a steady growth course in key markets, expanding name recognition, and a high level of repeat business. Franchises are currently available in all states and in selected overseas markets, but not in Canada.

Franchise Highlights

Began operating: 1963	**Monthly royalty: 5%**
Began franchising: 1970	**Advertising fee: Min. 1%**
Outlets currently open: 150	**Max. 5%**
Initial franchise fee: Min $6,000	**Training program: 2 weeks**
Max. $12,000	**Term: 15 years**

Command Performance

Industry experience:	★ ★ ★ ★	*Franchising experience:*	★ ★ ★ ★
Financial strength:	★ ★ ★ ★	*Training & services:*	★ ★ ★ ★
Fees & royalties:	★ ★ ★	*Satisfied franchisees:*	★ ★ ★

Command Performance
335 Middlesex Ave.
Wilmington, MA 01887
(617) 658-6586

Command Performance was one of the first enterprises to transform an independent hair salon into a nationwide franchise system. The success of this endeavor hinged on creating efficient business management techniques for what was traditionally regarded as a cottage industry. The franchise system expanded so rapidly in its first three years, the company found itself unable to keep up with its own growth rate. After a period of economic turmoil, the franchisor successfully regrouped to assume its present position as one of the nation's foremost chains of hairstyling salons. The company's meteoric rise is still evidenced by a widely recognized name, more than 340 franchises in 41 states, and $80 million in gross annual sales.

The Franchise: The franchise operates a retail hairstyling salon for men and women, under the trade name Command Performance. A typical outlet is a 1,500 sq. ft. retail space in a shopping center, mall, or other suitable commercial site, with ten full-time and six part-time employees. A contemporary, upscale decor creates an environment in which clients feel comfortable and confident. The company's reputation is based on the premise of moderate pricing and brightly lit, high-tech furnishings. Franchisees derive profits from haircutting, styling, and sales of hair care merchandise.

The Franchisee Profile: A cosmetician's license or prior experience in operating a haircutting salon is helpful, but not essential. The company allows the franchisee to hire a qualified manager to operate the outlet. Multiple unit ownership is common.

Projected Earnings: A projected earnings statement for Command Performance outlets is not available. However, based on reported sales figures, the average outlet generates approximately $260,000 in gross annual revenues.

Franchisor Services: New franchisees attend a 30-hour training seminar in either Massachusetts or Ohio. The curriculum focuses on the management aspects of the haircutting operation. A field representative will assist with selecting a site, negotiating the lease, and planning the construction and decor of the salon.

The franchisor employs a full-time staff of field consultants to provide on-site guidance, both before and after the outlet opens. Pre-opening assistance includes promotional, advertising, and marketing planning; personnel hiring and training; and help with ordering equipment and supplies.

The company's training center, Command Performance Hair Institute, conducts frequent workshops and seminars to keep franchisees and their employees abreast of hairstyling trends and techniques. The franchisor charges a fee for ongoing seminars. Command Performance distributes a private brand of hair care merchandise to franchisees for resale.

Initial Investment: The minimum cash investment required to start a Command Performance hair salon ranges from $70,000 to 130,000. The actual amount depends on the site, cost of improvements, staff, local economic conditions, and other variables. The franchisor has a financial assistance program for creditworthy franchisees.

Advertising: Command Performance does not operate a co-op ad fund. Franchisees do not pay any advertising royalties or fees for on-going promotions. The company administers a conscientious national advertising campaign and enjoys excellent name recognition in most major markets.

Fee and Royalties: The initial franchise of $21,500 is a reasonable reflection of the system's stature and size. A moderate royalty bite of six percent of gross monthly revenues is below the industry average, considering that the company does not exact advertising royalties.

Contract Highlights: The term of the franchise is 15 years, with a 15 year first renewal option. The franchisee has exclusive rights within his or her territory. Subfranchising rights are available under a separate agreement. The outlet must be open for business within six months after the signing of the franchise agreement. Franchisees may purchase hair care products for resale from the franchisor, but are not restricted from carrying other brands that meet Command Performance's quality control standards.

Summary: Command Performance emerged from economic difficulties to demonstrate new maturity and stability. Franchisee satisfaction is generally high, reflecting the company's role as a major U.S. franchisor. Franchisees benefit from strong name recognition and positive imaging, a solid base of outlets supported by a strong management team, and an effective — if conservative — advertising program.

Franchise Highlights

Began operating: 1976
Began franchising: 1976
Outlets currently open: 340
Initial franchise fee: $21,500
Monthly royalty: 6%
Advertising fee: None
Training program: 30 hours
Term: 15 years

Cost Cutters

Industry experience: ★★ *Franchising experience:* ★★★
Financial strength: ★★★ *Training & services:* ★★★
Fees & royalties: ★★★ *Satisfied franchisees:* ★★★★

Cost Cutters Family Hair Care Shop
300 Industrial Boulevard NE
Minneapolis, Minnesota 55413
(612) 331-8500

Cost Cutters has opened more than 200 franchises and 30 company-owned hair care salons since 1982 — a growth clip of more than 40 new outlets per year. Rather than catering exclusively to women or men, Cost Cutters successfully focuses on family hair care, based on standardized haircutting procedures in a modern, attractive environment.

The Franchise: The franchisee operates a retail haircutting salon, under the trade name Cost Cutters Family Hair Care Shops. A typical outlet is housed in a 1,500 sq. ft. retail site, with ten full-time and five part-time employees. Franchisees offer haircutting and styling services for men, women, and children.

Franchisee Profile: No prior experience in the hair care field is necessary. The company is seeking prospective franchisees with sound business abilities and 'people' skills.

Projected Earnings: The franchisor does not provide a statement of projected earnings.

Franchisor's Services: Cost Cutters conducts a training program from three to five days in length at the company's headquarters in Minneapolis. Franchisees must pay their own travel and lodging expenses to attend the program. One to five days of on-the-job training tare provided at the franchisee's salon.

Cost Cutters assists with selecting a site for the franchisee's outlet and negotiating a lease for the premises. Cost Cutters also helps plan the layout and construction of improvements, acquisition of equipment and supplies, and Grand Opening. After the outlet is open, a field representative visits the outlet periodically to provide ongoing advice and troubleshooting. The franchisor's support program also includes refresher courses and continuing education seminars, annual franchisee conventions, and a newsletter covering franchise events and industry trends.

Initial Investment: The total investment is estimated between $25,000 and $60,000. The amount includes lease deposits, improvements, equipment, supplies, and merchandise. The franchisor does not offer any direct financial assistance to franchisees.

Advertising: The four percent advertising royalty pays for national and regional campaigns, and the development of ad materials for use in local promotions.

Contract Highlights: The term of the franchise is 15 years, with a 15-year renewal option. The franchisee does not receive a protected territory, but multiple unit ownership is permitted. The franchisee does not have to participate full-time in the management of the business, providing that a qualified manager is employed to operate the outlet on the franchisee's behalf.

Fees and Royalties: The initial franchise fee of $12,500 is moderate for the hair care field. The four percent monthly royalty is on the low side. Even coupled with the four percent advertising contribution, the total royalty burden is a moderate eight percent.

Summary: Cost Cutters franchisees benefit from a moderate initial investment, a manageable royalty structure, and positive imaging. Established franchisees report a high level of ongoing business from repeat customers.

Franchise Highlights

Began operating: 1982	**Monthly royalty: 4%**
Began franchising: 1982	**Advertising fee: 4%**
Outlets currently open: 240	**Training program: 5 days**
Initial franchise fee: $12,500	**Term: 15 years**

Diet Center, Inc.

Industry experience:	★ ★ ★ ★	*Franchising experience:*	★ ★ ★ ★
Financial strength:	★ ★ ★	*Training & services:*	★ ★
Fees & royalties:	★ ★ ★ ★	*Satisfied franchisees:*	★ ★ ★

Diet Center, Inc.
220 South 2nd West
Rexburg, Idaho 83440
(208) 356-9381

When Sybil Ferguson, a 186-pound housewife in Rexburg, Idaho, dropped 50 pounds with her doctor's help, her friends began asking her for weight-control advice. In 1969, she made diet counseling her business and, four years later, sold her first franchise.

According to Ferguson, now Diet Center's founder and director, the company's phenomenal success is based on 'a comprehensive weight-loss program, not simply a diet.' With more than four million followers, Ferguson is one of America's most famous diet advocates and the author of a best-selling book, aptly titled The Diet Center Program.

Her franchise organization, Diet Center, Inc., offers an integrated package of counseling, diet control, vitamins, and a personalized regimen for weight loss. Since the first franchise opened its doors in 1974, the organization has bulged to more than 2,000 outlets in all 50 states and Canada.

The Franchise: The franchisee operates a weight-loss counseling and support business, operating under the name Diet Center. A typical outlet is a 1,500 sq. ft. space in a suitable retail, commercial, or professional site, such as a shopping mall, strip center, or medical or office building. Diet Center outlets offer daily counseling and sponsor weekly support groups as part of an individualized 'five-phase' plan. The program stresses motivational support, behavior modificiation practices, and education about nutrition-saving techniques. A two-day 'conditioning' diet rids the body of acquired cravings for high-calorie foods. Franchisees also sell brand-name vitamins and related nutritional supplements. The average outlet employs one full-time and one part-time diet counselor, catering to the dietary and nutritional needs of men, women, and children.

Franchisee Profile: Diet Center franchisees come from varied business or professional backgrounds. Experience in nutritional counseling is not required. Some existing franchisees were inspired to open their own Diet Centers after undergoing the program as clients.

Projected Earnings: The franchisor does not provide a written statement of the franchisee's projected earnings. However, based on reported sales figures, the average volume per outlet is about $85,000 before expenses.

Franchisor's Services: In a one-week training program in Rexburg, Idaho, franchisees learn all aspects of operating a Diet Center business. The curriculum covers the franchisor's five- phase weight-control program, counseling techniques, basic nutrition, business administration, financial planning, and personnel management. Although the cost of the training program is included in the initial franchise fee, attendees are responsible for their own travel and lodging expenses.

The franchisee is responsible for acquiring a site for the outlet and preparing the business for opening. The support program includes three months of telephone consultation with a corporate expert. Franchisee seminars and workshops are conducted at additional cost to franchisees.

Initial Investment: The franchisor estimates the total investment at between $22,000 to $39,000 depending on the location and size of the outlet. Diet Center, Inc. does not offer financial assistance to franchisees.

Advertising: The franchisor administers a co-op advertising program designed to facilitate franchise advertising on a local level. Apart from the ongoing licensing fee, there is no advertising royalty per se. The company supplies ad slicks for newspaper and magazine ads, radio and television commercials, promotional materials, and public relations aids. Diet Center also produces a series of videotaped presentations for use in client counseling sessions.

Fees and Royalties: The initial license fee ranges from $12,000 to $24,000. Franchisees pay a variable 'ongoing license fee' based on client volume. The fee is calculated at the rate of $1.20 per day for each client enrolled in the Diet Center weight reduction program.

Contract Highlights: The contract term is 10 years. The franchisee receives exclusive rights to a given territory but is not allowed to expand or subfranchise. Absentee ownership is not prohibited, and the franchisee may be sold, transferred, or assigned with the approval of the company. Area franchises are available under a separate agreement.

Summary: Diet Center franchisees benefit from a large base of outlets, increasing name recognition, and consistent demand in a health-conscious consumer market. Perhaps inadvertently, founder Sybil Ferguson has become an integral public figure in connection with the franchise. The Diet Center Program claims an 80 percent success rate for 'taking off weight and keeping it off.'

Franchise Highlights

Began operating: 1972
Began franchising: 1974
Outlets currently open: 2,100
Initial franchise fee: Min. $12,000
Max. $24,000

Monthly royalty: Varies
Advertising fee: Varies
Training program: 5 days
Term: 10 years

European Tanspa

Industry experience:	★★	*Franchising experience:*	★★
Financial strength:	★★★	*Training & services:*	★★
Fees & royalties:	★★★★	*Satisfied franchisees:*	★★★

European Tanspa, Inc.
1911 Ogden Avenue
Downers Grove, Illinois
(312) 963-2626

Founded in 1982, European Tanspa has opened an average of 30 tanning salons every year. In 1986, the company was purchased by a group of nine salon owners, headed by Sandy Lindholm, who had opened three salons herself. Today, ET is the uncontested leader in the tanning salon field. The company is currently seeking new franchisees in all U.S. regions, but not in Canadian or overseas markets.

The Franchise: The franchisee operates a retail tanning salon under the trade name European Tanspa. A typical outlet is located in approximately 1,000 sq. ft. of commercial space in a retail strip center or shopping mall, in close proximity to restaurants, video stores, or other service oriented businesses. The average salon has three tanning rooms and six tanning beds, and offers on-site use of state-of-the-art tanning equipment at hourly rates. Franchisees purchase the equipment required to conduct the business from the franchisor's distribution affiliate.

Franchisee Profile: There are no specific qualifications to own and operate a franchise, but applicants must have from $35,000 to $50,000 in available cash or collateral. The franchisor suggests the business is best operated as a second income source.

Projected Earnings: A statement of projected earnings is not available.

Franchisor's Services: ET conducts an intensive two-day training course at the company's headquarters in Downer's Grove, Illinois, an upscale suburb of Chicago. Attendees are responsible for their own travel and lodging expenses. Franchisees receive additional on-the-job instruction from company trainers at the franchisees' own tanning salons.

The franchisor provides site guidelines, but the franchisee is ultimately responsible for selecting the location, subject to ET's approval. Considerable freedom is permitted in the design and construction of the franchisee's tanning salon. Ongoing guidance and troubleshooting is available as required.

ET salon owners may also obtain comprehensive insurance coverage at reduced rates, through the franchisor's umbrella policy. The company's distribution affiliate, Midwest Suntan Products, sells tanning equipment, parts, and supplies to franchisees at an average discount of 20 percent.

The support package also includes seminars and workshops for franchisees and their staffs, unlimited access to telephone consultation, and a monthly newsletter to keep salon operators abreast of new products and developments.

Initial Investment: The franchisor estimates the franchisee's initial investment as follows:

	Low	High
Initial franchise fee	$5,000	5,000
Tanning equipment	15,000	24,000
Furnishings	600	800
Site improvements	7,500	7,500
Miscellaneous expenses	2,500	2,500
Total	30,600	39,800

The above breakdown does not include lease or utility deposits, or working capital required to sustain the business until it becomes profitable. Financing is available on tanning equipment purchased from European Tanspa.

Advertising: ET franchisees do not pay an advertising royalty. The franchisor provides guidelines and materials for local promotions.

Contract Highlights: The term of the franchise is ten years. The contract may be renewed for an additional term, if the franchisee is in compliance with all material provisions. The franchisee receives a protected territory for the duration of the agreement.

Fees and Royalties: The initial franchise fee of $5,000 is at the low end of the spectrum for both tanning salons and franchises in general. The fee covers the trade name license, reduced insurance rates, technical support, employee training, and $1,000 toward exterior signs. The franchise royalty is based on the number of hours for which the tanning equipment is used. The royalty is calculated at the rate of 40 cents per hour. A third of the monthly fee is applied toward insurance costs.

Summary: European Tanspa strongly reflects the cooperative aspects of a franchise organization, with liberal discount purchasing and a unique co-op insurance plan. Franchisees benefit from a low investment, a fashionable business motif, and a solid base of outlets.

Franchise Highlights

Began operating: 1982	**Monthly royalty: .40 per hour**
Began franchising: 1983	**Advertising fee: None**
Outlets currently open: 150	**Training program: 2 days**
Initial franchise fee: $5,000	**Term: 10 years**

Fantastic Sam's

Industry experience:	★ ★ ★ ★	*Franchising experience:*	★ ★ ★ ★
Financial strength:	★ ★ ★ ★	*Training & services:*	★ ★ ★ ★
Fees & royalties:	★ ★ ★	*Satisfied franchisees:*	★ ★ ★ ★

Fantastic Sam's
P.O. Box 18845
Memphis, Tennessee 38181
(901) 363-8624

Fantastic Sam's founder, Sam Ross, opened his first family haircutting business in 1974 and today, less than 15 years later, administers an enormous franchise system of more than a thousand salons. System-wide sales are an impressive $98 million per year. Whereas other hairstyling parlors may lean toward the trendy and fashionable, Fantastic Sam's based its phenomenal growth on the premise of 'one-stop' hair care for the entire family. The company is currently seeking new franchisees in all major U.S. and Canadian markets.

The Franchise: The franchisee operates a haircutting and styling salon offering quality hair care for men, women, and children at individualized rates, using the trade name Fantastic Sam's. A typical outlet is a 1,200 sq. ft. retail space in a suitable commercial site, such as shopping mall or strip center. To promote its family orientation, Fantastic Sam's employees don cartoon-character nicknames and greet arriving customers with coffee, bubblegum, and balloons. The heart of the business format is a patented haircutting process and a standardized package of equipment and procedures.

Franchisee Profile: The franchisor reports that a large percentage of its franchisees have no prior experience in the hair care business. An absentee owner may hire a qualified manager to operate the outlet. Multiple unit ownership is encouraged, and area franchises are available.

Projected Earnings: The franchisor does not provide a written statement of the franchisee's projected earnings. But based on reported sales figures, the average volume per outlet is around $150,000 per year.

Franchisor Services: Before opening, franchisees attend a one- week training program at company headquarters in Memphis, Tennessee or at a more conveniently located center elsewhere in the United States or Canada. The curriculum includes business administration and accounting, advertising, employee relations, and the franchisor's patented hair care techniques. Optional haircutting classes are available for employees, at no additional charge. The franchisor also courses in advanced marketing and advertising. The franchisor conducts continuing education seminars twice yearly.

Fantastic Sam's participates in site selection and lease negotiation, and assists with pre-opening activities, such as staff hiring and training. A field representative visits the outlet periodically to offer guidance and counsel. National franchisee conferences are held annually, and regional gatherings are conducted quarterly. The franchisor publishes a monthly newsletter to keep franchisees abreast of new products and techniques in the hair-care trade.

Initial Investment: The company estimates the total capital needed to start at between $55,000 and $67,000. The investment includes lease deposits, fixtures and improvements, equipment, and merchandise. The franchisor does not offer any direct financial assistance to franchisees, but the equipment package may be purchased on credit.

Advertising: According to a franchise representative, Fantastic Sam's company invests a sizable amount in national advertising and direct mail campaigns, based on weekly advertising royalties paid by franchisees. Target media include radio and television, newspapers, magazines, and outdoor advertising.

Contract Highlights: The franchise term is ten years. The company is flexible with regard to absentee ownership, allowing an owner to delegate management reponsiblities to another party. The franchisee has exclusive rights to a specific territory, with the possibility of expanding into multiple outlets. The franchisor will also consider granting area franchises to develop a large territory.

Fees and Royalties: The initial franchise fee of $25,000 is somewhat on the high side, reflecting the franchisor's status as the largest haircutting chain in North America. Fantastic Sam's franchisees pay a set royalty fee of $136.50 a week. Advertising royalties are paid to two funds: $63.18 is paid weekly into a regional fund, and $104.50 is earmarked for national advertising.

Summary: Fantastic Sam's has made a substantial commitment to advertising and training to make its franchise attractive to prospective investors. The number of units grew from 337 in 1984 to 1,064 in 1986; all but three are franchise stores. The phenomenal growth picture is often an ambiguous sign, but to date, the franchisor has successfully maintained a strong financial base and continued franchisee support, resulting in a nearly perfect franchise success rate.

Franchise Highlights

Began operating: 1974
Began franchising: 1976
Outlets currently open: 1,065
Initial franchise fee: $25,000
Monthly royalty: $135.50/week
Advertising fee: $167.68/week
Training program: 3 weeks
Term: 10 years

Great Expectations

Industry experience: ★ ★ ★ ★
Financial strength: ★ ★ ★
Fees & royalties: ★ ★ ★
Franchising experience: ★ ★ ★
Training & services: ★ ★ ★
Satisfied franchisees: ★ ★ ★

CutCo Industries
P. O. Box 265
Jericho, New York 11753
(516) 334-8400

Founded in 1955, Great Expectations has established more than 300 outlets since the company began franchising in 1974, opening an average of 33 new stores each year. Today, the parent company, CutCo Industries, is one of the largest retail chains of haircutting salons in North America, with outlets in almost every major U.S. market. CutCo also operates the HairCrafters franchise system and the Cut and Curl chain.

The Franchise: The franchisee conducts a retail haircutting and styling business, based on a standardized format and operated under the trade name Great Expectations Precision Haircutters. A typical outlet is situated in a retail strip center strip or shopping mall, employing up to ten full-time and five part-time hairstylists. Franchisees offer contemporary hair care for men, women, and children, in a comfortable atmosphere providing semi-privacy and modern furnishings.

Franchisee Profile: A background in haircutting or styling is not essential. The company is seeking prospective franchisees who are financially and managerially qualified to operate and expand the business. Absentee ownership is often encouraged, to promote the sale of multiple sites.

Projected Earnings: The franchisor does not provide a statement of projected earnings.

Franchisor's Services: CutCo provides a one-week training program at an operating Great Expectations hair salon. An additional week of on-the-job training is provided at the franchisee's own haircutting establishment. The curriculum focuses on business administration, inventory management, and advertising strategies.

The franchisor assists with selecting a site for the outlet and negotiating a lease for the premises. On request, CutCo will develop a complete turnkey hair care salon. After the outlet opens, a field representative will visit the salon periodically to provide ongoing guidance and troubleshooting. The support package also includes consolidated purchasing and continuing education on hairstyling trends and techniques.

Initial Investment: New Great Expectations franchisees should be prepared to invest between $80,000 and $160,000 to establish and develop the business. The amount includes lease deposits, site improvements, equipment purchases, and an initial inventory of hair care merchandise. CutCo offers a financial assistance program to qualified franchisees.

Advertising: Great Expectations does not currently exact an advertising royalty, but conducts national and regional campaigns on behalf of its franchises and company-owned outlets.

Contract Highlights: The term of the franchise is 15 years. The contract may be renewed for an additional five years, providing the franchisee is in compliance with all material provisions. The franchisee receives a protected territory for the duration of the agreement.

Fees and Royalties: The initial franchise fee of $18,000 is average for the industry. The six percent monthly royalty is moderate, especially in the absence of an advertising royalty.

Summary: The Great Expectations franchise is characterized by an upscale image, consistent customer demand, and solid name recognition in major markets. New franchisees benefit from a moderate investment, a light royalty burden, and the availability of financial assistance.

Franchise Highlights

Began operating: 1955	**Monthly royalty: 6%**
Began franchising: 1974	**Advertising fee: 2%**
Outlets currently open: 320	**Training program: 1 week**
Initial franchise fee: $18,000	**Term: 15 years**

HairCrafters

Industry experience:	★ ★ ★ ★	*Franchising experience:*	★ ★ ★
Financial strength:	★ ★ ★	*Training & services:*	★ ★ ★
Fees & royalties:	★ ★ ★	*Satisfied franchisees:*	★ ★ ★

CutCo Industries
P. O. Box 265
Jericho, New York 11753
(516) 334-8400

HairCrafters is a trade name of CutCo Industries, which also operates Great Expectations. Not surprisingly, many aspects of the HairCrafters franchise are identical to those of its sister chain. But whereas Great Expectations is upscale and trendy, HairCrafters caters to a more traditional, middle of the road clientele.

HairCrafters is an outgrowth of Cut & Curl hairstyling salons, which CutCo is presently revamping into HairCrafters outlets. With more than 400 salons in 30 states, the franchise system generates roughly $75 million in gross annual sales.

The Franchise: The franchisee conducts a retail haircutting and styling business, under the trade name HairCrafters. A typical outlet is a 1,200 to 1,800 sq. ft. commercial space in a suitable commercial retail site, such as a shopping mall or strip center. Franchisees perform hair care services for men, women, and children, based on a standardized format.

Franchisee Profile: A background in haircutting or styling is not essential. Absentee owners are welcome, but the company is not actively seeking area franchisees or subfranchisors.

Projected Earnings: The franchisor does not provide a statement of projected earnings. However, based on annual sales figures, HairCrafters outlets generate an average of about $190,000 in gross revenues.

Franchisor's Services: CutCo provides a one-week training program at an operating HairCrafters hair salon, plus an additional week at the franchisee's site. The curriculum covers business administration, inventory management, and advertising strategies. An additional seven to ten days of training are provided at the franchisee's place of business.

The franchisor will help select and build the site, or alternatively, will develop a complete turnkey hair salon, completely built out, furnished, and decorated. A field representative is available to provide ongoing guidance and troubleshooting in inspections. CutCo also sells hair care merchandise to franchisees for resale, and conducts frequent seminars and workshops.

Initial Investment: The following breakdown illustrates typical low and high investment requirements.

	Low	High
Initial franchise fee	$18,000	18,000
Site acquisition	——	3,500
Lease deposits	5,000	5,000
Improvements	25,000	50,000
Fixtures & equipment	5,000	25,000
Inventory	3,000	3,000
Miscellaneous	10,000	20,000
Total	66,000	124,500

CutCo offers a financial assistance program to qualified franchisees. The minimum cash down payment is $50,000.

Advertising: CutCo conducts national and regional campaigns on behalf of HairCrafters franchises and company-owned outlets. Advertising materials are available from the franchisor at additional cost.

Contract Highlights: The term of the franchise is 15 years. The contract may be renewed for an additional five years, providing the franchisee is in compliance with all material provisions. The franchisee receives a protected territory for the duration of the agreement. The outlet must be open within six months after the signing of the franchise agreement.

Fees and Royalties: The initial franchise fee of $18,000 is average for the industry. The six percent monthly royalty is moderate, especially in the absence of an advertising royalty.

Summary: The HairCrafters franchise caters to suburban families and shopping mall patrons, where high pedestrian traffic fuels both repeat business and new demand. Like Great Expectations, HairCrafters offers of a moderate investment and the competitive benefits of an industry leader.

Franchise Highlights

Began operating: 1955	**Monthly royalty: 6%**
Began franchising: 1968	**Advertising fee: 2%**
Outlets currently open: 420	**Training program: 1 week**
Initial franchise fee: $18,000	**Term: 15 years**

Jazzercise

Industry experience:	★ ★ ★	*Franchising experience:*	★ ★ ★
Financial strength:	★ ★	*Training & services:*	★ ★
Fees & royalties:	★ ★ ★	*Satisfied franchisees:*	★ ★ ★

Jazzercise, Inc.
2808 Roosevelt St.
Carlsbad, California 92008
(619) 434-2101

'Are you breathing? Are you smiling?' is the anthem of Jazzercise founder Judi Sheppard Missett. Misset has good reason to smile: the former jazz dancing instructor presently oversees a small business empire of more than 3,000 aerobic dance studios. Aerobic exercise first became popular in the late 1960s, with growing public awareness of the importance of cardiovascular stimulation to overall physical fitness. In 1972, Misset started conducting exercise classes, with nothing but a record player, a few leotards, and a couple of jazz records, using the facilities at the San Diego YMCA. Today, over 3,000 Jazzercise instructors are shouting Missett's anthem to more than 400,000 students nationwide.

Jazzercise prescribes hit-tunes, predesigned dance steps, and an entertaining milieu to get the heart pumping and the muscles toned. The format has been so successful that more than 800 franchisees have begun dancing to the Jazzercise tune every year since the company sold its first franchise.

The franchise: The franchisee operates a low-overhead fitness center, operating under the trade name Jazzercise. The outlet may be housed in virtually any suitable space that can be rented by the hour. Jazzercise instructors lead customers through pre-designed Jazzercize routines, to the accompaniment of upbeat dance tunes on records or tapes.

Franchisee Profile: Franchisees must be qualified to be aerobic exercise instructors — in perfect physical shape, adept at picking up movement routines quickly, and capable of exuding enthusiasm. Part of the training is actually a try-out in which the prospective franchisee is evaluated for potential as a Jazzercise instructor. Franchisees must also be certified in cardiopulmonary resuscitation (CPR) techniques.

Franchisor's Services: Jazzercise provides a four-day training/audition seminar at the company's headquarters in Southern California. Attendees are responsible for their own travel and lodging expenses. Franchisees who perform satisfactorily during the audition portion of the seminar receive further instruction in exercise training, business administration, and bookkeeping systems. Candidates who fail the training audition receive reimbursement for the cost of training materials but must absorb the cost of the trip.

When the franchisee's outlet is open for business, the franchisor supplies a monthly selection of dance routine tapes at additional cost.

Advertising: Jazzercise, Inc. does not administer a co-op advertising program, nor does it require any monthly advertising royalty fee. Ms. Missett writes a column on health and physical fitness published in popular health magazines.

Fees and Royalties: The Jazzercise company exacts a nominal initial franchise fee of $500, but takes 25 percent of the franchisee's gross monthly revenues. Though the royalty bite may seem ponderous, the franchise is a low-investment business with proportionately small overhead.

Initial Investment: The franchisor estimates the initial investment at about $2,000, including lease deposits and working capital. The investment includes the purchase or rent of a tape or hi-fi system and a video tape recorder.

Contract Highlights: The term of the franchise is five years. On expiration, the contract may be renewed at the franchisee's option for an additional five years. The franchise agreement prohibits the sale or transfer of the franchise to any other party.

Summary: The low startup costs and timely business format that fueled the company's phenomenal growth rate remain intact today, offering a vehicle for easily entering and rapidly penetrating one of the most lucrative consumer markets of the 80s.

Franchise Highlights

Began operating: 1976	**Monthly royalty: 25%**
Began franchising: 1983	**Advertising fee: None**
Outlets currently open: 3,300	**Training program: 4 days**
Initial franchise fee: $500	**Term: 5 years**

Nutri/System

Industry experience:	★ ★ ★ ★	*Franchising experience:*	★ ★ ★ ★
Financial strength:	★ ★ ★	*Training & services:*	★ ★ ★ ★
Fees & royalties:	★ ★ ★	*Satisfied franchisees:*	★ ★ ★

Nutri/System
3901 Commerce Ave., CS 925
Willow Grove, Pennsylvania 19090
(215) 784-5600

The Nutri/System Weight Loss Center offers customers a professionally supervised weight-reduction program based on a combined regimen of nutritional instruction, behavior modification, and exercise. Emphasizing overall health and safety, the franchisor does not advocate the use of drugs, injections, or diet pills. The core of the Nutri/System program is individualized evaluation and prescriptive measures to decrease fat and increase general health. Nutri/System also markets its own a diet food line under the trade name Nu System Cuisine, an exclusive assortment of frozen, canned, or freezed-dried foodstuffs.

The company recently introduced a line of flavor sprays that presumably restore the taste and scent of fattening foods without restoring the calories. The sprays were developed at Duke University, under a research grant from Nutri/System. Representative flavors include pizza, chocolate, and bread.

The Franchise: The franchisee operates a multi-faceted health center employing medically trained counselors, nutritional experts, and exercise facilities, and doing business under the trade name Nutri/System. Besides general fitness and weight control customers, the outlet also counsels clients with special nutritional problems, such as diabetes, hypoglycemia, or heart conditions. In some U.S. states, the law requires a physician to be on staff.

Each client is evaluated, presented with a reasonable goal, and prescribed a structured diet and exercise regimen. The facilities remain available to all customers until they acheive their individual goals.

Franchisee Profile: Nutri/System places no limit on applicants but suggests that experience in health, nutrition, or a related field, would be helpful.

Franchisor's Services: An intensive week-long training program at the company's headquarters in Philadelphia prepares the franchisee's staff to administer the Nutri/System weight-loss programs. The curriculum highlights important medical considerations in weight control and outlines procedures for evaluating client dietary and exercise requirements. Attendees receive a set of training manuals, tapes, and record keeping forms.

Nutri/System participates in both site selection and lease negotiation. Two weeks prior to opening, field representatives spend time at the outlet overseeing the set-up, helping plan promotions, and training the new staff.

After the outlet has opened for business, a franchise representative periodically inspects the operation and offers on-site troubleshooting. The franchisor conducts regional seminars and refresher courses and publishes a monthly newsletter.

Initial Investment: The total investment — including the initial franchise fee, deposits, and equipment — ranges from $70,000 to $135,000. The franchisor does not offer financial assistance, either directly or indirectly, to franchisees.

Advertising: Nutri/System franchisees do not pay a mandatory advertising fee and are responsible for conducting their own promotions. The franchisor will provide video tapes with prepared television commercials, audio tapes of authorized radio spots, and ad slicks for newspaper or magazine ads. Actual advertising costs are borne by the franchisee.

Fees and Royalties: The initial franchise fee of $49,500 is on the high side, reflecting the franchisor's involvement in pre- opening activities. The seven percent monthly royalty is moderate by industry standards.

Contract Highlights: The contract period is ten years with a ten year renewal option. Under the franchise agreement, the franchisees receives a protected territory. Absentee ownership is not prohibited, but no area rights or subfranchising rights are granted.

Summary: The Nutri/System franchise offers the benefits of a solid base of outlets, a proven multi-faceted business format, and a recent management overhaul that promises future financial stability.

Franchise Highlights

Began operating: 1971
Began franchising: 1972
Outlets currently open: 683
Initial franchise fee: 49,500
Monthly royalty: 7%
Advertising fee: None
Training program: 7 days
Term: 10 years
Renewal fee:

NuVision Optical

Industry experience:	★ ★ ★ ★	*Franchising experience:*	★ ★
Financial strength:	★ ★ ★	*Training & services:*	★ ★ ★
Fees & royalties:	★ ★ ★ ★	*Satisfied franchisees:*	★ ★ ★

NuVision, Inc.
P. O. Box 2600
Flint, Michigan 48501
(313) 767-0900

NuVision Optical has operated retail eye care outlets since 1949, with 150 company-owned optical centers. In 1983, the company began offering franchises based on its successful format that merges the services of a licensed optometrist with a fashion-oriented approach to filling eyeglass prescriptions. Roughly a fourth of the 200-plus NuVision stores in operation today are owned by independent franchisees.

The Franchise: The franchisee conducts a retail eye care business operated under the trade name NuVision Optical. A typical outlet is located in a retail, commercial, or professional site, offering one-stop optical services on the same premises. The store maintains a full-time optometrist on staff to conduct examinations and an optician to dispense lenses and frames.

Franchisee Profile: No previous experience in the optical field is necessary. Prospective franchisees do not have to be licensed optometrists, opticians, or ophthalmologists.

Projected Earnings: NuVision franchisor does not furnish prospective franchisees with a written claim of projected earnings.

Franchisor's Services: The franchisor provides a training program consisting of four to five days of intensive instruction at the company's training center in Flint, Michigan. Although the tuition for the program is included in the franchise fee, the costs of travel, lodging, and meals are borne by the franchisee. The curriculum covers business administration, accounting systems, merchandising techniques, and marketing strategies. All NuVision franchisees receive a manual containing confidential policies and procedures for managing the day-to-day operations of the business.

A NuVision field consultant assists with grand opening activities. Additional, ongoing consultation is available on request, including continuing education seminars at the franchisee's establishment.

The company operates its own optical laboratory to fill eyeglass prescritpions.

Initial Investment: NuVision franchisees should be prepared to invest from $10,000 to $75,000 to establish the business. The amount includes lease deposits, site improvements, equipment purchases, and an opening inventory. Financial assistance is available to qualified franchisees.

Advertising: NuVision franchisees contribute seven percent of gross monthly revenues to a co-op ad fund used to conduct national and regional campaigns on behalf of all franchised and company-owned outlets.

Contract Highlights: The term of the franchise is ten years, with an option to renew for an additional ten years. The franchisor derives a profit from the sale of prescription lenses and frames to franchisees for resale. The franchise agreement specifies that the franchisee must purchase merchandise either from the franchisor or from a company-approved vendor.

Fees and Royalties: The initial franchise fee of $8,000 is moderate the eye care industry. The eight and a half percent monthly royalty, added to the seven percent advertising contribution create a total royalty bite of fifteen and a half percent of gross revenues.

Summary: Although NuVision is an established retailer of eye care services and merchandise, the franchise program is relatively new. Nevertheless, franchisees benefit from strong name recognition, centralized purchasing and quality control, and the competitive strengths of an industry leader.

Franchise Highlights

Began operating: 1962	**Monthly royalty: 8.5%**
Began franchising: 1980	**Advertising fee: 7%**
Outlets currently open: 200	**Training program: 5 days**
Initial franchise fee: $8,000	**Term: 10 years**

One Hour Martinizing Dry Cleaning

Industry experience:	★★★★	*Franchising experience:*	★★★★
Financial strength:	★★★★	*Training & services:*	★★★
Fees & royalties:	★★★	*Satisfied franchisees:*	★★★

One Hour Martinizing
2005 Ross Avenue
Cincinnati, Ohio 45212

Founded in 1949, One Hour Martinizing is the largest dry cleaning chain in North America, with more than 1,000 outlets in all U.S. states and Canada.

The Franchise: The franchisee operates a retail dry cleaning business, using the franchisor's standardized equipment package, techniques, and trademarks.

Franchisee Profile: A background in the dry cleaning trade is beneficial, but not mandatory.

Projected Earnings: A written statement of projected earnings was not available at press time.

Franchisor's Services: Franchisees spend three weeks in training at the franchisor's headquarters in Cincinnati. An additional week of training and pre-opening assistance are provided at the franchisee's dry cleaning establishment. The One Hour Martinizing operation manual covers industry background, equipment operation, customer service, advertising, and business administration. Ongoing assistance is available from field advisers in personal visits to the outlet and from company operations and technical experts by phone.

Initial Investment: The start-up investment is estimated at about $150,000, including site acquisition, equipment purchases, supplies, and miscellaneous expenses. The franchisor does not offer any direct financial assistance to franchisees.

Fees and Royalties: The initial franchise fee of $30,000 is somewhat high for the dry cleaning industry, reflecting the chain's stature as the leader of the pack. One Hour Martinizing franchisees pay a set royalty of $1,500 per year. The franchise agreement is renewable every three years.

Summary: One Hour Martinizing offers a streamlined vehicle for entering the dry cleaning trade with the management support and competitive benefits of an experienced industry leader.

Franchise Highlights

Began operating: 1949	**Franchise royalty: $1,500 per year**
Began franchising: 1949	**Advertising fee: None**
Outlets currently open: 1,100	**Training program: 3 weeks**
Initial franchise fee: $30,000	**Term: 3 years**

Pearle Vision Center, Inc.

Industry experience:	★ ★ ★ ★	*Franchising experience:*	★ ★ ★
Financial strength:	★ ★ ★ ★	*Training & services:*	★ ★ ★
Fees & royalties:	★ ★ ★ ★	*Satisfied franchisees:*	★ ★ ★

Pearle Vision Center, Inc.
2534 Royal Lane Drive
Dallas, Texas 75229
(214) 241-3381

Pearle Vision is the brainchild of Dr. Stanley Pearle, whose creation in 1962 of a multi-faceted vision center was greeted with extraordinary success. By the time the company began offering franchises in 1980, Pearle Vision had already established one of the largest retail chains of its kind, boasting more than 300 outlets. Since then, the business has changed hands several times, and Dr. Pearle is not longer part of the management team. Today, more than half of the nation's 1,150 Pearle Vision Centers are independent franchises.

The Franchise: The franchisee conducts a retail optical outlet, operating under the trade name Pearle Vision Center and providing a comprehensive range of eye-care products and services. A typical outlet is housed in a 1,500 sq. ft. space in a suitable retail site, such as a shopping mall or strip center, with two full-time employees and one part-time employee. The franchisee sells frames, lenses, sunglasses, contact lenses, and related optical assessories, and may also provide diagnostic and prescriptive services from a trained optician, optometrist, and/or ophthalmologisit.

Some state laws do not permit prescriptive services to be performed on the same premises where retail optical aids are sold. In these markets, Pearle Vision allows the franchisee to operate a reduced-service business, with adjustments to the franchise fee and royalty.

The Franchisee Profile: The franchisee must be a licensed optician, optometrist, or ophthalmologist. The company also requires previous experience in the retail optical business.

Projected Earnings: Based on the company's reported annual sales, the average Pearle Vision Center grosses $330,000, with net earnings of $60,000 after expenses.

Franchisor Services: The franchisee has the option of selecting his own site, negotiating a lease, choosing contractors, and supervising construction — or paying Pearle to handle pre-opening activitier. In either case, the outlet must confirm to standardized specifications. The franchisor's participation is available on a fee-per-service basis, or for a flat fee of $15,000 to oversee the development of a complete turnkey optical center.

Pearle conducts an intensive three-day training program in Dallas or at a designated regional training center. The franchisee must pay travel expenses plus a $1000 tuition fee. The curriculum covers marketing practices, accounting systems, frame selection, contact lens insertion, fitting of multi-focals, quality control, and personnel relations. The training tuition entitles the franchisee to attend continuing education seminars at no charge during the first year of the franchise term.

Initial Investment: The franchisor estimates the initial investment at from $25,000 to $25,000, including the initial franchise fee, training tuition, site improvements, and opening inventory. Up to 90 percent of the investment can be financed.

Advertising: Franchisees contribute eight percent of gross monthly revenues to a co-op ad fund. A mandatory start-up advertising budget of $15,000 is stipulated by the franchise agreement, but the franchisor will provide matching funds to kick off the business. Pearle may also finance the franchisee's share of the start-up ad fund. The company supplies ad slicks for newspaper and Yellow Pages display ads, radio and television commercials, billboard art, and public relations aids.

Fees and Royalties: The initial franchise fee is $20,000. If the franchise is located in a state that restricts diagnostic and prescriptive exams, a reduced fee is assessed for a limited- service outlet. The eight and a half percent monthly royalty is moderate for the industry. But adding in the eight percent co-op ad contribution, the combined royalty burden is a hefty 16.5 percent of gross revenues.

Summary: Pearl Vision franchisees benefit from a proven operating system, effective national advertising, an experienced support team, and the competitive strengths of an industry leader. The franchise provides licensed vision professionals with a ready-made format for entering the field and penetrating the market.

Franchise Highlights

Began operating: 1962	**Monthly royalty: 8.5%**
Began franchising: 1980	**Advertising fee: 8%**
Outlets currently open: 1,150	**Training program: 3 days**
Initial franchise fee: $20,000	**Term: 10 years**

Supercuts

Industry experience:	★★★	*Franchising experience:*	★★★★
Financial strength:	★★★	*Training & services:*	★★★
Fees & royalties:	★★★	*Satisfied franchisees:*	★★★★

Supercuts
555 Northgate Drive
San Rafael, California 94903
(415) 472-1170

Founded in 1976, Supercuts has established more than 500 new outlets since the company began franchising in 1979, opening an average of more than 60 new salons each year. Today, Supercuts is one of the largest haircutting chains in North America. The company is currently seeking new franchisees in all U.S. states and Canada.

The Franchise: The franchisee conducts a retail haircutting salon, operated under the trade name Supercuts. A typical outlet is situated in a 1,200 sq. ft. retail space in a shopping mall or strip center. Customers of the franchise business include men, women, and children.

Franchisee Profile: A background in hair care or a cosmetologist's license is not required. The company is seeking prospective franchisees who have solid business skills. Absentee ownership is not prohibited, and multiple unit operation is common.

Projected Earnings: The franchisor does not provide prospective franchisees with a written statement of projected earnings.

Franchisor's Services: The franchisor provides a one-week training program at the company's headquarters in Northern California. Attendees are responsible for their own travel and lodging expenses. The curriculum covers the Supercuts haircutting technique, standard business procedures, employee hiring and training, and marketing strategies. An additional week of on-the-job training is provided at the franchisee's place of business.

The franchisee is reponsible for selecting a site for the outlet and negotiating a lease for the premises, with the franchisor's guidance. In addition, a field representative helps plan the development and opening of the francisee's haircutting salon. After the doors have opened for business, an area manager provides ongoing guidance and troubleshooting in periodic visits to the outlet. The support package also includes frequent seminars for franchisees and their staffs, videotape updates of new hair care products and techniques, and a company newsletter.

Initial Investment: New Supercuts franchisees should be prepared to invest from $52,000 to $103,000 to establish the business. The amount includes lease deposits, site improvements, equipment purchases, and an initial inventory of hair care merchandise. The franchisor does not offer any direct financial assistance to franchisees.

Advertising: Supercuts franchisees contribute five percent of gross monthly revenues for advertising. The franchisor conducts national and regional campaigns on behalf of all franchises and company-owned outlets. Franchisees receive ad slicks for newspaper and Yellow Pages ads, approved logo designs, and promotional aids for use in local campaigns.

Contract Highlights: The term of the franchise is ten years. The contract may be renewed for an additional ten-year term, providing the franchisee is in compliance with all material provisions.

Fees and Royalties: The initial franchise fee of $25,000 is moderate to high for the industry. The ten percent monthly royalty, added to the five percent advertising contribution, creates a total royalty bite of 15 percent of gross revenues.

Summary: The Supercuts franchise is characterized by a moderate initial investment, a proliferating base of outlets, and a high level of franchisee satisfaction.

Franchise Highlights

Began operating: 1976
Began franchising: 1979
Outlets currently open: 515
Initial franchise fee: $25,000
Monthly royalty: 10%
Advertising fee: 5%
Training program: 1 week
Term: 10 years

Real Estate Franchises

Real estate sales were sluggish in the late 1970s and early 1980s, primarily because interest rates were high. Two factors re-energized the industry: lower interest rates and the maturing, Post-War Baby Boom generation. The same consumers who bought records and tapes in the 1960s are more interested in buying homes in the 1980s. Tax Reform left intact the homeowner's deduction for interest on first mortgages, keeping the new real estate boom alive, at least for the foreseeable future.

The franchising of real estate brokerages first became popular in the early 1970s. Realtors discovered that they could increase their ability to compete in a field saturated with independents, by joining forces to create a national image and an inter-office referral network.

The leader in the field is Century 21, with more than 6,500 franchised brokers annually earning $1.6 billion in commissions on $40 billion worth of property transactions. Realty World runs a distant second, with approximately 1,500 franchisees. RE/MAX and Red Carpet round out the Big Four real estate chains.

Century 21

Industry experience:	★★★★	*Franchising experience:*	★★★★
Financial strength:	★★★	*Training & services:*	★★★★
Fees & royalties:	★★★	*Satisfied franchisees:*	★★★★

Century 21 Real Estate
18872 MacArthur Boulevard
Irvine, California 92715
(714) 752-7521

Every year, Century 21 real estate offices sell an estimated 600,000 homes worth $20.1 million. The organization was recently purchased from Transworld Corporation by Metropolitan Life Insurance Company, primarily to expand the outlets for the mortgage services which Metropolitan offers. Founded in 1971, Century 21 has established 7,000 outlets since the company began franchising, opening an average of more than 400 outlets every year. The company is still seeking new franchisees in all U.S. regions and Canada.

The Franchise: The franchisee conducts a real estate brokerage business, operated under the trade name Century 21 Real Estate. A typical outlet is situated in a suitable commercial or retail site, with a staff of two or more employees. Franchisees offer real estate sales and location services. Customers of the franchise business include individuals, families, and businesses seeking to purchase or sell residential or commercial properties.

Franchisee Profile: A background in real estate brokerage is required. Franchisees must possess a valid real estate license for the locality in which the outlet will be established.

Projected Earnings: The franchisor does not furnish prospective franchisees with a written statement of projected earnings.

Franchisor's Services: The franchisor provides a four-day training program at the company's headquarters in Irvine, California. Attendees are responsible for their own travel and lodging expenses. The curriculum includes client recruitment and relations, franchise policies and procedures, marketing, advertising, and sales.

The franchisor will assist with selecting a site for the outlet and negotiating a lease for the premises. After the outlet has opened for business, a Century 21 representative will visit the outlet periodically, to offer guidance and troubleshooting. Other ongoing services include on-site training, continuing education seminars, and franchisee conventions. Home financing and mortgage services are available through the parent company.

Initial Investment: New Century 21 franchisees should be prepared to invest $25,000 or more, depending on the location. The actual amount required to establish the business varies substantially from one outlet to another. The total includes the initial franchise fee, lease deposits, site improvements, equipment purchases, and an initial inventory of promotional materials. Century 21 does not offer direct financial assistance to franchisees.

Advertising: Century 21 franchisees contribute two percent of their gross monthly revenues for advertising. The franchisor conducts advertising on behalf of all Century 21 outlets. The franchisor supplies ad slicks, logo art, sign designs, and commercials for local advertising campaigns.

Contract Highlights: The term of the franchise is five years. The contract may be renewed at the franchisee's option. The franchisee does not receive an exclusive territory in conjunction with the franchise.

Fees and Royalties: The initial franchise fee of $12,000 is moderate for the industry. The six percent monthly royalty, added to the two percent advertising royalty, exacts a total of eight percent of gross revenues of the outlet.

Summary: The Century 21 franchise is characterized by strong name recognition and the competitive advantages of one of the largest real estate sales organizations in the world. The parent company, Metropolitan Life, is a financial giant.

Franchise Highlights

Began operating: 1971	**Monthly royalty: 6%**
Began franchising: 1971	**Advertising fee: 2%**
Outlets currently open: 7,000	**Training program: 4 days**
Initial franchise fee: $12,000	**Term: 5 years**

ERA

Industry experience:	★ ★ ★	*Franchising experience:*	★ ★ ★ ★
Financial strength:	★ ★ ★	*Training & services:*	★ ★ ★
Fees & royalties:	★ ★ ★ ★	*Satisfied franchisees:*	★ ★ ★ ★

Electronic Realty Associates
P. O. Box 2974
Shawnee Mission, Kansas 66201
(913) 341-8400

Founded in 1971, ERA has established 2,400 outlets since the company began franchising in 1971, opening an average of 150 outlets every year. The company is currently seeking new franchisees in the U.S. and Canada.

The Franchise: The franchisee conducts a licensed real estate listing and sales business, operated under the trade name Electronic Realty Associates, or ERA. A typical outlet is situated in a 1,800 sq. ft. commercial space in a self-standing site, strip center, or office complex, with a staff of 15 full-time employees. Franchisees offer nationwide property listings, residential and commercial sales and leasing, service contracts, and financing programs. Customers of the franchise business include individuals, families, and businesses.

Franchisee Profile: A background in real estate is required. ERA franchisees must possess valid real estate licenses in their respective localities.

Projected Earnings: The franchisor does not furnish prospective franchisees with a written statement of projected earnings.

Franchisor's Services: The franchisor provides a one-week training program at the company's headquarters in Shawnee Mission, Kansas. Attendees are responsible for their own travel and lodging expenses. The curriculum covers management, advertising, sales, financing, and the ERA nationwide referral system.

An ERA representative will visit the outlet periodically, to offer guidance and troubleshooting. Other ongoing services include an equity finance program for qualified customers, access to a computerized listing service, and a service contract program for residential properties.

Initial Investment: New ERA franchisees should be prepared to invest $15,000 for an established real estate office. Franchisees should be prepared to invest $35,000 or more to develop a new outlet for the franchise to establish the business. The amount includes the initial franchise fee, lease deposits, office equipment, and an initial inventory of sales literature, contracts, promotional aids, and supplies. ERA does not offer any form of direct financial assistance to franchisees.

Advertising: ERA franchisees contribute from $157 to $629 per month for advertising. The franchisor conducts national advertising campaigns on behalf of all ERA offices, using radio and television, magazines and newspapers. Franchisees also receive commercials and ad slicks for use in local advertising campaigns.

Contract Highlights: The term of the franchise is three years. The contract may be renewed at the franchisee's option. The franchisee does not receive an exclusive territory in conjunction with the franchise.

Fees and Royalties: The initial franchise fee of $15,000 is average for the industry. The $144 to $577 monthly royalty, added to the $157 to $629 advertising royalty, represents a combined royalty obligation of between $301 and $1,206 per month.

Summary: The ERA franchise is characterized by one of the most prolific organizations in real estate sales, providing ample name recognition and positive imaging for the independent realtor. Franchisees benefit from prominent national advertising, a coast-to-coast referral system, and the competitive advantages of an industry leader.

Franchise Highlights

Began operating: 1971
Began franchising: 1971
Outlets currently open: 2,400
Initial franchise fee: $15,000
Monthly royalty: $144 to $577
Advertising fee: $157 to $629
Training program: 1 week
Term: 5 years

Gallery of Homes

Industry experience:	★★★★	*Franchising experience:*	★★★★
Financial strength:	★★★	*Training & services:*	★★★
Fees & royalties:	★★★	*Satisfied franchisees:*	★★★★

Gallery of Homes, Inc.
P. O. Box 2900
Orlando, Florida 32802
(800) 241-8320

Founded in 1935, Gallery of Homes has established 800 outlets since the company began franchising in 1935, opening an average of more than 15 outlets every year. The company is currently seeking new franchisees in most U.S. regions and Canada.

The Franchise: The franchisee conducts a residential listing and sales business, operated under the trade name Gallery of Homes. A typical outlet is situated in a a 1,500 sq. ft. office facility, with a staff of five to ten full-time employees. Franchisees offer a broad range of residential real estate services, from listings to financial guidance. Customers of the franchise business include prospective home buyers, including families, individuals, and investment partnerships.

Franchisee Profile: A background in real estate sales is mandatory. Franchisees must be licensed real estate brokers and have demonstratable track records. The company stresses the importance of membership in professional real estate associations.

Projected Earnings: The franchisor does not furnish prospective franchisees with a written statement of projected earnings.

Franchisor's Services: The franchisor provides a five-day training program at the company's headquarters in Orlando, Florida. Attendees are responsible for their own travel and lodging expenses. The curriculum includes sales, management, and finance.

A Gallery of Homes franchise representative will visit the outlet periodically, to offer guidance and troubleshooting. Other ongoing services include a seminar series designed to keep franchisees abreast of industry trends and financial developments. Franchisees receive copies of the Gallery of Homes operating manuals, containing confidential policies and procedures for managing a successful real estate brokerage.

Initial Investment: New Gallery of Homes franchisees should be prepared to invest from $12,000 to $25,000 to establish the business. The amount includes the initial franchise fee, lease deposits, equipment purchases, and an initial inventory of sales contracts, promotional materials, and office supplies. Gallery of Homes does not offer any form of direct financial assistance to franchisees.

Advertising: The monthly advertising royalty varies, depending on the size of the outlet. The franchisor conducts advertising programs on behalf of franchisees, and supplies promotional materials, samples, and literature for use in local campaigns.

Contract Highlights: The term of the franchise is three years. The contract may be renewed at the franchisee's option. The franchisee does not receive an exclusive territory in conjunction with the franchise.

Fees and Royalties: The initial franchise fee of $7,000 is moderate for the real estate industry. The franchise royalty and advertising royalty are both variable, depending on the size and location of the outlet.

Summary: The Gallery of Homes franchise is characterized by a stable growth record, an ample base of outlets, and solid name recognition in major U.S. markets.

Franchise Highlights

Began operating: 1935
Began franchising: 1935
Outlets currently open: 800
Initial franchise fee: $7,000
Monthly royalty: Varies
Advertising fee: Varies
Training program: 5 days
Term: 3 years

Help-U-Sell

Industry experience:	★★★	*Franchising experience:*	★★★
Financial strength:	★★★★	*Training & services:*	★★★★
Fees & royalties:	★★★	*Satisfied franchisees:*	★★★★

Help-U-Sell, Inc.
57 W. 200 South
Salt Lake City, Utah 84101
(800) 345-1990

The Help-U-Sell franchise is based on a unique real estate counseling system that targets the 'For Sale By Owner' market. Founded in 1976, the company has enjoyed a steady growth course over the last decade, selling an average of 30 franchises every year. A subsidiary of Mutual Benefit Life Insurance Company, Help-U-Sell projects an organization of 6,000 outlets by the early 1990s. The company is currently seeking new franchisees in most areas of the U.S. and Canada.

The Franchise: The franchisee conducts a real estate marketing and counseling business, operated under the trade name Help-U-Sell Real Estate. A typical outlet is situated in a 1,000 to 2,000 sq. ft. commercial/retail space, with a staff of from three to 20 full-time employees. Franchisees offer counseling, advice, and support services to homeowners interested in locating buyers for their property. For a set fee, the outlet provides guidance in pricing the property, advertising, conducting an open house, and closing the sale. At the customer's option, the franchisee's staff will show the property to prospective buyers, for an additional fee. Customers of the franchise business include homeowners, passive property owners, and builders. According to a company spokesman, a traditional realtor spends as much as 80 percent of his time acquiring listings, whereas a Help-U-Sell franchisee is preoccupied with locating buyers.

Franchisee Profile: A background in real estate sales is mandatory. Franchisees must be fully licensed real estate brokers and thoroughly knowledgeable about industry practices.

Projected Earnings: The franchisor does not furnish prospective franchisees with a written statement of projected earnings. Based on the company's system-wide sales figures, the average gross revenues of a Help-U-Sell outlet are about $2 million.

Franchisor's Services: When a franchise agreement is struck, the new franchisee receives a startup kit containing work sheets, checklists, and preliminary training materials. The franchisor provides a five-day training program at the company's headquarters in Salt Lake City. Travel and lodging expenses are the responsibility of the franchisee. The curriculum focuses on professional counseling techniques, covering marketing, sales, communications, client relations, and business management.

The franchisor offers guidelines for selecting a location for the outlet and negotiating a lease for the premises, but the franchisee is responsible for acquiring the site. After the outlet has opened for business, a Help-U-Sell representative will visit the outlet periodically, to offer guidance and troubleshooting. Other ongoing services include annual franchisee conferences and seminars, unlimited telephone consultation, and a set of confidential manuals containing standardized procedures designed to streamline the operation of the business.

Franchisees are required to purchase a computer system linked with the franchisor's central database. An optional satellite receiver allows the franchisee's staff to receive continuing education programs via Help-U-Sell's own closed-circuit television channel.

Initial Investment: New Help-U-Sell franchisees should be prepared to invest from $25,000 to $75,000 to establish the business. The amount includes the initial franchise fee, lease deposits, site improvements, equipment purchases, and an initial inventory of forms, contracts, and sales literature. Help-U-Sell offers financial assistance to qualified franchisees.

Advertising: Help-U-Sell franchisees contribute seven percent of gross monthly revenues for advertising. The franchisor supplies franchisees with samples and specifications for direct mail campaigns and newspaper and magazine advertisements. In some markets, radio and television commercials are also available.

Contract Highlights: The term of the franchise is five years. The contract may be renewed at the franchisee's option. The franchisee receives an exclusive territory for the business. The franchisee must purchase a computer system in accordance with the franchisor's specifications. Absentee ownership is prohibited. The outlet may not be sold or transferred without the franchisor's consent; the purchaser must be qualified to be a Help-U-Sell franchisee.

Fees and Royalties: The initial franchise fee of $275 per 1,000 population is moderate for the industry. As an example, a franchisee in a territory with a population of 50,000 would pay an initial fee of $13,500. The minimum fee is $4,500. The seven percent monthly royalty, added to the seven percent advertising royalty, exacts a total of 14 percent of gross revenues of the outlet.

Summary: The Help-U-Sell franchise is characterized by an innovative business format combining real estate marketing strategies with a do-it-yourself counseling service. The franchisor's consistent growth rate is evidence of popular acceptance and increasing recognition of the Help-U-Sell name throughout the U.S. and Canada. Franchisees benefit from a flexible investment, an excellent training package, and a state-of-the-art support system.

Franchise Highlights

Began operating: 1976
Began franchising: 1976
Outlets currently open: 300
Initial franchise fee: $275 per 1,000 population
Monthly royalty: 7%
Advertising fee: 7%
Training program: 5 days
Term: 5 years

Realty World

Industry experience:	★ ★ ★	*Franchising experience:*	★ ★ ★
Financial strength:	★ ★ ★ ★	*Training & services:*	★ ★ ★
Fees & royalties:	★ ★ ★ ★	*Satisfied franchisees:*	★ ★ ★ ★

Realty World Corporation
12500 Fair Lakes Circle
Fairfax, Virginia 22033
(703) 631-9300

Founded in 1974, Realty World has established 1,520 outlets, opening an average of 117 offices every year. The company is currently recruiting new franchisees in all regions of the U.S. and Canada.

The Franchise: The franchisee conducts a real estate brokerage under the trade name Realty World. A typical outlet is located in a 1,400 sq. ft. office in a self-standing site or a suitable complex, with a staff of three or more full-time employees. The outlet offers residential and commercial real estate, including sale, leasing, and, in some cases, financial assistance. Customers of the franchise business include home buyers, commercial customers, and investors. Franchisee Profile: A background in real estate is required. The company only considers prospective franchisees who are fully licensed in their localities.

Projected Earnings: The franchisor does not furnish prospective franchisees with a written statement of projected earnings.

Franchisor's Services: The franchisor provides ongoing training at the company's headquarters in Fairfax, Virginia. Representative topics include finance, marketing, real estate trends, and promotion. Other support services include confidential operations manuals, a periodic newsletter, and a telephone hotline to put franchisees in touch with key support personnel. A national referral network provides access to residential and commercial listings throughout the U.S. and Canada. The franchisor offers its own home warranty program and an 'errors and omissions' insurance plan.

Initial Investment: New Realty World franchisees should be prepared to invest from $15,000 to $25,000 to establish a new office. The amount includes the initial franchise fee, lease, deposits, office equipment, and an initial supply of contracts, forms, and promptional materials. Realty World has a financial assistance program for qualified franchisees.

Advertising: Realty World conducts advertising programs on behalf of franchisees, promoting the Realty World name, image, and national home warranty program. Franchisees also receive advertising and public relations aids for conducting local promotions.

Contract Highlights: The term of the franchise is five years. The contract may be renewed at the franchisee's option. The franchisee does not receive an exclusive territory in conjunction with the franchise.

Fees and Royalties: The initial franchise fee ranges from $8,900 to $12,900 — low to moderate for the industry. The two percent monthly royalty is low by any standard.

Summary: The Realty World franchise offers the advantages of ample name recognition and positive imaging, associated with a progressive consumer protection program. Franchisees derive the reputation and competitive benefits of an international chain, while enjoying the managerial freedom of an independent brokerage.

Franchise Highlights

Began operating: 1974
Began franchising: 1974
Outlets currently open: 1,520
Initial franchise fee: Min. $8,900
Max. $12,900

Monthly royalty: 2%
Advertising fee: None
Training program: Ongoing
Term: 5 years

Red Carpet

Industry experience:	★ ★ ★ ★	*Franchising experience:*	★ ★ ★ ★
Financial strength:	★ ★ ★ ★	*Training & services:*	★ ★ ★
Fees & royalties:	★ ★ ★	*Satisfied franchisees:*	★ ★ ★ ★

Red Carpet Real Estate Services, Inc.
P. O. Box 85660
San Diego, California 92138
(619) 571-7181

Northern California realtor Anthony Yniguez opened the first Red Carpet office in 1966, in Contra Costa County, across the bay from San Francisco. His idea was to form a council of local brokers to join forces to generate referrals and fund cooperative advertising. Yniguez sold the first Red Carpet franchise for $500.

Today, Red Carpet's 1,300 offices handle an estimated 1.5 percent of all home sales in America. Recently, the company forged an agreement with Guild Mortgage Company of San

Diego to integrate mortgage services with the Red Carpet sales network. The company is currently seeking new franchisees in most U.S. and Canadian markets.

The Franchise: The franchisee conducts a residential and commercial real estate business, using the trade name Red Carpet Real Estate. A typical outlet is situated in a self-standing commercial site or an office in a suitable commercial/retail center, with a staff of five or more full-time employees. Franchisees offer real estate sales, leases, and rentals — primarily residential property. Customers of the franchise business include prospective home buyers and investment partnerships.

Franchisee Profile: A background in real estate sales is mandatory. A prospective franchisee must possess a valid real estate broker's license and be capable of demonstrating a sufficient net worth to handle the financial responsibilities of the business.

Projected Earnings: The franchisor does not furnish prospective franchisees with a written statement of projected earnings.

Franchisor's Services: The franchisor provides a three to four day training program at the company's headquarters in San Diego. Attendees are responsible for their own travel and lodging expenses. The curriculum includes sales procedures, marketing, closing techniques, advertising, and financing.

A Red Carpet field consultant provides on-site assistance in periodic visits to the outlet. Other ongoing services include sales and management training for associates, market research, and a coast-to-coast referral network. Red Carpet offers its own home warranty protection plan for customers. Franchisees and their staffs participate in a national sales incentive and awards program.

Through affiliation with Guild Mortgage, franchisees are able to offer mortgage services from the same office in which they close real estate sales.

Initial Investment: The total investment is estimated at between $18,500 to $45,000, including the initial franchise fee, lease deposits, equipment purchases, and an initial inventory of contracts, forms, sales literature, and promotional aids. Red Carpet offers financial assistance to creditworthy franchisees.

Advertising: Red Carpet franchisees do not pay a separate advertising royalty. The franchisor conducts national and regional advertising campaigns on behalf of all Red Carpet offices. Target media include television, radio, general- and special-interest magazines, newspapers, and billboards. Franchisees also receive ad slicks, logo art, sign designs, and commercials for use in local and co-op advertising programs.

Contract Highlights: The term of the franchise is five years. The contract may be renewed at the franchisee's option. The franchisee does not receive an exclusive territory in conjunction with the franchise.

Fees and Royalties: The initial franchise fee of $9,500 is below average for the real estate industry. The moderate eight percent monthly royalty includes advertising as well as support services and trademark benefits.

Summary: The Red Carpet franchise is characterized by a large network of affiliates throughout the U.S. and Canada, providing strong name recognition and imaging. The franchisor's advertising, home warranty, and national referral programs provide the independent broker with the resources of an industry giant.

Franchise Highlights

Began operating: 1966
Began franchising: 1967
Outlets currently open: 1,300
Initial franchise fee: $9,500

Monthly royalty: 8%
Advertising fee: None
Training program: 4 days
Term: 5 years

RE/MAX

Industry experience: ★★★
Financial strength: ★★★
Fees & royalties: ★★★
Franchising experience: ★★★
Training & services: ★★★
Satisfied franchisees: ★★★★

RE/MAX of America, Inc.
P. O. Box 3907
Englewood, Colorado 80155
(800) 525-7452

Founded in 1973, RE/MAX has established 1,100 outlets since the company began franchising in 1976, opening an average of 100 outlets every year. The company is currently seeking new franchisees in all U.S. and Canadian markets.

The Franchise: The franchisee conducts a real estate listing and sales business, operated under the trade name RE/MAX. A typical outlet is situated in a suitable commercial site, with a staff of commissioned sales associates who share the operating costs of the business. Franchisees offer residential and commercial properties for sale or lease. Customers of the franchise business include prospective home buyers, businesses, and investors.

Franchisee Profile: A background in real estate is required. Franchisees must possess valid real estate licenses.

Projected Earnings: The franchisor does not furnish prospective franchisees with a written statement of projected earnings. Based on the company's sales estimates, the average revenues of a RE/MAX office are about $650,000 per year.

Franchisor's Services: The franchisor provides a one-week training program at the company's headquarters in Englewood, Colorado. The cost of travel, lodging, and meals is borne by the franchisee. The curriculum includes management, operations, sales, marketing, financing, and advertising.

A RE/MAX field consultant calls on each outlet periodically, to offer on-site guidance and assistance. The franchisor also holds continuing education seminars and publishes a franchisee newsletter to keep RE/MAX brokers and associates abreast of current rules, regulations, financial news, and industry trends. Franchisees and their staffs have access to company technical and operations consultants via a toll-free hotline.

Initial Investment: New RE/MAX franchisees should be prepared to invest from $10,000 to $50,000 to establish the business. The amount includes the initial franchise fee, lease deposits, equipment purchases, and an initial inventory of sales materials, contracts, and promotional aids. RE/MAX does not offer any form of direct financial assistance to franchisees.

Advertising: Each month, RE/MAX franchisees contribute $50 per associate for advertising. For instance, an office with five associate realtors would pay a monthly advertising fee of $250. The franchisor uses these funds to conduct regional advertising campaigns on behalf of all RE/MAX offices. Franchisees are authorized to use the franchisor's trademarks on signs, advertisements, and printed materials.

Contract Highlights: The term of the franchise is five years — about average for the real estate trade. The contract may be renewed for an additional term at the franchisee's option. The franchisee does not receive an exclusive territory in conjunction with the franchise.

Fees and Royalties: The initial franchise fee ranges from $10,000 to $20,000 — moderate to high for the industry. Franchisees pay a monthly fee of $60 per associate. For example, an office with five associate realtors would pay $300 per month. Including the $50 per associate advertising royalty, the total monthly payment is $110 per associate.

Summary: The RE/MAX franchise is characterized by an expansive organization and the financial benefits of a cooperative business and financial relationship.

Franchise Highlights

Began operating: 1973
Began franchising: 1976
Outlets currently open: 1,100
Initial franchise fee: Min. $10,000
Max: $20,000

Monthly royalty: $60 per associate
Advertising fee: $50 per associate
Training program: 1 week
Term: 5 years

Recreation and Amusement

Americans spend more than $3.2 billion on recreation and amusement each year. In this section, you will find franchise opportunities ranging from miniature golf courses to campground facilities. Campground franchises, such as Kampgrounds of America, sprang up in the 1960s, as record numbers of Americans hit the roads on driving and camping vacations. The popularity of recreational vehicles and truck campers added fuel to the camping revolution.

In today's outdoor-oriented, fitness-conscious society, recreational camping is undergoing a new renaissance. Most recreational businesses are real estate-intensive, with the preponderance of the owner's investment tied up in property. As much as 80 percent of the cost of developing a campground or miniature golf course may go toward real estate.

KOA Kampgrounds of America

Industry experience:	★ ★ ★ ★	*Franchising experience:*	★ ★ ★ ★
Financial strength:	★ ★ ★	*Training & services:*	★ ★ ★
Fees & royalties:	★ ★ ★	*Satisfied franchisees:*	★ ★ ★ ★

KOA
P. O. Box 30558
Billings, Montana 59114
(406) 548-7239

Founded in 1960, KOA Kampgrounds of America has established 750 outlets since the company began franchising in 1962, opening an average of 30 outlets every year. The company is currently seeking new franchisees in all regions of the U.S.

The Franchise: The franchisee conducts a recreational campground business, operated under the trade name KOA. A typical outlet is situated in a rural or resort area, with a staff of four full-time and four part-time employees. Franchisees offer comfortable, convenient camping facilities featuring resort-style facilities in an outdoor environment. Representative facilities include a snack bar, general store, utility hookups, and showers. Customers of the franchise business include vacationing families and individuals.

Franchisee Profile: A background in campground or resort management is beneficial, but not mandatory.

Projected Earnings: The franchisor does not furnish prospective franchisees with a written statement of projected earnings.

Franchisor's Services: The franchisor provides a three-day training program at the company's headquarters in Billings, Montana. Attendees are responsible for their own travel and lodging expenses. The curriculum includes campground design, marketing, and operations.

The franchisor will assist with selecting a site for the campground. After the campground has opened for business, a KOA representative will visit the outlet periodically, to offer guidance and troubleshooting. Other ongoing services include a purchasing co-op for equipment and supplies, and periodic seminars.

Initial Investment: New KOA Kampgrounds of America franchisees should be prepared to invest $200,000 to $1 million to establish the business. The amount includes the initial franchise fee, site acquisition, construction and improvements, equipment purchases, and supplies. The franchisor does not offer any direct financial assistance to franchisees.

Advertising: KOA Kampgrounds of America franchisees contribute two percent of gross monthly revenues for advertising. The franchisor conducts national and regional advertising campaigns on behalf of all KOA outlets, using sports and travel publications, billboards, and radio.

Contract Highlights: The term of the franchise is five years. The contract may be renewed for an additional five-year term at the franchisee's option. The franchisee receives an exclusive territory in conjunction with the franchise.

Fees and Royalties: The initial franchise fee of $20,000 is moderate for the industry. The eight percent monthly royalty, added to the two percent advertising royalty, exacts a total of ten percent of the gross revenues of the business.

Summary: The KOA franchise is characterized by strong name name recognition, a prolific base of outlets, and a consistently strong demand for family-oriented campground facilities.

THE FOUR-WHEEL DRIVE THE HILLS AND

1989 FORD BRONCO II.

Eddie Bauer®

Take your pick. The plush hills of Beverly or the rough terrain of Baja. Either way, if you've got a Ford Bronco II Eddie Bauer, then you've got it handled.

HEAD FOR THE HILLS WITH STANDARD TOUCH DRIVE.

Now when you need to shift into 4-wheel drive you can do it at the touch of a button. Because now all Bronco II 4x4's come equipped with standard Touch Drive that lets you go from 2-wheel to 4-wheel drive on the move just by pressing a button. And when you're climbing those hills, you'll be doing it with fuel-injected V-6 power. Bronco II is also available in a 2-wheel drive model.

Welcome to Putter's Paradise

Miniature golf, a '20s fad, comes back in style

On Manhattan's West 21st Street, wooden bananas whirl over a patch of fake turf, while strutting pink flamingos pick at another patch. A wide-mouthed, 12-ft.-long Fiberglas alligator waits to swallow a fluorescent golf ball. No, it's not a discarded backdrop from *Miami Vice.* The gator's peristaltic mech-

ROB NELSON—BLACK STAR

Teeing off in Myrtle Beach, S.C., where sea beasts lurk

anism is just about the toughest hole at Putter's Paradise, a miniature-golf course in New York City's Chelsea district. "If you hit the ball too hard, it just bounces right back out of the mouth," explains co-proprietor Jeanne Horning. "If you hit it too soft, it just rolls around in there and doesn't go through."

Miniature golf, a craze of the late '20s, is staging a comeback. In 1930 more than 25,000 courses dotted the American landscape from Lookout Mountain in Tennessee to Los Angeles, with several of the most popular atop New York City skyscrapers. As many as 4 million Americans putted every day, and a popular song bore the title *I've Gone Goofy over Miniature Golf.* By the early '30s, the game's appeal withered as quickly as it had risen, though mini-courses remained a staple of beach resorts.

The boomlet can be credited to the upsurge in nostalgia for the pop culture of recent periods and the growing popularity of full-scale links. There are an estimated 1,800 courses in the U.S., 54% of them built since 1981, according to one survey. Upwards of 50 million Americans played the tiny greens last year. Some argue that the resurgence is the result of fancy new courses. Once played on flat bits of artificial turf with hollow logs and windmills as props, the modern versions are built around themes of jungle adventures, pirate ships and treasure hunts, with waterfalls, mountains and boat rides. "It's not that people are suddenly saying 'Let's go play miniature golf,'" notes Tim Troy, part owner of Lost Mountain Adventure Golf, a new course outside Chicago. "It's that they didn't have anyplace to play."

One of the latest links is Donald Trump's Gotham Golf, a nine-hole, 10,000-sq.-ft. course in Central Park.

FRANK MICELOTTA

In Central Park, as Miss Liberty looks on

Opened last month, it features, among replica landmarks like the Statue of Liberty, two of Trump's prized possessions, Trump Tower and the Plaza Hotel.

But not everyone is convinced that the mini-boom will last. Don Clayton, chairman of Putt-Putt Golf Courses of America, which has 325 U.S. franchises, says gross revenues from the links have quadrupled over the past ten years, but a glut of new courses could lead to a collapse. Still, a game that costs as little as $1.50 to play (or around $7 at the adventure setups) has a certain built-in demographic appeal. Says Gary Knight of Lomma Enterprises, a Scranton, Pa., company that builds miniature courses: "Baby boomers have children now and want something to do with their family. Miniature golf fits the bill, and it's cheaper than going to the movies." That doesn't sound very goofy at all. ***—By Sylvester Monroe. Reported by Michael Mason/Atlanta and Stephen Pomper/New York***

Milestones

EXPECTING. Kimberley Conrad, 26, former *Playboy* playmate, and *Playboy's* **Hugh Hefner,** 63, who were married in July.

DIED. A. Bartlett Giamatti, 51, erudite, passionate commissioner of major league baseball and former president of Yale; of a heart attack, eight days after he succeeded in barring Cincinnati Reds manager Pete Rose from baseball for betting on games; in Edgartown, Mass. A Renaissance scholar and Renaissance man, Giamatti wryly noted upon his 1978 installation as Yale president that his true dream was to be president of the American League. In 1986 he got his wish—only it was the National League; he became baseball commissioner last April. As learned about the subtleties of the balk call as he was about Dante, he liked to philosophize about the national pastime: "I grew up believing in values and also believing we'll often fall short of realizing them. The best hitters fail about 70% of the time. But that's no reason for them, or for any of us, to give up."

DIED. Giorgio Sant'Angelo, 56, avant-garde fashion designer known for snug, stretchy fabrics and such ethnic touches as leather fringe; of lung cancer; in New York City.

DIED. Joseph Alsop, 78, influential conservative newspaper columnist; in Washington. A New Deal liberal and staunch anti-Communist, the crusty Alsop was a strong supporter of the Viet Nam War.

DIED. Dorothy Schiff, 86, indefatigable former owner and publisher of the New York *Post;* in New York City. From 1939 to 1976, when she sold the daily to Rupert Murdoch, Schiff used her ample inherited fortune and editorial talents to keep the financially precarious afternoon paper afloat while rival dailies went under.

DIED. Irving Stone, 86, popular, prolific author who virtually invented the genre of the biographical novel and sold 30 million copies of his books; in Los Angeles. Among the best known of his two dozen lengthy, richly detailed and researched works are *Lust for Life,* based on the story of Vincent van Gogh, and *The Agony and the Ecstasy,* about Michelangelo.

BORN. To **Ling-Ling:** a 3½-oz. giant-panda cub; at the National Zoo, in Washington. Her four previous cubs died at birth.

717 346-5555

Franchise Highlights

Began operating: 1960
Began franchising: 1962
Outlets currently open: 750
Initial franchise fee: $20,000
Monthly royalty: 8%
Advertising fee: 2%
Training program: 3 days
Term: 5 years

Putt-Putt Golf Courses

Industry experience:	★★★★	*Franchising experience:*	★★★★
Financial strength:	★★★	*Training & services:*	★★★
Fees & royalties:	★★★	*Satisfied franchisees:*	★★★★

Putt-Putt Golf Courses of America
3007 Fort Bragg Road
Fayetteville, North Carolina 28303
(919) 485-7131

Don Clayton founded the first Putt-Putt miniature golf course on doctor's orders. More precisely, his family physician prescribed a relaxing diversion, and Clayton began puttering around at miniature golf. Since he opened the first course in 1954, Putt-Putt Golf Courses of America has soared to more than 400 outlets in all 50 states and 30 foreign countries, generating $25 million in annual sales.

The Franchise: The franchisee operates a miniature golf course under the trade name Putt-Putt. A typical outlet is situated on a 60,000 sq. ft. site near a high-traffic shopping mall, with a staff of two full-time and five part-time employees. Besides miniature golf, the franchisee may also operate an electronic gameroom and/or an ice cream snack bar, called Scoop-Scoop. The course may be 36, 72, or 54 holes, depending on the population of the area.

Franchisee Profile: Some prior business experience is beneficial. The franchisor does not encourage absentee ownership.

Projected Earnings: The average volume of a Putt-Putt Golf Course is about $62,500 per year, before expenses. Net profits range from 21 to 32 percent on the average.

Franchisor's Services: The franchisor operates a continuous training program at regional centers and at the company's headquarters in Fayetteville, North Carolina. Travel and lodging expenses must be paid by franchisees.

The franchisor has the right to approve the selected site, before construction begins. Franchisees receive assistance with the planning and layout of the facilities, and the acquisition of materials and supplies. When the golf course is open, a Putt-Putt representative will visit the outlet regularly, to offer ongoing troubleshooting and assistance. The franchisor also supplies business forms, merchandise, and equipment used in the conduct of the business. Putt-Putt publishes a monthly franchisee newsletter and organizes annual franchisee conventions. In addition, the company offers insurance plans for both the business and its employees.

Initial Investment: The initial investment is estimated at $70,000 to $900,000, depending on the location and size of the golf course. The franchisor does not offer any direct financial assistance to franchisees for any part of the initial investment.

Advertising: Putt-Putt franchisees contribute two percent of gross monthly revenues for advertising. The franchisor uses these funds to develop ad materials for use in newspaper, magazine, Yellow Page, radio, and television campaigns conducted by the franchisee.

Contract Highlights: The term of the franchise is five years, with a five-year renewal option. The franchisee receives a protected territory for the duration of the agreement. The franchisor has the right to approve the site for the golf course. New franchisees are obligated to attend the first available training program or convention after signing the franchise agreement.

Fees and Royalties: The initial franchise fee is $10,000 for the golf course package alone. An additional $5,000 fee applies for a course with an electronic gameroom. Including the monthly franchise royalty and advertising fee, the total royalty burden is just eight percent of gross sales.

Summary: The Putt-Putt franchise capitalizes on the timeless demand for miniature golf recreational facilities, coupled with the recent popularity of electronic gamerooms. Franchisees benefit from a detailed startup package and an experienced organization.

Franchise Highlights

Began operating: 1954
Began franchising: 1955
Outlets currently open: 430
Initial franchise fee: Min. $10,000
Max. $15,000

Monthly royalty: 3%
Advertising fee: 2%
Training program: 5 days
Term: 5 years

Safari Campgrounds

Industry experience:	★★★	*Franchising experience:*	★★★
Financial strength:	★★★	*Training & services:*	★★★
Fees & royalties:	★★★	*Satisfied franchisees:*	★★★

Safari Campgrounds
30 North 18th Avenue, Unit 9
Struegon Way, Wisconsin 54325
(414) 743-6586

The Franchise: The franchisee operates an upscale camping resort facility, under the trade name Safari Campground. Franchisees operate the campground year-round, selling ownership participation rights to individual camp sites.

Franchisor's Services: Safari franchisees spend one week in training at the company's headquarters in Sturgeon Bay, Wisconsin. The franchisor provides pre-opening assistance at the franchisee's site. A field adviser offers ongoing guidance in marketing and operations.

Initial Investment: The start-up investment is estimated at between $100,000 and $150,000, including site acquisition, improvements, equipment and signs, supplies, and miscellaneous expenses. Safari does not offer any direct financial assistance to franchisees.

Fees and Royalties: The initial franchise fee of $8,000 is moderate for a campground franchise. Safari franchisees do not pay a separate royalty for advertising. The total royalty obligation is a manageable five percent of gross sales.

Summary: The Safari franchise offers a timesharing alternative for operating a resort-style camping facility, backed by a savy staff of marketing professionals.

Franchise Highlights

Began operating: 1967	**Monthly royalty: 5%**
Began franchising: 1967	**Advertising fee: None**
Outlets currently open: 40	**Training program: 1 week**
Initial franchise fee: $8,000	**Term: 20 years**

United States Basketball League

Industry experience:	★	*Franchising experience:*	★
Financial strength:	★ ★	*Training & services:*	★ ★ ★
Fees & royalties:	★ ★	*Satisfied franchisees:*	★ ★ ★

United States Basketball League
5100 Poplar Avenue, Ste. 1219
Memphis, Tennessee 38137
(901) 761-3085

The United States Basketball League offers the opportunity to own an organized sports franchise. The USBL plays out its season in the spring, so as not to compete head-on for the attention of basketball fans of the NBA, which plays in fall and winter.

The Franchise: The franchisee operates an organized basketball franchise staging games with teams field by other league franchises. Besides team competition, franchisees participate in league coordination, management, and expansion decisions.

Franchisee Profile: Franchisees must have at least $250,000 in available cash or liquid assets. Absentee ownership is not prohibited.

Projected Earnings: The franchisor does not provide a statement of projected earnings.

Franchisor's Services: The USBL conducts a seven-day training and orientation program for franchisees at league headquarters in Memphis, Tennessee. Attendees are responsible for their own travel and lodging expenses. Additional training and startup assistance are provided at the franchisee's place of business.

USBL franchise owners receive a set of confidential manuals detailing league policies and franchise operating procedures.

Initial Investment: New USBL franchisees should be prepared to invest $485,000 to establish a new team franchise. The league does not offer any direct financial assistance to franchisees.

Advertising: Franchisees do not pay any separate royalties for advertising. The league conducts its own advertising programs, but franchisees are primarily responsible for promoting their own teams.

Contract Highlights: The term of the franchise is ten years. The contract may be renewed for an additional term, by mutual agreement. The franchisee receives an exclusive territory for the duration of the agreement.

Fees and Royalties: The initial franchise fee to field a team in the USBL is $250,000. Franchisees pay a royalty of four percent of their gross monthly revenues.

Summary: The USBL provides a ready-made vehicle for owning a low-profile sports franchise in team competition.

Franchise Highlights

Began operating: 1984
Began franchising: 1984
Outlets currently open: 8
Initial franchise fee: $250,000
Monthly royalty: 4%
Advertising fee: None
Training program: 7 days
Term: 10 years

Yogi Bear's Jellystone Park

Industry experience:	★★★	*Franchising experience:*	★★★
Financial strength:	★★★	*Training & services:*	★★★
Fees & royalties:	★★★	*Satisfied franchisees:*	★★★

Yogi Bear's Jellystone Park Camp-Resorts
30 N. 18th Avenue, Unit 9
Sturgeon Bay, Wisconsin 54235
(414) 743-6586

The Franchise: The franchisee operates a family-oriented campground-resort, under the trade name Yogi Bear's Jellystone Park. The property features resort-style facilities and playground equipment, with a motif based on Hannah-Barbera trademarked cartoon characters. Franchisees generate revenues from the sale of ownership shares in individual camp sites.

Franchisor's Services: The franchisor conducts a one-week training program in Sturgeon Bay, Wisconsin. Additional training and grand opening assistance are provided at the franchisee's selected property. The company offers ongoing management assistance through a team of field consultants and marketing specialists.

Initial Investment: The start-up investment ranges from $100,000 to $150,000, including site acquisition, property improvements, equipment, signs, and miscellaneous expenses. The franchisor does not offer any direct financial assistance to franchisees.

Fees and Royalties: The $9,000 franchise fee is moderate for a franchise in this category. The franchisee's total royalty obligation is six percent of the campground's gross revenues.

Franchise Highlights

Began operating: 1969
Began franchising: 1969
Outlets currently open: 60
Initial franchise fee: $9,000
Monthly royalty: 6%
Advertising fee: None
Training program: 1 week
Term: 20 years

Retail and Convenience Stores

The following section includes miscellaneous retail and merchandising franchises, ranging from specialty boutiques to convenience food marts.

The convenience store sprang up in the 1960s, in answer to the proliferation of supermarkets which threatened to wipe out the small, independent grocer. Southland Corporation, with $8.6 billion in annual sales and more than 7,000 7-Eleven Food Stores, has grown to become a retailing giant in its own right. Lately, convenience marts have begun to take on the aspect of diversified 'micromalls,' selling everything from groceries to airline tickets. For example, some 7-Eleven also sell Hardee's hamburgers or Church's fried chicken, in addition to Southland's own microwave fast food. In the western U.S., convenience marts are often piggybacked with gasoline service stations or retail liquor stores.

Hardware was one of the first retail sectors to be franchised, but rising wholesale prices and lagging sales have forced most hardware chains to diversify into other merchandise, such as home furnishings, children's apparel, and auto supplies.

Meanwhile, the retail floral trade has flourished, generating more than $5 billion per year. Americans buy almost as many live pets and pet supplies as floral arrangements — $4 billion annually.

The rise of the regional shopping mall breathed new life into specialty retailers hustling such merchandise as art goods and greeting cards. The huge, self-contained 'shopping cities' provide small boutiques with equal visibility and access as major department stores.

Almost Heaven Hot Tubs

Industry experience: ★ ★ ★ *Franchising experience:* ★ ★ ★
Financial strength: ★ ★ ★ *Training & services:* ★ ★ ★
Fees & royalties: ★ ★ ★ ★ *Satisfied franchisees:* ★ ★

Almost Heaven Hot Tubs, Ltd.
Route 5 FY
Renick, West Virginia 24966
(304) 497-3163

The most heavenly thing about Almost Heaven Hot Tubs is its franchise fees and royalties: There are none. For a minimum initial inventory purchase ranging from $5,000 to $10,000, franchisees receive a protected territory, advertising support, and personal assistance from seasoned hot-tub pros.

Founded in 1971, Almost Heaven has established more than 1,000 outlets since the company began franchising in 1978, opening an average of 130 outlets every year. The company is currently seeking new franchisees in all U.S. regions and selected overseas markets.

The Franchise: The franchisee operates a retail sales business, specializing in hot tubs, spas, and related leisure products, under the trade name Almost Heaven Hot Tubs. A typical outlet is situated in a retail strip center or free-standing commercial building, with a staff of two full-time and one part-time employees. Franchisees offer a comprehensive line of hot tubs, saunas, portable spas, accessories, and supplies.

Franchisee Profile: A background in business or retail merchandising is beneficial, but not mandatory. Absentee ownership is not specifically prohibited by the franchise agreement.

Franchisor's Services: The franchisor provides a one-week training program at the company's headquarters in Renick, West Virginia. Attendees are responsible for their own travel and lodging expenses. The curriculum includes hot tub design, installation, sales, and operation; marketing, advertising, and sales promotion; purchasing and inventory control.

Franchisees receive a set of confidential operations manuals, ongoing field seminars, and a franchisee newsletter.

Initial Investment: The total start-up investment is reportedly just under $30,000, including $10,000 in opening inventory purchases. Financing is available on the purchase of hot tubs and spas from the franchisor.

Advertising: Almost Heaven franchisees do not pay any advertising fees or royalties. The franchisor conducts national advertising and supplies franchisees with catalogs, brochures, and point-of-sale materials.

Contract Highlights: The franchise does not have a definite term. The franchisee receives an exclusive territory in which the franchisor promises not to compete with the franchisee's outlet.

Fees and Royalties: Aside from the initial inventory purchase, franchisees do not pay any franchisee fees or royalties. The franchisor derives profits from the sale of merchandise to franchisees.

Summary: The Almost Heaven Hot Tubs franchise is characterized by an easy-to-operate retail business in a highly competitive leisure products market. Franchisees benefit from a low investment, professional imaging, and access to an experienced staff of technical and marketing advisers.

Franchise Highlights

Began operating: 1971
Began franchising: 1978
Outlets currently open: 1,080
Initial franchise fee: None
Monthly royalty: None
Advertising fee: None
Training program: 2 weeks
Term: 1 year

am/pm Mini-Market

Industry experience:	★ ★ ★	*Franchising experience:*	★ ★
Financial strength:	★ ★ ★	*Training & services:*	★ ★ ★
Fees & royalties:	★ ★ ★	*Satisfied franchisees:*	★ ★ ★

Atlantic Richfield Company
515 South Flower Street
Los Angeles, California 90071
(213) 486-3939

A typical am/pm store is operated in conjunction with another business, such as an Atlantic Richfield service station. The franchisee must provide both the land and the building for the convenience store. Since the first market opened in 1979, the company has recruited more than 400 franchisees to supplement the chain's company-owned outlets.

The Franchise: The franchisee operates a retail convenience market under the trade name am/pm Mini-Market. A typical outlet is located on the same premises as a gasoline service station, selling a limited selection of groceries, microwave foods, beverages and sundries.

Franchisee Profile: Previous retail experience is beneficial, but not mandatory. The franchisee must be capable of purchasing or leasing suitable premises for the convenience store.

Projected Earnings: A written statement of projected earnings was not available at press time. Franchisor's Services: am/pm conducts a training program from two to three weeks in duration at the company's headquarters in Los Angeles. A franchise representative provides assistance with pre-opening activities. Ongoing counsel is available from field specialists, as required.

Initial Investment: The total investment to start a new store may range as high as $450,000, including site acquisition, construction, fixtures, equipment, inventory, and miscellaneous start-up expenses. A franchisee with existing property and/or a building for the outlet may spend substantially less. The franchisor does not offer any direct financial assistance to franchisees.

Fees and Royalties: The initial franchise fee of $30,000 is high for a convenience market. The franchisee's total royalty obligation, including the monthly franchise fee and the advertising fee, is six percent of gross sales.

Summary: The am/pm franchisee benefits from merchandising support, increasing name recognition, and the cooperative benefits of a well established organization.

Franchise Highlights

Began operating: 1980
Began franchising: 1980
Outlets currently open: 750
Initial franchise fee: $30,000
Monthly royalty: 4%
Advertising fee: 2%
Training program: 2 weeks
Term: 10 years

Annie's Book Stop

Industry experience:	★★★	*Franchising experience:*	★★
Financial strength:	★★★	*Training & services:*	★★★
Fees & royalties:	★★★	*Satisfied franchisees:*	★★★

Annie's Book Stop
15 Lackey Street
Westborough, Massachusetts 01581
(617) 366-9547

In 1974, Annie Adams, mother of six and former suburban housewife, went shopping for novels in a book store that had devoted a small section of its shelf space to 'pre-read' books. She envisioned an entire store dedicated to trading used books — not a haggard shop with a dog-eared inventory, but an appealing, upscale establishment with a drawing-room decor. The result was Annie's Book Swap, a pristine, curtained and carpeted book exchange in Worcester, Massachusetts. When she opened her third store six years later, people began offering her money to teach them the business. Ninety stores and two name changes later (for a spell, the stores were called Swap to Stop), Annie's Book Stop is a thriving franchise organization nearing a hundred outlets.

The Franchise: The franchisee operates a retail book exchange specializing in mass-market paperbacks and doing business under the trade name Annie's Book Stop. A typical outlet is situated in 800 sq. ft. to 1,000 sq. ft. of retail space and sells 'pre-read' paperback books for about half the original retail price and. The shop also accepts used books in exchange for credit towards other purchases.

Franchisee Profile: A typical Annie's franchisee is a college-educated female with a background in teaching or retail book sales. There are no particular qualifications, except a fondness of books and the desire to succeed.

Franchisor's Services: Annie's Book Stop conducts a training seminar in three to five days at the company's headquarters in Ann Arbor, Michigan. Additional training and grand opening assistance are provided at the franchisee's place of business.

Franchisees receive copies of the Annie's Book Stop operations manual, a comprehensive guide to the business. The content covers financial planning, site negotiation, censorship, the history of paperback books, business forms and procedures, and promotional techniques. Annie's provides a start-up stock of approximately 25,000 titles, delivered to the franchisee's store in the company's distinctive, red 'Magic Wagon' van.

Ongoing assistance is provided by a field consultant in periodic visits to the shop. Annie's Book Stop also publishes a quarterly franchisee newsletter and disseminates training videos to maintain a sense of community in the franchise organization.

Initial Investment: The total start-up investment is estimated at between $11,500 and $27,000, including lease deposits, site improvements, fixtures, and opening stock. The franchisor does not offer any direct financial assistance to franchisees.

Advertising: Annie's Book Stop franchisees do not pay a separate fee for advertising. The franchisor considers the store's presentation to be its most prominent advertising vehicle. Occasionally, Annie's conducts tasteful but low-profile promotions on a regional scale.

Contract Highlights: The Annie's Book Stop franchise has a ten-year term, renewable for an additional term at the franchisee's option.

Fees and Royalties: The $12,500 franchise fee reflects, in part, the franchisor's cost of training and start-up assistance. New franchisees pay a set royalty of $35 per month during their first year of operation, increasing to $50 per month in the second year. Thereafter, the royalty is calculated as a percentage of gross sales.

Summary: The Annie's Book Stop franchise offers a ready-to-go business format for entering the used book trade, enhanced by upscale imaging, a moderate initial investment, and keen personal assistance.

Franchise Highlights

Began operating: 1974	**Monthly royalty: Varies**
Began franchising: 1981	**Advertising fee: None**
Outlets currently open: 90	**Training program: 3 to 5 days**
Initial franchise fee: $12,500	**Term: 10 years**

Bathtique

Industry experience:	★ ★ ★	*Franchising experience:*	★ ★ ★
Financial strength:	★ ★ ★	*Training & services:*	★ ★ ★
Fees & royalties:	★ ★ ★	*Satisfied franchisees:*	★ ★ ★ ★

Bathtique International
247 North Goodman Street
Rochester, New York 14607
(716) 442-9190

Founded in 1969, Bathtique has established 100 outlets since the company began franchising in 1969, opening an average of five outlets every year. The company is currently seeking new franchisees in most U.S. markets.

The Franchise: The franchisee operates a retail store specializing in bath decorating products and related gift items, under the trade name Bathtique. A typical outlet is situated in a shopping mall or retail strip center, with a staff of one full-time and five part-time employees. Franchisees offer decorative products, gift items, and accessories for home bathrooms, ranging from scented soaps and ceramic dispensers to towels and rugs.

Franchisee Profile: A background in business or retail merchandising is beneficial, but not mandatory. Absentee ownership is not prohibited.

Projected Earnings: A statement of projected earnings was not available at press time.

Franchisor's Services: The franchisor provides a one-week training program at the company's headquarters in Rochester, New York. Attendees are responsible for their own travel and lodging expenses. The curriculum includes merchandising techniques, store procedures, customer assistance, sales promotion, and financial administration.

The franchisor will assist with selecting a site for the outlet and negotiating a lease for the premises. After the outlet has opened for business, a Bathtique representative will visit the outlet periodically, to offer guidance and troubleshooting. Other ongoing services include a franchisee newsletter and a toll-free hotline to franchise headquarters.

Initial Investment: New Bathtique franchisees should be prepared to invest from $50,000 to $100,000 to establish the business. The amount includes the initial franchise fee, lease deposits, site improvements, equipment purchases, and an initial inventory of merchandise. Bathtique does not offer direct financial assistance to franchisees.

Advertising: Bathtique franchisees do not pay a monthly advertising fee. The franchisor supplies franchisees with point-of-sale materials, preprepared advertising aids, and public relations tools. Co-op advertising is available at the regional level, on a voluntary basis.

Contract Highlights: The term of the franchise is ten years. The contract may be renewed at the franchisee's option. The franchisee receives an exclusive territory in conjunction with the franchise.

Fees and Royalties: The initial franchise fee of $25,000 is somewhat high for the industry — reflecting a high level of on-site support prior to opening. Including the monthly franchise royalty and advertising fee, the total royalty burden is a low five percent of gross sales.

Summary: The Bathtique franchise is characterized by a unique retail format catering to the do-it-yourself home decoration and gift markets, well suited for high-traffic shopping malls. The franchisor suggests that the business may be operated as either a primary or secondary income source.

Franchise Highlights

Began operating: 1969	**Monthly royalty: 5%**
Began franchising: 1969	**Advertising fee: None**
Outlets currently open: 100	**Training program: 1 week**
Initial franchise fee: $25,000	**Term: 10 years**

Coast to Coast Total Hardware

Industry experience:	★ ★ ★ ★	*Franchising experience:*	★ ★ ★ ★
Financial strength:	★ ★ ★	*Training & services:*	★ ★ ★
Fees & royalties:	★ ★ ★ ★	*Satisfied franchisees:*	★ ★ ★

Coast to Coast Total Hardware Stores, Inc.
10801 Red Circle Drive
Minnetonka, Minnesota
(612) 935-1711

Coast to Coast franchise stores have been in operation for 60 years — long enough to spread across the nation, survive two stock market crashes, and compete with all manner of entrepreneurial enterprise. Today, more than a thousand stores are scattered throughout 30 states, with the heaviest concentration in Minnesota, Iowa, and Wisconsin.

The Franchise: The franchisee operates a retail hard goods store, under the trade name Coast to Coast. A typical outlet sells hardware, electrical, plumbing, auto, sporting goods, home furnishings, appliances, building materials, housewares, paints, toys, and lawn and garden supplies. The exact inventory is geared to the needs of the surrounding community. Franchisees purchase merchandise — including a private line of Coast to Coast products — from the franchisor's distributors. A typical outlet is located in a free-standing commercial building or retail strip center, with four full-time and five full-time employees.

Franchisee Profile: Coast to Coast prefers applicants with previous business, retail or related experience.

Projected Earnings: The franchisor will furnish prospective franchisees with a statement of projected earnings on request. Based on the company's reported annual sales, the average volume of a Coast to Coast outlet is about $490,000 before deducting the cost of goods and operating expenses.

Franchisor Services: The franchisor analyzes the market in the franchisee's proposed territory and selects a suitable site for the store. A company representative negotiates a lease for the premises, then sublets the site to the franchisee.

A five-day training program in the lakeside community of Minnetonka, Minnesoat prepares the new franchisee for opening. The curriculum covers retail purchasing, inventory control, employee relations, and advertising and promotional techniques.

Ongoing support includes a computer ordering system, central purchasing, regular evaluations, and a franchise newsletter. Assistance with inventory control is offered for a fee.

Initial Investment: The startup investment ranges from $200,000 to $700,000, including construction, fixtures, signs, inventory, and miscellaneous expenses. The franchisor does not offer any direct financial assistance to franchisees, but offers credit terms on merchandise purchases.

Advertising: Franchisees do not pay any monthly advertising fees. Coast to Coast provides examples of point-of-sale displays and offers some materials at additional cost. Co-op advertising funds are available for local campaigns.

Fees and Royalties: The $3,000 initial franchise fee is low. A set royalty of $50 is paid monthly.

Contract Highlights: The contract term is five years — half the national average. The franchise may be extended for an additional five-year term on expiration. The franchisee does not receive any territorial rights, but has the option to open additional outlets by paying a separate initial franchise fee for each. The franchise may not be sold or transferred without the franchisor's consent.

Summary: The Coast to Coast franchise is characterized by low fees and royalties, a fabled history, and the competitive resources of an industry leader. Franchisees benefit from personal assistance with inventory, merchandising and market analysis.

Franchise Highlights

Began operating: 1928	**Monthly royalty: $50 per month**
Began franchising: 1928	**Advertising fee: None**
Outlets currently open: 1,100	**Training program: 5 days**
Initial franchise fee: $3,000	**Term: 5 years**

Conroy's

Industry experience:	★★	*Franchising experience:*	★★
Financial strength:	★★★	*Training & services:*	★★★★
Fees & royalties:	★★★	*Satisfied franchisees:*	★★★

Conroy's Florists
11260 Playa Court
Culver City, California 90230
(213) 390-9781

Chris Conroy opened his first flower shop in Southern California in 1964. He began franchising the business in 1974 and, since that time, has expanded into 80 sites, mostly in his home state. All but three of the chain's outlets are franchise operations.

The Franchise: The franchisee operates a retail floral shop based on the franchisor's standardized merchandising program and doing business the trade name Conroy's. A typical outlet is situated on a high-traffic thoroughfare, with four full-time and eight part-time employees. The most prominent feature of the shop is its streetside display of brightly colored floral merchandise, designed to attract the attention of passing motorists.

Franchisee Profile: A background in floral arrangement is not required. Conroy's stresses the need for strong business and financial aptitude.

Projected Earnings: Based on the company's reported sales, the average volume of a Conroy's outlet is about $460,000 per year, before deducting inventory costs and operating expenses. This figure does not take into consideration such variables as outlet size or location, and is not based on any earning claim furnished by the franchisor.

Franchisor's Services: Conroy's franchisees receive a total of six weeks of training at the company's headquarters in Culver City, California. Each franchisee receives a set of comprehensive operations manuals detailing the operation and management of the business. The franchisor's advertising program includes aggressive radio and newspaper campaigns conducted at the regional level. Franchisees receive ongoing support from Conroy's field specialists who visits each florist periodically.

Initial Investment: The total start-up investment is estimated between $75,000 and $100,000, including the initial fee, site acquisition, improvements, fixtures, inventory, and miscellaneous expenses. The franchisor does not offer any direct financial assistance to franchisees.

Fees and Royalties: The initial franchise fee of $75,000 covers a comprehensive start-up program. The franchisee's total royalty obligation, including the monthly franchise fee and the advertising fee, is just under 11 percent of gross sales.

Summary: The Conroy's franchise is characterized by positive imaging, extensive start-up assistance, and professional management support.

Franchise Highlights

Began operating: 1964	**Monthly royalty: 7.75%**
Began franchising: 1974	**Advertising fee: 3%**
Outlets currently open: 80	**Training program: 6 weeks**
Initial franchise fee: $75,000	**Term: 20 years**

Convenient Food Mart

Industry experience:	★ ★ ★ ★	*Franchising experience:*	★ ★ ★ ★
Financial strength:	★ ★ ★ ★	*Training & services:*	★ ★ ★ ★
Fees & royalties:	★ ★ ★	*Satisfied franchisees:*	★ ★ ★

Convenient Food Mart, Inc.
9701 West Higgins Road
Suite 850
Rosemont, Illinois 60018
(312) 692-9150

One of the first retailers to capitalize on quick-stop supermarket shopping, Convenient Food Mart opened its first franchise store in 1959. Today, nearly 30 years later, more than 1,000 franchisees carry the Convenient Food Mart trademark throughout the United States. The franchise system is a network of decentralized territorial divisions under the supervision of master area franchisees.

The Franchise: The franchisee operates a retail convenience store, under the trade name Convenient Food Mart. A typical outlet is located in a high-traffic retail mall, strip center, and or free-standing roadside location. The primary site selection criteria are convenient access and high population density. Franchise stores sell groceries, produce, staples, automotive supplies, hardware, and, often, gasoline. Franchisees are required to conform to a one-roof, one-stop shopping motif, but store size may vary. The average outlet employees two full-time and four part-time employees, and is open 24 hours a day, seven days a week.

Franchisee Profile: A strong business and management background is required of area franchisees. Unit franchisees may have varying qualifications. In general, some business or retail experience is beneficial, but not mandatory. Franchisor's Services: Within the limits of the franchisor's standards and specifications, the franchisee is allowed to make fundamental decisions regarding site selection and outlet design. Area representatives are available to help with site selection, lease negotiation, construction planning, interior design, marketing analysis, and purchasing.

The franchisor conducts a training program in Elmhurst, Illinois. When the store is open for business, a field consultant provides on-site guidance in periodic visits to the outlet. Franchisees receive continual support in employee relations, merchandising, inventory, financial analysis, purchasing, and promotion.

Initial Investment: The total investment for a new store ranges from $120,000 to $200,000, including site acquisition, construction, fixtures, and inventory. The franchisor does not offer any direct financial assistance to franchisees. Advertising: Convenient Food Mart franchisees do not pay any monthly advertising fees. The primary marketing thrust is location, on the premise that the store itself is its own best advertising medium.

Fees and Royalties: The initial franchise fee ranges from $5,000 to $15,000 depending upon the location and size of the outlet. Royalties range from 4.5 five percent of gross monthly sales.

Renewal and Assignment: The term of the franchise is ten years with a ten-year renewal option. Absentee ownership is permitted in individual cases, and subfranchising is encouraged.

Summary: Convenient Food Mart has a solid track record in the highly competitive quick-stop shopping field. Franchisees benefit from uniform imaging, adequate name recognition, centralized inventory control, and the keen personal attention of an experienced staff.

Franchise Highlights

Established: 1958
Began franchising: 1958
Outlets currently open: 1300
Initial franchise fee: Min. $5,000
Max. $15,000

Monthly royalty: 4.5% to 5%
Advertising fee: None
Training program: 12 days
Term: 10 years

Deck the Walls

Industry experience:	★ ★ ★	*Franchising experience:*	★ ★ ★
Financial strength:	★ ★ ★	*Training & services:*	★ ★ ★
Fees & royalties:	★ ★ ★ ★	*Satisfied franchisees:*	★ ★ ★

Deck the Walls
P. O. Box 4586
Houston, Texas 77210
(800) 231-6337

Deck the Walls is a subsidiary of WNS, Inc., which also operates the Wicks 'N' Sticks franchise system and the Wallpapers To Go chain. Founded in 1979, Deck the Walls has established 280 outlets over the last seven years, opening an average of 35 outlets every year. The company is currently seeking new franchisees in the midwestern and southern regions of the U.S.

The Franchise: The franchisee operates a retail art and frame store, under the trade name Deck the Walls. A typical outlet is situated in a 1,400 sq. ft. retail space in a large, high-traffic shopping mall, with a staff of two full-time and two part-time employees. Franchisees offer an exclusive line of traditional and contemporary art work, posters, prints, and framing supplies, including wood, metal, formica, and photo frames.

Franchisee Profile: A background in retail merchandising is beneficial, but not mandatory. Absentee ownership is prohibited.

Projected Earnings: Based on the company's annual sales, the average gross revenues of a Deck the Walls outlet are about $250,500 before expenses.

Franchisor's Services: The franchisor provides a ten-day training program at the company's headquarters in Houston, Texas. Attendees are responsible for their own travel and lodging expenses. The curriculum includes art merchandising, framing, marketing, bookkeeping, and business administration.

The franchisor will assist with selecting a site for the outlet and negotiating a lease for the premises. After the outlet has opened for business, a Deck the Walls field consultant will provide on-site guidance in periodic visits to the store. The franchisor's support program also includes a telecommunications system, ongoing field seminars, and a franchisee newsletter.

Initial Investment: New Deck the Walls franchisees should be prepared to invest $184,500 to establish the business. The amount includes the initial franchise fee, lease deposits, site improvements, fixtures, and an initial inventory of posters, prints, and framing supplies. Deck the Walls does not offer any form of direct financial assistance to franchisees.

Advertising: Deck the Walls franchisees contribute two percent of gross monthly revenues for advertising. The franchisor supplies franchisees with a marketing manual and point-of-sale materials, and offers an optional advertising package for conducting local ad campaigns.

Contract Highlights: The term of the franchise is five years. The contract may be renewed at the franchisee's option. The franchisee does not receive an exclusive territory in conjunction with the franchise.

Fees and Royalties: The initial franchise fee of $27,500 is high for the industry. Including the monthly franchise royalty and advertising fee, the total royalty burden is eight percent of gross sales.

Summary: The Deck the Walls franchise is characterized by high visibility, solid inventory support, and an easily managed but volume-intensive business. The company recently launched an aggressive marketing campaign aimed at heightening name recognition and setting the business apart from competition.

Franchise Highlights

Began operating: 1979	**Monthly royalty: 6%**
Began franchising: 1979	**Advertising fee: 2%**
Outlets currently open: 280	**Training program: 10 days**
Initial franchise fee: $27,500	**Term: 5 years**

Dial-A-Gift

Industry experience:	★★	*Franchising experience:*	★★
Financial strength:	★★★	*Training & services:*	★★
Fees & royalties:	★★★	*Satisfied franchisees:*	★★★

Dial-A-Gift, Inc.
2265 E. 4800 South
Salt Lake City, Utah 84117

Founded in 1980, Dial-A-Gift operates a unique direct-mail merchandising system specializing in gifts and novelties. Since the company sold its franchise in 1984, Dial-A-Gift has established 150 outlets, selling an average of 50 franchises every year.

The Franchise: The franchisee conducts a gift-wire service, selling gifts and novelties to catalog customers, under the trade name Dial-A-Gift. Customers order merchandise from a mail-order catalog, receiving fast delivery from locally stocked inventories. The catalog lists candies, cakes, gourmet foods, ceramic dishes and figurines, beverages, and other gift and novelty items.

Franchisee Profile: A background in mail-order merchandising is not required. The company is seeking prospective franchisees with sound business and financial aptitudes.

Projected Earnings: The franchisor does not provide a statement of projected earnings.

Franchisor's Services: The franchisor provides two days of training at the company's headquarters in Salt Lake City. Franchisees must pay for their own travel and lodging expenses to attend the seminar.

The franchisor operates a centralized purchasing program to support franchisees' inventories. Dial-A-Gift publishes a monthly franchisee newsletter and conducts periodic seminars to keep franchisees abreast of new products and sales trends. Company advisers are available for telephone consultations, as required.

Initial Investment: The franchisee's initial investment is estimated at $20,000. Dial-A-Gift does not offer any direct financial assistance to franchisees.

Advertising: Franchisees contribute $100 per month for advertising. The franchisor administers national marketing programs to promote the sale of catalog merchandise.

Contract Highlights: The franchise agreement has no set term; the franchisee receives perpetual rights to the gift-wire business. The franchisee receives an exclusive marketing territory for the duration of the agreement.

Fees and Royalties: The initial franchise fee of $10,000 is moderate for a gift and novelty franchise. The franchise royalty is just four percent of gross sales.

Summary: The Dial-A-Gift franchise is based on a unique gift-wire service, offering a low-investment, low-overhead business format requiring minimal training.

Franchise Highlights

Began operating: 1980	**Monthly royalty: 4%**
Began franchising: 1984	**Advertising fee: $100 per month**
Outlets currently open: 150	**Training program: 2 days**
Initial franchise fee: $10,000	**Term: 10 years**

Docktor Pet Center

Industry experience:	★ ★ ★	*Franchising experience:*	★ ★ ★
Financial strength:	★ ★ ★	*Training & services:*	★ ★ ★
Fees & royalties:	★ ★ ★ ★	*Satisfied franchisees:*	★ ★ ★

Docktor Pet Centers, Inc.
355 Middlesex Avenue
Wilmington, Massachusetts 01887
(617) 658-7840

Founded in 1966, Docktor Pet has cautiously expanded to 250 outlets, all but three of which are independent franchise operations.

The Franchise: The franchisee operates a retail pet and supply store under the trade name Docktor Pet Center. A typical outlet is situated in a high-traffic shopping mall, strip center, or other suitable retail site, offering a broad selection of live pets and related supplies. The inventory of puppies, kittens, and tropical birds and fish is prominently showcased to draw attention to the store. Employees are trained in pet handling, care, and grooming.

Franchisee Profile: A background in the pet business is beneficial, but not mandatory.

Projected Earnings: Based on the company's reported sales, the average volume of a Docktor Pet Center is in excess of $500,000 per year, before deducting wholesale costs and operating expenses.

Franchisor's Services: Docktor Pet franchisees receive 21 days of training at the company's headquarters in Wilmington, Massachusetts. Another two weeks of on-site training and grand opening assistance are provided at the franchisee's pet center. Each franchisee receives a set of operating manuals covering store operations, pet handling and merchandising, and business administration. Field representatives visit the store periodically to inspect the operation and offer ongoing guidance.

Initial Investment: The total start-up investment is estimated at from $150,000 to just under $200,000, including the initial fee, lease deposits, improvements, fixtures, inventory, and working capital. Docktor Pet does not offer any direct financial assistance to franchisees.

Fees and Royalties: The initial franchise fee of $15,000 is moderate for a retail franchise and competitive for a pet store. The franchisee's royalty obligation is less then five percent of gross sales. The franchisor does not exact a separate advertising royalty.

Disputes and Litigation: In 1986, Docktor Pet was sued by a customer who had bought a dog at a franchisee's store. The store had misrepresented the dog's authenticity, and the disgruntled purchaser sued both the franchisee and the franchisor. The court ruled in favor of the customer, finding both Docktor Pet and its franchisee liable for misrepresenting the pet's credentials.

Summary: The Docktor Pet franchise is characterized by growing name recognition, an ample base of outlets, and a retail motif catering to a market that is traditionally immune to fluctuating economic conditions.

Franchise Highlights

Began operating: 1966	**Monthly royalty: 4.5%**
Began franchising: 1967	**Advertising fee: None**
Outlets currently open: 250	**Training program: 3 weeks**
Initial franchise fee: $15,000	**Term: 20 years**

Flowerama

Industry experience:	★★★★	*Franchising experience:*	★★★★
Financial strength:	★★★	*Training & services:*	★★★
Fees & royalties:	★★★	*Satisfied franchisees:*	★★★★

Flowerama of America
3165 West Airline Highway
Waterloo, Iowa 50703
(319) 291-6004

Flowerama blossomed from a floral supply business founded by horticulturists Maurice and Herbert Frink, who heralded from the green meadows of Cedar Falls, Iowa. The company has flourished to 100 outlets since the company began franchising in 1972, opening an average of seven outlets every year. The company is currently seeking new franchisees in the northeastern, midwestern, and southern regions of the U.S.

The Franchise: The franchisee operates a retail flower, plant, and gift store, under the trade name Flowerama. A typical outlet is situated in a retail shopping mall, with a staff of two or three full-time employees. Franchisees offer cut flowers, floral arrangements, potted plants, and related gift items. The franchisee leases a turnkey flower store, completely developed by the franchisor.

Franchisee Profile: A background in the floral business or retail merchandising is beneficial, but not mandatory. Absentee ownership is not prohibited.

Projected Earnings: A statement of projected earnings was not available at press time.

Franchisor's Services: The franchisor provides a nine-day training program at the company's headquarters in Waterloo, Iowa. Attendees are responsible for their own travel and lodging expenses. The curriculum includes floral arrangements, plant and flower merchandising, store operations, marketing, customer relations, and financial administration.

The franchisor secures the site for the store and completely develops the outlet before turning over the keys to the franchisee. When the store is open for business, a Flowerama representative calls on the outlet periodically, to inspect the outlet and offer on-site troubleshooting. The franchisor provides each franchisee with a confidential store operations manual and publishes a mopnthly franchisee newsletter. Company operations experts are available for consultation by phone, as required.

Initial Investment: New Flowerama franchisees should be prepared to invest between $40,000 and $70,000 to open a new flower shop. The amount includes the initial franchise fee, lease deposits, and an initial inventory of cut flowers, potted plants, and gift merchandise. Flowerama does not offer direct financial assistance to franchisees.

Advertising: Flowerama franchisees do not pay any monthly fee for national advertising. The franchisor provides franchisees with preprepared advertising materials, Yellow Pages art, and point-of-sale aids.

Contract Highlights: The term of the franchise is ten years. The contract may be renewed for an additional term, at the franchisee's option. The franchisee receives an exclusive territory in conjunction with the franchise.

Fees and Royalties: The initial franchise fee of $17,500 is moderate for the industry. Including the monthly franchise royalty and advertising fee, the total royalty burden is a low five percent of gross sales.

Summary: The Flowerama franchise offers an easy-to-operate retail format for the erstwhile floral designer and gift merchandiser. The retail floral market is a $5 billion industry, with strong seasonal and holiday influences. Flowerama franchisees benefit from a turnkey development package, a quaint European-style motif, and the resources of an industry leader.

Franchise Highlights

Began operating: 1967
Began franchising: 1972
Outlets currently open: 100
Initial franchise fee: $17,500
Monthly royalty: 5%
Advertising fee: None
Training program: 9 days
Term: 10 years

Foremost Liquors

Industry experience: ★★★★
Financial strength: ★★★
Fees & royalties: ★★★
Franchising experience: ★★★★
Training & services: ★★
Satisfied franchisees: ★★★

Foremost Liquors
5252 N. Broadway
Chicago, Illinois 60640
(312) 334-0077

The Foremost franchise offers a head start for liquor retailers, by supplying inventory and offering general operating guidance.

The Franchise: The franchisee may operate a retail liquor store, or a discount liquor supermarket, using the franchisor's trademark, inventory selection, and merchandising system.

Franchisee Profile: A valid liquor license is required for the site where the outlet will be located.

Projected Earnings: A written statement of projected earnings was not available at press time.

Franchisor's Services: Foremost franchisees receive training and grand opening assistance are at their own locations. An operations manual covers inventory control, sales and marketing, and business administration. A Foremost representative calls on the store periodically to check inventory and offer on-site troubleshooting.

Initial Investment: The total start-up investment ranges from $100,000 to $150,000, including lease deposits, fixtures, signs, opening inventory, and miscellaneous expenses. Foremost does not offer any direct financial assistance to franchisees.

Fees and Royalties: The initial franchise fee varies, depending on the type and size of the liquor store. Apart from inventory purchases, Foremost franchisees do not pay any franchise fees or royalties.

Summary: The Foremost franchise is characterized by a high-volume merchandising format, supported by inventory assistance and the know-how of an experienced organization.

Franchise Highlights

Began operating: 1949
Began franchising: 1949
Outlets currently open: 130
Initial franchise fee: Varies
Monthly royalty: None
Advertising fee: None
Training program: Ongoing
Term: 1 year

Framin' Place/Frame Factory

Industry experience: ★ ★ ★
Financial strength: ★ ★ ★
Fees & royalties: ★ ★ ★
Franchising experience: ★ ★ ★
Training & services: ★ ★ ★
Satisfied franchisees: ★ ★ ★

Framin' Place/Frame Factory
9605 Dalecrest Street
Houston, Texas 77080
(800) 231-2564

Framin' Place/Frame Factory is the brainchild of attorney Thomas Devine, a specialist in franchising. His retail picture-frame chain has opened 120 outlets since the it began franchising in 1971. The company is currently seeking new franchisees in all major U.S. markets.

The Franchise: The franchisee operates a retail business specializing in custom and do-it-yourself picture framing supplies and services, under the trade name Framin' Place/Frame Factory. A typical outlet is situated in a suitable retail space in a shopping mall, strip center, or free-standing commercial site, with a staff of two full-time and two part-time employees. Franchisees sell custom picture frame supplies and services to the general public, based on a selection of 250 different styles displayed in the retail showroom. Outlets also offer advice on the use of framing materials and techniques, including museum-style mounting and needlepoint blocking.

Franchisee Profile: A background in business or retail merchandising is beneficial, but not mandatory. Absentee ownership is discouraged.

Projected Earnings: A statement of projected earnings was not available at press time.

Franchisor's Services: The franchisor provides a three-week training program at the company's headquarters in Houston, Texas. Attendees are responsible for their own travel and lodging expenses. The curriculum includes marketing, merchandising, customer assistance, and business administration.

The franchisor assists with site selection, lease negotiation, and pre-opening site preparation. After the shop has opened, a Framin' Place field advisor provides on-site assistance in periodic visits. The support program also includes a daily operating manual, a franchise newsletter, and ongoing telephone consultations.

Initial Investment: New Framin' Place franchisees should be prepared to invest $75,000 to open a new store. The amount includes the initial franchise fee, lease deposits, signs, fixtures, and an initial inventory of picture frames and supplies. Framin' Place has a financial assistance program for qualified franchisees.

Advertising: Framin' Place franchisees contribute two percent of gross monthly revenues for advertising. The franchisor supplies franchisees with point-of-sale materials, catalogs, and public relations aids for use in local promotions.

Contract Highlights: The term of the franchise is ten years. The contract may be renewed at the franchisee's option. The franchisee does not receive an exclusive territory.

Fees and Royalties: The initial franchise fee of $17,500 is slightly high for the industry. Including the monthly franchise royalty and advertising fee, the total royalty burden is just seven percent of gross sales.

Summary: The Framin' Place franchise is characterized by a ready-to-go business format in a stable market for do-it-yourself home decoration services and supplies.

Franchise Highlights

Began operating: 1971
Began franchising: 1971
Outlets currently open: 120
Initial franchise fee: $17,500
Monthly royalty: 5%
Advertising fee: 2%
Training program: 3 weeks
Term: 10 years

The Great Frame Up

Industry experience:	★ ★ ★	*Franchising experience:*	★ ★ ★
Financial strength:	★ ★ ★	*Training & services:*	★ ★ ★
Fees & royalties:	★ ★ ★	*Satisfied franchisees:*	★ ★ ★

The Great Frame Up Systems, Inc.
9335 Belmont Avenue
Franklin Park, Illinois 60131
(800) 553-7263

The Franchise: The franchisee operates a retail art goods store, specializing in custom picture frame supplies and doing business under the trade name The Great Frame Up. A typical outlet is situated in a shopping mall or retail center, with three full-time employees and on part-time. Franchisees sell picture frames, do-it-yourself framing materials, and art prints and posters.

Franchisee Profile: A background in a retail business is beneficial, but not mandatory. The franchisor will grant area franchises to develop large territories.

Projected Earnings: An estimate of the franchisee's average or projected earnings was not available at press time.

Franchisor's Services: Franchisees receive six weeks of training in Franklin Park, Illinois. A field specialist spends a week at the franchisee's store to provide additional training and pre-opening assistance. Franchisees receive help with store design and layout, purchasing, stocking, and merchandising. A field consultant provides ongoing management assistance in periodic visits to the outlet.

Initial Investment: The total start-up investment is estimated at $56,500, including deposits, improvements, fixtures, signs, opening inventory, and miscellaneous expenses. The franchisor does not offer any direct financial assistance to franchisees.

Fees and Royalties: The $15,500 initial fee is about average for a retail franchise. The franchisee's total royalty obligation, including the monthly franchise fee and the advertising fee, is eight percent of gross sales.

Summary: The Great Frame Up franchise is characterized by high visibility and a ready-to-operate business in the home decoration field.

Franchise Highlights

Began operating: 1971
Began franchising: 1975
Outlets currently open: 85
Initial franchise fee: $15,500
Monthly royalty: 6%
Advertising fee: 2%
Training program: 6 weeks
Term: Varies

Jr. Food Mart

Industry experience:	★ ★ ★ ★	*Franchising experience:*	★ ★ ★ ★
Financial strength:	★ ★ ★	*Training & services:*	★ ★ ★
Fees & royalties:	★ ★ ★	*Satisfied franchisees:*	★ ★ ★

Jr. Food Mart/Jitney Jungle, Inc.
P. O. Box 3500
Jackson, Mississippi 39206
(601) 944-0873

The Franchise: The franchisee operates a retail convenience market, under the trade name Jr. Food Mart. A typical outlet is situated in a strip center or free-standing site with four full-time and two part-time employees. Franchisees stock a basic selection of groceries, supplemented by the sale of fast food and fresh baked goods — including the chain's trademarked Creole Fried Chicken and Morning Fresh Bakery products. The store may also vend gasoline and selected auto supplies.

Franchisor's Services: Franchisees spend two weeks in training at the company's headquarters in Jackson, Mississippi. Attendees must pay their own travel and lodging expenses. Additional training and grand opening assistance take place at the franchisee's store.

Each Jr. franchisee receives an operating manual detailing the management, finance, and daily operation of the convenience store. An area representative provides ongoing management assistance in periodic visits to the outlet.

Initial Investment: The total start-up investment is estimated at around $130,000. Jr. Food Mart does not offer any direct financial assistance to franchisees.

Fees and Royalties: The initial franchise fee of $25,000 is high for the retail trade, but about average for a convenience-mart franchise of this stature. The franchisor does not charge any monthly fees for advertising. The franchisee's total royalty obligation is just one percent of gross sales.

Summary: The Jr. Food Mart franchise offers a competitive convenience-mart format with diversified profit centers, backed by the resources of an experienced organization.

Franchise Highlights

Began operating: 1919
Began franchising: 1920
Outlets currently open: 410
Initial franchise fee: $25,000

Monthly royalty: 1%
Advertising fee: None
Training program: 2 weeks
Term: 15 years

Koenig Art Emporium

Industry experience:	★★★★	*Franchising experience:*	★★★★
Financial strength:	★★★	*Training & services:*	★★★
Fees & royalties:	★★★	*Satisfied franchisees:*	★★★★

Koenig Art Emporium
1777 Boston Post Road
Milford, Connecticut 06460
(203) 877-4541

The first Koenig Art Emporium was opened in 1933, selling art and art supplies direct to the public. The company began franchising in 1979, opening 75 outlets in less than a decade. The company is currently seeking new franchisees in the northeastern, southern, and southwestern regions of the U.S.

The Franchise: The franchisee operates a retail store, specializing in art supplies and frames, under the trade name Koenig Art Emporium. A typical outlet is situated in a a regional shopping mall, with a staff of three full-time and two part-time employees. Franchisees offer artist's supplies, posters, prints, and picture frames.

Franchisee Profile: A background in the art supply business is beneficial, but not mandatory. Absentee ownership is prohibited.

Projected Earnings: A statement of projected earnings was not available at press time.

Franchisor's Services: The franchisor provides a two-week training program at the company's headquarters in Milford, Connecticut. Attendees are responsible for their own travel and lodging expenses. The curriculum includes store management, merchandising strategies, framing, sales promotion, financial administration, and inventory control.

The franchisor will assist with selecting a site for the outlet and negotiating a lease for the premises. After the outlet has opened for business, a Koenig representative will visit the outlet periodically, to offer guidance and troubleshooting. Other on-going services include a franchisee newsletter and a toll-free hotline.

Initial Investment: New Koenig franchisees should be prepared to invest from $50,000 to $80,000 to establish the business. The amount includes the initial franchise fee, lease deposits, site improvements, equipment purchases, and an initial inventory of art supplies, posters, and picture frames. Financial assistance may be available to qualified franchisees.

Advertising: Koenig Art Emporium owners do not pay a separate royalty for advertising. The franchisor provides display aids, sign designs, and advertising materials for use in local promotions.

Contract Highlights: The term of the franchise is ten years. The contract may be renewed at the franchisee's option. The franchisee receives an exclusive territory in conjunction with the franchise.

Fees and Royalties: The initial franchise fee of $25,000 is somewhat high for the industry, but the franchisee's royalty obligation is only six percent of gross sales.

Summary: The Koenig Art Emporium franchise is characterized by a diversified inventory catering to art hobbyists and do-it-yourself home decorators, backed by the know-how and resources of an experienced organization.

Franchise Highlights

Began operating: 1933
Began franchising: 1979
Outlets currently open: 75
Initial franchise fee: $25,000

Monthly royalty: 6%
Advertising fee: None
Training program: 2 weeks
Term: 10 years

Little Professor Book Centers

Industry experience:	★ ★ ★	*Franchising experience:*	★ ★ ★
Financial strength:	★ ★ ★	*Training & services:*	★ ★ ★
Fees & royalties:	★ ★ ★	*Satisfied franchisees:*	★ ★ ★

Little Professor Book Centers
110 N. Fourth Avenue
Ann Arbor, Michigan 48104
(800) 521-6232

Founded in 1969, Little Professor today oversees 130 franchised book and magazine stores. According to a company spokesman, the franchise organization generates over $25 million in annual sales.

The Franchise: The franchisee conducts a retail book store under the trade name Little Professor Book Center. A typical outlet is located in a 1,600 sq. ft. space in a shopping mall, strip center, or other suitable commercial site, with a staff of one full-time and two part-time employees. The merchandise mix includes roughly 2,000 hardcover titles, 5,000 paperback, and 200 magazine titles. Magazine sales account for about 18 percent of the average store's sales.

Franchisee Profile: A background in book retailing is not required. Absentee ownership is permitted, but not encouraged. Area franchises are available.

Projected Earnings: According to the franchisor, the average volume of a Little Professor outlet is about $340,000 per year, before expenses, with profits of $36,000 — about 10.6 percent of gross sales.

Franchisor's Services: Little Professor conducts a five-day training program at an operating Book Center in Ann Arbor, Michigan. Attendees are responsible for their own travel and lodging expenses. The curriculum includes book purchasing and merchandising, retail operations, business administration, marketing and sales. An additional four days of on-site training are provided prior to opening. Franchisees receive copies of the confidential Little Professor Book Centers franchise manual, documenting the company's daily operating procedures.

The franchisor will assist with selecting a site for the outlet and negotiating a lease for the premises. After the store has opened, a field representative will visit the outlet periodically, to offer on-site guidance. Litte Professor assists with purchasing, inventory control, and bookkeeping systems. The franchisor also publishes a franchisee newsletter and offers annual on-site training. Company advisers are accessible by phone as required.

Initial Investment: The initial investment is estimated at $76,000. The minimum cash requirement is about $35,000. The total includes lease deposits, improvements, fixtures, furnishings, equipment, and signs. Little Professor may assist with obtaining financial assistance from a third party lender.

Advertising: Little Professor franchisees contribute one half of one percent of gross monthly revenues for advertising. The franchisor supplies ad slicks for newspaper and magazine campaigns, a Yellow Pages layout, radio and television commercials, point-of-sale materials, and public relations aids.

Little Professor also collects retail display allowances (RDA) for franchisees. These allowances are financial incentives offered by some publishers in exchange for prominent displays of their titles. The RDA funds are used to pay a rebate to stores, based on 4.2 to 5.5 percent of their total magazine sales.

The franchisor recently initiated an annual scholarship fund for college-bound high school seniors. The national award is presented at the annual American Booksellers Association convention. Participating franchisees offer local prizes of $100.

Contract Highlights: The term of the franchise is 15 years. The contract may be renewed for an additional term, at the franchisee's option. The franchisee receives a protected territory for the duration of the agreement.

Fees and Royalties: The initial franchise fee of $15,000 is average for the retail industry. The 2.75 percent monthly royalty is low by any standard. Including the one half of one percent advertising contribution, the total royalty burden is slightly more than three percent of gross sales.

Litigation and disputes: The Little Professor franchisee in Wilmington, North Carolina became a local hero and made national headlines, when he successfully overturned a city ordinance that forbade the sale of merchandise on Sunday.

Summary: Little Professor Book Centers is the largest franchise chain of book stores in America. Franchisees face formidable competition from Waldenbooks and Dalton's — chains many times larger than Little Professor. A moderate investment, low royalties, and favorable imaging give franchisees a competitive stance.

Franchise Highlights

Began operating: 1969
Began franchising: 1969
Outlets currently open: 130
Initial franchise fee: $15,000
Monthly royalty: 2.75%
Advertising fee: .5%
Training program: 5 days
Term: 15 years

M.G.M. Liquor Warehouse

Industry experience:	★ ★ ★	*Franchising experience:*	★ ★
Financial strength:	★ ★ ★	*Training & services:*	★ ★ ★
Fees & royalties:	★ ★ ★	*Satisfied franchisees:*	★ ★ ★

M.G.M. Liquor Warehouse
1124 Carpenteur Avenue West
St. Paul, Minnesota 55113
(612) 487-1006

The Franchise: The franchisee operates a discount liquor supermarket under the trade name M.G.M. Liquor Warehouse. A typical outlet is situated in a 5,000 sq. ft. retail or commercial site with one full-time and five part-time employees.

Franchisee Profile: Franchisees must be creditworthy and be capable of handling the initial investment. A valid liquor license is required for the site where the outlet will be located.

Projected Earnings: A written statement of projected earnings was not available at press time.

Franchisor's Services: M.G.M. holds a two-week training program at the company's headquarters in St. Paul, Minnesota. The franchisor also offers on-site training and grand opening assistance. The design and layout of the store must comply with M.G.M.'s specifications and standards.

Each franchisee receives a set of operations manuals documenting the franchisor's policies and procedures for running the liquor store. Franchisees meet monthly in regional advisory ocuncils. An M.G.M. representative visits the liquor store peridoically to offer ongoing managerial support. The franchisor's centralized inventory and purchasing system helps to streamline the store's merchandising activities. Franchisees may purchase merchandise from M.G.M. at competitive prices. Only liquor labels approved by the franchisor may be purchased at wholesale from other suppliers.

Initial Investment: The start-up investment is estimated at around $350,000, including lease deposits, improvements, signs, equipment, and working capital. The franchisor does not offer any direct financial assistance to franchisees.

Advertising: M.G.M. franchisees contribute one percent of gross sales for advertising. The contributions are pooled to administer a promotional organization — called the Wine Club — which sponsors wine tastings and marketing campaigns.

Fees and Royalties: The initial franchise fee ranges from $25,000 to $50,000, depending on the location. The monthly franchise royalty also varies.

Summary: M.G.M. franchisees benefit from administrative support, inventory assistance, and personal management attention.

Franchise Highlights

Began operating: 1971
Began franchising: 1979
Outlets currently open: 35
Initial franchise fee: Min $25,000
Max. $50,000

Monthly royalty: Varies None
Advertising fee: 1%
Training program: 2 weeks
Term: 15 years

The Medicine Shoppe

Industry experience:	★ ★ ★	*Franchising experience:*	★ ★ ★
Financial strength:	★ ★ ★ ★	*Training & services:*	★ ★ ★ ★
Fees & royalties:	★ ★ ★	*Satisfied franchisees:*	★ ★ ★ ★

Medicine Shoppe International
10121 Paget Drive
St. Louis, Missouri 63376
(314) 993-6000

The Medicine Shoppe franchise was devised in 1970 as a retail vehicle for the licensed pharmacist. Since, the chain has grown into the nation's largest drugstore organization, with 720 outlets. More than 40 Medicine Shoppes have opened every year of the company's existence. The franchisor is currently seeking new franchisees in most U.S. markets.

The Franchise: The franchisee operates a retail drugstore, under the trade name The Medicine Shoppe. A typical outlet is situated in a a 1,000 sq. ft. space in a strip center or other suitable retail site, with a staff of three full-time and one part-time employees. Franchisees offer prescription drugs, over-the-counter medications, and sundries.

Franchisee Profile: A background in pharmacy is required. The owner/manager of the business must be a licensed pharmacist. Absentee ownership is not prohibited.

Projected Earnings: Based on the company's reported annual sales, the average volume of a Medicine Shoppe outlet is about $500,000 per year, before expenses.

Franchisor's Services: The franchisor provides a one-week training program at the company's headquarters in St. Louis. Attendees are responsible for their own travel and lodging expenses. The curriculum includes store operations, purchasing, inventory control, marketiong, accounting, and customer relations.

The franchisor will assist with selecting a site for the outlet, negotiating a lease, and building out the interior. An area representative will visit the store periodically, to offer guidance and troubleshooting. Other ongoing services include a confidential store operations manual, a franchisee newsletter, and unlimited access to retail operations experts via a toll-free hotline.

Initial Investment: The start-up investment is estimated at $75,000 for a new store. Pharmacists with existing drugstores may convert to a Medicine Shop for much less. The investment amount includes the initial franchise fee, lease deposits, site improvements, fixtures, and opening inventory. Financial assistance is available to creditworthy franchisees.

Advertising: Medicine Shoppe franchisees contribute two percent of gross monthly revenues for advertising. The franchisor supplies franchisees with ad slicks, point-of-sale materials, and guidelines for conducting local ad campaigns. Franchisees may also participate in voluntary co-op advertising programs.

Contract Highlights: The term of the franchise is 20 years. The contract may be renewed at the franchisee's option. The franchisee receives an exclusive territory in conjunction with the franchise.

Fees and Royalties: The initial franchise fee of $18,000 is moderate for a retail drugstore franchise. Including the monthly franchise royalty and advertising fee, the total royalty burden is less than eight percent of gross sales.

Summary: The Medicine Shoppe franchise is characterized by growing name recognition and an ample base of outlets. Franchisees benefit from professional training and a ready-to-go business format for the licensed pharmacist.

Franchise Highlights

Began operating: 1970
Began franchising: 1970
Outlets currently open: 720
Initial franchise fee: $18,000
Monthly royalty: 5.5%
Advertising fee: 2%
Training program: 1 week
Term: 20 years

Petland

Industry experience:	★ ★ ★	*Franchising experience:*	★ ★ ★
Financial strength:	★ ★ ★	*Training & services:*	★ ★ ★
Fees & royalties:	★ ★ ★	*Satisfied franchisees:*	★ ★ ★

Petland, Inc.
195 North Hickory St.
Chillicothe, Ohio 45601-5606
(800) 221-5935

The Petland franchise capitalizes on America's love for creature companionship. Since the original Petland store opened in 1967, more than 100 franchise outlets have sold retail pets and pet supplies in 14 states. The chain is predominately clustered in the Ohio valley and Florida.

The Franchise: The franchisee operates a retail pet center, under the trade name Petland. A typical outlet occupies 2,500 to 4,000 sq. ft. of commercial space in a shopping mall or retail strip center, with three full-time and three part-time employees. An optional 'superstore' may run as large as 8,000 sq. ft. All Petland outlets stock a diverse inventory of puppies, kittens, tropical and marine fish, birds, and related pet supplies and accessories. Franchisees purchase most inventory items from Petland distributors, presumably at discount prices. The merchandise line includes Petland's own private line of pet care products and supplies.

Franchisee Profile: Prospective franchisees do not need prior experience in pet handling or retailing. The franchisor provides training in all phases of store operation, including the care and training of animals. Petland is actively seeking new franchisees in the west, southeast, midwest and middle Atlantic states. The franchisor discourages absentee ownership, but may be willing to negotiate subfranchising rights.

Franchisor Services: Petland conducts a four-week training program in Chillicothe, Ohio. Attendees receive comprehensive instruction in animal care and pet center operations. Field trainers also spend up to two weeks at the franchisee's store prior to opening.

Petland selects the site for the business and develops a complete, turnkey pet center before turning the store over to the franchisee. When the outlet is open for business, a Petland representative pays regular visits to the site, to inspect the operation and offer continuing guidance.

Initial Investment: New franchisees should be prepared to invest $60,000 to establish and develop the store. The total working capital requirement may run as high as $150,000 to $450,000, depending on the size of the outlet. Petland does not offer direct financial assistance, but will help franchisees secure financing from a third party lender.

Advertising: Franchisees contribute one half of one percent of gross monthly sales for advertising. The franchisor supplies ad mattes, Yellow Pages art, and public relations tools for conducting local promotions.

Fees and Royalties: Petland does not charge an initial franchise fee. The franchisee assumes the site lease on taking over the business. The monthly franchise royalty is four percent of gross sales.

Renewal and Assignment: The term of the franchise is 20 years. The franchise may not be sold or transfered without the franchisor's consent. Area franchises are available by separate agreement.

Summary: Petland's growth objective is to double the size of its franchise network by 1990. The franchise offers professional imaging and a fine-tuned business system for rapidly entering the retail pet trade.

Franchise Highlights

Began operating: 1967
Began franchising: 1971
Outlets currently open: 100
Initial franchise fee: None
Monthly royalty: 4%
Advertising fee: 0.5%
Training program: 4 weeks
Term: 20 years

7-Eleven Food Store

Industry experience:	★★★★	*Franchising experience:*	★★★
Financial strength:	★★★★	*Training & services:*	★★★
Fees & royalties:	★★★	*Satisfied franchisees:*	★★★

Southland Corporation
2828 North Haskell Avenue
Dallas, Texas 75221
(214) 828-7763

Southland Corporation, the parent of the 11,000-store 7-Eleven convenience store chain, has one of the most sterling track records in the retail trade. The company's original business was vending ice. By mixing in a few groceries with its ice cubes, Southland inadvertently created an entirely new retail sector. Despite a recent sales slump and some highly publicized misadventures in the petroleum business, the company continues to dominate the worldwide convenience retail industry. Southland recently invested $50 million to develop its own videotape rental network for 7-Eleven stores.

The Franchise: The franchisee operates a retail convenience store under the trade name 7-Eleven. A typical outlet is situated in 2,400 sq. ft. of commercial space in a retail strip center or free-standing site, stocking a limited selection of groceries, automobile supplies, hardware, and, household goods. Some stores also vend gasoline, or operate in conjunction with other, related businesses or franchises.

Franchisee Profile: A background in retail business is beneficial, but not mandatory.

Franchisor's Services: 7-Eleven conducts a two-week training program at the company's headquarters in Dallas, or at a designated regional training center. The company acquires a site for the store and leases the property to the franchisee.

Franchisees receive copies of the confidential 7-Eleven franchise operations manual, detailing store procedures and maintenance standards. The franchisor helps stock the outlet's shelves prior to opening, but the franchisee is responsible for ongoing inventory control. An area representative visits each store periodically, to inspect the operation and provide management assistance, as required.

The franchisor sells merchandise to franchised stores through its wholesale affiliates and offers a group insurance plan to franchisees and their employees.

Initial Investment: The total start-up investment is estimated at around $70,000, including the initial fee, site lease, fixtures, equipment purchases, and supplies. Included in the investment are initial inventory purchases amounting to about $38,800. The initial fee varies, depending on the location. Financial assistance is available to qualified franchisees.

Advertising: 7-Eleven franchisees do not pay a separate monthly royalty for advertising. The franchisor conducts aggressive regional and local ad campaigns, using television, radio, and newspapers.

Contract Highlights: The 7-Eleven franchise has a ten-year term, renewable for an additional term if the franchisee is in compliance with all material provisions. The franchisee is not required to purchase merchandise from the franchisor.

Fees and Royalties: The initial franchise fee is calculated at 15 percent of the annual profits of store's annual profits. In the case of a new store, the calculation is based on the profits of other stores in the area. For example, the fee for an established outlet that generated $200,000 in profits over the last 12 months would amount to $30,000. The monthly franchise royalty varies, depending on the location.

Summary: The 7-Eleven franchise is characterized by strong name recognition, competent start-up assistance, and stunning growth and earnings.

Franchise Highlights

Began operating: 1927	**Monthly royalty: Varies**
Began franchising: 1964	**Advertising fee: None**
Outlets currently open: 11,200	**Training program: 2 weeks**
Initial franchise fee: Varies	**Term: 10 years**

Swiss Colony

Industry experience:	★ ★ ★ ★	*Franchising experience:*	★ ★ ★
Financial strength:	★ ★ ★	*Training & services:*	★ ★ ★
Fees & royalties:	★ ★ ★ ★	*Satisfied franchisees:*	★ ★ ★

Swiss Colony Stores, Inc.
1 Alpine Lane
Monroe, Wisconsin 53566
(608) 328-8803

Swiss Colony has been marketing specialty foods and novelties since 1926, mailing sausages, cheeses, cakes, and candies to gift recipients throughout the continent. The retail chain of the same name supplements the firm's mail-order line with delicatessen-style sandwiches, fresh baked goods, yoghurt, and desserts. Swiss Colony oversees more than 100 stores in all U.S. states and is actively seeking new franchisees in most major markets.

The Franchise: The franchisee operates a retail food store supplemented by limited fast-food service, under the Swiss Colony trade name. A typical outlet is situated in a high-traffic shopping mall or retail center, with five full-time and five part-time employees.

Franchisee Profile: A background in retailing or merchandising is beneficial, but not mandatory.

Projected Earnings: A written statement of projected earnings was not available at press time.

Franchisor's Services: Swiss Colony franchisees must successfully complete a two-week training program at the company's headquarters in Monroe, Wisconsin. Additional staff training, inventory planning assistance, and grand opening coordination are provided at the franchisee's place of business. The Swiss Colony operations manual documents the franchisor's policies and procedures for the retail store. Ongoing management assistance is available from a Swiss Colony field consultant, who visits each store periodically, or from company operations experts via a franchisee hotline.

Initial Investment: The total start-up investment may range from $100,000 to $250,000, including lease deposits, improvements, fixtures, inventory, and miscellaneous expenses. Swiss Colony does not offer any direct financial assistance to franchisees.

Fees and Royalties: The initial franchise fee of $10,000 is moderate for a specialty food retail operation. Swiss Colony franchisees do not pay any monthly advertising fees. The total royalty obligation is just six percent of gross sales.

Summary: The Swiss Colony franchise is characterized by strong brand recognition, a pronounced seasonal orientation, and demonstrated consumer appeal.

Franchise Highlights

Began operating: 1926	**Monthly royalty: 6%**
Began franchising: 1963	**Advertising fee: None**
Outlets currently open: 120	**Training program: 2 weeks**
Initial franchise fee: $10,000	**Term: 20 years**

Taylor Rental

Industry experience:	★ ★ ★	*Franchising experience:*	★ ★ ★
Financial strength:	★ ★ ★	*Training & services:*	★ ★ ★
Fees & royalties:	★ ★ ★	*Satisfied franchisees:*	★ ★ ★

Taylor Rental Center
P. O. Box 8000
New Britain, Connecticut 06050
(203) 229-9100

Taylor Rental Centers rent a diversity of equipment, appliances, and goods to homeowners, businesses, and contractors. The franchisee's inventory ranges from televisions to construction equipment.

The Franchise: The franchisee operates an equipment rental business under the trade name Taylor Rental Center. A typical outlet is situated in a business park or freestanding site, with a staff of three full-time and two part-time employees. The franchisee rents small appliances, tools, light industrial equipment, furniture for wedding receptions and parties, lawn mowers, seeders, spray painters, welding torches, and camping equipment.

Franchisee Profile: A background in the equipment rental business is beneficial, but not mandatory.

Projected Earnings: A written statement of projected earnings was not available at press time.

Franchisor's Services: Taylor conducts a two-week training program at the company's headquarters in New Britain, Connecticut. Inventory planning and pre-opening assistance are provided at the franchisee's site. The franchisor supplies each franchisee with a set of manuals for planning, marketing, operating, and managing the business. Ongoing guidance is available from a field consultant who visits each outlet periodically.

Initial Investment: The total start-up investment is estimated at around $220,000, including site acquisition, equipment purchases, signs, supplies, and miscellaneous start-up expenses. Taylor does not offer any direct financial assistance to franchisees.

Fees and Royalties: The initial franchise fee is $20,000 and includes the cost of the training program. The franchisee's total royalty obligation is less than three percent of gross sales. Taylor franchisees do not pay any monthly fees for advertising.

Summary: The Taylor franchise is characterized by ample name recognition and consistently strong demand for rental goods and equipment.

Franchise Highlights

Began operating: 1963
Began franchising: 1963
Outlets currently open: 360
Initial franchise fee: $20,000
Monthly royalty: 2.75%
Advertising fee: None
Training program: 2 weeks
Term: 10 years

Travel Franchises

Travel and tourism is the third largest segment of the U.S. retail economy, with more than $160 billion in domestic sales — roughly six percent of the Gross National Product. Travel, both domestic and international, continues to increase every year. As an industry, travel employs 4.8 million people and supports more than 22,000 retail travel agencies booking nearly $16 billion worth of airline tickets each year. Agents' commissions amount to more than $1.5 billion.

Travel agencies thrive by serving as a one-stop resource for business and leisure travelers. Hotels, tour operators, airline carriers, automobile rental chains, and cruise ships pay the agency a commission for business sent their way. Contrary to popular belief, travelers cannot obtain better fares or rates by bypassing a travel agency.

A travel franchise offers the enterprising businessperson an opportunity to learn the trade and rapidly penetrate the market, with the managerial independence of owning one's own agency.

Empress Travel

Industry experience:	★ ★ ★ ★	*Franchising experience:*	★ ★ ★
Financial strength:	★ ★ ★	*Training & services:*	★ ★ ★
Fees & royalties:	★ ★ ★	*Satisfied franchisees:*	★ ★ ★

Empress Travel
5 Penn Plaza
New York, New York 10001
(212) 563-0560

Founded in 1957, Empress Travel is one of the oldest and most established travel agency chains in North America. The company has pursued a conservative growth course, opening 60 agencies — more than half of which are located in New York State. The Empress Travel franchise is currently registered in New York, Maryland, Virginia, and Washington. Company president Jack Cygielman plans to begin offering franchises in California by 1989.

The Franchise: The franchisee operates a retail travel agency under the trade name Empress Travel. A typical outlet is situated in a commercial building or retail strip center, employing a staff of four full-time travel specialists. Franchisees book air reservations, tour packages, cruises, hotel space, and other travel arrangements. The agency derives income from commissions on airline, hotel, car rental, and tour reservations, with the majority of business devoted to commercial travel.

Franchisee Profile: A background in the travel and tourism industry is considered beneficial, but not mandatory. The company is seeking prospective franchisees with solid business credentials. Absentee ownership is not prohibited by the franchise agreement, provided that the franchisee hires a qualified manager to oversee the operation.

Projected Earnings: A statement of projected earnings was not available at press time.

Franchisor's Services: The franchisor provides a one-week training program at the company's headquarters in New York. Attendees are responsible for their own travel and lodging expenses. The curriculum covers travel industry background, agency operations, airline reservations, and accounting.

An Empress Travel representative will visit the outlet periodically, to offer on-site guidance and troubleshooting. The company's management, technical and operations experts are available for telephone consultation as required.

Initial Investment: New franchisees should be prepared to invest from $10,000 to $75,000 to establish the travel agency. The amount includes lease deposits, furnishings, equipment purchases, and miscellaneous start-up expenses. The franchisor does not offer any direct financial assistance to franchisees.

Advertising: Franchisees contribute an advertising royalty calculated at the rate of .04 of one percent of gross sales. The franchisor supplies ad materials, commercials, point-of-sale aids, and public relations tools.

Contract Highlights: The term of the franchise is 20 years. The franchisee receives a protected territory for the duration of the agreement. The contract does not specifically prohibit absentee ownership.

Fees and Royalties: The initial franchise fee of $15,000 is average for the travel industry. The 1.5 percent monthly royalty is moderate, reflecting the fact that the agency's primary income source is commissions.

Summary: Empress Travel is an established chain with strong name recognition in the northeast. Franchisees benefit from a refined business motif, industry training, and keen personal support from an experienced management team.

Franchise Highlights

Began operating: 1957
Began franchising: 1974
Outlets currently open: 60
Initial franchise fee: $20,000
Monthly royalty: 1.5%
Advertising fee: .04%
Training program: 1 week
Term: 20 years

Travel Travel

Industry experience:	★★★	*Franchising experience:*	★★★
Financial strength:	★★★	*Training & services:*	★★★
Fees & royalties:	★★★	*Satisfied franchisees:*	★★★

Travel Travel
4350 La Jolla Village Drive
San Diego, California 92122
(619) 546-4350

Travel Travel enjoys a high profile on the west coast, with a high concentration of outlets in California and Colorado. Besides assisting new franchisees with start-up programs, the company also 'converts' established travel agencies that are capable of meeting the franchisor's qualifications and standards.

The Franchise: The franchisee operates an upscale, retail travel agency under the trade name Travel Travel. A typical outlet is located in an office site, retail facility, or mall location, with a staff of three full-time employees. The primary activity of the business is airline ticketing, but franchisees also offer travel planning and counseling, tour and cruise arrangements, and related services.

Franchisee Profile: A background in the travel industry is beneficial, but not mandatory. Absentee ownership is not prohibited by the franchise agreement.

Projected Earnings: Travel Travel does not currently provide a statement of projected earnings.

Franchisor's Services: The franchisor provides a one-week training program at the company's headquarters in San Diego, or at a designated regional site near the franchisee's location. Attendees are responsible for their own travel and lodging expenses. The curriculum covers agency operation, staffing, travel industry background, air reservations, and bookkeeping.

A Travel Travel representative will assist with selecting a site for the agency and designing the outlet. Ongoing consultation is provided in periodic visitations by a field adviser. Franchisees receive copies of the confidential Travel Travel operations manual, detailing the day-to-day conduct of the business.

Initial Investment: New Travel Travel franchisees should be prepared to handle an initial investment of about $60,000. The amount includes lease deposits, improvements, equipment purchases, signs, and miscellaneous start-up expenses. Financial assistance may be available to qualified franchisees.

Advertising: Franchisees contribute a monthly advertising royalty of $200 per month. The franchisor's advertising support includes radio, magazine, and newspaper advertising, radio and television commercials, and public relations materials.

Contract Highlights: The term of the franchise is 10 years. On expiration, the contract may be renewed for an additional 10-year term, if the franchisee is not in violation of any material provisions. The franchisee receives a protected territory for the duration of the agreement.

Fees and Royalties: The initial franchise fee of $27,500 is somewhat on the high side, but lower than other franchises of similar stature. The 6.5 percent monthly royalty, added to the 2.5 percent advertising royalty, exacts a total royalty burden of nine percent.

Summary: The Travel Travel franchise offers industry training and considerable flexibility in outlet design and operation. The chain is currently expanding into undeveloped markets in the U.S., Canada, and overseas territories.

Franchise Highlights

Began operating: 1979
Began franchising: 1979
Outlets currently open: 160
Initial franchise fee: $27,500
Monthly royalty: 6.5%
Advertising fee: 2.5%
Training program: 2 weeks
Term: 10 years

Uniglobe Travel

Industry experience: ★★★
Financial strength: ★★★
Fees & royalties: ★★★
Franchising experience: ★★
Training & services: ★★★
Satisfied franchisees: ★★★

Uniglobe Travel
90-10551 Shellbridge Way
Richmond, British Columbia, Canada V6X 2W9
(604) 270-2241

Founded in 1979, Canadian-based Uniglobe Travel is arguably the most recognizable franchise chain in North America. With 450 outlets in a dozen states and Canada, Uniglobe offers one of the most thorough franchise packages in the travel industry. The company is currently expanding in California, the northeastern U.S., and eastern Canada.

The Franchise: The franchisee operates a retail travel agency using the Uniglobe trademark. A typical outlet is situated in a 1,000 sq. ft. office site in a commercial building, strip center, or freestanding facility, with a staff of three full-time employees. Franchisees offer travel consultation and reservation services for both commercial and leisure travelers, based on the franchisor's training and standardized business system.

Franchisee Profile: A background in travel is beneficial, but not mandatory. Absentee ownership is discouraged, but not strictly prohibited.

Projected Earnings: The average gross sales of a Uniglobe outlet are about $1.5 million, before expenses.

Franchisor's Services: The franchisor provides a training program in four days at the company's headquarters in British Columbia. Additional training takes place at the regional level. Attendees are responsible for their own travel and lodging expenses. The curriculum includes travel agency operation, airline reservation systems, agency accounting, marketing and sales.

The franchisor will assist with selecting a site for the outlet and negotiating a lease for the premises. When the agency is open for business, a Uniglobe consultant will visit the outlet periodically, to offer on-site assistance as required. The franchisor helps develop new and ongoing business for franchisees, by cultivating corporate accounts and establishing industry ties. Franchisee conventions are organized annually.

Initial Investment: The total investment is estimated at about $125,000, including the initial franchise fee, lease deposits, furnishings and equipment, supplies, and miscellaneous expenses. Uniglobe may provide direct financial assistance to creditworthy franchisees.

Advertising: Uniglobe franchisees contribute $560 per month for advertising. The franchisor plans national and regional campaigns on behalf of all Uniglobe outlets. Franchisees also receive ad slicks, radio and television commercials, and public relations aids.

Contract Highlights: The Uniglobe franchise has a standard 10-year term, renewable for an additional ten years by mutual agreement. The franchisee does not receive a protected territory for the travel agency.

Fees and Royalties: The initial franchise fee of $42,500 is high for the industry — reflecting the franchisor's investment in training and start-up assistance. The monthly franchise royalty on gross sales is one percent or less.

Summary: The Uniglobe franchise offers strong name recognition, a progressive training program, and aggressive advertising support.

Franchise Highlights

Began operating: 1979	**Monthly royalty: 1%**
Began franchising: 1980	**Advertising fee: $560 per month**
Outlets currently open: 450	**Training program: 4 days**
Initial franchise fee: $42,500	**Term: 10 years**

Name Index

Category Index